CW00540701

The Covenant and the Kingdom

Charles Simpson

Sovereign World

Sovereign World Ltd
PO Box 777
Tonbridge
Kent TN11 9XT
England

Copyright © 1995 by Charles Simpson Ministries

All rights reserved. No part of this publication may be reproduced, stored in a retrieval system or transmitted, in any form or by any means, electronic, mechanical, photocopying or otherwise, withou⁺ the prior written consent of the publisher.

Short extracts may be used for review purposes.

Scripture quotations unless otherwise noted, are from The Spirit-Filled Life Bible, New King James Version, Thomas Nelson Inc., 1991.

New American Standard Bible © Copyright 1960, 1962, 1963, 1968, 1972, 1975 by the Lockman Foundation, La Habra, CA 90631.

NIV – The Holy Bible, New International Version © Copyright 1973, 1978, 1984 International Bible Society. Published by Hodder & Stoughton.

ISBN: 1 85240 102 8

Typeset by CRB Associates, Norwich, England

FOREWORD

Welcome to the new edition of *The Covenant and the Kingdom*. The book you hold in your hand is the product of countless hours of preparation and distillation from many dedicated people. Some of the material in this edition has been re-written and re-formatted in order to make it as accurate, concise, and user-friendly as possible.

The information it contains is both **timeless** and **timely**. That is, we seek to proclaim biblical truth, which is the same yesterday, today, and forever. God's eternal Word, settled in heaven before time began, is as relevant, practical, and encouraging today as it was in the beginning.

Within the pages of the Bible are the keys to life from the One Who creates and sustains all life. As we read His Word, we not only gain wisdom, but we actually commune with our Creator. Our aim in *The Covenant and the Kingdom* is to work under the Holy Spirit's leading to inspire you toward further examination and 'feeding' in God's Word.

Acts chapter 8 records the story of how Philip the Evangelist was led by the Holy Spirit to an Ethiopian official who was reading God's Word. 'Do you understand what you are reading?' Philip asked. 'How can I, unless someone teaches me?' the official replied honestly.

Those who contributed the material within this book share the burden of Philip . . . to seek to study the whole counsel of God, the full Gospel, and then to pass on this wisdom to all who would hear. We do not profess to 'have it all' or to have 'cornered the market' on truth. Nonetheless, such as we do see, we share within these pages.

It is so appropriate that this book would be published in the year that noted pastor and Bible teacher Charles Simpson celebrates his fortieth year in the ministry. Dad's mission throughout these years has been to sow good seed that would bear good fruit . . . to affect the people who affect the world. This book is part of that good fruit.

In late 1986, a project was begun by my father under the Lord's direction to compile a systematic overview of Scripture that was scholarly, yet practical . . . structured, yet infused with the life and dynamic of the Holy Spirit.

Over the course of more than seven years, in seven different volumes, we have published and distributed this curriculum project widely among the nations, and we've received exciting testimonies indicating that thousands of lives have been blessed. Then, upon conclusion of that first phase, we began re-structuring this material for publication into one user-friendly volume.

More than twenty-five ministers, teachers, business leaders and scholars contributed material for this project overall. Key contributors are listed in the next section.

I have been so honored to play some part in this process, to share in the vision, and to give myself into its completion. I cannot think of a better investment of time or energy.

Throughout the challenging process of putting this book together, my wife, Susanne, was not only a great encouragement to me, but she put in many long nights of proofing and editing the material as well, for which I am eternally grateful.

So many others are a part of this new phase of the project in terms of typing and proofing: Brenda Ring, Lois Robinson, Kathy Tyrrell, Bonita Harris, Sue Grant, Evelyn Brisendine, Carynn Lanier, Candace Dyess and others. I thank each one so much for being a part of the mission.

Special thanks to Chris Mungeam at Sovereign World for his vision and patience throughout the long months of final preparation. He has been a major catalyst in moving this project along, and we are honored to be associated with him.

Our lessons are designed to give you a concise overview in systematic fashion of what the Word of God has to say about His redeeming love for us and His rulership over all areas of life and creation. There are numerous Scripture references listed within each lesson. These references are placed next (or as close as possible) to the material to which they pertain. **Your study of each lesson is incomplete without exploring these valuable Bible passages.**

Certain themes run throughout this entire volume, and we examine these same themes from many different angles, as one might examine the different facets of the same fine diamond. In this seeming repetition, a more complete beauty may be seen.

We pray that the final product is a book that makes an excellent study for the individual reader, a devotional tool for the intercessor, a practical outline for the home group or Sunday School teacher, and sound doctrinal teaching for the pastor or minister.

Charles Simpson Ministries (CSM) provides many valuable resources 'Equipping you for victorious Christian living.' In addition to its award-winning publications, CSM provides audio tapes by outstanding Bible teachers, as well as missionary support through its subsidary, International Outreach Ministries. For a free catalog or more information on CSM, please contact:

CSM
PO Box Z
Mobile, AL 36616 USA
(334) 633-7900

May the Lord bless you greatly as you explore the following pages.

Stephen Simpson
Associate Editor

PREFACE

Covenant is the voluntary binding together of two or more persons for a common purpose. Unique among all covenants is the one that God Himself established with those who accept Jesus Christ as Lord. This covenant joined the sovereign God to fallen mankind through the blood of His Son. The reconciling of man to God through Christ re-establishes God's Kingdom – His reign on earth as in heaven.

Governments are based on covenants. Before a common purpose can be carried out, there must be a mutual commitment of the parties to one another, to the administration, and to the purpose. Covenant civilizes man. It binds him to purpose and benefits higher than his own appetites, and enables him to achieve more lofty goals through cooperation. Covenant, therefore, is the decision to give up some personal freedoms in order to realize the common good.

In the case of the New Covenant, those who receive Christ do more than give up some of their personal freedoms. Because they recognize His divine nature and their sinfulness, they submit their entire lives to His will and purpose. The resulting reign of Christ by the Holy Spirit produces righteousness, peace and joy.

Covenant transforms a group of individuals into a unit. The Bible speaks of the Jews as 'a people' or 'the people of God'. Its references to the Gentiles are that they are not a people. Gentiles were not covenanted or united with God. 1 Peter 2:10 puts it succinctly. 'For you once were not a people, but now you are the people of God' (NAS). The New Covenant in the blood of Christ joins us to God, and to His people, from Abraham on until the present. We are one in Christ.

It is this union with God and His people that enables Him to govern through Christ, Who sits at His right hand. His government is a one-to-one relationship between Christ and individuals. And beyond that, it is a relationship between a King and His people. Receiving Jesus as Christ means receiving Him as the anointed King. 'Christ' is not Jesus' last name; it is His title and function as Lord and Savior.

The New Covenant is eternal. The covenants of the Old Testament were ratified with the blood of animals and were mediated in an earthly sanctuary, through earthly priests. However, the New Covenant was ratified with the divine blood of Christ in the heavenly sanctuary, through His eternal priesthood. Therefore, the New Covenant is eternal, and the Kingdom it establishes is eternal.

If Christ is King, how then does His Kingdom operate? What are its precepts? This is what we hope to express in this book, with the Holy Spirit's help. Acknowledging that we 'know in part' and 'see through a glass darkly', it is our desire to set forth a systematic presentation of God, His purpose, and activity in history. Furthermore, we will describe what He has provided for mankind that mankind cannot provide for itself, and what our response to His grace and provisions should be. Then we will see how His government functions in our personal lives, families, the Church, and world once we have acknowledged His Lordship.

This material will be presented in seven sections compiled by proven and practical authors and scholars. It comes from the labor of those who have not only studied, but have committed themselves to the Covenant and the Kingdom. They come from widely diverse theological and social backgrounds, to the common ground of faith in Christ. These lessons are presented in the conviction that the Holy Bible is the Word of God, and is the standard for faith and practice. They are presented with the conviction that the Holy Spirit is the instructor of divine truth and a relationship to the Holy Spirit is essential to understanding the message of the Bible.

These lessons are presented in a simple, direct manner with additional resources available. We encourage a commitment from the outset to complete the 126 lessons in the seven sections, so that we can be fully established in Christ and His eternal purpose: 'Thy Kingdom Come'.

My personal thanks to the writers, editors and instructors who join me in presenting *The Covenant and the Kingdom*.

Charles Simpson
Editor

FACULTY

CHARLES SIMPSON – Editor and Author

The son of a Baptist pastor, Charles Simpson is an internationally-known author, Bible teacher, pastor and church planter. He responded to God's call into ministry in 1955, and received his Bachelor's Degree in History from William Carey College before attending New Orleans Baptist Theological Seminary. In 1964, Charles was baptized in the Holy Spirit and became a pioneer in the Charismatic Renewal movement. He was part of the editorial leadership of *New Wine* Magazine from its inception in 1969. In 1985, the ministry of *New Wine* gave birth to a new worship ministry, which eventually grew into a separate, highly-successful outreach known as Integrity Music. Charles is the author of numerous books, including *The Challenge to Care*, *Courageous Living*, *Your Home or His?* and *A New Way to Live*, and he has personally ministered around the world in more than thirty nations. Charles is the Senior Pastor of Covenant Church of Mobile, a congregation he helped launch in 1973. This year, 1995, marks the celebration of thirty-five years of marriage for Charles and his wife, Carolyn.

STEPHEN SIMPSON – Associate Editor and Author

Since 1981, Stephen has been a part of the editorial staff of CSM Publishing, and in the same year, he responded to God's call into the ministry. He received his Bachelor's Degree in Journalism from Spring Hill College, attended Reformed Theological Seminary, and participated in the Liberty Ministry Training Institute. Stephen and his wife, Susanne, have served on the ministry team at Covenant Church of Mobile since 1985, with special focus on ministry to youth and young married couples. In 1987, he was part of the launching of *Christian Conquest* Magazine, a publication for which he continues to serve as Editor. Stephen is the Founder of Entertainment and Arts Renewal (EAR), a resource for concerned consumers.

ROBERT GRANT – Contributing Editor and Author

A longtime pastor and Bible teacher, Robert completed undergraduate studies in religion at Southern California College and further graduate studies in New Testament and Church history at George Washington University. He received his Master's Degree in counseling psychology from Valley Christian University. For more than five years, he served as the Director of Biblical Research for CSM Publishing. Robert has helped to launch churches across the United States and Canada and now serves as the Senior Pastor of Summit View Covenant Church in Colorado Springs, Colorado. He is heard each week with his wife, Sue, on their popular radio program, 'The Grant Connection'.

DR. DOW ROBINSON – Contributing Editor and Author

For more than 50 years, Dow Robinson has given his life for training and encouraging individuals and leaders in the Word of God. Many of these years have been spent among the

Developing Nations, including more than 25 years with his wife, Lois, in Mexico as Wycliffe Bible translators. While in Mexico, he and Lois translated and dedicated the New Testament for the Aztec-speaking peoples. He received his Bachelor's Degree in English Literature, Greek, and History from Houghton College, and his Master of Divinity Degree in Greek, Hebrew, and History of Doctrine from Fuller Theological Seminary. In 1966, Dow earned his PhD. in Linguistics and Cultural Anthropology from the Hartford Seminary Foundation. He has taught at the University of Oklahoma and served as Academic Dean for Liberty Theological Seminary in Pensacola, Florida. Dr. Robinson is presently the Dean of Cross-Cultural Studies for the American Center of Theological Studies, and continues to travel widely teaching on Christian education, church planting and missions.

DR. ERICK SCHENKEL – Contributing Author

After receiving his Bachelor's Degree from Harvard College and his Master's of Theology from Harvard Divinity School, Erick earned his PhD. from Harvard University in American Church History. He and his wife, Elizabeth, have five children and they reside in the Boston area, where Erick serves as the Pastor of Covenant Church in Arlington. With more than twenty years of pastoral experience, he remains a popular speaker among students and educators, and continues to be actively involved with Christian education.

GARY BROWNING – Contributing Author

Gary's ministry spans more than twenty-five years as a pastor, worship leader, and counselor. He received his Bachelor's Degree in Religion from the University of Mobile and is completing his Master's Degree in Counseling. Gary is the Founder of The Discovery Group, a healing gathering for those who are being restored. He is also active in business and service, with a burden for 'inner city' residents.

BRUCE LONGSTRETH – Contributing Author

An anointed musician and speaker, Bruce graduated from Simpson College in San Francisco with a Bachelor's Degree in Religion, and attended Golden Gate Baptist Theological Seminary. He was the Editor of *New Wine* Magazine for two years, as well as his role for five years as Editor for *FatherGram*, a resource for families. Bruce has served as a pastor within the Christian Missionary Alliance churches, Covenant churches, Presbyterian churches, and presently serves as the Pastor for Jacksonville Christian Center in Jackson Hole, Wyoming, where he resides with his wife, Janet.

DR. FRANK LONGINO – Contributing Author

Born to Salvation Army officer parents, Frank was raised in an atmosphere where biblical training and world outreach were lifestyle priorities. He received his Bachelor's Degree in History and Philosophy from the University of Richmond and his Master's of Divinity Degree from the Louisville Southern Baptist Theological Seminary. He earned his Doctorate in Christian Education from Liberty Theological Seminary, located in Humble, Texas, where he resides with his wife, Betty. Dr. Longino is now the President of Liberty Theological Seminary and Director of Adult Education for Deerbrook Church in Humble. An accomplished musician, arranger and conductor, Frank also is the President of Selah Music Ministries, providing published music and instructional material for church intrumentalists.

SPECIAL THANKS TO OTHERS WHO CONTRIBUTED

Eduardo Andrade, Duke Bendix, Keith Currie, Michael Davis, Bill DeCleene, Dennis Harris, Oliver Heath, Gary Henley, Steve Humble, Richard McAfee, John Moreland, Larry Mullins, Dennis Peacocke, Steve Rannells, David Redish, Glen Roachelle, Vernon Simpson, Sam Soleyn and Bob Terrell.

'*The Covenant and the Kingdom* is one of the most comprehensive Bible study curriculums I have ever seen. It is replete with powerful truth, all cross-referenced with Scripture. I recommend this material to anyone who is serious about studying God's faithfulness to His covenant.'

Tommy Barnett
Pastor
Phoenix First Assembly of God

CONTENTS

SECTION 5: CHRIST'S KINGDOM AND THE CHURCH   235

SECTION 6: CHRIST'S KINGDOM IN THE MARKETPLACE

SECTION 7: CHRIST'S KINGDOM IN THE WORLD

SECTION 1:

GOD AND COVENANT HISTORY

LESSON 1 – THE ONE TRUE GOD

PURPOSE

Jesus said, 'This is eternal life that they may know You, the only true God, and Jesus Christ Whom You have sent' (John 17:3). Jesus' statement concerning eternal life is very important to our study of God. We live in a 'pluralistic' culture which has many 'gods'. A prevailing philosophy of today is 'Have it your way.' People have created their own special gods based upon their own particular beliefs. Therefore, it is important for us to look at how God has revealed Himself in Scripture.

GLOSSARY

Immanent – nearness or closeness.

Pluralistic – when used in a religious context, refers to a multitude of different religions and philosophies.

Sovereign – one who possesses ultimate authority to rule.

Supreme – above and higher than all others.

Transcend – to be prior to, above, or beyond.

WHO IS GOD?

Perhaps no other question has been asked more frequently, pondered more deeply, or discussed more widely than, 'Who is God?' At some time or another in the lives of each person, we wonder, 'Is there a God, and if so, how does that relate to me?'

The Good News is that not only is there a God, but that He deeply desires to reveal Himself to us. God has provided us with an account of Himself, His relationship to mankind, and His plan for all the Earth . . . and that account is recorded in The Holy Bible.

More will be said about the Bible, its authority and its authenticity, later in this book. In this lesson, we want to present the picture that the Bible paints of God.

Ephesians 4:6
Genesis 1:1–31
Psalm 33:6–9
Revelation 4:11
Isaiah 40:21–31
Colossians 1:16–17
Nehemiah 9:6; Job 38–39
Psalm 104; Hebrews 1:3

GOD IS THE SOVEREIGN ONE

The Bible tells us that there is only one true God. He rules and reigns over all creation and all people. In fact, He created all things, He controls all things, and He sustains all things. God is not only the Lord, but He is the Father of all.

Psalm 90:1–2
Psalm 102:25–27
Isaiah 44:6–8; Isaiah 57:15

GOD IS THE ETERNAL ONE

Not only is God the Sovereign Ruler of all things, but He is eternal . . . that is, He is without beginning or end. God was God before time

Hebrews 13:8
2 Peter 3:8

Revelation 1:4–18

existed and He will be God when time comes to an end. In fact, God Himself created time and He stands outside of it.

Or, to put it another way, He is:

The God Who was – He transcends time
The God Who is – He created time
The God Who is to come – He will end time

GOD IS COMPLETE AND ALL-KNOWING

John 5:26; Acts 17:25
Genesis 1:1

God is not reliant upon anything or anyone. He is absolutely complete in Himself and He depends on nothing else. Though He is **distinct** from creation, He is not **divorced** from creation.

In fact, creation itself is dependent upon Him.

Matthew 5:45
Isaiah 46:9–11
Psalm 147:4–5
Hebrews 4:13

Psalm 139

God is all-knowing and is acquainted with every detail of His creation. We refer to this as His **Omniscience** ... simply put, God knows everything!

He knows all events, all creatures, and all time ... past, present, and future. God knows all people, for He created each one.

God knows you better than anyone else – He even knows you better than you know yourself. God knows your:

Proverbs 15:11
Ezekiel 11:5
Proverbs 15:3

Motives – what is in your heart
Thoughts – what is in your mind
Status – whether you are saved or lost

No one can know creation better than the One Who is the Creator.

GOD IS HOLY

The word 'Holy' is much-misunderstood. In the Hebrew language, the word used for holy is *qadosh*, which indicates being set apart, or dedicated for a righteous cause. It is separation from that which is unrighteous, defiling, or impure in order to fulfill that which is righteous and pure.

Isaiah 6:1–5
Revelation 4

Leviticus 19:2

God is unique ... there is no other like Him. He is holy and perfect in His character and in His actions. His nature and His presence are majestic.

Yet, He calls us to be like Him ... to dedicate ourselves to His righteous purpose. Because of His holiness – and His great love and grace – we can also participate in His righteous cause.

Proverbs 6:16–19
Psalm 119:104
Psalm 119:163
Proverbs 8:13

Because of His holy nature, God despises sin. Sin, *hamartia* in the Greek language, means simply 'missing the mark.' It can mean failure, impurity, degradation, wrongdoing, and other negative forms of behavior, but the ultimate problem with sin is that it causes us to miss the target; to move away from the blessed purpose for which God created us. Sin is against God's nature. He hates the sin, but provides redemption for the sinner (which we will discuss momentarily).

2 Corinthians 6:17

Sin causes separation. It cannot exist in God's presence. God's holy nature calls for separation from anything that is unclean. The road to restoration with a Holy God for those who have fallen into sin is called **repentance**, or a turning away (separation) from the sin.

While sin itself leads to separation from God – and ultimately death – the Good News is that we are called out of sin, and God's holy nature influences us toward redemption and holiness.

GOD IS THE LOVING ONE

If the end of the matter was simply that God is holy, and humanity is sinful – and the wages of sin is death – then that would not be very good news at all!

But the majestic, holy, all-powerful God loves us, and He has provided a way for us to escape the curse and bondage of sin.

God's love for us is unique in that it is self-sacrificing and completely pure in motivation. In the New Testament Greek, the word for God's kind of love is *agape*.

It was this divine love that motivated God to send His only Son, Jesus Christ, into the world to die on a cross for our sins. He died that we might live. No one has ever loved so much. This is the standard by which all other love is measured.

The death and subsequent Resurrection of Jesus Christ demonstrates to us His love and His desire to deal redemptively with us. He continually causes good to triumph over evil, and He promises that nothing can separate us from His love.

APPLICATION

Review the characteristics of God given in this lesson. Have you always viewed God this way? How did you view God prior to reading the lesson? Are there any other characteristics to add to this list?

CONCLUSION

The world is filled with many false views of God. People without a knowledge and relationship with God tend to create their own 'gods' – either a god who is made up of nature and creation, or a god who is totally absent and separated from creation. The One True God is neither of these. The God of the Bible is the Creator, not the creation; He is transcendent; He is holy. Yet, He has not separated Himself from that which He has made. He is actively involved. He is near. He is immanent. It is in knowing Him that we have eternal life and blessing. Only in knowing Him can we understand and fulfill our purpose for living.

Romans 6:23
1 John 1:7
1 John 3:2–5

John 3:16
Romans 5:1–11

Romans 8:28
Romans 8:35–39

LESSON 2 – GOD: THE TRINITY

PURPOSE

The doctrine of the Trinity is a fundamental truth of the Christian faith. So important is this truth that it has been called 'the heart of Christianity.' Because of this strategic importance, it is one doctrine that has been attacked most severely. Therefore, before we go any further, we must take a look at the fact that the God of the Bible is one in nature, yet three in personhood. In God, there is a perfect balance between unity and diversity.

GLOSSARY

Doctrine – authoritative teaching.

Diversity – the quality of having many different members.

Unity – oneness; especially in an entity having varied parts.

Trinity – God revealed in the Bible as Father, Son (Jesus), and Holy Spirit.

THE DIVERSITY OF THE TRINITY

First, let us recognize that when we are dealing with the Trinity, we are dealing with a mystery. The Bible, God's Word, is our source and our standard for examining this most profound revelation of Who God is.

Romans 1:7
John 6:41–45
Matthew 6:6–15

Scripture says plainly that the Father is God. Jesus Himself acknowledged God as Father, and taught us to pray to 'Our Father, Who is in heaven . . .'

Isaiah 9:6–7; John 1:1–5
Colossians 2:8–9
John 5:16–47
John 6:26–59
John 8:25–59
John 10:25–39
John 14:1–24
John 20:28–29

Scripture also reveals that the Son, Jesus Christ, is God. One grossly erroneous claim made by atheists and deceivers is that Jesus never claimed to be God or the Son of God. Scripture proves clearly that not only is Jesus God, but that He believed it and stated it. Yet many people, perhaps due to a lack of knowledge of the Bible, have fallen prey to this false teaching. Jesus Christ is God, and He says so!

Acts 1:1–8
Acts 2:1–21
Romans 8:5–14
John 14:15–18
John 15:26–27
Acts 5:1–5

Perhaps the most often ignored or misunderstood Person of the Trinity is the Holy Spirit. Yet, the Bible tells us that the Holy Spirit is God, which ought to make us want to get to know Him better. Jesus spoke of the Holy Spirit as the Comforter or Helper, the Promised One Who would guide us in all Truth. And when Ananias and Sapphira lied to the Holy Spirit concerning their giving, Peter told them that they had lied to God Himself.

THE UNITY OF THE TRINITY

Deuteronomy 6:4–6
Mark 12:29–30

In the Bible, we see that though God is Three Persons, He is One in His nature. All three members of the Trinity function in perfect harmony and union. We should therefore love Him with all of our heart, soul, mind, and strength.

John 10:30
John 5:19
John 8:29

There is perfect unity between the Father and the Son. Jesus said that Father and Son were one and the same, and that He could do only those things that He saw the Father doing ... it is His heart's desire to please the Father.

John 16:5–15

Likewise, there is perfect unity between the Son and the Holy Spirit. The Holy Spirit declares what is from Jesus, He brings glory to Jesus, and He represents Jesus in the earth.

John 15:26–27
1 Corinthians 2:9–16

And, it is critical to understand that there is perfect unity between the Father and the Holy Spirit. The Spirit proceeds from the Father, and He is the One Who makes the Father's will known to us.

Matthew 28:18–20
2 Corinthians 13:14

Finally, there is perfect unity between the Father, Son, and Holy Spirit together. Jesus Himself commanded believers to baptize in the name of the Father, in name of the Son, and the name of the Spirit. The Apostle Paul blessed the Church in Corinth in this manner also ... he speaks of all three co-equally. In the Trinity there is grace, love, and communion.

THE ACTIVITY OF THE TRINITY

Genesis 1:1–27

During Creation, before making Adam, God said, 'Let us make man in our own image.' In God, there is distinction without separation. We must realize that throughout history, **all of God** does **all that God does**. Creation provides a picture of this:

The Father Initiates – the thought
The Son Mediates – the Word
The Holy Spirit Administrates Through Action – the dynamic power

The late Bible teacher Ern Baxter put it clearly when he said, 'The Father thinks it; the Son speaks it; the Spirit does it.'

Matthew 3:16–17
Luke 3:21–22

Another picture of the Trinity is found at the Baptism of Jesus by John the Baptist. The Father spoke from Heaven, Jesus obeyed, and the Spirit anointed and empowered Jesus.

APPLICATION

Ephesians 4:4–6
1 Corinthians 12:3–31

Why is it important for us to understand that God is One? Is there disunity in your family or church? If so, what are positive steps that can be taken to have unity with diversity of gifts and functions? Finally, do a study of the Gospel of John, taking special notice of the Persons of the Trinity.

CONCLUSION

John 17:6–26

God reveals Himself in Scripture as both One and Three – a difficult doctrine to fully comprehend. But as we accept, affirm, and apply the model of the Trinity to our own lives, we are better able to keep a balance between unity and diversity ... the one and the many.

Sometimes, people are tempted to choose one to the exclusion of the other. This could produce either irresponsibly independent individuals on the one hand, or overly controlling communities on the other. Neither extreme is proper nor desirable. Unity with diversity should be a goal for all of us. The Trinity is the model for the life of the individual in the community ... distinction without separation ... differences without division. This is God's desire for His people.

LESSON 3 – GOD THE FATHER

PURPOSE

Luke 11:1–4
Matthew 6:9–13

'Lord, teach us to pray,' the disciples of Jesus asked. Jesus' response to them is now commonly known as 'The Lord's Prayer,' and begins with, 'Our Father, Who is in Heaven...' God is not impersonal, neither is He uninvolved with His creation. Instead, His Word tells us that He is a Father who desires a close fellowship and relationship with His children.

The previous lesson discussed the Father's role within the Trinity. This lesson will also discuss His relationship with us.

GLOSSARY

Adoption – the act of receiving into a family one that is not naturally a part of that family.

Begotten – term used to describe the eternal relationship of God the Son with God the Father.

Covenant – in its primary biblical usage, a bond which God has established between Himself and His people and between His people with one another.

THE FATHER OF ALL

Ephesians 4:6

John 3:16

Romans 8:14–16

Exodus 4:22
Deuteronomy 32:6
Hosea 11:1; Jeremiah 31:9
Matthew 6:1–15
Galatians 3:26–4:7

God is not simply a father; He is the Father, and He has deliberately revealed Himself as such in the Bible.

First, as we saw in the last lesson, God is the Father of the Lord Jesus. Jesus is the only begotten Son of the Father in that He is uniquely the eternal Son.

When we believe that Jesus Christ is the Son of God, and we confess Him as Lord of our lives, an amazing and wonderful transition occurs ... we are adopted into the Father's family. We become His children by adoption.

Scripture repeatedly reveals God as the **Father of Israel**, having created and preserved the nation by means of His power.

For those who are believers in Christ, God is the Father, and each believer becomes an 'heir' of His promises.

THE FATHER AS CREATOR

1 Corinthians 8:6
Nehemiah 9:6
Matthew 5:45
Matthew 6:26–32
Titus 2:11–14
1 Peter 1:13–19

Before God created the heavens and the earth, He existed as the Father. Out of His Fatherhood has come everything else. God the Father created all things, and by Him are all things sustained. The Father is a generous provider for His creation – indeed, He loves His creation. God has even provided redemption for His creation.

Jeremiah 31:1
2 Corinthians 6:18
Hosea 11:1
Romans 8:31–39
Hebrews 12:5–7
Deuteronomy 8:5
Deuteronomy 1:30–33
Psalm 59:16
Psalm 105:37–45
Exodus 33:14–16
Hebrews 13:5; Genesis 3:9
Isaiah 43:5–7
Matthew 10:10–14
Luke 15:11–32
Psalm 10:14–18
Psalm 146:9

Genesis 9:8–9
Genesis 15:18
Exodus 19:1–6
2 Samuel 7:1–17
Jeremiah 31:31–34

THE FATHER OF HIS CHILDREN

God wants to be your Father, and for you to be His child. How does God relate to His children? We can see His nature as Father expressed in many ways: love, discipline, protection, provision, and presence.

And, as a loving Father, He will seek out His children who are lost ... those who may turn away from Him and fall into trouble. The Father loves His children, and does not forget them.

Finally, we see His Father's heart revealed in that He is a defender of the fatherless ... those left destitute by natural circumstances have a Father ... and a friend ... in God.

THE FATHER INITIATES COVENANT

As our Father, God desires to dwell with us. The way that He accomplishes this is by making covenant. Throughout the Bible and history, we can see God continually initiating covenant with man.

The Father initiated covenant with Noah, Abraham, the people of Israel, and David, just to name a few. And, He initiates covenant with all people through Jesus Christ, the promised New Covenant.

FATHER KNOWS BEST

God is the perfect Father, the model for all fatherhood. He provides a pattern for earthly fathers to follow in:

> **Headship** – He leads us
> **Care** – He provides for our every need
> **Nurture** – He gives life
> **Commitment** – He never leaves or forsakes us

In fact, God not only provides an example for earthly fathers to follow, but as the loving Father of all who will believe in Him, He will help and strengthen fathers who call upon His Name.

APPLICATION

Does it make any difference if God is revealed as Father or mother? If so, why? Then, read John 8:28-29. Whom did Jesus come to reveal? God is the perfect example of love and concern for others. Can you think of one person who is in need of your love? In what tangible, practical way will you express your love to them?

CONCLUSION

Throughout Scripture and history, God has consistently revealed Himself as Father. He was the Father of Israel, and prophets referred to God as the Father. He is the Father to all who confess Jesus Christ as Lord. Fatherhood is the heart of God, and He wants no one to be left fatherless. In fact, in Psalm 68:5, God is called 'a father to the fatherless.'

LESSON 4 – GOD THE SON

PURPOSE

God the Son is eternal with the Father, and He became man in Jesus Christ. Jesus declared, 'I am the way, the truth, and the life. No one comes to the Father except through Me' (John 14:6 NKJ). The question being asked today by many people is, 'Are there many different ways to reach God, or is there only one true way?' Do all of the various religious paths eventually lead to God? This is a very serious question. In this lesson, we will look at the only way to God ... the only 'go-between' for God and man. His name is Jesus Christ, the Son of God.

GLOSSARY

Mediator – a 'go-between' or agent who acts to settle disputes.

Messiah – refers to 'The Anointed One' in Hebrew language; Greek equivalent is 'Christ'.

Incarnation – the act in which God the Son became a man.

THE ETERNAL SON

John 1:1
John 8:58

Matthew 14:33
Hebrews 1
John 17:5
Colossians 1:13–23

As we noted earlier, the Trinity is a great mystery. Yet, Scripture does tell us plainly that God the Son is eternal with God the Father. The Son existed in the beginning with the Father at creation. And, Jesus Himself said, 'Before Abraham was, I AM.'

The Son receives worship, and shares the Father's glory. He not only acts in creation, but is in fact the Ruler of it all.

We see the Lordship of Jesus demonstrated in many ways, including His Lordship over:

Matthew 8:23–37
Mark 6:56
Luke 8:26–36
John 11:38–44

Nature – He calms the wind and the sea
Disease – He heals the sick
Demons – He expels evil spirits
Life – He raises the dead

GOD BECAME MAN

John 3:16–17
Isaiah 9:6–7
Matthew 1:18–25
Philippians 2:7
John 1:1–18
Hebrews 2:14–18
Matthew 4:2
Matthew 21:18
Matthew 8:24
John 4:6
1 Peter 4:1
1 Corinthians 15:3

God the Father was so concerned for man's condition of sin and death, that He sent the Son to earth to become man and to deliver all those who would believe Him. God the Son was incarnated as a man named Jesus. He is called Jesus Christ, because 'Christ' means Savior or Anointed One.

Jesus was both fully man and fully God. While we will examine the importance of this in future lessons, it is important to note that God became man in birth, in development, and in likeness. God became a servant, in flesh and blood, who faced temptation, physical limitations, hunger and thirst, weariness, pain ... and ultimately, death.

THE MEDIATOR BETWEEN GOD AND MAN

1 Timothy 2:5

God is completely holy and righteous. Humanity, because of sin, became separated from God. Who can mediate this terrible separation?

Who can go between God and man, to restore a right relationship? There is only One Who is able: Jesus Christ, the Son of God. Why is He the only One qualified to be our Mediator before the Father?

Sin brought a curse of separation and death to humanity. Mankind needed a Deliverer ... One Who could pay the price for sin and break the curse. But there was no one person without sin, no one who was worthy to pay the price for the sins of man. God alone was holy and without sin. But it was humanity that had sinned; not God. In order to break the curse of sin, a man must pay the price. How could this impossible impasse be broken?

Hebrews 4:14–16

God became man in Jesus, and He lived a completely sinless life. Though He faced temptation in all areas, He did not ever give in. He never 'missed the mark'.

Romans 6:1–11

Then, He died in our place. He died for all of the sins that had ever been committed before His day, as well as for all of the sins that have been committed since then.

Thank God, the story does not end there; because Jesus triumphed even over death, rising again just as He had promised.

John 11:23–26
1 Corinthians 15:12–22
Hebrews 9:16–22
Acts 1:9–11; Romans 8:34

After His Resurrection, He taught His followers about the kingdom of God, and then ascended into Heaven, where He now sits at the right hand of the Father ... praying for you. He is our one and only Mediator.

PRIEST, PROPHET AND KING

The Son is God's 'Ultimate Office Bearer'. He is the supreme example of service to the Father.

John 2:13–22
Matthew 21:12–16
Hebrews 9:23–28

Jesus is a **Priest** who cleansed the Temple in Jerusalem, declaring it to be a house of prayer. And by His great sacrificial death, once and for all, He prepared the heavenly temple. At this moment, Jesus, our Great High Priest, is 'making intercession' on our behalf.

Hebrews 7:24–28

John 1:1
Matthew 4:23
Luke 4:18–19
Mark 13:1–23
Hebrews 1:3

He is also a **Prophet** who reveals God's Word. In fact, He is the 'Word made flesh'. Jesus proclaimed the Good News of God's Kingdom, but also prophetically warned of the coming judgement. We also see in Scripture that all things are held together by His Word. There has never been a greater prophet than Jesus.

Acts 2:33–36
John 18:36–37
Matthew 28:18

And, Jesus is the **King**, the Ruler of all things. He was crowned Lord and King by God the Father, and He Himself declared that He was the King. All authority in heaven and on earth belongs to Jesus Christ.

THE OBEDIENT SON

Luke 2:41–52

Even at the age of 12, it was clear that Jesus was a remarkable young man. All were amazed by Him, even the great wise men of that day. Jesus understood clearly that He was to do the will of the Father, and He said this to his earthly parents, Joseph and Mary. Yet, He was also

Mark 1:35
John 8:26–29

Matthew 26:39
Hebrews 12:2

Hebrews 1:2

able to submit Himself to them as the parents to whom the Father had entrusted Him. Because of this, He grew in favor with God and all those who were around Him.

Jesus prayed daily, seeking the Father's will. He only wanted to do those things that pleased the Father, and He was attentive to the Father's voice.

The obedient Son was not even willing to allow death to stand in the way between Him and His Father's will. When He faced the prospect of a terrible death on the cross, He plainly did not wish to inflict it upon Himself. But He was willing to endure it to fulfill the Father's purpose and 'because of the joy that was set before Him.' The Father's will was His overriding motivation.

Having fulfilled His mission in death, resurrection, and ascension, He obtained an excellent inheritance and reward from the Father ... the Name of Jesus is above every name that has ever been named.

APPLICATION

What Scriptural evidence can you find that reveals Jesus to be co-equal with the Father? What proof exists of Jesus' humanity? How does His obedience to the Father apply to your own life? Memorize John 14:6 and share it with someone who believes there are 'many paths to God.'

CONCLUSION

Many individuals throughout history have claimed to be 'messiahs'. There are even those today who claim that they are the 'way to God' or that some novel philosophical notion will bring salvation. But Jesus said, 'If you abide in My word, you are My disciples indeed. And you shall know the truth, and the truth shall make you free' (John 8:31–32 NKJ). The truth is, we are not the ones who make the decision on who can be our Mediator. The Father has sent Jesus Christ, His only Son as the Mediator between God and man. There is only one way to God, and that is through Jesus, the promised Messiah. Only in believing Him can we find reconciliation, reality, and resurrection life.

LESSON 5 – GOD THE HOLY SPIRIT

PURPOSE

God the Father initiates the covenant, God the Son mediates the covenant, and God the Holy Spirit makes the covenant a reality in our lives. The Apostle Paul wrote in Romans 14:17 that the kingdom of God is 'righteousness, peace, and joy in the Holy Spirit.' Through the Spirit, God empowers us to do His will 'on earth as it is in heaven.' In this lesson, we will see how the Spirit is sent by the Father and the Son. He is God . . . present with us right now.

GLOSSARY

Kingdom – the domain over which one rules; the extension of the rulership itself.

Paracletos – Greek word used in Scripture translated as 'One called alongside to help'; The Comforter and Helper promised by Jesus.

Righteousness – rightness in relationship to God and man.

WHO IS THE HOLY SPIRIT?

Genesis 1:2
Genesis 2:7
Psalm 33:6
John 15:26
Acts 15:29
John 16:13
Revelation 2:7
1 Corinthians 12:11
John 14:26
Romans 8:27
Hebrews 9:14
Psalm 139:7
Acts 1:8
1 Corinthians 2:1–11

When we talk about the Holy Spirit, we are not referring to a vague essence, nebulous power, or abstract force; the Holy Spirit is not simply a funny feeling in the pit of our stomachs or goosebumps! No, the Holy Spirit is God . . . a person of the Holy Trinity.

He is called 'Spirit' because He is the 'Breath' and 'Wind' that was present at creation. He proceeds from the Father and the Son, and there are many personal actions ascribed to Him, such as: Searching, Judging, Hearing, Speaking, Choosing, Teaching, and Interceding.

The Holy Spirit, because He is God, has the characteristics of the Divine Nature. He is eternal, present everywhere, all-powerful, and all-knowing.

THE POWER OF THE HOLY SPIRIT

Acts 1–2

Genesis 1:2
2 Peter 1:20–21

Matthew 1:20; Luke 1:35
Luke 4:18–21
Romans 1:4

Hebrews 2:4
John 16:8; Acts 2:4

The Holy Spirit is God in action in the earth and in our lives. He empowered the disciples and He empowers us to witness to the reality of Christ's eternal Kingdom.

At creation, the Holy Spirit was present and active. Throughout the entire recording of Holy Scripture, the Spirit inspired and directed 'holy men of God'.

And, the Holy Spirit was active in God's redemptive plan in Jesus Christ. Jesus was **conceived** by the Spirit, **anointed** by the Spirit, and **raised from the dead** by the Spirit.

The Spirit Himself is a witness to Kingdom reality through signs and wonders, convicting hearts, and in putting His Word in our mouths.

Titus 1:4–7

We are **renewed** by the power of the Holy Spirit. He washes and regenerates us because of His mercy and grace. The Greek word *anakainosis* for renewing, suggests a transformation and change of heart. Because of this transformation, we become 'heirs according to the hope of eternal life.'

BE FILLED WITH THE SPIRIT

John 16:7

The Holy Spirit is the Helper promised to us by the Lord Jesus, and He dwells within the heart of every believer. If we will hear His voice, and obey, we can receive the power to fulfill God's wonderful purpose for our lives.

1 John 2:20–27
John 16:13
1 Corinthians 2:10

The Spirit **teaches** us, and helps us to know the truth. Without His guidance, we could easily fall into error, deception, and sin. He is the source of God's truth and the revealer of God's wisdom.

Romans 8:14
Philippians 3:3
Acts 8:26–39
Matthew 10:19
Acts 4:8–12
Acts 4:31
Acts 6:10
Acts 13:9–13

The Holy Spirit **leads** us, if we are God's children. By the Spirit, we are led in worship, 'putting no confidence in the flesh.' He motivates and guides us in evangelism ... the sharing of the Good News of Christ's Kingdom with other people. He will even give us the right words to say when our own wisdom fails us.

We are **controlled** by the Spirit as we yield our lives to Him. 'Control' is a word that has a negative connotation in modern culture ... perhaps that is why so many people are 'out of control' like a fast-moving automobile without a steering wheel on a treacherous road. When viewed in this context then, we can see how control could be very positive, especially in light of the blessings that the Spirit's control produces in our lives. By His control, we receive:

1 Peter 1:2
Ephesians 1:13
Galatians 5:22–23
1 Corinthians 12:1–11

Sanctification – a Spirit-filled life
Assurance – a Spirit-sealed life
Fruitfulness – a Spirit-led life
Dynamic – a Spirit-gifted life

John 15:26
Romans 8:26
Ephesians 6:18

We are **empowered** by the Spirit, Who is our Helper and Comforter. He helps us in our weaknesses and helps us in our prayers. The Spirit gives us boldness, because our confidence is in Him and in the strength that He gives.

Ephesians 5:18–19

With all of these blessings in mind, is it any wonder that the Apostle Paul urged the young Christians in the city of Ephesus to 'be filled with the Spirit'? He encouraged them to speak to one another with songs from Scripture, hymns that they had written, and songs that the Spirit put in their hearts, and to do these things continually and repeatedly.

One of the greatest evangelists in modern history was Dwight L. Moody. On one occasion, he was asked, 'Brother Moody, why do you testify to so many different infillings of the Holy Spirit?' He replied, 'Because I leak.' Truthfully, though we may have experienced an infilling of the Spirit yesterday, we need to ask for 'our daily bread' today ... be filled with the Spirit ... right now ... as you read this!

APPLICATION

How do we know that the Holy Spirit is a person? Can you list four characteristics of the Holy Spirit that reveal He is God? In what area of your life do you most need the Holy Spirit's help right now? Take a moment to seek Him.

CONCLUSION

Historically, far too little attention has been paid by theologians to the person and work of the Holy Spirit. This has resulted in a distortion of Christian doctrine and a lack of His dynamic in the lives of many believers. But in recent years, the Holy Spirit Himself has inspired a fresh emphasis on His role, resulting in dramatic renewal in every area of Church life. Let His life renew yours.

LESSON 6 – MAN AS THE IMAGE OF GOD

PURPOSE

God created man in His image. Though man was created to be like God, he was not to be God. Many people today are confused by the notion that humanity is improving, evolving, and becoming more 'godlike'. This is a terrible deception, as any study of modern history will show that human progress has been merely technological, not moral and spiritual. In this lesson, we will see God's intention when He created man 'in His image.' It is only as we acknowledge our Creator and our need to be restored to our Creator's image that we can be delivered from the curse of sin and death.

GLOSSARY

Image – a likeness or reflection.

Man – unless context obviously indicates otherwise, 'man' refers to humanity in general, both males and females.

THE CROWN OF CREATION

Genesis 1–2

When God completed His work at creation, He looked and saw that it was good. The Lord was pleased with it all – He made no mistakes. But He did not create all things equally. Man was the crown of creation, and the Lord created him to have dominion over all other created things.

Man's creation was unique. The Trinity took counsel before creating man. Not only was man created in God's image, but God Himself breathed the life into the first man, Adam. Then, God gave man authority over creation.

THE IMAGE OF GOD

The image, or likeness, of God distinguishes man from animals and plants ... even angels. Though we share some common traits with other created beings, we are also very different because of our unique nature.

Man is a person, not an animal. This very statement, once accepted as common sense, has been increasingly under attack by those who neither know their Creator nor His purpose for their lives and for humanity. But Scripture and history show us clearly that man has some very distinct characteristics:

Genesis 2:16–17
Romans 5–6

Reason – God spoke to and commanded man.
Response – Man is called upon to respond to God; each person is either a covenant keeper (righteous) or a covenant breaker (rebellious). And each individual is held accountable for the choices that they make.

Psalm 8
Genesis 1:28
Genesis 2:15
John 4:23

Representation – Man reflects the glory of God in a special sense. God has given man purpose for living and work to do. And man gives back to God worship ... we are called to give continual thanks to the Lord.

Genesis 1:27–28

Another Scriptural truth that is under attack today is that God created the male and female identities. Men are distinct from women. While there is equality in value, there is also diversity in purpose. Male and female together reflect the image of God. In creating male and female, God also created family and called the 'two to become one.'

Genesis 2:24

This is another way in which man is created in the image of God – this reflection of the unity and diversity of the Trinity.

Genesis 2:18

As male and female, humanity is distinguished from the angels. Man is called to relationship, and is able to reproduce.

MAN IS A CREATURE

Psalm 100:3

Though man is in the image of God, man is not God, nor is mankind on the way to becoming 'gods'. Man is distinct from God. God made us ... not the other way around!

Genesis 2:7
Job 10:12
Ecclesiastes 12:6–7
Matthew 6:31–33

God created man out of the dust of the earth, and man depends upon God for life. We are mortal and must eat, drink, and rest in order to survive. We can never be God because we were created by Him.

GROWING IN GLORY

2 Corinthians 3:7–18

How can mankind, fallen and sinful as it is, be restored to God's glorious purpose? The answer is in beholding the glory of our Redeemer – the One Who has been provided as a Ransom for our sins ... Jesus Christ. As we see Him and receive His nature, we are set free from our sinful nature and changed 'from glory to glory.'

In His earthly life, Jesus provided the supreme example of this:

Luke 2:52
1 Corinthians 15:47–58

Wisdom – intellectually
Stature – physically
Favor with God – spiritually
Favor with man – socially
From earthly to heavenly – from a physical body to a spiritual one

MAN'S FUNCTION

Genesis 1:24–31

A created entity cannot function properly apart from that which it was created to do. We, as God's creation, cannot be at peace nor can we find fulfilment apart from the purpose of our Creator. We need to discover what it is we were created to do. (We will look at Man's Purpose further in the next lesson.) While each individual has a unique, God-given purpose for their lives, there are three basic directions in which we all need to function.

John 4:23; Colossians 1:16
Ephesians 2:10
Matthew 6:19–34
Philippians 2:13
Hebrews 13:20–21

Romans 13:9–10
Romans 15:1–7
Hebrews 10:24–25

Psalm 8
Genesis 1:28

First, we must be directed toward God and His will for our lives. Each person owes their very existence to the Lord and we depend upon Him for daily living. God is a gracious and merciful Father, who gives us life and in return receives our worship and our accountability.

Next, we must be directed toward our fellow man. God did not make any individual complete in and of themselves. We were created by Him to be interdependent upon one another. Each person has within them a need for fellowship. Also, we cannot completely fulfill our worship to God apart from other believers. As each person and each gift finds its place and function, then everyone is blessed.

Finally, man must see himself as a steward over nature. We are not the owners of the earth, but we have been given authority by the Creator to rule over it. It is both for our benefit and our care.

APPLICATION

Can you list three ways in which God's image in man is distorted in popular entertainment? How can we adjust our attitudes about what it means to be human? In the *Humanist Manifesto* of 1933, the following is declared: 'Religious humanists regard the universe as self-existing and not created' (page 8). What does this statement reveal about humanists? Finally, since man is a steward over creation, how are we to approach environmental concerns?

CONCLUSION

Mankind was created to reflect the image of God. Many people believe they are merely animals, and many people behave as though they were. It is this fallen view of man which helps perpetuate the fallen behavior of man. It is only as we look to God and His purpose that we are able to properly reflect His image. As we behold the Lord, we are transformed from glory to glory by His Spirit. We must never lose sight of the distinction between God the Creator and man the creation. As we relate properly to God, our fellow man, and nature, we can truly reflect God's glory.

LESSON 7 – THE PURPOSE OF MAN

PURPOSE

The Bible teaches us that we have a purpose for living. God does not just randomly allow people to haphazardly inhabit the earth. He has a plan for your life that will not only bless you as you follow it, but will bless His creation. As we look back to the beginning – to Adam and Eve – we can see more clearly God's purpose for our own lives. In the beginning, God gave man work to do. Man was not to be idle, but to subdue and take dominion over the earth. In addition to man's general task in the world, he had a specific two-fold task in the Garden of Eden. As we closely examine man's two-fold task, we can better understand our purpose in creation.

GLOSSARY

Consecrate – to set apart to God.

Cultivate – to foster growth and development.

Dedicate – to offer to God.

Keep – to guard, protect, and watch over.

Sanctuary – place of God's presence; a holy place; a place of safety.

IN THE GARDEN – A SPECIAL PURPOSE

Genesis 2:8–19

The Lord planted a Garden of exceptional beauty and abundance in Eden. Out of this Garden flowed a river, which became four river-heads. Many scholars place the Garden in the region of Mesopotamia in the Middle East.

Into this Garden, God placed Adam, the first man that He created. God gave Adam a special two-fold purpose: to cultivate the Garden and to protect it.

Adam was called to cultivate – to dress and tend – the Garden and take it 'from glory to glory.' To do this, he would need to understand creation (science), and he would need to restructure creation (art).

Genesis 2:20–24

But Adam could not do this alone. There was certainly no compatible helper among the animals. And, besides, Adam was lonely. So God gave him a suitable helper in the first woman, Eve. God caused Adam to sleep, and took from him a rib, from which He created Eve. She was 'bone of his bone, flesh of his flesh,' and is called woman ('out of man'). God brought Eve to Adam, creating a union. Together, they carried out their task as co-labourers.

IN THE WORLD – MAN'S GENERAL PURPOSE

Genesis 1:28
Genesis 2:10–14

There was literally a garden and literally a river flowing out of that Garden. But that Garden is also a picture of God's intent for the world.

The river flowing in four different directions symbolized God's purpose and concern for the 'four corners' of the earth. Man was to: Be fruitful, multiply, fill the earth, subdue the earth, and rule over all creation.

A ROYAL PRIEST

Exodus 19:6
Revelation 1:6

Scripture refers to God's people as a 'kingdom of priests,' and a 'royal priesthood.' Jesus Himself is both the King of Kings and our Great High Priest. How do the Kingly and Priestly tasks affect our lives? How do they relate to one another?

The **Kingly** task is not simply rulership, but service. From the beginning, man was to cultivate the Garden, to export the culture of the Garden out into the world, and to extend the glory of God by filling the earth with godly children.

In the **Priestly** task, man was to guard the earth (his world), Eden (his home), the Garden (his sanctuary), Eve and their children (his bride and family), and himself (his heart).

Man's priestly role centers on the adoration of God. Our royal activity must be directed towards the goal of our engagement as priests. These tasks must flow together in our lives in order for us to effectively carry out our God-given purpose:

Cultivation	**Consecration**
Production	**Presentation**
Service	**Sacrifice**
Work	**Worship**

APPLICATION

How does the two-fold task affect our families and our jobs? What areas has God given to you to cultivate and protect? What happens when we let our guard down, and how can we keep this from happening again? Are you functioning in your priestly role – praying, reading Scripture, and worshipping as you should? What are the blessings that come from properly functioning in our kingly and priestly tasks?

CONCLUSION

God's purpose is to fill the earth with His glory and blessing. Mankind is His agent to fill the earth with the knowledge of His purpose. Specifically, the Church is called upon to fulfill this great task. We are to cultivate all of the earth so that it becomes an increasing revelation of God's glory. Mankind's ability to do this depends upon his willingness to minister to the Lord as a priest.

LESSON 8 – THE FALL OF MAN

PURPOSE

In previous lessons, we have seen God's wonderful purpose for man. What happened between that blessed creation and the twisted world in which we live today? Is there any hope for restoration? The Bible teaches that sin entered the world as a result of the disobedience of Adam and Eve in the Garden. Satan, a fallen archangel and the enemy of God and creation, came to Adam and Eve in the form of a serpent and tempted them to disobey their Creator. Against God's specific instructions, they ate the fruit from the Tree of the Knowledge of Good and Evil. In doing so, they sinned by rebelling against the will of their wise and loving Creator. This sin resulted in unimaginable disaster, not only for Adam and Eve, but for every person who has ever lived after them. In examining this historical event, we can gain valuable insights that will help us overcome sin when we are tempted.

GLOSSARY

Satan – evil angel who opposes God's will; thrown out of heaven by God; also known as Lucifer or the devil.

Serpent – animal used by Satan to tempt Eve; a symbol of Satan himself (see Genesis 3:1–15; John 8:44; Romans 16:20; 2 Corinthians 11:3; Revelation 12:9).

Sin – a violation or transgression of a command; the state of being alienated from God.

Temptation – a circumstance that may entice someone into sin.

GOD'S COMMAND

Genesis 1:29
Genesis 2:15–17

The Lord had planted a beautiful and abundant Garden, and had given it to man for his cultivation and protection. Everything in this Garden was available as a blessing to Adam and Eve, and there was abundant food and provision. However, the Lord told them that the only tree that they should not touch was the Tree of the Knowledge of Good and Evil. God told them that if they ate from that tree, it would result in their death.

TEMPTATION AND FALL

Genesis 3:1–7

The nature of temptation and rebellion has not changed since the days of the Garden. Satan's strategy then was not much different from the ways in which he tempts us today.

He appeared to Eve in the form of a serpent, and questioned the words of God, seeking to bring confusion. Satan knows Scripture and will sometimes try to twist it in our minds and cause us to doubt what God has said.

Then, he called God a liar and questioned God's motives. Sowing dissention, mistrust, and cynicism is another favorite tactic of the enemy. Finally, he appealed to the human ego, promising that they would be like God if they ate of this forbidden fruit. The devil is a cunning liar who knows how to tell people what they want to hear in order to manipulate them for his own evil ends.

Eve took the fruit and ate it, also giving some to Adam who also ate. Adam had failed, not only in eating the fruit, but as a priestly guardian. He did not guard the Garden against the serpent, nor did he protect Eve. Finally, he failed to guard his own heart against the sin.

TWO TREES IN THE GARDEN

Genesis 2:9

The Tree of the Knowledge of Good and Evil was not the only special tree in the Garden. The Tree of Life was also placed there by God as a representation of the blessings of obedience. It was not forbidden.

But the Tree of the Knowledge of Good and Evil represented God's curse for disobedience ... death. Even though it was forbidden, Adam and Eve chose it over the Tree of Life.

NATURE OF SIN

In sin, we make a futile attempt to transcend our being and become that which we were not created to be. Adam's sin reveals that man wants to decide right and wrong for himself. In a sense, man is attempting to be God. Another aspect of Adam's sin is impatience ... we grasp at what we want without allowing God to bestow His blessing. Man has a very damaging and frustrating tendency to seize by human effort what can only be given by God.

Isaiah 14:12–15

Satan himself sinned in the same way. He boastfully said in his heart:

I will ascend into heaven
I will exalt my throne
I will sit on the mount
I will ascend above the clouds
I will be like the Most High

However, instead of exaltation, Satan's sin caused him to be cast out of heaven ... 'like lightning' was the swiftness and severity of his fall.

Romans 6:23
2 Corinthians 11:1–3

That is the nature of sin – instead of bringing us up, it brings us down. In fact, the pathway to sin leads ultimately to death. There is a downward spiral involved with sin that begins with a seemingly innocent seed of doubt and ends in the pit of destruction.

Romans 1:21–23

The Apostle Paul paints a vividly accurate picture of sin's fruits in Romans: **Irreverence** leads to **Ingratitude**, which leads to **Irresponsibility**, which leads to **Ignorance**, which leads to **Insanity**, which leads to

Idolatry. Ultimately, when man refuses to acknowledge or worship his Creator, he will end up serving and worshipping foolish creatures.

APPLICATION

Why did God approach Adam first after he and Eve fell? Are there areas in your life where you are attempting to seize control from God? Do you have any idols ... anything that comes in-between you and God? There is a way to break out of the downward spiral: 'The wages of sin is death, but the gift of God is eternal life in Christ Jesus our Lord' (Romans 6:23 NKJ).

CONCLUSION

Philippians 2:5–11

Man cannot transcend his being. We cannot be God. Whenever we cast aside His wisdom or care in favor of our own control, we will find failure and destruction. Instead, we should look to Jesus, who humbled Himself and was therefore exalted to God's right hand. Receive His example and His gift of life.

LESSON 9 – THE EFFECTS OF THE FALL

PURPOSE

When Adam and Eve fell, it was not an isolated event without consequence to the present day. This fall affected all of mankind, from that moment until now. Sin brought a curse upon all of humanity and creation. The problems that we face today can be directly traced back to the sin in the Garden. Understanding these effects of the fall gives us a proper perspective on humanity's present predicament.

GLOSSARY

Curse – the evil that comes upon man and creation because of sin.

Enmity – hostility toward another.

Restoration – bringing back a former condition or position.

Inheritance – a blessing or possession received as a gift, particularly to an heir.

SIN AND CREATION

Genesis 3:8–13

Immediately after the sin of Adam and Eve, God came to them, as He always had, for fellowship and blessing. However, their rebellion caused them to flee from the Lord and to be separated from His Presence. And so, in accordance with His own Word, God pronounced judgement.

First, He cursed the serpent. There is a literal curse upon the serpent species in terms of its humiliation, uncleanness, and enmity with humanity. But there is also a curse upon the devil who had moti-vated the serpent, and a prophetic promise that there would come a Holy Seed Who would crush the devil's head.

Genesis 3:14–15

Then, God addressed Eve. Without directly cursing her, He told her that her sin had severely marred her roles as wife and mother. There would be multiplied sorrow, great pain in childbirth, and conflict in her marriage.

Genesis 3:16

Finally, the Lord spoke to Adam. Again, He did not directly curse him, but told Adam that by listening to Eve instead of God, he had brought a curse upon the ground. Adam's role as a laborer and pro-vider were marred by his failure, resulting in a struggle against thorny ground in order to bring forth fruit. This difficult struggle against the ground would ultimately result in death and a return to dust from which he was taken.

Genesis 3:17–19

SIN AND RELATIONSHIPS

Ephesians 2:12–22

Sin had a dramatic affect on man's relationships. First and foremost, it caused man to lose peace with God. In fact, because of sin, humanity

Genesis 4:1–11

became like strangers and aliens in the world, separated from their Creator. Only in Christ can we be reconciled to God and receive His peace.

Because of sin, man lost peace with man. If you have read a newspaper today, you know that this affect of sin continues to dramatically manifest itself in our world. But tragically, Adam and Eve did not have to wait very long to see it happen ... one of their sons murdered the other. Cain, the eldest, became jealous of his brother Abel, and killed him in the field. Surely, this was one of the 'multiplied sorrows' that Eve experienced most grievously, as have countless mothers throughout history.

Genesis 3:17–19

Sin also caused man to lose peace with creation. Nature itself revolted, and animals which were once named and subjugated by man became hostile snarling beasts, predators upon themselves and even upon man.

SIN AND INHERITANCE

God had given the Garden to Adam, and had provided Adam with trustworthy guidelines for successfully stewarding that Garden. Because of Adam's failure to guard the Garden, he lost his inheritance.

Adam and Eve were driven out of the Garden sanctuary, and never permitted to return. Cain, following the murder, was driven out of Eden itself, his home. Finally, as mankind continued to pile sin upon sin, the Great Flood in the days of Noah drove men from the face of the earth. Sin causes man to lose his sanctuary, his home, and ultimately, his life.

APPLICATION

What happened to man's nature after the fall? Read Romans 7:13 and Romans 8:3 ... describe man's problem. Does man have the ability within himself to do good? How can man be delivered from the power of sin? Finally, examine your own life for any broken relationships. Are you seeking reconciliation?

CONCLUSION

The sin of Adam brought about tremendous change and affected all of creation, bringing it under a curse. But even on the day that Adam fell, God had a plan to redeem him and restore to him that which was lost. Sinful man does not seek after God; instead, man runs away ... but a loving God seeks out mankind with His redemptive purpose. The Bible, therefore, is the redemptive history of a fallen race.

LESSON 10 – THE RELENTLESS REDEEMER

PURPOSE

God is a Redeemer, always at work to advance His great purpose, and able to turn human failure and dark circumstance into opportunities for greater good. In fact, God has worked through the prophets, the Incarnation of Jesus Christ, the Holy Spirit, and also the Church in order to demonstrate His multi-faceted wisdom. Man's tragic fall did not stop God. Therefore, we can see history as the story of God's relentless redemptive activity in restoring all things ... it is literally 'His story'.

GLOSSARY

Redeem – to buy out of slavery; to ransom or deliver from bondage, both physically and spiritually; to bring good out of bad.

Seed – offspring or descendant; used particularly in Scripture to speak of that Descendant of woman who would defeat the serpent and produce a redeemed race (see Lesson 9).

Relentless – unstoppable, incessant, sustained, unbroken, persistent.

REDEMPTION AFTER THE FALL

Genesis 3:15

Immediately after Adam and Eve fell into sin, God's heart was for redemption. Though their sin brought a curse upon the land and a marring of their appointed roles and their descendants, God had a plan for restoration.

Genesis 3:7

He promised that a Seed of the woman would ultimately crush the serpent's head – thus the deceiver would be defeated by the Seed of the one deceived.

Genesis 3:21

Because of their sin, Adam and Eve felt shame at their nakedness and attempted to cover themselves with fig leaves. But God sacrificed animals in order to provide fur skins for adequate clothing for the fallen couple. This is also a picture of the sacrificial system which was to come, whereby the innocent suffers to provide a covering for the guilty.

Galatians 3:19–29

Ultimately, Jesus – without sin – became the sacrifice once and for all to cover the sins of humanity. Our sins are covered by His sacrifice rather than our own vain attempts at good works.

REDEMPTION AND THE FLOOD

Romans 5:14–21
Romans 6:23
Genesis 6:1–8

Because of Adam's sin, mankind received a bent toward sin. The sinful nature became a part of every descendant of Adam, causing all to sin. Within just a few generations, the sins of mankind had become so grievous that the Lord determined that He must wipe man from the face of the earth. But there was one man named Noah who found grace in the eyes of the Lord.

Genesis 6–9

God instructed Noah to build a large ship, an ark, which would carry Noah and his family – along with at least two of every animal – safely through the coming flood . . . for God would cause tremendous rain for forty days and nights.

Even in the midst of awesome and righteous judgement, God's heart was toward His redemptive purpose for mankind. He not only saved Noah's family and the animals, but He preserved the Redemptive Seed . . . His promise.

REDEMPTION AND THE PATRIARCHS

Genesis 12–50

Exodus – Joshua

God called Abraham, Isaac, and Jacob to form the family from which the Seed would come to bless all nations and peoples of the world.

Later, when the descendants of these Patriarchs were enslaved in Egypt, God called Moses, and through him formed the nation from which the Seed would come.

REDEMPTION AND ISRAEL

Judges – Chronicles

Judges 3
Isaiah – Malachi
Ezra – Esther
2 Samuel 7
Psalm 72
Psalm 78

Throughout the history of Israel, the special nation from which the Redemptive Seed would come, the people experienced great seasons of turning toward God and tragic seasons of turning toward wickedness and destruction. But God never forgot His purpose or His promise.

God raised up judges to save the people and He sent prophets to warn them. Even in the midst of suffering and defeat, He mercifully and miraculously spared a remnant of the people.

Finally, God raised up a young man named David to produce a Kingly lineage for the Seed Who would reign forever.

REDEMPTION AND JESUS CHRIST

Hebrews 1:1–12
Galatians 4:4–7
John 3:16–17

Hebrews 4:15
Matthew 20:28
Colossians 2:13–15

Ultimately, we see God's Redemptive nature revealed in the Seed Himself, Jesus Christ. God sent His own Son – not the seed of man, which was corrupted by sin – Who was conceived by the Holy Spirit and born to a young virgin named Mary. Jesus lived a sinless life, though He was tempted in every way. He died on the cross, becoming the sacrifice for our sins, and then rose again from the dead, conquering death and Satan (the serpent) and saving mankind.

Jesus now reigns, even as His Church proclaims His victory and His redemptive purpose in all of the earth. Scripture promises that all creation will be redeemed and the Kingdom will be handed back to God the Father . . . the relentless Redeemer.

APPLICATION

In relation to God's eternal purpose, why are you here on earth? Read 2 Corinthians 5:17–20 . . . How does the knowledge of God's redemptive nature change the way you think about other people? Meditate on the fact that God is a Redeemer by nature, and let this glorious truth strengthen your security in Him. Talk to God about your part in His redemptive purpose and begin to identify some people with whom you can share His redemption.

CONCLUSION

Our knowledge of God's redemptive nature will cause us to love Him even more, and to trust Him to complete our salvation. Understanding His redemptive purpose will help you to face every situation with faith and hope, and motivate you to seek your place of service in that purpose. In His purpose, we discover our destiny, seeking to make His redemption known to everyone, that they, too, might be redeemed.

LESSON 11 – THE MEANING OF COVENANT

PURPOSE

God relates to people by means of covenant. In fact, the Bible consists of the Old and New Covenants, or Testaments. Scripture shows God establishing covenantal relationships with people through whom He accomplishes His purpose. He is a covenant-making and covenant-keeping God Who continues to relate to His people in this way today. Therefore, it is critical that we have an understanding of the significance and nature of covenant, a concept that is greatly misunderstood in modern society.

JOINED TOGETHER

Our highest understanding of covenant is that it is a bond which God has established to **join His people to Himself**, and to **join His people together**. The basic meaning of covenant is 'to bind together'.

Genesis 15:8–21
Jeremiah 34:8–22

The root meaning of the Hebrew word *Berith*, ('covenant' or 'to cut covenant') probably derives from a common covenant-making ceremony from Bible times. Animals were cut in half, and the pieces laid out side by side with a path between them. The parties making the agreement would then walk between the pieces, symbolizing the fact that they were giving up separate lives to begin a new relationship. They pledged their lives to be faithful to the relationship, and death could be the common penalty for breaking the covenant.

The English word *covenant* comes from a Latin word meaning, 'a coming together', and means 'a binding and solemn agreement' (*Webster's Dictionary*, 1828 Edition).

Exodus 19–24

Though there are covenants between equals, the covenants of God are Sovereign. God initiates the covenant and establishes its terms. Man then either accepts or rejects God's covenant.

Genesis 2:21–24
Malachi 2:13–16
Ephesians 5:22–32

Covenant causes two to become one. Marriage is a covenant whereby the partners are to lay down their lives for one another. The marriage covenant is to be a prophetic picture of the relationship between Christ and the Church.

GOD AND COVENANT HISTORY

Genesis 1:26–30
Genesis 2:15–17

God has unfolded His purpose – and His relationships with people – through a series of covenants.

His first relationship with man was established in the **'Dominion Covenant'** with Adam. God established mankind as His representative authority on the earth, and specifically set out man's responsibility. He gave man freedom, with certain boundaries and restrictions. And, God clearly warned man of the penalty for disobedience.

Genesis 9:1–17
Genesis 12; Genesis 15
Genesis 17; Genesis 22

Exodus 19–24
2 Samuel 7
Psalm 89

After the Great Flood, God re-established His covenant with Noah and his descendants. God made covenant with Abraham and his descendants, that they would be the family through which redemption would come to the nations.

It was by covenant that God formed the children of Israel into a nation through which He would reveal Himself in the earth. Later, God made covenant with David to bring the Redeemer King from among his offspring.

THE NEW COVENANT

Jeremiah 31:31–34

God's Law in the old covenant was written upon tablets of stone, and proclaimed by the prophets. But the prophet Jeremiah declared that there would come a New Covenant that was written upon the hearts of the people.

Luke 22:14–20
Hebrews 7:11–28
Hebrews 10:11–23

The new covenant was initiated by Jesus Christ Himself at the Last Supper. According to the writer of Hebrews, this New Covenant is a better covenant, with a better priest, a better sacrifice, and better promises.

Romans 4–8

There is nothing wrong with the Law whatsoever, except for the people who are supposed to keep it. In the New Covenant, there is not only forgiveness for the occasions when we sin, but there is power to help us stop sinning.

Ephesians 2:11–22

The new covenant includes both Jews and Gentiles, and forms all who believe into one Body, with Christ as the Head.

COVENANT AND GOD'S WORLD PURPOSE

Romans 5:12; Isaiah 59:2

Romans 5:12–21
2 Corinthians 5:18–21
Colossians 1:15–20
John 1:1–14
Philippians 2:5–8
Hebrews 2:9–18
Matthew 5:17
Hebrews 7:22–28
Luke 4:1–12
Luke 22:39–46
Hebrews 4:15
John 12:49–50
Hebrews 10:5–7

Genesis 22:15–18
Galatians 3:6–29
Acts 2:22–36
Matthew 1:1–18
Luke 3:23–38

Hebrews 2; Hebrews 7
1 Peter 2:21–24
Hebrews 9:11–28

Through covenant, God has bound Himself to fulfill His purpose on the earth through man. Adam, the first man, failed and broke the relationship between God and man.

However, God sent another man, His own Son Jesus ('The Second Adam'), Who kept the covenant and reunited God with those who believe. Jesus was both fully God and fully man, and because of this, He fulfilled the covenant for both parties.

Jesus fulfilled the covenant by withstanding every temptation ... He was tempted in every way possible that any person can be tempted, but He never sinned. Jesus was fully obedient to the Father, and only wanted to please Him.

According to God's covenants with Abraham and David, Jesus is in their lineage. He is in the royal line of descent through Joseph, His earthly (though not natural) father, and He is in their natural line of descent through His mother, Mary.

Jesus is the High Priest of a better covenant, and is the perfect sacrifice offered on behalf of those who have broken the covenant. In Jesus, God is fulfilling His original intent for mankind.

APPLICATION

Fulfillling covenant – whether with God or with other people – requires loyalty and faithfulness. Read Psalm 15 . . . how does God reward faithfulness? How has God demonstrated His covenant faithfulness to you? What does your loyalty to the covenant require?

CONCLUSION

When we believe upon the Lord Jesus Christ, we enter into a covenant with God, complete with blessings and responsibilities. All of history meets at the cross of Christ. There, the full penalty of the broken covenant was paid when Jesus, fully God and fully man, became the perfect sacrifice, once and for all (2 Corinthians 5:21). Indeed, Jesus not only speaks and reveals the Covenant Word of God, but He is the Living Word . . . Covenant is part of His very being. Through the work of the Holy Spirit in the Church, Christ's Kingdom is being extended throughout the whole earth (Matthew 28:18–20; Matthew 24:14). Through mankind, Jesus Christ, and the Church, God is fulfilling His original covenantal intent.

LESSON 12 – ABRAHAM, FATHER OF FAITH

PURPOSE

History belongs to God ... it's **'His Story'**. We are part of that history, created by God and serving His purpose in the unfolding drama. For God's people, the calling of Abraham is a momentous development and a significant beginning. The life of Abraham, 'Father of the Faithful', provides a model for God's dealings with man and for man's response to God. Abraham is the human vessel through whom God's redemptive purpose began to unfold.

GLOSSARY

Justification – the legal declaration that one is not guilty before the Law of God; the word 'Justified' can be broken down into 'Just-as-if-I'd never sinned'.

GOD SPOKE TO ABRAHAM

Genesis 12–15

The Lord came to Abram, as he was known at that time, and told him to leave the land of his family and go to a new land. God promised Abram that He would bring forth a great nation from Abram's descendants. Abram's name meant, 'Father of a multitude', which was very awkward considering that he and his wife, Sarai, had no children at that time.

Genesis 22:18
Galatians 3:16

But God told him that he would have land, an heir, and countless descendants. All of those who blessed him would be blessed, and those who cursed him would be cursed. And, there would be a special Seed, a descendant from his family line, Who would bless all nations.

Genesis 15

God confirmed His promises by making a covenant with Abram ... and Abram became Abraham, 'Father of many nations.' Abraham made a covenant sacrifice, and God Himself passed between the pieces of meat, signifying that the covenant would be fulfilled by a pledge unto death. Furthermore, God swore an oath on His own name and character that these promises were sure.

Genesis 22:16–18
Genesis 17:15–16

God also changed Sarai's name to Sarah. The added 'h' in Abraham's and Sarah's names is the breath of God which was a sign of God's favour and blessing upon them both.

ABRAHAM'S RESPONSE TO GOD

Genesis 15
Genesis 17
Genesis 22:1–14

Despite his circumstances and the extraordinary nature of God's promises, Abraham believed God. He did not simply believe in God ... he believed what God had said so much that he obeyed God. He submitted himself to circumcision, the covenantal seal, and was even willing to sacrifice his son Isaac in order to fulfil God's purpose.

Romans 4
James 2:20–24

OUR RESPONSE TO GOD

We are justified (declared righteous) before God as we respond to Him like Abraham, our father in faith. Justification happens when we believe God, and then complete our faith through obedient action to God.

APPLICATION

Was Abraham's faith based upon circumstantial evidence, or on the nature of God? Do you believe God enough to obey Him, even when circumstances are difficult? God gave Isaac to Abraham because Abraham would train Isaac in righteousness (Genesis 18:19). Are you committed to passing godly teaching on to the next generation? Read and meditate upon Hebrews 11:8–19 ... what is your attitude toward the things of this life?

CONCLUSION

Abraham provides us with a model for responding to the Living God. Not only is Abraham a model, but he is the father of the family of faith ... a family in which all who believe in Christ are a part (Romans 11; Galatians 3). Learning about Abraham is to discover our own roots. Learning his destiny is to discover our own destiny.

LESSON 13 – PATRIARCHS OF FAITH

PURPOSE

God's covenant with Abraham established the lineage through whom the promised Seed would come. God began to work with certain descendants of Abraham to reveal more of His own nature and purpose. In the Patriarchs, we see God preparing a family and a national context through which His covenant would be revealed and the Seed would come.

GLOSSARY

Patriarch – father, especially the founder of a family or tribe.

ISAAC, THE SON OF PROMISE

Genesis 16
Genesis 21:1–5
Genesis 25:1–2
Genesis 17:5
Genesis 15:1–4

Genesis 17:15–21
Romans 4:16–21
Genesis 22:1–14
Hebrews 11:17–19
Genesis 24

Genesis 26:23–24
Genesis 25:21–26

By the end of his life, Abraham had produced a total of eight sons. Each one of them gave birth to one or more nations in fulfilment of God's promise. But only one of them, Isaac, son of Sarah, was chosen to be in the redemptive line that God was preparing.

Isaac (which means '*Laughter*') was born out of an impossible situation. Later, Abraham prepared to offer him up as a sacrifice, only to have God spare him at the last moment ... he was reckoned to be dead, only to be 'resurrected'. Later still, God watched over the selection of his wife, Rebekah.

The Lord personally confirmed His covenant with Isaac, and promised to bless him and multiply his descendants. However, Rebekah was also barren. In answer to Isaac's prayer, she conceived and twin sons were born. Esau was born first, but Jacob was born holding on to his brother's heel. (Jacob means '*heel-grabber*' or '*supplanter*'.) God prophesied to Rebekah that in the rivalry between the two boys, the younger would prevail.

Genesis 27
Hebrews 11:20

Despite the rivalry, Isaac's trust in God's promises enabled him to speak blessing on his sons' future.

GOD SOVEREIGNLY CHOSE JACOB

Malachi 1:1–3
Romans 9:10–13

Genesis 25:27–34
Genesis 27:1–40

Though Jacob was the younger son, and as such was not in the natural line to receive the blessing, God sovereignly chose him to continue the redemptive family.

This, despite the fact that Jacob was a schemer, and he and Rebekah sought to gain precedence over Esau through bargaining and deception. For his part, Esau seemed to initially disdain his birthright, choosing a meal of beans instead. Then, Isaac deceived his father into giving the blessing to him, instead of Esau.

Genesis 28:10–22
Genesis 29–31

Fleeing a wrathful Esau, Jacob encountered the Lord, Who confirmed His covenant with Jacob. Then, Jacob himself was deceived by his Uncle Laban. After completing his struggles with Laban and determining that he should face Esau, Jacob again encountered the Lord.

Genesis 32:22–32

A man that Hosea 12:4 identifies as an angel of the Lord wrestled with Jacob. Jacob would not give in until he received a blessing. When he confessed that his name was Jacob, the angel told him that from that point onward, he was to be called 'Israel' (one who rules). The angel left Jacob with a limp as a reminder of God's strength and mercy in the face of Jacob's own weakness.

Genesis 33

Jacob did reconcile with Esau, before each went their separate ways again.

Genesis 49

Before his death, Jacob called his sons together and prophesied over them. He specifically pointed out Judah's place in God's covenant purpose. He looked ahead to God's covenant and asked to be buried with Abraham and Isaac in the Land of Promise.

Genesis 47:28–31
Hebrews 11:21

In the course of Jacob's struggles, he gained two wives and twelve sons. These sons became heads over the tribes of Israel. The eldest son of Jacob's beloved wife Rachel was named Joseph, and he was to play a special role in covenant history.

GOD USES JOSEPH

Genesis 37

Jacob loved his eleventh son, Joseph, more than any other. Thus, his elder brothers hated him. They were jealous of their father's love and bitterly resented the fact that God revealed (through Joseph's dreams) that Joseph would rule over the entire family. And so, his own brothers sold him into slavery, after first considering murder.

Genesis 39–41

This was not to be the last setback for Joseph. Yet, in every difficult situation, God caused Joseph to prosper. While a slave of Potiphar in Egypt, Joseph and his master prospered. After being thrown into prison, he became the chief administrator. And through God's favor, Joseph was raised to lead Egypt.

Genesis 42–48

Hebrews 11:21–22

His dreams were fulfilled and God used him to save the covenant family. He was restored to his father and his brothers, and they came to live with him in Egypt. While there, God again confirmed the covenant with Israel and his family. Joseph's sons were adopted by Israel and became tribal heads.

Genesis 50:22–26

Knowing God's faithfulness, Joseph believed that He would one day bring His people back to the land promised to Abraham and instructed his descendants to return his bones there.

APPLICATION

Consider your own history. How has God's hand been upon your life in preparing you to enter the covenant family and to serve in God's redemptive purpose? Read Genesis 50:15–21 ... How was Joseph able to have such a forgiving spirit? If there is some person or circumstance that has caused you to be hurt or offended, ask God to help you see things redemptively, and choose to offer forgiveness.

CONCLUSION

Through the lives of the Patriarchs, we see the faithfulness of God to His covenant Word. Judah was the family from which Jesus would descend. God sovereignly selected, prepared, and preserved the lineage for the promised Seed in spite of the weakness and the sinfulness of the people involved and in the face of life-threatening circumstances.

LESSON 14 – A CHOSEN NATION

PURPOSE

Exodus 2:23–25

After 400 years in Egypt, the children of Israel numbered more than one million, and they were enslaved by the Egyptians. They cried out to God for their deliverance, and God was concerned for them and remembered His covenant with Abraham. In this lesson, we will see that God is faithful to His Word and to His world purpose.

GOD PREPARED A DELIVERER

Exodus 1–2

Hebrews 11:23
Acts 7:20–36

The Pharoah, Egypt's leader, was a cruel tyrant, and he decreed that all of the male children born to the Hebrew slaves should be thrown into the river and drowned. But God gave extraordinary determination and wisdom to a woman from the tribe of Levi (the Priestly tribe) who was also the wife of a Levite. After this courageous and loving woman gave birth to a son, she took him and hid him for three months.

When she could no longer spare his life in this way, she made a small basket boat for him and placed him at the water's edge near the place where the daughter of Pharoah bathed. When Pharoah's daughter saw the infant, she had compassion on him, though she knew he was one of the Hebrew children.

The child was named Moses, and God sovereignly made a way for his own mother to serve as his nurse. And so, she not only saved his life, but had the opportunity to train him.

Though he was raised in Pharoah's household, Moses identified with the Israelites, and wanted to aid them ... he even killed an Egyptian who was beating one of his Hebrew brethren. Pharoah sought to kill Moses, but God led Moses into the Sinai desert wilderness, where He trained Moses for 40 years. When Moses was ready, God sent him back to lead Israel out of Egypt.

GOD USED MOSES TO DELIVER THE CHILDREN OF ISRAEL

Exodus 4–15

Exodus 11:1–8

Exodus 12
Hebrews 11:28

Through Moses, God demonstrated His power and authority, by miracles, signs, and wonders. The Lord used Moses to deliver the Israelites from their oppressors in Egypt. God sent nine terrible plagues upon Egypt, and when Pharoah would not release the slaves, He decreed the death of every firstborn Egyptian son.

But God preserved the firstborn sons of Israel by providing lambs as sacrifices. When the Hebrews placed the blood of the lambs on their door posts, the Lord 'passed over' their homes, touching only the unmarked homes of their oppressors.

There was a dreadful cry in Egypt ... Pharoah and the Egyptians urged the Israelites to leave their country at once. The Egyptians even gave to them silver, gold, and clothing.

The Lord instituted the Feasts of Passover and Unleavened Bread as continuing memorials throughout the generations, to remind the Israelites that He had saved their firstborn sons and delivered them from Egypt.

Exodus 13–15

Hebrews 11:29

But Pharoah changed his mind. He sent out an army to bring the Israelites back to Egypt. Against one of the greatest armies of that day, God protected His people with a pillar of cloud by day and a pillar of fire by night.

Then, God parted the waters of the Red Sea, and brought the people through to the other side. When Pharoah and his army tried to pass through the sea, God caused it to close back in over them so that they were all completely destroyed. The people rejoiced and the name of the Lord was exalted.

A NATION FORMED BY COVENANT

Exodus 19–24

Exodus 19:3–6

There is a tremendous difference between being a grouping of former slaves and becoming a holy nation. But after crossing the Red Sea, God led the people into the wilderness of Sinai, where He reminded them of His delivering power and His covenant choice of them as His people. He offered them a special place of service in the earth if they would obey His covenant.

Exodus 19:7–8
Exodus 20–23

The people committed themselves to obey God, and then God gave Moses the Ten Commandments. The Lord also gave instructions for how these commands were to be applied. He reaffirmed His covenant concerning the land promised to Abraham, and gave instruction concerning it.

Exodus 24

The people of Israel affirmed the covenant, saying, 'All the words which the Lord has said we will do.' Moses wrote God's words into a book and they offered up a sacrifice to the Lord. Then, Moses and the elders of Israel went up onto the mountain of God, where they ate and drank in His Presence. The covenant between God and the nation of Israel was established.

Exodus 25:8

It was God's desire that He could dwell among His people. God gave them the pattern for the Tabernacle, a tent dedicated to Him for His Presence.

Exodus 25–31

The Lord laid out specific instructions for the furnishings of the Tabernacle, including the ark of the covenant, as well as instructions concerning those who would minister within the tabernacle.

Finally, He revealed the system for sacrificial offerings. They were to look to Him to provide the sacrifice necessary for forgiveness of sin.

APPLICATION

In what ways did the Passover Lamb foreshadow Jesus Christ, the Lamb of God? (For further insight, read Isaiah 53:4–7; John 1:29; 1 Corinthians 5:7; and 1 John 3:16.) There were more than 400 years between God's covenant with Abraham and the formation of Israel as a covenant nation. What does this history show us about the fulfilment of God's covenant promises? Is God's perspective on time and generations different than ours?

CONCLUSION

2 Peter 3:8–9

The Lord is patient and is not slack concerning His promises. He brought the children of Israel out of slavery, and made them a covenant nation . . . just as He had promised. And though that nation was to be tested many times, and the faithfulness of its people was frequently found to be lacking, God remained faithful. In fact, He was continuing in His covenant purpose, to prepare the true Passover Lamb. There would be another mountain on another day, and a better way for us to stand righteous in His Presence.

2 Corinthians 5:21
Hebrews 12:22–24

LESSON 15 – GOD'S PEOPLE IN THE WILDERNESS

PURPOSE

Psalm 103:7
1 Corinthians 10:1–11

The history of Israel is very important to us today. One reason is that human nature remains much the same today ... their problems, challenges, attitudes, and responses are not unlike our own. Therefore, we have much to learn from them and their experience. Also, in them, we see the continuity of God's covenant purpose. As we look at their history, we see what God is like, what He has done, and the way He expects us to respond to Him.

PROVISION IN THE WILDERNESS

Exodus 16–18

James 1:1–8

Exodus 16

Exodus 17:1–7

Exodus 17:8–16
Exodus 18
Deuteronomy 1:9–18

Before the people of Israel had ever reached Mount Sinai, they began to show their basic mistrust of God, and his appointed leaders, Moses and Aaron. Their behavior also revealed their own double-mindedness.

Despite their behavior and doubt, the Lord blessed and upheld them. When they grumbled about food, God supernaturally supplied them with quail and manna – and a test of their obedience. When they complained about the lack of water, God gave them water from a rock. The first time they encountered an enemy, God gave them the victory. He even gave Moses a practical system for governing and caring for the people.

NO PATIENCE FOR THE PROMISES

Hebrews 6:12

Exodus 32

In spite of these amazing lessons, Israel still could not endure patiently in order to see God's promises fulfilled. While Moses was still on Mount Sinai with God, the people made a golden idol to worship ... and credited it with their deliverance!

Numbers 11–25

Numbers 13–14

Even after God's righteous and awesome judgement for that folly, the people continued to murmur and complain ... even refusing to obey on occasion. Most significantly, when they reached the Promised Land, they refused to enter in, choosing to believe the word of ten frightened spies, rather than the covenant Word of the Lord.

Numbers 14:28–38

Because of this disobedience, a whole generation was condemned to die in the wilderness, wandering and unable to inherit the promise. Only two men from that generation, Joshua and Caleb, were allowed to eventually enter into the land because of their outspoken faith in God's promise.

Nehemiah 9

A two-year journey tragically became forty years of wandering in the wilderness of death. Yet, even in the midst of their rebellion and judgement, God provided them with care, leadership, provision, food, and protection.

But because of their rebellion and their impatience, an entire generation missed out on the blessings of the Promised Land.

APPLICATION

Read 1 Corinthians 10:1–13 . . . compare the experiences of Israel with our experience in Christ. What lessons should we learn from Israel's wilderness experience?

CONCLUSION

Deuteronomy 4:32–40
Deuteronomy 7:6–8
Exodus 19:5–6
Deuteronomy 28:1–2
Deuteronomy 28:15

In Israel's deliverance, we see that God's salvation is based on His Sovereign grace and not upon human merit. Receiving the full inheritance, however, depends upon our obedient response to His grace. Seeing the failure of this generation in Israel should motivate us to follow the Lord more closely.

LESSON 16 – GOD'S PEOPLE GO INTO THE LAND

PURPOSE

Numbers 20:1–13

The day came when the rebellious generation in Israel had all died . . . only the younger generation remained. Moses was also dead, having also been refused entry into the Promised Land because of sin and frustration. Yet, in the midst of that difficult wilderness situation, the multitude of former slaves had become a united force of young warriors, perfected and toughened in the wilderness. They had also learned from the mistakes of their parents. These were ready to go in and take possession of the Land that God had promised to their fore-fathers. This lesson will examine the necessity of obedience and cour-age to claim the inheritance that God has for us.

A NEW LEADER

Joshua was one of two men who survived from the former generation. He and Caleb were the only two who had expressed faith in God's promises, and God rewarded them by allowing them the opportunity to enter into the Land.

Joshua was uniquely qualified to serve as the new leader for the Israelites:

Exodus 24:13
Exodus 17:10
Numbers 13–14
Deuteronomy 34:9
Joshua 1:1–19

He had faithfully served Moses
He was prepared by warfare in the wilderness
He was proven faithful in spying out the land
He received authority from Moses
He was commissioned by God Himself

GOD PREPARED THE WAY

Joshua 2

Joshua 2:9–14

There were still many obstacles facing the Israelites in the Promised Land . . . the same obstacles that had terrified the earlier generation. But this generation was determined to be obedient to the Lord.

Hebrews 11:31

Matthew 1:5

God Himself prepared the way for them. Joshua sent two spies into the fortress city of Jericho, where they encountered a prostitute named Rahab. She not only hid the spies and helped them, but she prophesied to them saying, 'I know that the Lord has given you the Land,' and told them that the inhabitants of the Land were terrified of the Israelites. This heathen harlot was greatly used by God and was spared when the city of Jericho was destroyed. Even more amazing was that God sovereignly grafted her into the family tree that eventually produced King David and the Holy Seed, Jesus Christ!

Joshua 3–4

The Israelites were led through the Jordan River by God, just as He had led their forefathers through the Red Sea.

Joshua 5

Joshua 6

The Lord renewed His covenant with them. They were circumcised and they celebrated the Feasts of Passover and Unleavened Bread.

Then, as they obeyed His specific instructions, the Lord gave the city of Jericho to them, supernaturally bringing down its walls.

THE PEOPLE OBEYED

As we have already seen, obedience is critical to receiving the inheritance that God has for us. This generation of Israelites was prepared to obey God and to fight for their inheritance:

Joshua 1:12–18
Joshua 2
Joshua 3–4
Joshua 5:1–9
Joshua 5–6
Joshua 7

They were committed to God's delegated leader
Their spies were faithful
They followed God's instruction at the Jordan
They received circumcision
They followed unusual instructions at Jericho
They carried out God's judgement on Achan

The exploits of Joshua and the Israelites in His day are numerous and God's favour was greatly upon them. Unlike the previous generation, this generation was willing to obey God and had great faith in His Word.

APPLICATION

Like the children of Israel of that day, we have an inheritance that is promised to us if we have faith in Christ. Read Acts 26:15–18 ... what two things do we receive when our eyes are opened to turn from darkness to light? According to Acts 20:32, what builds us up so that we might receive our inheritance?

CONCLUSION

1 Corinthians 10
Hebrews 3–4

Exodus 20:20–33
Joshua 23–24

Someone once said, 'Israel received a Promised Land, and the Church of Jesus Christ receives a land of promises.' Israel's example shows us that true faith will produce obedience, and obedience will open the way for us to receive our inheritance. For seven years, the Israelites advanced under Joshua's leadership, taking all of the major strongholds in the Promised Land. Then, at God's command, they divided the Land according to tribe and family, and then each tribe and family completed the task of taking and occupying the Land. In this way, God gave them the Land little by little, as they grew and became able to rule it. He also tested their willingness to obey Him, though they had no strong national leadership. God directed them to obey in their families and through the generations. This command was critical, as we are to see in the next lesson.

LESSON 17 – ISRAEL UNDER THE JUDGES

PURPOSE

Scripture tells us that Joshua's generation was faithful and accomplished great things in God's will ... except in one area. The next generation grew up 'who neither knew the Lord nor what He had done for Israel.' This generation was evil, and served false gods. A pattern began whereby following generations would forsake the covenant, then experience God's judgement, then repent, and then fall back into sin once more. A key to this tragic period is the failure of parents to train their children in covenant heritage, covenant life, and personal knowledge of God. Yet, even in the midst of this dark time, God raised up Judges to rescue the people, thereby preserving the covenant.

GLOSSARY

Judge – from the Hebrew word '*Shaphat*' meaning a ruler or deliverer; God used the Judges to deliver Israel from its enemies, to maintain justice, and to settle disputes among the people.

TRAINING THE NEXT GENERATION

Exodus 12:21–27
Deuteronomy 6:4–9

True obedience to God's covenant means more than just keeping it ourselves ... by its very nature, God's covenant requires us to pass it on to others, particularly the next generation. God gave Israel clear commandments to train their children regarding their history and the covenant with God.

Exodus 20:1–11

And, He made it clear that He was the only God and there was no other god that could take His place. For anyone to reject their Creator – the One Who has given them life, sustained their life, and provided practical guidelines for successful living – is the height of ingratitude and foolishness.

Genesis 18:19

But in this time, Israel failed to train their children as their father Abraham had done ... and were therefore disobedient to the covenant.

Joshua 24:15

It was of paramount importance to Joshua that his own household should continue to serve the Lord after his death. Not long before he died, he renewed his family's stand for God and for the covenant.

Joshua 23–24

Joshua carefully reviewed covenant history with the leaders, and to the tribes. He challenged them to choose God or the idols ... but warning them of the seriousness of the choice and of their sinfulness. This was the very generation that had come into the Land with him, but had failed to train their children.

Judges 2:10
Proverbs 22:6

Israel had also disobeyed God in not persevering to drive out all of the Canaanites whom God had judged. Thus, they left temptation and false religion in the Land to entice and confuse their untrained children.

Exodus 23:27–33
Deuteronomy 7:1–6
Joshua 15:63
Joshua 16:10
Joshua 17:12–13

It is important to note that even among these wicked generations, there was always a remnant of faithful people who remembered the covenant and served the Lord. And, there were the Judges whom God raised up at strategic times to save the nation.

Ezekiel 18

Every person and every generation has their own responsibility to accept or reject God and His ways. Parental failure is no acceptable excuse to prevent a child from serving God.

SERVING THE ENEMY

Judges 2:11–15

The people of Israel fell into a terrible pattern of turning away from God. Whenever they would, God would allow their enemies to defeat them, and they would be forced to serve their enemies in misery.

Judges 2:16–19

Then, the people would cry out to God for deliverance, and He would raise up a judge to save them. But after that judge would die, the people would revert to their wicked behavior, becoming even more corrupt.

Judges 2–3

They were unable to pass the test of driving the Canaanites from the Land, and finally, they had to live in temptation among them. They intermarried with the Canaanites and their culture became affected by the pagan culture among them.

HEROES OF FAITH

In this time during Israel's history, the people simply went their own ways, doing what was right in their own eyes, rather that following the covenant or the common good. Often, what seems right or convenient in the eyes of men is wicked in the eyes of God. And so it was in Israel during the time of the judges.

Nonetheless, some of the greatest heroes of faith emerged during this time ... there are never any heroes apart from crisis. God raised up judges such as Othniel, Ehud, Deborah, Barak, Gideon, Jepthah, and Samson, who did great exploits and brought salvation to the people.

APPLICATION

Exodus 29:45
Leviticus 26:12
Isaiah 52:11
Isaiah 43:6
Hosea 1:10

Many of the forefathers of Western nations sought to establish their nations upon Scriptural precepts and under God's rule. For example, in the United States, many of its founding documents such as the First Charter of Virginia and the Mayflower Compact express the clear intent to establish a godly nation with godly people and godly government. In this history of the United States and other nations, there have been periods of judgement and renewal. In what ways are nations today like Israel was in the days of the Judges; particularly, what are the similarities with Western culture? Read John 17:14–19 ... what does it mean to be 'in the world, but not of the world'? What has Jesus given to us that sets us apart from the world? Read 2 Corinthians 6:11 – 7:1 ... why does the apostle Paul use these promises from the Old Testament, and what can we learn from Israel about how to live out these commands?

CONCLUSION

God's covenant included His Law, which was given for the benefit of wayward mankind, who needs the guidance and protection that it provides. In His Law, we discover how to submit to God and how to live under His leadership. Nevertheless, sinful man cannot, in his own will and strength, consistently obey God. Every person – and every generation – needs a deliverer who can save them from their enemies. Every person must know God's personal dealings, just as Abraham, Isaac, Jacob, and Moses did. Like Israel in the wilderness, each person must come face-to-face with their own rebellious nature and enter into His gracious provision. Life is a war that lasts until death . . . only by faithfully and consistently responding to God's grace through obedient faith can we inherit the Land.

Finally, we are reminded that being faithful to the covenant requires that we share it with the next generation. To do anything less is to disobey God and to perform a grave disservice to our children. God has given the next generation to us for us to train and shape . . . to command them in His ways and to commend them to His care.

There may be times when, after a parent has done all to train and teach a child in God's ways, the child may make poor decisions, or even turn away from the faith . . . God does allow each of us to make choices concerning His Lordship in our lives. The possibility that your child may make a wrong choice should not dissuade you from making the vigorous effort to train them rightly . . . after all, our own disobedience hasn't stopped the Lord. And, the Good News is that as we place our children in God's care, He is able to speak to and rescue them even in the midst of difficulty, so never cease praying for them.

If we are afraid to train and shape our children, we must remember that there is a godless, alien culture 'out there' that is more than willing to fill the vacuum. Take a stand in this day, that we might have the joy of seeing the next generation serving the Lord in the earth.

LESSON 18 – THE UNITED KINGDOM

PURPOSE

Judges 17:6

Israel as a nation had turned away from God, the Sovereign Almighty Lord Who had called the Patriarchs, delivered Israel from Egypt, offered them covenant relationship at Sinai, and established them as a kingdom of priests in the Land He provided. He had given them His Law and the book of the covenant, which had given unprecedented opportunity for self-government to each person and family under God.

Judges 21:25

1 Samuel 8:5

Yet, they did not acknowledge Him as their King, and told the prophet Samuel to appoint a king for them ... so that they might be like other nations. In this lesson we will again see God's redemptive purpose unfolding, as He demonstrates His covenant faithfulness to His Word and His people, and provides the Kingly lineage for the Promised Seed.

A HUMAN KING

Deuteronomy 4:39
Deuteronomy 10:14–22
Isaiah 33:22
Isaiah 43:15
Isaiah 44:6

In the covenant that God had made with Israel, there was none higher than Him. He declared His ownership and rulership over all of the heavens and the earth. The prophet Isaiah refers to God as the King of Israel, and indeed, He was the Ultimate Ruler.

Numbers 24:17–20

Psalm 2
Psalm 72:1–11
Psalm 110

Yet, His intention for Israel also included a human king. Balaam prophesied the rulership and victories of King David centuries before David's birth, as well as King Saul's victory over the Amalekites. Through Israel, God planned to produce a King who would rule the nations.

1 Samuel 8

But God had an appointed time and an appointed man for His purpose, and the people were not willing to wait, and they rejected God's wisdom and rulership. Nonetheless, God had compassion upon His people and prepared the heart of Saul – a tall and strong man – to be their king. However, after being appointed king, Saul became disobedient to the Lord, and began to trust in his own wisdom and resources.

1 Samuel 9
1 Samuel 10:9
1 Samuel 13
1 Samuel 15

A MAN AFTER GOD'S OWN HEART

1 Samuel 13:14
Acts 13:22
Ruth 4:13–21

Even as Saul was turning away from the Lord, God was preparing a young man for rulership ... a young man named David whose heart was inclined toward the Lord. David was in the tribe of Judah. His great-grandparents were Boaz and Ruth, the Moabite woman celebrated in Scripture for her faithfulness.

Besides his heritage and his fulfilment of covenant promises to his ancestors, there were many ways in which David was uniquely qualified to serve as king:

1 Samuel 17:34–37

He was prepared as a shepherd, protecting and caring for his father's sheep

1 Samuel 16:10–13

2 Samuel 7:18–29
1 Chronicles 29:10–20

1 Samuel 17:20–26

1 Samuel 17:38–51

1 Samuel 16:14–23
1 Samuel 18–31

He was anointed and the Spirit of God was upon him

He worshipped God and inspired others to praise the Lord

He was courageous and concerned for the name of the Lord

He knew the true source of victory and had God's wisdom in choosing resources and weapons

He was trained and disciplined through serving Saul, even as Saul tried to kill him

THE REIGN OF DAVID

2 Samuel 2:4
1 Chronicles 29:26–30

After the death of Saul and his son Jonathan, who was David's best friend, David was anointed King of Judah, and reigned for seven years before all of Israel recognized his rule. In all, his reign lasted for forty years.

2 Samuel 8:1–14
1 Chronicles 18:1–13
1 Chronicles 29

Under his leadership, Israel conquered all of the territory promised to Abraham, and the nation became very wealthy. David prepared for the building of the Temple in Jerusalem, and he left the kingdom to his son Solomon at the peak of its glory.

2 Samuel 11–12
Psalm 51

Though David did tragically sin, he repented and found mercy with God.

A KING FOREVER

2 Samuel 7
1 Chronicles 17

God made a covenant with David, to establish his son as King forever. This was not a natural son, but One Who was the Son of God, to rule on David's throne forever and build God's house.

1 Chronicles 29:25
1 Kings 4
1 Kings 6–8
1 Kings 10
1 Kings 11

David's natural son, Solomon, was glorious, and he did build an earthly Temple. But Solomon did not rule forever ... indeed, he was not even faithful to God within his lifetime. He married many foreign wives, who led him astray toward false gods. Therefore, God judged Solomon by dividing his kingdom after his death.

Matthew 1:1–17
Acts 2:25–35

Romans 1:1–4

There was yet a more glorious King to come from the line of David ... Jesus Christ. Peter declared that David had spoken of Jesus, His Resurrection, and His eternal reign. And, while Jesus was David's son in the natural, He was also shown to be the Son of God by His Resurrection, according to Paul's letter to the Romans.

Despite the sins of Israel, and the failures of its kings, God was merciful and faithful to keep His covenant promise.

APPLICATION

Matthew 28:18–20
2 Corinthians 5:17–20

In your opinion, why did God approve of David and not Saul? Jesus taught us to pray, 'Thy Kingdom come, Thy will be done, on earth as it is in heaven' (Matthew 6:10). What part did David play in fulfilling that prayer? What part do you have to play? In what ways does this lesson illustrate God's mercy and covenant faithfulness? How does that apply to our lives?

Hebrews 2
Ephesians 2:19–22

CONCLUSION

And so, God's covenant purpose continued to unfold during the period of the united kingdom of Israel. He chose David to produce the Kingly lineage of the Promised Seed. Though the nation failed to follow God wholeheartedly ... though even many of David's descendants were unfaithful ... God was faithful to His promise.

David and Solomon provide glimpses of the One Who would eternally reign in wisdom and build God's living temple.

LESSON 19 – THE DIVIDED KINGDOM AND EXILE

PURPOSE

Deuteronomy 17:14–20

The Lord knew there would come a time in Israel when they would want a human king, so He set forth commands to govern kings. The king was to fear God and obey His commands, reading the Law daily. The king in Israel was not to be above the Law, nor was he the Law, but he was to represent God and live and govern according to God's Law. This was a radical political concept, and is the key to understanding the history of the kingdom of Israel. In this lesson, we will see how disobedience led to division, and then to exile and captivity.

SOLOMON'S HEART TURNED

1 Kings 3
Matthew 6:33

Deuteronomy 17
Deuteronomy 7:1–11
Exodus 23:32–33
Exodus 34:12–16

At the beginning of his reign, Solomon asked the Lord for His wisdom, rather than for wealth, long life, or the death of his enemies. This was pleasing to God, and God granted His request, as well as giving him the other blessings also.

Despite God's provision, Solomon did not take God's Law into his heart, and he sinned in ways that were grievous to God and devastating to the nation:

1 Kings 3:1
1 Kings 11:1–13

He made alliances with foreign nations and married non-covenant women . . . he took 700 wives

1 Kings 10:14–29

He accumulated great wealth through taxation and acquired large numbers of horses and chariots

1 Kings 11:4–10

He turned his heart toward foreign gods

A KINGDOM DIVIDED

1 Kings 11–12

2 Kings 9–10

2 Kings 10:32
2 Kings 17

Solomon's sin caused the kingdom to be divided during the reign of Solomon's weak son, Rehoboam. This divided kingdom consisted of:

Israel – Northern 10 tribes; capital in Samaria
Judah – Southern tribe, incorporating the tribe of Benjamin, with its capital in Jerusalem and ruled by David's descendants

During this tragic period, Israel was led by wicked kings. One king, Jehu, did do some good, but he nonetheless persisted in sin. Because of their idolatry and sin, Israel began to lose territory to its enemies. Finally, in 722 BC, God allowed the Assyrians to destroy Israel and take the people into captivity.

2 Chronicles 14–16
2 Chronicles 29–32
2 Chronicles 34–35
2 Chronicles 36

In Judah, there were a few good kings, but many more bad ones. Asa, Hezekiah, and Josiah stand out as kings who led in times of covenant renewal. But many other kings of Judah sinned terribly. Because of His covenant with David and the reforms of the few good kings, God allowed Judah to stand until 586 BC, when He sent Nebuchadnezzar to destroy Jerusalem and take the people into exile.

Though there was great wickedness during these centuries of division, God faithfully sent prophets to warn the kings and the people, calling them back to the covenant.

Those who prophesied to Israel included: Elijah, Elisha, Hosea, and Amos.

Those who prophesied to Judah included: Isaiah, Jeremiah, Ezekiel, Joel, Habbakkuk, Zephaniah, Haggai, Zechariah, and Malachi.

God used key prophets to speak to other nations also. These include: Obadiah, Daniel, Jonah, and Micah.

EXILE AND RETURN

Matthew 1:12
Ezra 3–5

Though they were exiled for seventy years in Babylon, God re-established Judah in Jerusalem and in the Promised Land. Thus, God continued to honor His covenants with Abraham and David, preserving their descendants and land. In fact, one of David's descendants, Zerrubabel, played a significant role in rebuilding Jerusalem and the Temple.

Daniel 9

In answer to Daniel's intercessory prayer, based upon Jeremiah's prophecy, God caused the Persian King Cyrus to send Ezra and the exiles back to rebuild the Temple.

Nehemiah 8–13

Later, Nehemiah, sent by King Artaxerxes, led the people in a powerful time of covenant renewal. Though Nehemiah faced many obstacles, he was able to say, 'The joy of the Lord is my strength.'

Nehemiah 8:10

And so it was that the covenant was preserved and renewed after a severe test.

APPLICATION

God sought to get the attention of His wayward people through prophets, discipline, and finally exile. Is God trying to get your attention concerning any area of your life? Remember, no matter what our sins are, He is a God of mercy Who desires that our fellowship be restored with Him.

CONCLUSION

Romans 7
Romans 3
Romans 6

Romans 4
Galatians 3

Though the Law is good and holy, it cannot change the sinful nature of man . . . and all people have this sinful nature. The Law cannot save; it can only demonstrate the wickedness of the human condition. However, God's covenant promise to Abraham preceeds the giving of the Law, and His promise is to extend His grace to all those who believe. This period in Israel's history demonstrates these truths – whenever the people would repent and believe, covenant life was renewed. Whenever they refused to hear the Lord, sin and death reigned. But the promise withstood this season, and God continued to call upon those who would look for the Seed Who was coming to bless all nations.

LESSON 20 – THE PROPHETS AND THE NEW COVENANT

PURPOSE

God's sent special human messengers – prophets – who spoke to His people, their kings, and other nations. These prophets declared the Word of the Lord to the people for their times and situations. As they were inspired by the Holy Spirit, these prophets also saw down the corridors of time itself. In the midst of speaking of their own times, the prophets also spoke of the new covenant that God would make, and also of the Messiah, who would mediate this Covenant. In examining the words of these prophets, we can be assured that they point toward Jesus Christ, the Messiah and promised Seed Who is our salvation.

GLOSSARY

Messiah – the Hebrew word for 'Christ' or 'Anointed One'. The Old Testament includes hundreds of references to the Messiah who was to come and deliver God's people.

Ceremonial Aspects of the Law – portions of the Old Testament, especially the first five books, that prescribe the religious rituals of Israel.

Moral Aspects of the Law – portions of the Old Testament, including the Ten Commandments, that provide God's unchanging moral principles and remain in force for all people at all times.

PROPHECY CONCERNING THE NEW COVENANT

Jeremiah 31:31–34

In this series, we have discussed God's eternal purpose regarding the covenant, and we have examined many passages of the Old Testament that point toward the Messiah to come. Let us look briefly at two major prophets and what they had to say about the new covenant.

Jeremiah declared that the new covenant would be a more personal covenant, written on human hearts rather than simply on tablets of stone. From the least to the greatest, all of God's people would know the Lord personally as their God. And God promised that He would forgive their iniquity and forget their sin.

Ezekiel also prophesied concerning the new covenant that would help us to recognize it:

It would be with the House of David

God's people would have one Shepherd

It would be an everlasting covenant of peace

God would multiply His people and dwell with them

The nations would know that the Lord is God

THE NEW COVENANT AND THE OLD COVENANT

Hebrews 8–10

In the letter to the Hebrews, the writer explains the relationship between the new covenant and the old covenant.

Quoting directly from Jeremiah, the writer points out that the new covenant is superior to the old covenant because it is enacted upon better promises. The problem with the old covenant was not the covenant itself, but with the people who had to carry it out ... in fact, no person – no matter what race, nationality, sex, or age – is able to carry out the covenant fully and without sin. The moral commands of God are righteous and good, but corrupt man is unable to keep them.

In the new covenant, God unveiled the answer to this terrible dilemma ... He would change man's nature in Christ, writing His commandments on man's heart. What people needed was not more rules ... there was nothing wrong with the rules. Instead, we needed was the Way to walk in righteousness.

Exodus 20:1–17

The moral aspects of the Law remain the same in the new covenant as they were in the old covenant. For example, worship of other gods, idolatry, murder, adultery, stealing, false testimony, and covetousness are sins in the new covenant, just as the are in the old.

Matthew 5:17–48

Jesus stated that He had not come to abolish the Law but to fulfill it. In fact, He took the Law to a new level, saying that the righteousness of those who believe in Him should even exceed the righteousness of the Pharisees. The Pharisees were very concerned with fulfilling the letter of the Law, but Jesus was even more concerned with what was in the hearts of the people.

Galatians 2:14–21
Galatians 3:2–25
Hebrews 11
Galatians 5:13–26

Zechariah 4:6

At the same time, the New Testament carefully warns us that we are not justified by our obedience to the Law, but rather by faith in Jesus. Nor can we live with a constant dependence upon the Law, but by the power of the Holy Spirit. Note that this does not contradict the Old Testament ... the Old Testament sets forth these principles, and they are fulfilled in the New Testament.

Hebrews 4:3–11
Hebrews 9–10

In fact, the Ceremonial Aspects of the Law ... the sacrifices, the Sabbath, the festivals, and other signs pointing to God's provision ... are fulfilled in Jesus Christ Himself.

Hebrews 8:13

The new covenant is characterized by grace and mercy, and its glory makes the Old obsolete. All people, Jews and Gentiles, are saved by God in the same way: through the new covenant in the blood of Jesus Christ.

Romans 4:13–25
Ephesians 2:14–22

A FOUNDATION IN THE OLD COVENANT

Luke 24:44
Matthew 26:56
John 5:39–47

Many aspects and events in the life of Jesus were foretold by the Old Testament prophets, and this was a significant tool for evangelism in the hands of the New Testament apostles.

Jesus Himself spoke of His life and ministry as fulfilling prophecies written in the Law of Moses, the Prophets, and the Psalms.

Acts 3:18–26
Acts 17:2–3
1 Corinthians 15:3–4

The preaching and writing of the apostles largely depended upon Old Testament Scripture. Of course, when they were making these proclamations, there was no written or compiled New Testament, so

Genesis 22:18
Matthew 1:1
Galatians 3:16
Matthew 28:18–20
Psalm 110
Luke 2:11
Matthew 22:43–45
Hebrews 5:5–11
Isaiah 7:14
Matthew 1:18–25
Colossians 2:9
Psalm 2
Matthew 27:11–37
1 Timothy 1:15–17
Revelation 19:11–16

Micah 5:2–5
Luke 2:1–11
Isaiah 7:14
Matthew 1:18–25
Isaiah 11:2–5
Isaiah 61:1–3
Luke 3:22
Luke 4:17–21
Psalm 22
Isaiah 53
John 1:29
Mark 15:14–39
2 Corinthians 5:21
Psalm 16:9–10
Luke 24
Acts 2:22–36

whenever a New Testament writer refers to Scripture, he is referring to the Old Testament.

Examine the irrefutable evidence that Jesus is indeed the Christ, the Messiah, of Whom the prophets spoke:

He is the Seed of Abraham who blesses all the nations of the earth according to God's promise.

He is the Lord who rules and is also our Great High Priest after the Order of Melchizedek . . . He reigns and intercedes.

He is God with us, born of the Holy Spirit to a virgin, in accordance with Scripture.

He is the King of Kings who rules over all nations and all rulers, bringing judgement on the unrighteous and deliverance to those who put their trust in Him.

Other events in the life and ministry of Jesus were foretold in the Old Testament, including:

The Messiah would be born in Bethlehem

The Messiah would be born of a virgin

The Messiah would receive a special anointing by the Holy Spirit

The Messiah would be the Lamb of God, who would be tortured and crucified, taking the sins of the world upon Himself

The Messiah would be Resurrected from the dead

The Old and New Testaments are inextricably linked. It has been said that 'The New is in the Old concealed . . . the Old is in the New revealed.' In the Old Testament, we have the foundation of the Law and the prophetic promise of the Holy Seed Who would come to fulfill all righteousness. In the New Testament, we see Jesus Christ as the fulfilment of all that had been spoken in the Old.

APPLICATION

What does it mean to you in your daily life to have access to God in the new covenant? How does it affect you to have the covenant written on your heart, rather than in a book of rules? Use the section on fulfilled prophecy to share the Good News with someone.

CONCLUSION

We cannot properly understand how God relates to us apart from the old covenant. It was in the context of the old covenant that He progressively revealed Himself to the world. And, it was in this context that He sent His Son to establish the new covenant. Without understanding this, we are left with a shallow 'gospel' that is robbed of its intended fullness. Jesus and the apostles understood this, and used it effectively to reveal that Jesus was indeed the promised Messiah.

LESSON 21 – A HOLY NATION

PURPOSE

1 Peter 2:9–10

The apostle Peter was inspired by the Holy Spirit to declare to the Church of Jesus Christ that we are a chosen people and a holy nation, called by God to function as royal priests and as proclaimers of the Good News. Like Israel, the Church has a special calling and destiny as a chosen nation. The Church, Christ's body, is the primary realm of God's rulership in the earth. 'The kingdom of God' is not a vague religious concept or abstract term; it is the rulership or government of God in practical daily living. Just as God ruled Israel by His Law, He intends to rule the Church – His Holy Nation – by His Word and His Spirit. Just as Israel fell short of God's purpose, the Church can also fall short at times. Yet, the same high calling remains, to proclaim by our life together the praises of the One Who called us 'out of darkness into His marvelous light.'

CHILDREN OF ABRAHAM

John 8:13–59

John 8:39

The Book of John records a significant debate between Jesus and the Pharisees. In response to their assertion that Abraham was their father, Jesus told them that the true children of Abraham were those who did the works of Abraham. While recognizing their racial ties to Abraham, Jesus pointed out that if they were truly his children in the Spirit, they would rejoice to see Him as Abraham had done. These statements so infuriated the Pharisees that they considered killing Him on the spot.

John 1:10–11

God's covenant promise to Israel – that from this nation would come the Holy Seed – was fulfilled in Jesus Christ. The Seed of Abraham, Who was also the Holy One from the House of David, came into the midst of His own people . . . but they rejected Him.

Matthew 23:37–39

Psalm 118:22

1 Peter 2:1–10

As they had in times past, God's chosen nation rejected God's chosen Messenger. Jesus Himself lamented over Jerusalem, being reminded not only of His own rejection, but of the rejection of so many prophets from God. But, 'the stone that the builders rejected became the Cornerstone,' as the Psalmist prophesied concerning Israel's rejection of Jesus. And from Jesus, God built a new nation.

Matthew 21:33–46

Jesus declared to the religious officials that because they had not brought forth fruit according to God's commands – and the grace to which He had extended to them – the kingdom of God would be taken away from them and given to this new nation. The new nation would bear fruit among all of the nations, in accordance with God's covenant promise to Abraham and His stated purpose from the beginning of creation.

Galatians 3:6–29

In fact, those who receive Christ, whether they be Jew or Gentile, are the true children of Abraham, and heirs of the promise.

1 Peter 2:9
Isaiah 9:2

Revelation 5:9–10
Colossians 1:9–14

Romans 11

The heritage of Abraham has passed to the Church, God's Holy Nation. Our task is the one which He spoke to Israel: 'proclaim the praises of Him who called you out of darkness into His marvelous light.'

In Christ, God has created a nation of believers from every family, tribe, and nation. By God's great mercy and love, we have been delivered out of darkness and become 'partakers of the inheritance of the saints in the light.'

ISRAEL NOT REJECTED

In his letter to the Romans, the apostle Paul compares the Church to a branch from a wild olive tree that is grafted into a rooted, healthy olive tree. He warns that the Church should not boast against the root – Israel – because branches do not support roots … roots support branches.

He reminds us that he himself is an Israelite of the Tribe of Benjamin, and that God has not cast away Israel, His chosen people. Though blessing has come to the Gentiles, they should not be haughty, considering that if God did not spare the natural branches, He may not spare the Gentiles either. Paul asks, 'If wild branches can be grafted into a cultivated olive tree, then how much more can the natural branches be grafted back into their own tree?'

Finally, Paul reminds the Church that the Jews are beloved by God, and that the gifts and callings of God are irrevocable. Through the Jews came the covenant and the Covenant Seed, Jesus Christ, Who offers salvation to all who will believe in Him, whether they be Jew or Gentile.

PRIVILEGES AND RESPONSIBILITIES

Matthew 6:9–10

Matthew 3:2
Matthew 5:2–10
Matthew 10:7
Matthew 12:28
Mark 1:15
Luke 10:9
Acts 1:3
Acts 8:12

Being a part of the Holy Nation is a privilege that has responsibilities. Jesus is not merely our Savior … He is our Lord and King. In fact, it is only in allowing Him to be our Lord that He becomes our Savior. He rules over us by His Word, His Spirit, and His delegated representatives.

Jesus taught us to pray that the Father's Kingdom would come, and that His will would be done on earth as it is in heaven. This is a request that God's government would be established in our hearts and extended through our lives. The message of the kingdom of God was the central theme in the preaching of John the Baptist, Jesus, and the disciples. Scripture references to their teaching are too numerous to list here. Later in this book, we will discuss aspects of the kingdom of God in greater detail.

Nonetheless, it is important to remember that by entering into the blessings of His Kingdom, we have also entered into responsibilities before Him and one another.

DON'T MISS IT

1 Corinthians 10:1–11

John 6:41–59

Hebrews 3–4

Israel did not attain the full heights of God's calling, and Scripture reminds us that the Christians can also miss out on God's highest calling if Christians do not listen to His Word.

God's dealings with Israel are a clear example to the Church. Israel's baptism with Moses in the cloud and in the sea was a foreshadowing of the Christian's baptism in water and in the Spirit.

The provision of manna and water for the children of Israel in the wilderness was a picture of the One Who is our spiritual provision, Jesus Christ. Like the Israelites who were tried in the wilderness, Christians will also encounter trials ... but God has also made provision for us.

In order to grow and mature in Christ and to faithfully fulfill our high calling, we must understand God's ways in dealing with His people. We glorify God when we stand in faith and obedience in time of trial.

Moses understood God's ways and was blessed; Israel as a nation only saw God's works. Faith toward God and obedience to God were critical issues that the people of Israel faced; likewise, we as the Holy Nation must also have both faith and faithfulness.

Israel failed to enter into God's rest because of disbelief and disobedience. The only way for us today to enter into God's rest in Christ is to believe and obey God's Word in times of trial, without provoking the Lord through grumbling and complaining.

Hebrews 10

It is vital that we encourage one another every day, so that our hearts do not become hardened against the Lord and grumble against Him, as Israel did.

LOVE ONE ANOTHER

Galatians 5:14
John 13–17

God has called His Holy Nation to be one people, bound together in covenant by love for Him and for one another. In fact, the Law can be fulfilled by loving your neighbour in the way that your love yourself. Love that produces unity is the central commandment that Jesus has given to us.

John 17:20–23

God is glorified in His people when they are one in love ... in fact, Christian love and unity is the sign which should speak to the world of Jesus' Lordship. The unity reflected in the diversity of God's people is the unity in diversity that is rooted in the Trinity ... we are one Body, even as God is one God.

John 13:34–35

Furthermore, the way that the world knows that we are His disciples is by our love for one another.

John 15:1–17

Because we are commanded to bear fruit, we must consider the key that Jesus provided in John 15. This key is shown in a progressive revelation that Jesus shared with His disciples. He said that if we are to be fruitful, then we must abide in Him and keep His commandments in the same way that He keeps His Father's commandments. In doing this, He promised that our joy would remain full.

He then clearly told His disciples His command: to love one another in the same way that He had loved them. Jesus provides the standard for love ... laying down your life, or considering others above ourselves. As we do His will, He no longer calls us servants, but friends. It is in the context of this teaching that He said, 'Whatever you ask the Father in My name He may give you.'

As His Holy Nation, we are to love one another, thereby bearing good fruit and testifying to all the nations of the Good News of Christ's Kingdom.

APPLICATION

In what ways does the government of God affect and bless your personal life? Are you succeeding as an 'Ambassador' of His Kingdom to the world? Think about times when your faith or obedience were tested ... how did you respond? What can you do to strengthen the unity of God's people? How can you avoid weakening that unity?

CONCLUSION

1 Peter 2:12

Becoming a Christian is not simply a matter of 'going to heaven when you die.' When we receive Christ's Lordship in our lives, we are actually 'changing governments' and that ought to affect the way we live each day. The Gospel commands us to live as obedient subjects of King Jesus, and if we fail, we are to seek out His abundant grace and be restored. We should be a people that not only say, 'Glory to God,' but – by our behavior – cause the world to glorify God.

LESSON 22 – THE RESTORATION OF ALL THINGS

PURPOSE

1 Corinthians 15:20–28

History is going somewhere. God established His covenant in order to accomplish the restoration of all things to Himself. Moses and the prophets spoke of God's intention to restore creation, and Jesus Christ is the One appointed by the Father in Whom this restoration takes place. Jesus must rule until He has made all enemies subject to Him, including death. Having completed His role as Conqueror and Mediator, He will Himself become subject to the Father, in order that God may be 'all in all.' In this, we see that redemptive history – foreshadowed in God's promise to Eve, begun in His covenant with Abraham, made victorious in the work of Christ – will culminate in the Father. The 'Relentless Redeemer' has been present throughout history, bringing it inevitably back to Himself.

GLOSSARY

Eschatology – the study of events pertaining to the end of the world.

OLD TESTAMENT REFERENCES TO RESTORATION

As we have seen throughout this book, covenant restoration is a thread that runs throughout Scripture, and both the Old and the New Testament offer promises and pictures of God's redeeming work.

Numbers 14:21

In one of the darkest moments in the history of the Israelites, when they had fearfully and rebelliously turned away from the Promised Land, the Lord promised Moses that no matter what the circumstance, the whole earth would be ultimately filled with His glory.

Isaiah 2:2–4
Micah 4:1–4

Prophets foretold of the glorious time of peace, when the 'mountain of the house of the Lord' would be established as 'the chief of all mountains.'

Psalm 110:1
Matthew 22:44
Mark 12:36; Luke 20:42–43
Acts 2:34–35
1 Corinthians 15:25
Hebrews 1:13

David prophesied concerning Christ that He would conquer all of His enemies – indeed this is the most often-quoted Old Testament Scripture in the New Testament, speaking of Christ's present reign and denying any defeatist eschatology. Jesus reigns now, and will reign until He 'makes all His enemies His footstool.'

PRESENT RULE OF CHRIST

Hebrews 2:5–10

Even now, all things have been put under subjection to Christ by God the Father, though we do not yet see it. Jesus has been appointed over all the works of God, and He is crowned with glory and honor. He brings blessing by turning us from our wicked ways.

Acts 3:19–26

Jesus will remain in heaven until the time comes for 'the period of the restoration of all things.' When He returns for His people, He will complete the task of bringing all things into subjection and bringing 'many sons to glory.'

Matthew 24:14

The end will come when the Gospel of Christ's Kingdom is preached in all the nations. Much more about the 'end times' will be said later in this book.

THE GLORY TO COME

Romans 8:18–25

While we do not yet fully see His present rule in that we may experience 'sufferings in this age,' we must know that these sufferings will pale in the light of the glory that is to be revealed at the resurrection and redemption of our bodies.

The apostle Paul described in his letter to the Romans how we 'groan within ourselves' as we eagerly await our full adoption and redemption. Furthermore, creation itself is groaning and suffering as though in childbirth, eagerly awaiting the day of full restoration ... the day of resurrection. And when all things have been made subject to Christ, God's wonderful redemptive work ... His mighty act of love and restoration shown to a fallen creation ... will be completed.

APPLICATION

How does the present reality of Jesus' rulership affect the way you live? What does it mean to live in the time of 'groaning' when the glory of God is not yet fully manifested within us? How should we live until Christ's Return?

CONCLUSION

Jesus Christ is the first and the last ... the 'Alpha and Omega' ... the beginning and end of all creation. He created all things, redeemed creation by His blood, and rules now at the Father's right hand. Because He rules, we can live triumphantly in this life and proclaim His Kingdom throughout the earth. The promise of God in the Holy Spirit assures us that He shall conclude this age with His appearance to complete our transformation, and creation's full redemption. The Church with this perspective has proclaimed the kingdom of God with boldness in every generation. We are strengthened in this revelation: even though we do not yet see everything subject to Christ, we have this confidence that ultimate victory belongs to Him.

SECTION 2:

GOD'S PROVISIONS IN CHRIST

LESSON 1 – JESUS CHRIST, FATHER'S INCARNATE GIFT

PURPOSE

Galatians 4:4
John 1:14
Matthew 1:21

In the fullness of time, God sent forth His Son, born of a woman, born under the Law. God's Son took on human form, became a man and received the name Jesus. Jesus of Nazareth lived on earth as totally man and completely God, not half and half. Jesus, as God Incarnate, fulfilled all previous prophesies, promises, and covenants. He accomplished for us what we could never accomplish on our own – a right relationship with the Father. Jesus provided the means for us to live righteously and covenantally with the living God. This lesson shows the detailed preparation for and the significance of God Incarnate … Jesus, Son of God.

GLOSSARY

Incarnation – invested with flesh, human body, nature, and form. The transcendent God became a human being, a man.

Original Sin – the stain of disobedience and willfulness that indelibly overspread Adam's nature. All born as descendants of Adam inherit these characteristics. Physical death is the consequence of original sin.

Transcendent – God, by nature, lives apart from His creation. He created it; He is not dependent on it. He transcends the human plane on which we live.

PREPARATION: SOMEONE IS COMING!

Genesis 3:15

Genesis 12:1–3

Genesis 22:18
Genesis 3:16

Genesis 49:10

Numbers 24:17

2 Samuel 7:12
Psalm 89:1–4
Psalm 89:19
Joel 1:15; Joel 2:1, 11
Micah 5:2
Matthew 2:1, 6

From the time of Adam's fall, God indicated His plan to defeat Satan through Eve's Descendent – her Seed. God further clarified His intentions in the covenantal promise He established with Abraham and his family. Through Abraham's offspring, God would convey His blessing to all peoples on earth.

Jacob, grandson of Abraham, prophesied that a ruler would come forth from the tribe of his son, Judah. This tribe would provide victorious leadership for the nation of Israel for generations to come, finally culminating in the birth of the Prince of Peace. The Old Testament writers continually reaffirm this Messianic prophecy.

Nathan, the prophet during David's reign, spoke clearly that the Holy Seed would come through King David. Both king and kingdom would continue forever. Many prophets, like Joel, refer to the coming 'Day of the Lord'. Micah calls Him 'the Ruler of Israel', and specifically notes Bethlehem as the place of His birth.

Isaiah 4:2
Isaiah 52–53
Isaiah 7:14

Isaiah gives the most details concerning the features and characteristics of the coming king. He names Him the 'Promised Seed, the Branch, Immanuel (God with us), the Lord's Servant and the Savior.'

THE MEANS OF INCARNATION

Isaiah 7:14
John 1:14
John 3:16–18
1 John 4:9
Luke 1:35
1 Peter 1:23
1 Corinthians 15:22
1 Corinthians 15:45

Romans 5:12
Galatians 4:4

Genesis 3:15

2 Samuel 7:12

Jeremiah 22:30

Luke 3:23
Luke 2:4–27

God the Spirit overshadowed the Virgin Mary, and by His power produced a miraculous conception. Mary bore the Child, the 'only begotten Son of God.' By God's creative Power, the Spirit began a spiritual nation ... people who experience a 'new birth' through faith in Christ their King. He became the First, the Leader, the New Adam.

The unique conception through the Virgin Mary enabled Jesus to avoid the curses of Original Sin. Had He been born of both Joseph and Mary, He would have carried the sin inherent in all people. God's Word in the Garden established that the Seed of woman, not man, would crush the Serpent's head.

God promised David that his descendants would sit on the throne forever. But Jehoiachin (Coniah) – David's legal and royal descendent – was cut off by a curse from God. Jesus was a descendent of David through Mary's lineage. That line came through Jehoiachin's brother Jonah.

Joseph, a descendent of David through Jehoiachin, adopted Jesus as 'supposedly' the son of Joseph. Thus Jesus avoided the curse of sin and still qualified legally for the throne of David.

INCARNATION AND THE NEW COVENANT

Deuteronomy 4:13
1 Peter 1:18
1 Corinthians 11:25
2 Corinthians 3:13
Luke 22:20
Jeremiah 31:31

Hebrews 8:8–13
Hebrews 9:12–15
Hebrews 190:16–18
Luke 22:20

God initiated and maintained the old covenant in terms of animal sacrifices. These terms he wrote on tablets of stone. God writes the new covenant on the tablets of human hearts. Jesus of Nazareth through His life sacrifice, once and for all met all requirements of God's holiness. All that the sacrificial system of the old covenant meant in terms of human failure, this Jesus, the God-Man, gathered up in Himself and paid the price. Jesus ratified the new covenant in His own blood. He fulfilled all the terms of the new covenant. Therefore, He and He alone, was able to inaugurate the new covenant, set it in motion, and maintain it.

APPLICATION

How does Jesus Christ uniquely qualify as the One who could break the curse of sin and death over mankind? In what ways does He uniquely fulfill the promises given to King David?

CONCLUSION

Old Testament prophesies and allusions abound concerning the One who would fulfill all righteousness, and remedy with cosmic finality, all the temporary solutions to the wreckage caused by mankind's sin. The Messiah would personify all that the Old Testament sacrificial system represented. God alone had the insight and power to effect any real change in humanity's sinful condition. Therefore, God Himself became a Man (Incarnation) in a unique way (virgin birth) that avoided the curse of Original Sin. Jesus established the new covenant through His own blood.

LESSON 2 – JESUS CHRIST, GOD'S SERVANT AMONG US

PURPOSE

Hebrews 2:17
Ephesians 1:20–22
Isaiah 42:1–7
Philippians 2:5–11

Jesus of Nazareth, as the Servant of the Lord, embodies His earthly ministry, from Incarnation to Ascension. In order to understand Jesus as God's Word (Prophet), great High Priest and King, we need first to look at His servanthood. Jesus' servanthood qualifies Him to function as Priest and King. Isaiah's 'Servant Hymns' look forward to this extraordinary Servant. The Apostolic writers, after Pentecost, look back and marvel at the depth of servanthood Jesus demonstrated among them. Jesus bequeathed His servanthood to His Church as the most transparently identifying feature of His followers. This lesson shows Jesus as Servant: prophesied, at work, in death, and in Resurrection.

GLOSSARY

Servant – the title of an office, the idea of a subordinant King ruling for the Great King; also (Greek: *doulos*) a bond-servant, a slave.

Subordinate King – a legal term, from the Hittite covenantal structure of 2,000 BC, signifying the responsibility and covenantal bond between the Supreme Sovereign and his subordinate rulers.

Servant-King – a legal term, signifying the subordinate ruler who rules in covenant relationships with the Supreme Sovereign.

THE SERVANT PROPHESIED

Isaiah 42:1–7
Isaiah 49:1–9
Isaiah 50:4–9
Isaiah 52:13–53

Matthew 12:18–20
Isaiah 42:8–10

Isaiah 42:6
Isaiah 43:10
Isaiah 49:6
Isaiah 49:5

Isaiah 52–53

Isaiah, the evangelical Prophet, foresaw the Messiah in an aspect which largely escaped the attention of Jewish writers. The Jewish leadership interpreted Isaiah's Servant as the nation Israel. The Apostolic writers lived in the midst of Jesus' ministry and named Him as the Servant. Isaiah sees the Servant as the Chosen of the Father, strengthened and upheld by the Father's hand ... the One who is the Father's covenant to the nations. He bears witness to the Father; He comes as Light to the Gentile nations of the earth. Formed from the womb to be the Father's Servant, He brings restoration to Israel.

Isaiah portrays the suffering Servant, disfigured and marred beyond all human likeness, a root out of dry ground, despised and rejected by people. Isaiah sees Him as struck by the Father, smitten, afflicted, pierced, crushed, and wounded. As the guilt offering, the Father lays on Him all the sins of the world. By knowing the Righteous One, the Father's Servant, many will find justification and salvation.

Little wonder that readers and scholars of Isaiah's time mis-read the Servant-Person! Yet in the light of salvation completed, we re-read

Isaiah and marvel at the Servant. Jesus, His disciples, and those who heard Him carried in their hearts Isaiah's prophecies.

THE SERVANT AT WORK

1 John 1:1
Isaiah 61:1–3
Luke 4:18

Matthew 12:18

Matthew 9:30

Matthew 6:30
Matthew 8:26

John wrote that he had seen Him, observed Him, and touched Him. Luke recognized Him as Isaiah's Messiah, anointed with the Good News for the poor and captive, to release them into sight, healing, and God's favour. Matthew observed His self-effacing manner. More than once Jesus cautioned His followers not to divulge His real identity or work. In Jesus' healing events, the Gospel writers stand in awe at the range of diseases and demonic spirits which Jesus addresses. In the face of this extraordinary Person, the Apostles, more than once, pulled back in disbelief. He was not the stereotype – public nor scholarly – of the long-anticipated Messiah.

Matthew 5:17
Luke 24:27

Matthew 23:13
Mark 9:31
Matthew 16:21

Matthew 16:22

In serving His Father, Jesus undertook to fulfill all the Old Testament Scripture spoke concerning the Messiah. Popular belief saw the Messiah as a kingly figure from the presence of the Father with sufficient troops to defeat Rome and re-establish Jerusalem as the capital of the earth. Instead, Jesus came as the Servant, meeting the needs of ordinary people, cautious about divulging His true identity, and exposing the hypocrisy of religious leaders. Jesus explained to His disciples three times the necessity of His going to Jerusalem to die. Even Peter rebuffed Him, saying, 'God forbid it, Lord. This shall never happen to You.'

John 6:38
John 5:19
John 7:16
John 5:36

John 10:18

To complicate the picture more, Jesus avowed in John's writings that He came to earth because the Father sent Him; that He came to accomplish the Father's will; He does nothing on His own initiative, but only what He sees the Father doing; His teaching is not His own, but the Father's who taught Him; the very works which He does are the ones the Father sent Him to accomplish; He carries the Father's authority, not His own. The only authority He carried was that of laying down His own life at the cross – and that commandment He received from His Father.

This Servant posture, prophesied in Old Testament detail, but nowhere anticipated, Jesus maintained until the end of His earthly life and ministry. He saw Himself as His Father's Servant, sent on the Father's initiative, carrying the Father's words, accomplishing the Father's works and representing the very essence of the Father's nature.

John 14:9
Psalm 40:6–8
Hebrews 10:5–7

Mark 1:11
Mark 9:7

He confronted Philip: 'He who has seen Me has seen the Father.' For Jesus, His delight was to accomplish His Father's purposes. As the joyful, consistently yielded Servant, Jesus received the Father's verbal and audible approval as the 'Beloved Son, the One in whom the Father is well-pleased.'

Let us not think that Jesus came to earth with a grudging attitude, or a sense of being humiliated. Rather, by the Spirit, Jesus savored every day on earth as His opportunity to please His Beloved Father. Such an attitude, then, He leaves with us for our lifestyle in the Spirit.

THE SERVANT IN HIS DEATH

Mark 8:31
Mark 9:31
Mark 10:33

Luke 18:31

John 12:7

John 13:1–38

John 14:1–31
John 15:1–27
John 16:1–33

John 17:1–26

The Gospel writers faithfully recorded their response to Jesus' thrice-stated intention of going to Jerusalem to lay down His life for the people of the world. Astounded, they responded in unbelief at such a demise. Though Jesus specifically stated that resurrection followed in three days, His intinery so differed from popular teaching for the Messiah that they could not comprehend it. Jesus rebuffed His disciples for despising Mary's pre-burial anointing of Him.

Jesus took a few days just before His arrest, trial, and execution to work privately with His disciples. He washed their feet, recognized the betrayer and gave them His New Commandment. He promised them His abiding Presence through the Holy Spirit. He showed them the vine-branch relationship. He described the work of the coming Holy Spirit and told them farewell. Then, He spent His last hours alone in the Father's Presence, interceding for His disciples and all subsequent believers. To the end of His earthly existence, Jesus maintained His Servant posture.

THE SERVANT IN HIS ASCENSION

Luke 24:25

Acts 2:31

Hebrews 5:7

On the road to Emmaus, Jesus chides His friends for their foolish and slow-hearted attitude in not grasping all that the prophets spoke: it was necessary for the Christ to suffer these things and to enter into His glory. He knew He came to die; He knew the Father would raise Him from the dead. The servant attitude pre-eminently is that of trust, of willingness to follow the Father's wishes. God accepted this 'reverent submission' as a lifestyle, and raised Jesus from the dead.

Paul describes Jesus' journey from Heaven to earth and return succinctly as a seven-step process:

Philippians 2

Ephesians 1:20–21

(1) Jesus recognized His equality with the Father
(2) Jesus emptied Himself of His rights and privileges
(3) Jesus took on the nature of a servant, the likeness and nature of man
(4) Jesus humbled Himself
(5) Jesus became obedient, even to the point of death on a cross
(6) The Father exalted Jesus to the Father's Right Hand as Ruler
(7) The Father gave Him the Name that is above all names

1 Corinthians 15:25
1 Corinthians 15:24

From the obedient, suffering Servant, the Father fashioned the Sovereign Servant. Jesus rules at the Father's right hand until all things are in subjection under His feet. Then He shall deliver up the Kingdom to His God and Father. Jesus came to earth as Servant-King; He continues in Heaven as Servant-King.

APPLICATION

How does the Servanthood of Jesus affect our own attitudes toward serving? Why must we be servants in order to rule? Why was Jesus' servanthood so difficult for society and even the disciples to accept?

CONCLUSION

Jesus of Nazareth, the Bond-Servant, and the Servant-King, came to fulfill His Father's purposes for mankind. The Old Testament prophesies saw Him as Servant-King, and Isaiah saw Him as both Bond-Servant and Servant-King. Jesus' earthly colleagues expected Him as Servant-King and could not believe their eyes as He lived before them in His identity as Bond-Servant. Jesus publicly stated that He came from the Father's Presence, on the Father's initiative, to declare the Father's Presence, to declare the Father's words, and to accomplish the Father's works. He only and always claimed the Father's authority, not His own. He willingly laid down His life to fulfill His Father's incomprehensible love for fallen mankind. And the Father raised Him from the dead, placed Him at His own right hand and gave Him all authority in Heaven and on earth. There, the Bond-Servant rules as Servant-King.

LESSON 3 – GOD'S WORD TO US

PURPOSE

John 1:1–2

John 7:16
John 8:28

Jesus Christ is the Word of the Living God, forever in His presence, forever God. As Eternal Word, Jesus expresses the heart of the Father in communicating with fallen mankind. Jesus is the Father's communication with people ... He is Word and Prophet. And Jesus came to declare to us the words that His Father had taught Him while still together in Heaven. As the Father's expressed Word, or Prophet, Jesus gave to His disciples His own prophetic words, teachings, and gifts. When the Father poured out the Holy Spirit through Jesus Christ, the Church received Jesus' mantle as Prophet to the Church and society. As His Church, we are called to live as His corporate prophetic voice on earth.

GLOSSARY

John 1:1–14

Prophet – (Hebrew: *Nabi*) authorized spokesman, one who speaks for God; a foreteller or 'forth-teller' of God's purpose.

Word – the designation of Jesus of Nazareth as the giver and expression of God's teachings, both in an eternal and temporal sense.

Pentateuch – first five books of the Old Testament, collectively regarded as the 'Books of the Law', also referred to as the 'Torah'.

Messianic Poems – a collection of poems in Isaiah, chapters 40–53, that speak of the nature and ministry of the coming Messiah, the Anointed One. Much of the material applies to the Messiah as God's prophetic voice.

THE MINISTRY OF THE PROPHET IN THE OLD TESTAMENT

Exodus 3–4

Exodus 4:15–16

Exodus 7:1–2

In Moses' testy exchange with God concerning his projected leadership for the slave-nation Israel in Egypt, we find a clear picture of the Hebrew concept of the prophet. God chose Aaron to be the mouthpiece for Moses, given Moses' reluctance to carry God's Word by himself. 'You are to speak to him and put the words in his mouth ... I will teach you what you are to do ... he shall be as a mouth for you, and you shall be as God to him.' If effect, the prophet is God's mouthpiece, or God's 'mouth'.

Genesis 12:1–3

Job 11:8

Jeremiah 18:6

The Old Testament prophets revealed the nature of God to Israel and surrounding nations. Abraham expressed God's Fatherhood to Israel and the Gentile nations. Hosea demonstrated God's redemptive love, His faithfulness and forgiveness in the midst of Israel's unfaithfulness. Jeremiah demonstrated God's Sovereign response to Israel's sin.

Exodus 34:5

Yet Moses emerged as the principal prophet speaking for God to Israel. He experienced God's very Presence, and listened as God declared His own nature for all the world to know ... 'compassionate and gracious.' God used Moses to reveal more about Himself than any other prophet. Some seventeen names of God flow through Moses' writing, such as, '**Jehovah-Jireh**', God our Provider and '**Jehovah-Nissei**', God our Banner. Each name presented another aspect of God's Person.

God established Samuel as a prophet and 'let none of his words fail.' The Word of the Lord came to Elijah, confronting Ahab and Jezebel, leading to the destruction of 400 false prophets. Elisha, as heir to Elijah, received a double prophetic portion and went on to make life difficult for kings and commoners who criticized his work as prophet of the Lord. God revealed the strategy of Israel's attacker to His prophet, such that the Army Commander looked in vain for the traitor within his own camp. God had made Israel a prophetic community, His voice on earth.

Israel became the only nation on earth to know God's mind and heart concerning itself and the surrounding Gentile nations. Kings of Israel consulted with the prophets on matters of state. Those who disregarded His voice, though Israel's kings, suffered and died. Much of Israel's identity as a nation is due historically to the input of God's prophets. Even foreign nations respected Israel because of the testimony of their relationship to God. Early in Israel's history, Moses identified the great prophet who was to come, God's final and greatest prophet ... Jesus Christ.

THE MINISTRY OF THE PROPHET IN THE NEW TESTAMENT

John the Baptist arrived as the first authentic prophet in Israel in more than 400 years. His biting critique of popular religion and leaders, and his uncompromising insistence on righteousness endeared him to the masses within Israel. But royalty took personal offense at his righteous demands and put him in prison for execution. Jesus considered him the greatest of the prophets.

Jesus of Nazareth exemplified, to the highest degree, God's prophet and God's prophetic voice on earth. He insisted on receiving John's baptism, thereby identifying with John's ministry as well as the entire line of Old Testament prophets. In baptism Jesus indicated His own consecration to and approval of God. Further, He personally identified with man's own sin and failure, though he Himself experienced neither.

The masses of Israel recognized Jesus as Prophet, fulfilling the prophetic office so clearly stated in the Old Testament. And Jesus referred to Himself as Prophet. As the 'Word made flesh,' He expressed in word and deed what all the previous prophets had said. Jesus spoke uniquely as the Father's Prophet. His voice and manner carried astounding authority, certainly absent from the religious teaching of His day. Jesus' voice powerfully affected His listeners, because He spoke the words He had heard from the Father. And His words impelled demonic spirits to reveal themselves to be cast out. To the end of His days, Jesus represented Himself as Spokesman for the

---

1 Samuel 3:19
1 Kings 17–18

1 Kings 18:30

1 Kings 19:19
2 Kings 3:13
2 Kings 2:23

Isaiah 13–23

2 Kings 3:11
2 Kings 23:29
Chronicles 16:31

Jeremiah 1:5, 10
Numbers 11:10
Deuteronomy 18:15
Acts 3:19
Acts 7:37

Luke 3:1–6
Matthew 3:7
Luke 3:7–9
Luke 3:10–14
Matthew 14:1–12

Mark 6:25
Luke 7:28

Matthew 3:15

Mark 1:9–11

Luke 4:14–15
John 4:43–5

Mark 6:4
Matthew 13:57

Matthew 21:46

Hebrews 1:1–2
Matthew 21:46

John 5:36

John 8:28
Mark 1:23
John 5:43
John 14:6
John 8:28–29

Father, the 'Way, the Truth, and the Life,' who leads others into the Father's presence.

THE MINISTRY OF THE CHURCH AS GOD'S PROPHETIC VOICE

Ephesians 1:17
John 14:26
Ephesians 4:11–16
Ephesians 2:20
Ephesians 3:5

After Jesus' Ascension into Heaven, He provided three ways of ongoing ministry among His Church:

(1) His Word and the revelation that comes from it;
(2) the indwelling Holy Spirit as Teacher; and
(3) the five ministry gifts for equipping Jesus' followers. The Apostles and Prophets, as foundational for the Church, carry the revelation given by the Spirit.

Acts 11:28

Acts 21:10
1 Corinthians 14:1
1 Corinthians 14:4
1 Corinthians 14:22

1 Corinthians 14:39

1 Corinthians 14:29

As one of the apostolic ministries, prophets today carry the Spirit's insight for interpreting the Church's place in the world. They carry God's perspective for life within the Church. Paul exhorts the Corinthian Elders to pursue prophesy, for prophesy exhorts and edifies the Church. Further, he exhorts the Church to use prophesy as a sign to those who believe. As in Paul's day, we should 'desire earnestly to prophesy.'

As the prophetic ministry emerges in Christ's Church today, we see once again Jesus Christ, the Father's greatest prophet, speaking, exhorting, confronting, and edifying. We must learn to recognize the prophetic voice, encourage yet challenge it, until we can once again receive Jesus' on-going prophetic voice to His Church.

APPLICATION

In what sense can proclamation be prophetic today? Can you name any present-day ministers who proclaim in a prophetic way? How do you express a prophetic burden which you feel God gave you? What are the similarities and differences between the 'prophetic community' of Israel, and that of the Church? How can the local church move into its prophetic function?

CONCLUSION

Through the Old Testament prophets, God revealed His nature, His purposes for Israel, and for the Gentile nations. Moses pointed to the 'great' prophet who was to arise from within Israel. In His day, people recognized Jesus as the 'Prophet'. Jesus' prophetic uniqueness lay in the fact that His authority exceeded any of His predecessors. Further, He came from the Father's Presence with the highest and final revelation of the Father. As God's supreme Prophet, Jesus reveals God in His inspired Word, by the indwelling Holy Spirit, and through His anointed prophets in the Church.

LESSON 4 – GOD'S HIGH PRIEST FOR US

PURPOSE

God appointed Jesus Christ, His Son, as High Priest forever. As High Priest, Jesus stands before God on behalf of all mankind, particularly His followers. His uniqueness comes from His dual role: advocate-mediator, but more importantly, sacrificial Lamb, or propitiation for sin. Now glorified, Jesus represents us before the Father in intercession. This lesson explores Jesus varied ministry as our great High Priest, as well our call to be priests here on earth.

GLOSSARY

Priest – a man appointed to act for others in matters pertaining to God.

Mediator – a go-between; one who stands in an intermediate position.

Intercession – the act of mediating or pleading in behalf of another for the purpose of agreement.

Covenant – (1) An arrangement established and maintained by God whereby He grants a bond, blessing, and benefits to those who receive Him; (2) a binding agreement between two or more parties decided by dialogue. In both cases divine retribution accompanies those who break covenant.

Vicarious Atonement – substitutionary sacrifice of Jesus Christ to satisfy the penalty of sins which separate mankind from God, an act to make reconciliation possible.

Reconciliation – the act of settling a disagreement and returning the parties to friendship and harmony.

THE OLD TESTAMENT PRIESTHOOD AS PREPARATORY

Genesis 14:17–20

Exodus 3:1
Exodus 4:18

Exodus 20
Exodus 19:1–9
Exodus 29:44
Deuteronomy 10:8
Exodus 29
Leviticus 9

Exodus 19:6
Exodus 19:5
Hebrews 7:11

Hebrews 7:12

Before the Mosaic Law, we find priests representing the Living God, but with no explanation as to their origin or functions. Abraham met Melchizedek, priest of the Most High God, and received his blessing. Moses' father-in-law, Jethro, lived as the priest of Midian and gave Abraham his blessing.

At Mount Sinai, God gave His Law to Moses and established Israel as His covenant people. Aaron and the tribe of Levi received appointment and ordination as priests to represent Israel before God. By specific ritual of animal and grain sacrifices, the Lord granted forgiveness and access to Himself in a limited way. He called Israel to become a kingdom of priests, a holy nation, a people special to Him among all nations on earth. But perfection (completion) was not possible under the Levitical priesthood. God, in establishing the new covenant, changed both the priesthood and the Law behind it.

GOD APPOINTS JESUS AS HIGH PRIEST FOREVER

Psalm 110:4
Hebrews 7:21
Hebrews 7:21
Hebrews 7:17

Hebrews 8:6

In the timeless counsel of God, He appointed Jesus, His Son, the High Priest; the Psalmist recorded it around 1,000 BC. Unlike Aaronic priests who received their priesthood by inheritance, God took an oath in appointing Jesus as '...Priest forever after the order of Melchizedek.' Jesus Christ has an eternal unchangeable priesthood, based on the Father's oath. Jesus' priestly function enables Him to inaugurate a new covenant, based on better, or more effective promises.

JESUS CHRIST, THE MEDIATOR OF THE NEW COVENANT

Hebrews 8:13
Hebrews 10:1
Hebrews 9:12

Hebrews 9:26
Hebrews 9:28
Hebrews 9:12
Hebrews 9:14
Hebrews 10:10

The Scriptures consider the old covenant (Mosaic Law) as '...obsolete and growing old, ready to disappear, a shadow of the good things to come and not the very form of things.' The new covenant, made effective through the life, ministry, and death of Jesus of Nazareth, obtained for us eternal redemption. The sacrifice need not be repeated; He offered Himself once and bore the sins of the people. Jesus laid down His own life and offered His own blood, not that of bulls and goats. We, His Church, have been sanctified through the offering of the body of Jesus Christ once and for all.

JESUS CHRIST, THE GUARANTEE AND SACRIFICE

Hebrews 7:22
Hebrews 10:12
John 1:29–36
Romans 3:24–5
1 John 2:2
Hebrews 7:26–7
Hebrews 9:11–14
Hebrews 10:12–14

As the 'Guarantee of the New Covenant,' Jesus became legally responsible for our sin. He made one sacrifice 'for sins for all time.' As Lamb of God, Jesus became the sacrifice that propiated (satisfied) the righteous requirements of an all-holy God. Jesus needed no sacrifice for His own sin – He had no sin. His own body and blood became our sacrifice and provided the removal of the curse of sin in our lives. His sacrifice was perfect, complete, and eternal, rendering any further sacrifice unnecessary.

JESUS CHRIST, OUR INTERCESSOR

Luke 22:31–2
Matthew 26:36–46
John 17

Matthew 6:9
Romans 8:34

Hebrews 7:25

Romans 8:26
Romans 8:27
Hebrews 7:25

Jesus' intercession for Peter helps us understand His intercession today. Jesus interceded for all His disciples in the Garden. Also, He interceded for all those who would come to believe in Him later. His prayer in the Sermon on the Mount also helps us comprehend how He prays and how He wants us to pray. We, as His Church, take courage from His earthly intercession, knowing that He continues that intercessory role in Heaven as High Priest. Today, the indwelling Holy Spirit carries out Jesus' ministry of intercession. The Spirit knows the mind of Christ and intercedes for us according to the will of God.

OUR ROLE AS PRIESTS

1 Peter 2:9

God names us, as His children, a 'Royal Priesthood'. We represent God to others; we plead to God for them. As earthly priests, we no longer make sacrifices for sin; Christ's was sufficient. Rather, we represent

Hebrews 7:27
Hebrews 10:19–20
Romans 12:1–2

2 Corinthians 5:18

Jesus Christ before our families, our neighbours, and colleagues at work. We plead with God in their behalf. We convey to them the Person and work of God in Jesus Christ. We lay down our lives for them, as Christ laid down His life for us. We share with them the reconciliation that God made possible through Jesus Christ.

APPLICATION

What is the nature of Jesus' intercession today at the Father's right hand? What qualifies Jesus to be the Mediator and guarantee of the new covenant? What is our participation in the Royal Priesthood? What is the best way to bring people to be friends with God (reconciled)?

CONCLUSION

God directed that the covenant He established with Abraham, Moses, and David be ratified by animal blood, showing them to be symbolic, temporary, and repetitive. Christ, our High Priest, established the new covenant in His own blood. His sacrifice was the authentic, the eternal, and the only effective one in removing sin forever. The God-Man, Jesus Christ, as Mediator between God and all people, now intercedes for us at the Throne of Grace. The indwelling Holy Spirit shows us how to intercede.

LESSON 5 – GOD'S KING REIGNING OVER US

PURPOSE

After the Resurrection, the Father seated Jesus Christ at His right hand and placed all things under His feet. Jesus now manages the Church, the earth, and all matters in both spheres. He rules over the Father's Kingdom, both believer and non-believer, in heaven and on earth. The Father granted Jesus this rulership as a result of His faithfulness in life and death. This lesson explores the rationale and dynamics of the Father's Kingdom, ruled over by Jesus Christ.

GLOSSARY

Kingdom – (Greek: *basileia*) rulership or government; refers to God's active rule or government past, present, and future.

Sovereignty – the condition of superiority to all rank, powers, or authority; Father's absolute rule in Jesus Christ over all other authorities.

JESUS CHRIST, SUPREME RULER OVER GOD'S KINGDOM

Matthew 28:19–20

Ephesians 1:19–22

Philippians 2:9–10

Matthew 28:18

The Scriptures show four aspects of Jesus' receiving all authority and power. The Father raised Him from the dead, seated Him at His own right hand, put all things in subjection under His feet, and gave Him as Head to the Church over all things. Paul adds that the Father gave Him the name that is above every name. And to that name every created thing will bow in heaven and earth. Upon His Resurrection, Jesus states that the Father has given Him all authority and power in heaven and on earth. Jesus Christ is truly Lord today.

THE KINGDOM OF GOD IN THE OLD COVENANT

Psalm 99:1–5

Exodus 19:5

2 Samuel 7:10–17
Psalm 89:20–29

Psalm 89:30–37

Isaiah 9:6–7

Acts 13:22–23
Daniel 2:44
Daniel 7:13–14
Hebrews 1:3

Although God Almighty has always ruled over His kingdom of heaven and earth, He focused on Moses, the elders and Israel in the old covenant. He established His gracious dominion over not simply a family and clan (Abraham), but over a nation of some two million people.

God covenanted with David to establish his household and throne as eternal. We find in the Davidic covenant an earthly as well as an heavenly pattern. For the promises to King David went far beyond a human throne and dynasty. Later, Isaiah linked David's throne to a Messianic Person for whom there would be no end to the increase of government and peace. From David's descendants, God brought forth Jesus and gave Him David's eternal throne and Kingdom. Daniel also foresaw the coming kingdom and its leader ... 'One like the son of

Man.' Upon Jesus' sitting down at the right hand of the Father, He became the Ruler of the present phase of God's eternal Kingdom.

THE KINGDOM OF GOD IN THE NEW COVENANT

Luke 1:32–33

Matthew 3:2
Matthew 4:17

Matthew 17:20

The archangel Gabriel announced the manifestation of God's eternal Kingdom at the point of Jesus' conception. Mary's Son would fulfill God's promise to King David. John the Baptist then declared, forcefully and publicly, that God's Kingdom was at hand. Just after successfully avoiding the Tempter's snare, Jesus began to proclaim the same message, explaining that God's Kingdom was right among them. Since all Israel expected only an earthly Kingdom, won by angelic forces, they misunderstood Jesus' message.

Matthew 1:15

Matthew 13:11
Luke 8:10
Acts 28:30–1
Hebrews 6:5

Matthew 6:10
John 17:15–16

Jesus proclaimed the kingdom of God as His central message, that around which all other teachings and events revolved. His preaching, His miracles, and parables all focused on the coming of God's Kingdom. His Body on earth today carries the same apostolic message that Paul shared in Rome. We share in the 'powers of the age to come,' not in fullness but in authenticity and quality. Whenever we touch the new birth, the Spirit's work, sanctification, and healing, we witness that the powers of the future Kingdom have arrived. Jesus' Kingdom is sourced in heaven, not in the world system; His Kingdom is 'in' this world, not 'of' this world.

John 3:3, 5

Colossians 1:13

Matthew 1:23–24
Matthew 24
Matthew 13

As we enter God's Kingdom through the new birth, the Father transfers us out from under the world's authority into the Kingdom of His beloved Son. The presence of God's Kingdom forces demonic powers to reveal themselves and release God's people. Yet we await the coming of the King to walk into the fullness of all that the Father has planned for us as members of His Kingdom.

THE KINGDOM OF GOD AS FUTURE

Matthew 24:19
Philippians 2:10–11
1 Corinthians 15:24
1 Corinthians 15:25–6
2 Peter 3:3–13
Titus 2:13
1 Thessalonians 4:13–5:11

The future aspect or phase of the Father's Kingdom begins when the Son of God returns in power and subjects all creation to Himself. Completion, fullness, and perfection become reality; nothing less will be tolerated. Even death yields to the Christ. The issue of the timing and accompanying events is not in focus here. He will come again. Our 'blessed hope' is the 'appearing of the glory of our great God and Savior, Christ Jesus.' God asks us to 'occupy until He comes.' We are to live faithful, fruitful lives, by the power of His Spirit, anticipating the arrival of King Jesus.

APPLICATION

If Christ reigns in Heaven now, how can we reign with Him now? What are the practical limitations? Just how does God's active ruling (Kingdom) touch our lives at home and work? Just how does God's active ruling today impact Satan's dominion?

CONCLUSION

God used David's throne and dynasty to establish the pattern for His eternal and righteous dominion. Jesus fulfilled this pattern and established His Kingdom in earth in a limited way. The Church continues to express and extend Christ's Kingdom on earth. He will return one day and bring to completion all that lacks. Until then, we reign with Him through our placement within His church on earth.

LESSON 6 – CHRIST PERSONALLY KNOWS MAN'S NEED

PURPOSE

When Adam and Eve sinned, rebelling against His ways and choosing their own, God introduced judgement into the human race. The willfulness and self-centeredness passed from Adam to all subsequent generations, resulting in physical death. Jesus came, took our human form, and without sin learned our pitiable condition. This lesson explores God's view of sin, its incurable nature and its terrible effects in our lives.

GLOSSARY

Original Sin – Adam and Eve's initial disobedience to God, the effect of their sin, passed genetically to all descendants.

Total Depravity – the effect of Original Sin in peoples' psyche and body, permeating every aspect of their being, rendering them unable to submit to God's ways, making them unable to please God. Total depravity does not mean that every person is as bad as he could possibly be. Rather, that the infection has spread irreversibly throughout a person's being.

Self-Centerdness – sin's pervading effect that shapes people to concentrate first on themselves, ignoring the needs of others.

Willfulness – the effect of sin in one's heart that makes us automatically choose our own self-developed pathways, ignoring God's gracious purposes and help.

SIN IS UNIVERSAL

Psalm 14:3
Romans 3:23
Psalm 58:3
Isaiah 1:4–6
Romans 6:6
Romans 6:12–14
Genesis 3
Romans 11:20
Hebrews 3:12, 19

Our inheritance through Adam brings to all humans the irresistible tendency to ignore God's purposes and ways. This all pervading sin-principle passes without exception from one generation to another. The sin-principle is the root cause of all our individual sins. The core of sin is rebellion, pride, and unbelief. We, like Adam and Eve, choose to believe the liar, Satan, rather than God. For we really want to become like God. The New Age movement today, as in the Garden of Eden, espouses this view.

GOD'S VIEW OF SIN

Romans 3:18
Romans 36:1–4
Romans 1:18

The modern, politically-correct view of sin is to trivialize; to dismiss it as an antiquated and medieval mindset, out of date with the scientific mind. The person, untouched by God, sees sin as a mistake, a slip-up,

Romans 1:21
Romans 1:25
Romans 1:28

Romans 1:20
Romans 1:19
Acts 14:17
Acts 17:30–31

Romans 5:8–11

Psalm 51:5
Romans 3:19
Romans 7:21
Romans 7:8–11
Romans 8:7
Romans 7:23

Romans 7:18
Isaiah 59:2
Ephesians 4:17–19

an error in judgement or simple misbehavior. On the contrary, God views sins as rebellion against Himself, the essential sin of Satan and his angelic forces. God clearly expressed His view of sin while maintaining the witness about Himself in creation, conscience, and providence. He has overlooked peoples' times of ignorance and asked them to repent.

The clearest expression of God's view of sin lies in the price He paid for providing the remedy: He sent His own Son to pay the cost for removing sin. In other words, if sin is not a desperate issue, then why Calvary and the cross?

Scripture identifies sin, not only as a series of acts that offend God, but rather a state of complete alienation from God. The old nature in people does not submit to the Law of God, it is unable to do so. We have become prisoners to the law of sin, which results in death.

The current Humanist view of people misses completely God's perspective. The 'spark of goodness' allegedly indwelling all people has turned out to be a bonfire of willfulness and disregard for one another. The more clearly we see our 'total depravity', our total inability to walk in God's ways, the more thankful we become for God's full provision in Jesus Christ.

THE EFFECTS OF SIN IN OUR LIVES

Romans 1:21
Romans 1:23
Romans 1:25
Romans 7:15–16
Romans 7:17–24
Romans 6:19

Romans 7:23–24
Romans 6:23
Romans 3:10–18
James 1:14–15
2 Thessalonians 1:9

Over the generations since Adam, the effect of sin in peoples' lives worldwide spread inexorably into all features of our nature and personality. The knowledge of God grows dimmer. God's standards become less relevant. Now we are caught in a bondage, a bondage that requires us to live only in terms of our own desires and purposes. Impurity and lawlessness grow individually and culturally. The willful lifestyle that parents practice pass to the third and fourth generation of their offspring. Sin becomes culturally acceptable, the cultural norm.

The law of sin and death produces guilt, alienation, and deep resentment in families and societies. The separation between people and God grows inevitably wider, producing physical death and eternal separation from God.

JESUS CAME, WITHOUT SIN, TO KNOW OUR CONDITION

Philippians 2:7
Hebrews 2:14
Matthew 1:25
Hebrews 2:17
Hebrews 2:18
Hebrews 4:15

Romans 8:2–4
Romans 7:24

Jesus of Nazareth came to earth as the second Adam. He took on the form and nature of people. His Virgin Birth kept Him from inheriting Adam's sinful nature. Satan tested Him from the days of the wilderness until the Garden of Gethemane. Jesus entered the human condition, yet without Adam's fallen nature. Jesus came to walk in our pathway, to experience our testings, to know our relationships, living in joyful obedience to His Father by the power of the Spirit. He brought the Law of the Spirit of Life and finally provided the release from the law of sin and death.

APPLICATION

What view do your neighbours take of sin? Do you see sin as rebellion against God? What other forms of daily activity can you label as sin? How does sin affect our daily walk with God? How does one confront people with the reality of sin without condemning them as sinners?

CONCLUSION

The sin of the first couple, Adam and Eve, spread upon all their descendants, including our own generation. We easily and willingly follow our own pathway instead of God's. Sin for us has become not just a series of rebellious acts or events. Rather, sin took over our natures and, as a sin-principal, directs our natural activities in a direction away from God. Apart from God's consistent intervention in lives, families, societies, and nations, we would have become all that sin could become. The effect of Original Sin in our lives brings us finally to the grave. Jesus of Nazareth came to live among us, to know our situation and needs. He walked by the power of the Holy Spirit, without the taint of Adam's nature. He endured the testing and the suffering and fulfilled the Father's purposes in our behalf. By this act, we truly know what love is.

Romans 5

LESSON 7 – JESUS CHRIST PERSONALLY PAYS FOR OUR SINS

PURPOSE

Jesus of Nazareth announced to His followers that He was on His way to Jerusalem to die. They ignored His words in disbelief. After the Resurrection and the coming of the Holy Spirit, they began to understand what He meant. This lesson explores the vital meaning of Christ's atoning death on the cross, its significance to God and the effects in our lives.

GLOSSARY

Atonement – to avert punishment, especially divine anger, by the payment of a ransom: a life, an animal, or money.

Propitiation – turning away God's wrath towards us by the sacrificial (atoning) death of Jesus Christ.

Reconciliation – the bringing together of two offended and separated parties, referring to Christ's death that brought together God and people, resulting in our salvation.

Redemption – the payment of a ransom or sacrifice by which Jesus Christ secured our salvation.

THE IMPORTANCE OF CHRIST'S DEATH

Exodus 29:10
Exodus 29:15
Exodus 29:19
Leviticus 1:4

Leviticus 2:1
Leviticus 3:1
Leviticus 17:11
Hebrews 10:1

Hebrews 10:2

Genesis 15:6

Numbers 15:30

Deuteronomy 18:15

The Old Testament sacrificial system bore witness to God's involvement in enabling mankind to approach Him once again. The Mosaic Law stipulated certain sacrifices and rituals which God would receive, and then pardon the supplicant and re-establish relationship with Him. Without the shedding of blood, there was no forgiveness for sin. The Law, however, could never perfect the worshipper, or clear him permanently of guilt. Continual sacrifice was necessary. The worshipper still carried a consciousness of his sin. The offerings covered (atoned for) the sin, but never completely removed it.

There were two factors influencing the Old Testament sacrificial system. First, the Abrahamic covenant, justification by faith, still held force. The worshipper under the Mosaic Law had to approach God in faith; his faith would be counted to him for righteousness. Second, the Israelite must not sin 'with a high hand,' or with defiance. He must not despise God, in pride and arrogance, and still expect the sacrifices to avail for him. On the contrary, he would be cut off and expelled from Israel, if not executed. God provided the sacrificial system for those who would approach Him in faith and in repentance, not with a high hand.

Psalm 95:7
Isaiah 1:11–17
Psalm 22:1
Isaiah 53:4,5
Acts 3:22
Deuteronomy 18:15
Deuteronomy 18:19
Galatians 3:21
Galatians 2:21

Matthew 1:25

Matthew 4:1–11
John 7:3–5
Mark 3:21

Matthew 9:1–11

Hebrews 2:17
Hebrews 2:18
2 Corinthians 5:21
Hebrews 4:15

Mark 10:45
Hebrews 2:9

1 Corinthians 15:1–5
Galatians 6:14
1 Corinthians 1:18
John 3:14
John 12:24
Acts 17:3

2 Corinthians 5:21
Hebrews 2:9
Exodus 12
1 Corinthians 5:7

Hebrews 9:22
Leviticus 17:11
Romans 3:25; 9:28
2 Corinthians 5:19

Exodus 34:7
Romans 8:3
Romans 10:4
Leviticus 4:13–20
Leviticus 2:6–7
Psalm 103:12
Hebrews 10:22
Romans 3:25
1 John 2:2
Romans 5:10
2 Corinthians 5:18–21

Matthew 20:28
Galatians 3:13
Romans 6:2–14
Romans 8:2–4

Many Old Testament prophets challenged the Israelites for their unbelief and spiritual blindness. They also carried the message that God would provide One who was to take on Himself the punishment and rejection due to the sinner. Moses Himself foresaw in the Spirit that God would raise up a 'prophet like me from among you ... you shall listen to Him.' He who does not listen to that prophet will be utterly destroyed from among the people. Yes, God provided a sacrificial system, but there is no Law that can impart life. So God provided a 'better way' in Jesus Christ.

QUALIFIED TO PAY FOR OUR SIN

Since Jesus experienced a Virgin Birth, He did not inherit the sinful nature, passed down from Adam. He carried a human nature; clean but untested. The temptations from Satan challenged Jesus deeply to walk His own pathway, rather than what the Father desired. Even from His family, Jesus experienced disbelief and rejection. Yet Jesus walked in the awareness that He pleased His Father, as His Beloved One. An unrelenting testing (tempting) pursued Jesus all His days. He was made like His brethren in all things. He was tempted in all points like us, yet without sin.

The importance of Jesus' death cannot be overstated. The Gospel writers devote one-fifth of the materials to Jesus' death. As the fundamental theme of the Gospel message, the death of Jesus Christ is the Good News. It demonstrates that man need not die for his own sin. Paul's proclamation always centered on the death of Jesus. For Christianity without the cross loses its power to change peoples' lives and societies.

THE TRUE MEANING OF CHRIST'S DEATH

All of Scripture shows us that Christ did not die for His own sins, since he was sinless, but that He offered Himself as a substitute for us – the sinless One for the sinner. He died in our place as the true Passover Lamb. Three Scriptural elements form the backdrop for Jesus' sacrificial death. First, the fact that blood atones for, or covers sin. The second is propitiation, or the turning away of God's anger over sin. And third, is substitution, wherein Jesus willingly took our place (as condemned sinners) and paid the price for us.

Christ's death satisfied the justice and holiness of God. Jesus fulfilled all that God's Law and holiness required. In His death on the cross, He made atonement for our sin. He not only covered over our sins (Hebrew: *kaphar*); He removed these sins from existence. Today we have no more remembrance of past sin; He has washed our hearts from an evil conscience in His own blood. Since our sin has been removed, then God's justice has been satisfied. Christ's propiatory death opens the way for our reconciliation with God.

The Scripture also defines Jesus' death as a ransom for sinners (Greek: *lutrosis*). His life was the ransom to provide our release; His ransom frees us from the penalty and power of the Law of sin and

2 Timothy 2:26
Colossians 1:13
Hebrews 9:14
Jeremiah 31:31–34
Jeremiah 26:28
Hebrews 9:18–20

death. We live now under God's grace by the power of the Spirit and, thus, fulfill all the requirements of God's righteous Law. We are freed from the power of sin and the power of the Evil One. Finally, Christ's death ratifies the new covenant, making it effective. We stand washed and forgiven before God. Jesus died to bring His people into this new covenant relationship with God.

APPLICATION

Discuss some of the Old Testament provisions for atonement. Show how they represent the atonement Christ was to provide. What are the provisions of the new covenant given in Jeremiah 31 and Ezekiel 36? How can we communicate to people the terrible consequences of their sin?

CONCLUSION

The Death of Jesus Christ on the cross provided a substitute so that people do not have to die eternally for their sin. Jesus satisfied the justice and holiness of God, forever fulfilling all that God requires in Law. Christ's atonement paid the ransom, redeemed us from the law of sin and death, and restored us to fellowship with God. The atonement makes possible the establishment of the new covenant. Sacrifice views atonement from the perspective of peoples' guilt. Propitiation views atonement from the perspective of God's wrath. Reconciliation views atonement from the perspective of peoples' guilt. Reconciliation views atonement from the perspective of peoples' alienation. Redemption views atonement from the perspective of release from bondage. Atonement has been defined as **'At-one-ment'** ... we who were separated from God are now rejoined to Him through the blood of Jesus Christ. That **is** Good News!

LESSON 8 – HIS RESURRECTION

PURPOSE

The purpose of this lesson is to examine the nature, importance, and results of Christ's Resurrection and its implications for us today. The Resurrection is the first of the four states of Christ, known as His Exaltation. The other three are His Ascension, Session, and Return in glory. These last three will be dealt with in the next lesson.

GLOSSARY

Immanence – God's intimate relationship with His creation, which He both created and sustains. It means the **reachableness** of God.

Transcendence – that which speaks of God's separateness from His creation. He was before it, is not dependent upon it, and in some sense is wholly apart from it. It means the **unreachableness** of God.

THE RELEVANCE OF CHRIST'S RESURRECTION

1 Corinthians 15:12–19

Everything we believe as Christians stands or falls with the truth of Christ's Resurrection. It was the central message of apostolic preaching and makes Christianity unique among religions of the world.

Ephesians 1:20–22

Acts 1:5
Acts 2:32–33

Romans 5:8–10

It is vital in the application of salvation because it made Him Head over all things to the Church. It was necessary for Him to be raised from the dead before He could baptize the believer in the Holy Spirit. While Christ's death reconciled us to God, His Resurrection and present life **perfects** our salvation.

John 11:14–26
Matthew 27:52, 53

Ephesians 1:9–23

Christ's Resurrection is an exhibition of divine power even more important than the saving power God demonstrated in the deliverance of the Hebrews from Egypt. This power that raised Christ from the dead is the same power that raised Lazarus and others from the dead. It is the same power that accomplished all the miracles in the Old and New Testaments, and it is available for Christians today.

THE REALITY OF CHRIST'S RESURRECTION

Matthew 15:45
John 19:33
Mark 15:45
John 19:33
Matthew 23:17
Luke 24:37–43

It was an actual resurrection. He did not just faint and then regain consciousness by the cool air of the tomb. The Centurion and Roman soldiers declared Him dead, and His appearance 'alive' greatly surprised His disciples.

Luke 24:34–39
John 20:25–30

John 5:20–30

It was a bodily Resurrection. Early heresies in the Church viewed Christ's Resurrection as just a phenomenon. They claimed that He 'appeared' to be in the flesh, but in reality, He was just 'spirit'. The fact is, there are many proofs that He rose bodily. For example, He ate food with the disciples, the imprint of the nails was in His hands, and

Thomas was even invited to put his fingers in the holes. Also, many Scriptures would make no sense if Christ did not rise in glorified flesh.

It was a unique Resurrection in that all other resurrections were not to a glorified body, and they all died again. Also, there were some unusual features to Christ's resurrected body: it was a real body; it was recognized as the same body, not another (the marks of His Crucifixion helped identify Him, and will be visible at His return); and finally, He was not limited by time or space after His Resurrection (passing through doors and appearing at widely separated places in short periods of time, for example).

THE RESULTS OF CHRIST'S RESURRECTION

Christ's Resurrection attests to His Deity. Christ was declared to be the Son of God with power by the Resurrection from the dead. Christ Himself said that the Resurrection was the sign that would be given to the people of Israel.

It assures us of the accomplishments of all Christ's work. He died for our sins, and was raised up for our justification.

It also made Christ our High Priest. Through the Resurrection, He became our Intercessor and Protector.

Finally, it provided for many additional blessings: personal salvation for all who believe; assurance that all help from God is abundantly available; a guarantee that our bodies will be raised from the dead (like His); and that there will be a judgement for the godly and the ungodly.

APPLICATION

Discuss the implications of the fact that the Holy Spirit is the power that raised Christ from the dead. What can that power do in and through us?

What did it do in and through those early disciples who spread out all over the empire, motivated and empowered by the Truth that 'Jesus Christ is risen from the dead?'

Is it as important now in our Christian lives to re-examine the power of the Resurrection as it was when we were seeking salvation?

What proofs of the Resurrection are evident in our own lives right now? How can we avail ourselves of this power in our lives and ministries today, especially in terms of being a witness like the early Church was?

CONCLUSION

The Resurrection of Jesus Christ is the most important doctrine of the Bible in terms of the authenticity of the Christian faith. Without it there is no focus to all the events or prophecies in the Old Testament. Without it there is no validity to any of the statements in the New Testament. The Resurrection allows the immanence of God to be joined with the transcendence of God.

Matthew 28:9
Luke 24:39
John 20:27

Revelation 1:7

Romans 1:4
Matthew 12:38–40

Romans 4:25
Romans 5:9–21

Romans 8:34
Ephesians 1:20–22
1 Timothy 2:5–6

Romans 10:9–10
Ephesians 1:18–20

John 5:28–30
Acts 17:31

Acts 1:8

LESSON 9 – HIS EXALTATION

PURPOSE

The purpose of this lesson is to learn what the exaltation of Christ entails, to understand the heavenly significance of it, and to understand the earthly, personal impact it produces.

GLOSSARY

The States of Jesus Christ – Christ experienced two states in relationship to God's Law for mankind. The doctrine of the two-fold state of Christ teaches that Christ first experienced the state of **humiliation**, and then the state of **exaltation**.

The State of Humiliation – the four aspects of Christ's humiliation are incarnation, suffering, death, and burial. Sometimes a fifth aspect of His descent into Hell is included.

The State of Exaltation – the four aspects of Christ's exaltation are Resurrection, Ascension, Session (seated at the right hand of the Father), and Return in glory.

HIS RESURRECTION FROM THE DEAD

The Resurrection in this lesson is significant, because it was the transition point from Christ's state of humiliation to His state of exaltation. It is the link between the cross and the crown.

HIS ASCENSION INTO HEAVEN

John 6:62
John 20:17
Acts 1:9
1 Timothy 3:16
John 14:2

2 Corinthians 12:2

John 14:2–3

John 1:14
1 Timothy 3:16

Heaven refers to a **place**, not just a spiritual state. Just because God is pure Spirit does not mean that heaven is just a state of being. The apostle Paul indicated three heavens: the visible heavens or earth's atmosphere, physical heavens beyond our planets and constellations, and the dwelling of God.

We do not know all that Christ is doing in heaven, but we are sure He is preparing a place for us, and that tells us of His present interest and activity on our behalf. So the Ascension points to His present work. The great wonder of the Ascension is that glorified flesh now sits on the throne in heaven. Dust of earth is now in majesty on high.

HIS SESSION AT THE THRONE

Hebrews 1:3

Ephesians 1:19–20
Acts 2:33–36

Having completely fulfilled the Father's will in the work of redemption, Christ is now seated at the right hand of the Father reigning over the Church and the universe, and interceding on our behalf.

As believers, we share in Christ's Session by receiving authority over demonic power and the receiving of power to gain increasing victory over sin.

HIS RETURN IN GLORY

Matthew 25:31–46
Acts 1:11–12
2 Thessalonians 1:7–8
Revelation 1:7
Revelation 22:12

Revelation 11:15
Revelation 22:3–5

When Christ returns to earth in glory, His exaltation will be complete. Upon His return, Christ will reign in triumph publicly, cast down all His enemies, and judge the living and the dead.

Then His Kingdom will be established and 'He shall reign forever and ever.'

APPLICATION

What are the benefits of having 'one of our own' on the throne (someone who knows our frame; someone who can really represent us to the Father)?

Discuss the benefits of Christ's constant intercession on our behalf, especially in light of the spiritual warfare in which we find ourselves.

Discuss the personal and corporate bestowing of the fruit and gifts of the Holy Spirit that results in a dynamic manifestation of the body of Christ on earth now.

CONCLUSION

The exaltation of Christ vindicates all His claims about Himself, particularly those statements about His absolute identification with God. His Resurrection, Ascension, and Session place 'one of us' on the throne of heaven. Possessed of all authority in heaven and on earth, Christ intercedes constantly for us at the throne of God. From there, He pours forth the Holy Spirit upon the Church to enable it to minister as a Body as He ministered in the flesh. He not only oversees the Church, but also exercises authority over unbelievers. Finally, He will come in His glory to judge the living and the dead and to set up His everlasting Kingdom.

LESSON 10 – THE ENABLING WORK OF THE HOLY SPIRIT

The purpose of this lesson is to learn how the Holy Spirit, proceeding from the throne of the exalted Christ, makes God's provisions in Christ accessible to the believer and to the body of Christ, the Church.

THE WORK OF THE HOLY SPIRIT AND THE SCRIPTURES

1 Corinthians 2:10–16

The Holy Spirit works as a means of **illumination** whereby the mind of the believer may understand the Scriptures as God intends.

2 Timothy 3:16

His work includes the **inspiration** of the Scriptures which means that the authors of the Bible wrote as He influenced them to do so. The Scriptures are 'God-breathed.'

Jeremiah 1:12

Not only this, but the Holy Spirit continues to work in the **preservation** of the Scripture's original meaning throughout the passing of time and throughout all the various translations and versions.

THE WORK OF THE HOLY SPIRIT AT SALVATION

Romans 8:29
2 Corinthians 3:18
Ephesians 4:23
1 Thessalonians 4:3
2 Thessalonians 2:13
Romans 6:22
Galatians 6:14
Romans 6:4, 6
Romans 8:1

Since we have been predestined to be made like the image of God's Son, the Spirit of God undertakes the work of transforming us into that image. He works to renew the entire person, separating us from a sin-induced lifestyle and consecrating us to God and His purposes. He enables us to be 'crucified to the world and the world to us.' He enables us to die to sin and live to righteousness. He sets us free from the law of sin and death. His work continues, obstructed only by our stubbornness, until the coming of our Lord Jesus, either in death or at His return.

THE CONTINUING WORK OF THE HOLY SPIRIT

Acts 2:4
Acts 10:45
Ephesians 5:18

Acts 9; 19:2
Galatians 5:16, 25
Acts 8:29
Acts 13:2
Acts 15:28
Acts 16:6
John 14:6

1 Peter 1:8
1 Peter 1:12

Jesus fills us by a baptism in the Spirit initially, but commands us to keep on being filled with the Spirit. Even though the baptism in the Holy Spirit can happen at the time of the new birth, both in New Testament times and now, it is often subsequent to conversion. The Spirit guides, directs, appoints, makes decisions, prohibits, and teaches. He creates in us both the **life** of Christ, as well as the **work** of Christ. The Spirit engenders fruit, the qualities of Jesus' life, in believers. (See Galatians 5:22–23; Romans 8:11; Galatians 2:20; Galatians 4:19.) The Spirit fills us with the joy of Christ and reveals the things of God to His followers. All that Jesus won for us at the Cross, all that Jesus Christ inherited from His Father – all this, the Spirit makes available to us, His Church.

APPLICATION

Discuss three ministries of the Spirit in respect to the Word of God. How does the work of the Holy Spirit affect your daily life? How does genetic gifting differ from the gifts of the Holy Spirit? What would happen to you if God withdrew His Spirit from the world?

CONCLUSION

The Holy Spirit is the Counselor-Helper whom Jesus promised to send. He mediates all the work of Christ for us into our daily experience. He works with the Word of God to inspire and maintain it, to inscripturate it, and interpret it so that all believers may come to know the depths of God's love for us in Christ. The Spirit initiates the salvation of each believer, convicting us of sin, unrighteousness, and judgement. He regenerates us, places a seal of adoption on each of us, and undertakes the lifelong process of changing us into the image of Christ. He fills us with His power, imparts His gifts, and cultivates His fruit in our lives. He guides, teaches, and comforts each child of God. He is the Life of God freely given to us.

LESSON 11 – RECEIVING THE HOLY SPIRIT THROUGH JESUS CHRIST

The Father poured forth His Holy Spirit through His Son Jesus upon the waiting crowd in Jerusalem. The Father had promised that He would do so, upon the Son's completion of His earthly ministry, sacrificial death, and Resurrection. In fulfilment of many prophesies and types, the Holy Spirit came upon God's covenant people gathered for Pentecost celebration. He came to establish Christ's Body, the Church, and to enable the Church to fulfill the covenantal promises given through Abraham nineteen centuries earlier. This lesson explores the Person and work of the Holy Spirit as He makes effective to the believer all of God's provisions in Jesus Christ.

GLOSSARY

1 Corinthians 2:10–16

Illumination – the work of the Holy Spirit whereby He brings light to the believer's minds to understand the Scriptures as God intends.

2 Timothy 3:16

Inspiration – the work of the Holy Spirit whereby He directed the writers of the original Scriptures to express God's Word infallibly and without error. The Scriptures are literally 'God-breathed.'

Jeremiah 1:12

Preservation – the work of the Holy Spirit whereby He stands guard over God's Word in translation and exposition to protect the original meaning.

Regeneration – the inner re-creating of fallen human nature, a radical and complete transformation worked in the soul so that we become new people, no longer conformed to this world system.

Sanctification – the work of God's free grace to renew us in the image of God, enabling us to die to sin and live righteously.

THE PERSON OF THE HOLY SPIRIT IN THE SCRIPTURES

Matthew 10:16–20

John 15:25
John 14:18

John 14:16–17

John 14:26

John 15:26

John 16:7–10

Jesus encouraged His Disciples by showing them that the Spirit of their Father will speak in and through them at the moment of arrest and trial.

When He shared with them in the Upper Room (see John 13–16), Jesus presented five sets of instructions concerning the Person and work of the Holy Spirit. Jesus promised to send the Spirit from the Presence of the Father to bring comfort, so they not be left as orphans. The first instruction identifies the Spirit as the Helper (Counselor, Comforter) who abides with them forever. He is the Spirit of Truth whom non-believers cannot receive, behold, or know. But the disciples know Him because He is with them. The second instruction further identifies the Spirit as Teacher, the One who will remind them of all that Jesus had taught them. The third instruction adds the fact that the Spirit will bear witness to Jesus.

John 16:11
John 16:13–15

The fourth instruction explains the Spirit's work in convicting people of sin, righteousness, and judgement. The Spirit will demonstrate through His work that the Ruler of this world has been judged. The fifth instruction shows the Spirit as the Guide into all truth, for He speaks on Jesus' initiative, not His Own. He will glorify Jesus Christ by taking what belongs to Jesus and disclosing that to the Disciples. From Jesus' perspective, the Spirit comes to believers as God, to stand in for Jesus, enabling believers to continue receiving Jesus' life and ministry.

1 Corinthians 2:10

1 Corinthians 2:12

1 Corinthians 2:13
1 Corinthians 2:14
1 Corinthians 2:16

The Apostle Paul reveals the Spirit as the One who searches the depths of God to bring revelation to us. He comes that we might know the things freely given to us by God. And we teach these things by the wisdom of the Spirit, with thoughts and words from the Spirit. He enables us to evaluate all things, that we might have the mind of Christ. From these and other verses, we discern the work of God's Spirit to **inspire** the original Scriptures, to **illumine** our minds to comprehend God's message, and to **preserve** the Word of God throughout the ages, in all languages and societies.

THE WORK OF THE HOLY SPIRIT AT SALVATION

John 16:8–11

The Spirit convicts us of our actual situation before God (sinner) and enables us, with godly sorrow, to repent, leading to a change in lifestyle. His conviction shows us our unrighteousness compared to Jesus' righteousness and the judgement due to unrepentant sinners. The Spirit defines sin as rebellion against a righteous God, not social misconduct defined differently in different societies.

John 3:3,5
Timothy 3:5

1 Peter 1:3
1 Thessalonians 1:5

The Spirit regenerates us, producing new life in us. We are born 'from above,' and by God's mercy, we are washed and renewed. Our spiritual birth, like natural birth, may take place over a protracted period of time. But there is a point in time when we recognize that New Life has happened in us. The Spirit grants us a 'living hope,' and imparts a 'full assurance' that we are God's children. Spiritual rebirth is a free and mysterious exercise of the Spirit's power that cannot be explained simply in terms of human capabilities or resources.

Ephesians 1:13
Ephesians 4:30

The promised Spirit of God seals us in Jesus Christ, assuring us that we are secure in Him. The Spirit is the down payment or guarantee of the fullness of the inheritance that comes to us in Jesus Christ.

THE WORK OF THE HOLY SPIRIT IN SANCTIFICATION

Romans 8:29
2 Corinthians 3:18
Ephesians 4:23
1 Thessalonians 4:3
2 Thessalonians 2:13
Romans 6:22
Galatians 6:14
Romans 6:4, 6

Romans 8:1

Since we have been predestined to be made like the image of God's son, the Spirit of God undertakes the work of transforming us into that image. He works to renew the entire person, separating us from a sin-induced lifestyle and consecrating us to God and His purposes. He enables us to be 'crucified to the world' and the world to us. He enables us to die to sin and live to righteousness. He sets us free from the law of sin and death. His work continues, obstructed only by our stubbornness until the coming of our Lord Jesus, either in death or at His return.

THE CONTINUING WORK OF THE HOLY SPIRIT IN THE BELIEVERS

Acts 2:4
Acts 10:45
Ephesians 55:18
Acts 19:2
Galatians 5:16–25
Acts 8:29
Acts 13:2

Acts 15:28
Acts 16:6
John 14:6
Romans 8:11
Galatians 2:20

Jesus fills us by a baptism in the Spirit initially, but commands us to keep on being filled with the Spirit. Even though the baptism in the Holy Spirit can happen at the time of the new birth, both in New Testament times and now, it is often subsequent to conversion. The Spirit guides, directs, appoints, prohibits, and teaches. He creates in us both the life of Christ, as well as the work of Christ. The Spirit engenders fruit – the qualities of Jesus' life – in believers. The Spirit fills us with the joy of Christ and reveals the things of God to His followers. All that Jesus won for us at the Cross and all that Jesus Christ inherited from His Father . . . all this, the Spirit makes available to us, His Church.

APPLICATION

Discuss the three ministries of the Spirit in respect to the Word of God. How does the work of the Holy Spirit affect your daily life? How does natural genetic gifting differ from the gifts of the Holy Spirit? What would happen to you if God withdrew His Spirit from the world?

CONCLUSION

The Holy Spirit is the Counselor-Helper whom Jesus promised to send. He mediates all the work of Christ for us into our daily experience. He works with the Word of God to inspire and maintain it, to inscripturate it and interpret it, so that all believers may come to know the depths of God's love for us in Christ. The Spirit initiates the salvation of each believer, convicting them of sin, righteousness, and judgement. He regenerates us, places a seal of adoption on each of us, and undertakes the lifelong process of changing us into the image of Christ. He fills us with His power, imparts His gifts, and cultivates His fruit in our lives. He guides, teaches, and comforts each child of God. He is the Life of God freely given to us.

LESSON 12 – FATHER CHOOSES US AND CALLS US

PURPOSE

Romans 8:28–30

God, by His great mercy, predestined us to be conformed to the Image of His Son so that Christ Himself might be the First-Born Leader among His believers. That act of choosing us in ages past includes His call to us, justification from our sins, and eventual glorification in our new bodies. God's sovereign act of choosing (predestining) us in no way rules out man's responsibility to choose to follow Jesus by repenting of sin and receiving the Holy Spirit. This lesson explores the sovereign pathways of God in our behalf and the pathways of people who respond to the gracious overtures of the Holy Spirit.

GLOSSARY

Predestine – to chose or settle an issue ahead of time; to foreordain; refers to God's choosing people to come to know Jesus Christ and follow Him.

Election – a sovereign act of God's choice in reference to choosing people to know and follow Jesus Christ.

Sovereign – God's authority to operate the Universe as He chooses, without external influences pressuring Him to behave in a certain way.

Calling – a work of God's Spirit whereby He convinces us of our sin, enlightens our minds to know Christ, renews our wills, and enables us to embrace Jesus Christ.

Paradox – an apparently self-contradictory idea or statement, derived from two opposing truths each of which represents valid inferences. The term is not useful in describing statements about God and people which are difficult to reconcile in logic or life.

Antinomy – (Greek: *'against the law'* of reason.) An opposition between two apparently conflicting or contrasting truths. God reveals His essential nature in merely human terms. At times, some of His truthful statements carry the quality of 'antinomy,' because we cannot reconcile the logical quality of each statement with the other. How can God be Three, yet One? How can Christ be fully God and yet fully man? How can a Sovereign God choose a person to belong to Him while requiring accountability from that person in choosing to follow or not follow Him? Most heresies (or extreme belief and practice) in the Church come from attempting to simplify doctrine by ignoring or denying 'antinomies.' Clarification of such antinomies await further revelation of God or the time of our glorified minds and bodies. In the meantime, we receive God's revealed Word; we ask for His Spirit of wisdom and revelation, we prayerfully wait on Him and refuse to hate the one who disagrees with us.

GOD THE FATHER'S WORK OF PREDESTINATION

To decide or set apart beforehand (predestine) is an act of our Sovereign God. He set us apart (Greek: *prooridzo*) that we might share the likeness of His Son Jesus Christ. The goal of our predestination is to be transformed into the likeness of Jesus. Also, God set us apart for His purposes, not for our own self-fulfilment. He prepared ahead of time certain good works that we might fulfill them.

Several types of God's choosing (election, predestination) appear in Scripture. The Father elected Israel as His 'chosen' people. And He considers us, the Church, His chosen generation. He elected, or chose, certain individuals for special service, such as Moses, Aaron, David. He chooses His Servant, the One in whom He delights. Scripture also refers to His elect angels. God's choosing or electing is a free act of His sovereign grace. No one forces God to do anything. One point of contention among Christians is this: Did God choose only a certain number of people to be saved? Or did God choose all people to come to Him? We cannot hope to reconcile these viewpoints here; we commend you to the study of the Word of God. On this we all agree: God chose us in Jesus Christ because our rebellion and unworthiness made it impossible for us to save ourselves. He chose us in Christ, not in ourselves.

FOREKNOWLEDGE

According to this interpretation, God knew ahead of time who would respond to His offer of salvation in Christ. Therefore, He chose (elected, predestined) them to come to Christ. Another interpretation is that God, from eternity past, looked with favour on certain people and elected them to salvation. Scripture ties God's foreknowledge with our being predestined or called. Yet the same Scriptures in innumerable ways make it abundantly clear that individuals are responsible for receiving or rejecting Christ's salvation. This suggests that our response to Christ does affect election. God's grace or salvation has appeared to all men, not just the elect. Scriptures unequivocally show that Christ died for all and that whoever calls on the name of the Lord will be saved. These exhortations to turn to God presuppose peoples' responsibility to do so.

GOD'S CHOICE

According to this interpretation, God's foreknowledge affected His choice in no way. The 'potter' has the right over the clay to fashion the vessel he wishes. God chose Jacob over Esau before their birth. God raised up Pharaoh, King of Egypt, to demonstrate His power in the King's life and empire. The issue depends on God, who chooses to have mercy ... not on the person involved. Many godly scholars and churches believe this interpretation most fully represents the Scriptures.

We suggest several objections to this latter view because of the following limitations or implications of that perspective:

(1) Man's ability to choose God has no meaning; God chose for him
(2) Atonement is limited to those who are chosen, not the entire human race
(3) God takes the responsibility for choosing some to perish
(4) Evangelism has no real imperative, for God has already decided the saved and lost
(5) This prompts pride and a false sense of security as the 'chosen' of God, discouraging the whole process of sanctification

These comments are not designed to convince you on a particular position, but rather to show the kinds of verses and arguments that exist.

BIBLICAL THEOLOGY SHEDS LIGHT ON THE ISSUE

If we pursue the exegesis of Scripture itself, without concern for systematizing structures, then we find two clear illustrations of the mix of God's choosing and our response:

(1) The circumstances of Christ's death on the cross represent God's choosing or election (foreordination), yet God holds the participants responsible for killing Christ.
(2) In the book of Esther, we see how God allows peoples to have all their choices, yet His Sovereignty accomplishes the results He desires.

APPLICATION

In your life, what do you see as God's foreordaining work in the midst of your daily choices? How does God's sovereign choices affect the nations of the earth? In what way is God's election at work in your own children?

CONCLUSION

Based on His omniscience (knowing all), God chooses all things, from grasshoppers to people and nations. However, He has chosen to give people the responsibility for making valid choices, choices which He Himself honours – either salvation or Hell. As His followers, we learn to live 'by every word that proceeds out of the mouth of God.' In our permissive age, people are so totally convinced of 'freedom and rights' that they completely ignore the overtures and demands of a Sovereign just God. There is no fear of God in their eyes. Any attempt to resolve with finality these 'antinomies' brings us to a rational impasse. But it's better to live and work with an impasse than to lack the Word of God.

LESSON 13 – FATHER CALLS US TO HIMSELF

PURPOSE

God's provision in Christ Jesus includes His choosing us, then His calling and justifying us. The fact that He calls us assures us that He will continue in the process of justifying and glorifying us. His calling us to Himself differs from the calling, or vocation, to which He leads us as we follow Him. The lesson explores the biblical call to know God and then the vocation to which He calls us as we serve Him here on earth.

GLOSSARY

Calling – (Greek: *klesis*) in Reformation theology, the calling is said to be effectual; the call carries God's power to effect or to produce the desired results. The term 'call', refers not simply a call in greeting a person. Rather, the term carries the sense of a summons. God calls us to Himself, to know and serve Him.

Vocation – (Latin: *vocare*) the particular vocation, profession, trade or specialty through which God has called His children to serve Him, the Church, and the non-believing world.

CALLING IN THE OLD TESTAMENT

Genesis 12:1–3
Exodus 19:4–6
Hosea 11:1
Isaiah 43:1

Amos 7:14–15

God called Abraham and family to follow Him and receive the covenantal promises. God called Israel out of bondage in Egypt, to become His people and to live by His Law. He redeemed and called Israel as precious and honoured in His sight. In the sense of vocation for special service, God called Amos to prophesy to the house of Israel.

CALLING IN THE NEW TESTAMENT

Mark 3:13
Matthew 10:1–4
Acts 2:39
Matthew 9:13

1 Peter 2:10–11

1 Corinthians 1:9

1 Corinthians 1:26

1 Corinthians 7:20
1 Timothy 6:12

Acts 14:22
1 Peter 2:21

Jesus of Nazareth called His disciples to Himself, that they might be with Him. In turn, they became the team around which God began to call Israel and the Gentile Nations to Himself. Jesus came to call sinners and the sick, not the righteous and healthy. God called us, His believers, out of darkness into His marvelous light that we might proclaim His most excellent nature and Person. He called us into fellowship with His Son, Jesus Christ our Lord.

We find other examples of callings in the New Testament Paul mentions the wise ... the mighty ... the noble as callings which God resists with His choices of the foolish ... the weak ... the base, that no one might boast before God. Paul discusses marriage or single life in terms of calling. We are called to eternal life; therefore, we fight the good fight of faith. We are also called to suffer for Jesus Christ, as Christ suffered for us and left us an example.

Philippians 2:5–13
Luke 22:26
John 13:14–16
Philippians 2:1–4

Romans 1:1
1 Corinthians 1:1
Ephesians 4:11

THE CALL OF GOD TO SERVE HIM

God calls us into servanthood, like His Son, in attitude and lifestyle. The calling as servant is the highest in the kingdom of God. It underscores all other vocations or ministries. The humility of mind that enables one to serve, Paul exhorts us to find in Christ and use in serving Him and the Church. God calls people to specific function, offices, and giftings within the Church. He calls some to be apostles, prophets, evangelists, pastors, and teachers. Whatever our vocation in business or ministry, the call is to serve Jesus.

2 Timothy 1:9

Acts 2:37
Acts 26:18
Ezra 36:26
John 6:44
Philippians 2:13

THE HOLY SPIRIT AND GOD'S CALLING

In the Reformation theologies, the term 'calling', referred to the work of God's Spirit, an effectual or effective calling undertaken in the life of an individual. The calling involves a conviction that we are indeed sinners. The Spirit enlightens our minds, for we live and move in darkness apart from His illuminating work. The Spirit renews our wills and imparts to us the capacity to commit ourselves to Christ. Finally, the Spirit persuades us to embrace Jesus Christ, as Son of God and Redeemer.

Isaiah 6:1–7
Isaiah 6:8

Jeremiah 1:4–8

1 Kings 19:12

Romans 10:14

THE MEANS GOD USES TO CALL PEOPLE

Often God uses providential circumstances to make His call clear. God called Isaiah through an overwhelming vision of God's Sovereignty. Isaiah responded to the Lord's question: 'Whom shall I send, Who will go for Us?' Very simply, he said, 'Here am I, Send me.' Jeremiah responded to God's inner Word: 'Before you were born, I consecrated you, I have appointed you a prophet to the nations.' Elijah experienced a 'quiet, gentle voice,' or the 'sound of a gentle blowing' for the Lord's direction. Sometimes God calls us through the voice of His servants. God may use healings or miracles, the common or the special, the old or the new. If our hearts are willing, we will hear God's call.

APPLICATION

Discuss the difference between God's call on you to know the Living God and His call on you to serve Him. What are the indications, the clues, by which you know God is calling you? What is the difference in our work as a job and as a calling? How did you know God was calling you to marriage, or not?

CONCLUSION

Our most fundamental call: to come to know God in Jesus Christ. This call to belong to God as His child begins the process whereby God, through His Spirit, works in us His grace. His grace enables us to respond to His call to serve Him. And as we learn to serve Him, we begin to recognize His call to be servant of the Most High God in all areas of life. As His grace grows in us, then our profession or job takes on aspects of His calling. We see our spouses and children as more than human choices, but God's calling in our lives. Suddenly it dawns on us that life itself is a high calling of God in Jesus Christ.

LESSON 14 – JUSTIFIED BY THE SPIRIT

PURPOSE

God the Father introduced to Abraham a remarkable perspective unknown within any other religious system on earth: Abraham believed God and it was counted to him for righteousness. Instead of people striving to become acceptable to God by fulfilling certain duties or requirements, God simply credited righteousness to people based on their faith in Him. This faith results in obedience to the One who justifies people. This lesson explores the grounds, means, and results of justification for all believers.

GLOSSARY

Justify – (Hebrew: *sadeq*; Greek: *dikoo*.) the act of God's free grace whereby He pardons all our sins and accepts us as righteous in His sight, only because of Christ's righteousness imputed to us and received by faith alone.

Regeneration – the act of God's free grace whereby the Holy Spirit creates new life within the believer who has repented and come to trust in Jesus.

Conversion – the response of a sinner to God's gracious call in repenting from his own dead works and placing his faith in Jesus Christ.

Aspects of our Salvation from the theological viewpoint:

Election (Predestination) – God chooses me

Calling – God calls me

Justification – God declares me free from sin

Regeneration – the Spirit creates life in me

Conversion – I respond in repentance and faith

Adoption – God adopts me into His family

Union with Christ – Christ identifies me with Him

Reconciliation – God places me in right relationship to Himself

OVERVIEW OF JUSTIFICATION

Romans 3:24, 26
Romans 4:5
Isaiah 53:6,11
1 John 2:2
2 Corinthians 5:19

Romans 5:1
Romans 3:28
Romans 8:4

Justification is a declared act of God; He decides to count us as free from sin. He imputes to us Christ's own righteousness; He imputes to Christ our sin. God does this based on His gracious nature and the sacrifice which Christ made for all people on the cross.

This gracious declaration does not make us perfect or holy; rather, we are reckoned as legally righteous before God. This is the backdrop over which regeneration and conversion take place experientially in our lives. Justification produces peace in our lives and sets us free from the demands of the (Mosaic) Law. Now the righteous requirement of the Law is fulfilled in us who walk according to the Spirit, not according to the flesh. We obey God out of a loving gratitude for all His gracious work in our behalf. Our obedience does not gain us acceptance with God. Christ's obedience gained Him acceptance with the Father. And it is Christ's righteousness that has been so freely imputed to us.

THE GROUNDS OF JUSTIFICATION

Exodus 34:7
Genesis 15:6

2 Corinthians 5:19

1 Peter 3:18

2 Corinthians 5:21

God, from His earliest self-disclosures, calls all people into account for their sin. Yet even before the Mosic Law, God had already justified Abraham and family by faith. To reconcile this conflict, one must interpose the 'grounds' for justification. God called Jesus of Nazareth into account, not for His own sin, but the sin of all people. Based on Jesus' perfect and sinless lifestyle, the Father counted Jesus' righteousness as our own. The Father removed the conflict between His own righteous nature and our sinful selves. We now have His righteousness; He has disposed of our sin.

THE MEANS OF JUSTIFICATION

Galatians 3:11
Romans 3:20
Galatians 3:24
Galatians 3:21
Romans 5:1, 9

Romans 3:24

Ephesians 2:8–9

Acts 13:38–39

Galatians 2:16
Galatians 3:11

No one can be justified before God by the works of the Mosaic (or any) Law. God gave the Mosaic Law as a tutor to lead us to Jesus Christ, for the Law is unable to impart life. We are justified by faith in Jesus Christ; we are justified by His blood. We are justified as a gift by God's grace through the redemption which is in Christ Jesus. By faith in Jesus' life sacrifice for us, God justifies us freely by His grace. Even the faith we can sense is another gracious gift from God to us. The major theologies within Roman Catholicism point to faith and works as leading to justification. Protestant theology insists that 'faith alone' leads to justification and justification leads to good works. God's act of justification, accompanied by regeneration and conversion, moves us to accomplish His purposes (good works) in a response of gratitude and loving obedience.

THE RESULTS OF JUSTIFICATION

Romans 4:7–8

Ephesians 2:19
Romans 8:14–17
1 Corinthians 1:30
2 Corinthians 5:21

First, God remits or wipes out, the penalty for our sin. He has already laid it on Jesus Christ. Then, God restores us to His favour; He dissolves the broken relationship started in Adam's lifetime. Our continued rebellion had placed us outside of God's favour. Now, when we receive Christ's provision, we are counted as God's friends and receive all the blessings and privileges of family members with God. Finally, God imputes to us His own righteousness; we are righteous because of Christ.

APPLICATION

How do we fulfill the requirements of the Law? What blessings and privileges come to us as belonging to Christ (see Ephesians 1:1–14)? Is Justification the only basis for Christian morality? Why is Jesus Christ the only Person who can express both the judgement and mercy of God? What are the three results of justification? What other means of justification have people attempted?

CONCLUSION

Justification is a legal term from the first century law courts. God declares the repentant sinner justified. But it says nothing about the character of the justified one, just his legal standing before God. Justification displays God's **justice** in condemning and punishing sin. Justification expresses God's **mercy** in pardoning and accepting sinner. Justification manifests God's **wisdom** in exercising both justice and mercy to people through Jesus Christ. The grounds for justification are the substitutionary atonement accomplished by Christ's sacrificial death. We are never justified by the works of Law, but by the blood of Jesus, by faith, and by His grace. The results of justification are pardon, restoration to a right relationship with God, and receiving the very righteousness of Christ.

LESSON 15 – FATHER REGENERATES US IN JESUS CHRIST

PURPOSE

When a person comes to know Jesus Christ, life for them starts over. God works in them a 'new birth', and their old nature is put to death on the cross. Then they rise, with Christ, to walk in newness of life. This complete renewal changes the basic orientation of the believer so that they can live for Jesus Christ and not just for themselves. This lesson explores the Scriptural basis for regeneration, the means, and results.

GLOSSARY

Born again – (Greek: *gennao*) the idea of re-birth, a new birth, being born again or born from above by the Spirit.

Regeneration – an inner re-creating of fallen human nature by the gracious sovereign action of the Holy Spirit.

Monergism – the view that the grace of God alone makes our salvation happen; people have no strength to bring themselves to salvation. See the teachings of Augustine, Luther, and Calvin.

Synergism – the view that people somehow cooperate with the grace of God in effecting one's salvation. See Arminius, John Wesley, and others.

REGENERATION AND THE WILL OF GOD

James 1:18

1 Peter 1:3

The apostle John taught that the will (purpose and strength) of God makes our renewal or new birth happen. God works this in all those who believe in the name of Jesus. And the new birth takes place, not based on mere human genetics (blood) or by the natural process of childbirth. Regeneration happens not by virtue of one's parentage nor national origin. It is sourced in God. John goes on to say that the emotional or sexual desires of the flesh cannot accomplish regeneration. One's volition, the sheer force of personal will, cannot bring a person to regeneration. God intervenes and accomplishes regeneration based on His purpose and strength.

REGENERATION AND THE KINGDOM OF GOD

John 3:3

John 3:5

Without regeneration, we remain unaware and unseeing in reference to God's Kingdom rule. John states that without regeneration, or the new birth, one cannot even see that God's Kingdom exists. And if one cannot see it, how then is he able to experience it? Further, John quotes Jesus' dialogue with Nicodemus, 'Unless one is born of water and the Spirit, he cannot enter the kingdom of God.' Jesus insists on an act of

God, being born from above, as requisite for seeing and entering God's Kingdom. The decisiveness of the New Birth shows that a person ceases to be the one he was; his old life is over, a new life begins. He becomes a new person in Christ Jesus. He is buried with Christ, out of reach of condemnation and raised with Christ into a new life of righteousness. Paul summarizes it: God delivers us out of the dominion of darkness and transfers us into the Kingdom of His beloved Son. Without regeneration, we remain caught in Satan's rulership of darkness.

2 Corinthians 5:17

Romans 6:3–11

Colossians 1:13

THE MEANS OF REGENERATION

The new birth rests upon one's faith in Jesus Christ, His Crucifixion, and Resurrection. John speaks of being born from above in terms of the Spirit of God, and water. God's Spirit accomplishes the regeneration in us; no human agency or strength can do this. Water refers to the action of the Word of God in cleansing us of sin. Further, Peter speaks of the 'living and abiding Word of God' as the means by which we are born again. As we proclaim the Word of God, the Spirit uses that Word to bring people into the new birth. For the Spirit of God acts on the Word to make it clear to people concerning their sin and need of Jesus. The Spirit brings us to repentance and faith.

John 3:14–16
1 Peter 1:3
John 3:5

Ephesians 5:26
Titus 3:5
1 Peter 1:23

James 1:18

Romans 10:14
Acts 16:14
Philippians 2:13
Galatians 4:19

The Church in her long history of defining 'healthy teaching,' struggled with the idea of people's ability to bring about regeneration. One group chooses Monergism, which says only one person is involved in the New Birth: God Himself. Just as infants have no will or strength to induce their conception or birth, so the human being has no moral strength to accomplish his new birth. Other groups choose synergism, a working together of God and man in the New Birth. The two biblical truths we discussed earlier produce a conflict in human minds: the Sovereignty of God and peoples' moral responsibility. Is there enough moral strength left in people to cooperate with the Spirit of God in regeneration? Or, has sin so permeated our entire being, will emotion, and mind, that only God Himself can create in us the new birth?

THE RESULTS OF REGENERATION

Regeneration works in us a new life-focus so that we resist sin and temptation. God's life in us alters our attitudes, our perspectives, and works in us His strength to follow His ways. We do not become perfect or sinless just because we are born from above. Rather, our new life in Christ focuses us on serving Jesus, or pleasing the Father. And, when we sin, He forgives us and we resume our walk in the Spirit. In regeneration, we experience a new love for God and for all those who belong to His family. We find that He leads us to love our enemies and especially love those who do not know Him. We find a love for His Word.

1 John 3:9
1 John 5:4, 18
2 Corinthians 5:17

1 John 1:9
Galatians 5:16

1 John 5:1–2

Matthew 7:11
1 Peter 2:2
Psalm 119:97

Ephesians 1:3
Philippians 4:19
1 Corinthians 10:13
Ephesians 1:9, 17
Romans 8:17

Daily we discover other privileges that come with regeneration: God supplies all our needs. He assures us of His power to protect and hold us in all circumstances. We begin to perceive what God's will is in all facets of life. The person born of God becomes an heir of God and fellow-heir with Christ. Few of these results are visible to the non-believer. But to the one renewed in Christ, life is a constant discovery of the inexhaustible riches that come to us through Jesus Christ.

APPLICATION

In what sense does the media today use the term born again? How would you explain this biblical term to one not in the Church? What is the difference between rebirth and conversion? Do these happen at the same time? What differences in your life can you see, now that you have experienced regeneration? How would you explain these differences to a non-believer?

CONCLUSION

Regeneration is God's gracious action by which He makes us alive in our spirits. Though we were spiritually dead because of selfishness and rebellion, God accomplishes a new birth in us. By regeneration, we see, enter, understand, and participate in the kingdom of God. The image for regeneration is the new birth. Like natural birth it happens at a point in time with the awareness of the one being born.

We are regenerated by the will of God through the death and Resurrection of Jesus Christ, based upon our response to the Word of God. Regeneration results in our change of life-perspective and habits. We can overcome temptation by the Spirit's power. We begin to love God Himself, His Word, and His people. We enjoy the privileges of an heir in the family of God. God meets all our needs and keeps us by His grace.

LESSON 16 – HEALING IN JESUS CHRIST

PURPOSE

Jesus restored physical health to innumerable sick people during His earthly ministry. During the days of the Apostolic Church, the Spirit of God used a series of remarkable healings to draw people to Jesus Christ and establish new churches. In the life of the Church since then, healings have continued to occur sporadically. But especially in mission situations, the records show an abundance of healings accompanying the planting and growth of churches in non-Christian lands. During the current explosion of the Gospel worldwide, the Spirit of God empowers the healing gifts and ministry in and through local churches. This lesson explores the healing ministry as a provision of the new covenant and the Kingdom, and gives the Scriptural basis for releasing God's healing.

GLOSSARY

Healing – (Greek: *Sozo*) to save, deliver, heal or make whole. The term has a range of meaning from physical healing to the salvation experience in its entirety.

Healing – (Greek: *Therapuo*) to heal or make whole. Mostly used in the New Testament for physical healing.

GOD'S COVENANTS PROVIDE FOR HEALING

Exodus 15:26

Deuteronomy 28:4, 11
Deuteronomy 30:9
Psalm 103:3
Deuteronomy 28:18–22
Numbers 21:8–9

Deuteronomy 29:5

Luke 4:18
Matthew 9:35
Luke 5:17

Luke 6:19
Luke 5:30

Acts 10:38
Luke 4:40–43
Matthew 9:35
John 5:5
Mark 6:5, 6
Mark 9:23
Luke 11:23
John 11:40
Mark 2:4

Under the old covenant, God proclaimed Himself: 'I Am the Lord your Healer.' As the Israelites obeyed the terms of the Mosaic covenantal Law, God would provide for physical healing among the people and livestock. Disobedience brought judgement, sickness, and death. All healing begins with the believers's recognition that God desires to bring healing to us. Faith and obedience are the necessary responses to God's offer of healing. God's healing power among the Israelites kept even their clothes and shoes from wearing out.

Jesus of Nazareth demonstrated healing as part of the new covenant He came to inaugurate by His blood. He healed by the power of the Holy Spirit, at the direction of His Father. Jesus showed us the way of healing by emptying Himself of His divine privileges and living by the power of the Spirit, 'God anointed Him with the Spirit and with power and He went about healing the oppressed.' At times Jesus healed all those who came to Him; other times, He healed only certain individuals, whether Jew or Gentile. The Scriptures point out that Jesus did not heal all people on every occasion. He taught the link between the sick person's faith and His power to heal. On one occasion, Jesus healed because of the faith of those who brought the sick person to Him.

HEALING AND DELIVERANCE: SIGNS OF GOD'S KINGDOM POWER

Matthew 9:35

Luke 4:18
John 6:26
John 2:11
John 4:54
John 6:14
John 9:16
John 11:47

Matthew 12:28

Hebrews 6:5

In Jesus' ministry, He went about proclaiming the Good News of the Father's Kingdom and healing every sickness among the people. These healings validated Jesus as the Messiah, the Messenger and Prophet of God. John built his Gospel around seven extraordinary miracles – some physical healings – each of which the Scripture views as a sign of God's Presence. These signs pointed the observer away from just the physical situation to the Son of God, sent from the Father's presence. Further, the anointing power of God broke Satan's grasp in sickness and demonization. The healing and expulsion of demonic spirits, by the power of the Spirit, demonstrated that the kingdom of God had come among the people. The writer to the Hebrews calls this 'the powers of the age to come.' Whether in Jesus' ministry, or the Apostolic proclamation, or the Church today, God demonstrates the power of His future Kingdom by releasing healing signs, wonders, and gifts of the Spirit.

HEALING IN THE LOCAL CHURCH TODAY

2 Corinthians 1:20–21
Ephesians 1:3
John 14:12
Acts 4:10
Acts 5:16
James 5:14–15
1 Corinthians 12:9
1 Corinthians 12:28

Titus 3:4

Proverbs 4:20–23

Psalm 107:20

Acts 3:16

Acts 4:7–10
Acts 4:12–30
Acts 14:9

In Jesus Christ, God makes available to us all His covenantal provisions. He places within our hands as individuals and churches the gracious opportunity of continuing Jesus' earthly ministry of healing. When Jesus sent the Holy Spirit at Pentecost, He became the Healing Presence of Jesus Christ on earth among His Church. God distributes Jesus' healing Presence among church members, through the gifts and ministries of the Holy Spirit.

There are three primary methods God uses to minister Jesus' healing Presence by the Holy Spirit:

(1) **The grace of God represents the Father's compassion and power to heal**
(2) **The Word of God, used by the Spirit to heal**
(3) **The name of Jesus brings healing to people**

Often one cannot distinguish which combination conveys the healing. The presence of faith activates the power of God in His grace, His Word, and Jesus' name. We learn to walk in Jesus' healing work and virtue by faith and patience.

APPLICATION

What are some of the ways we can activate and implement the healing ministry? How can you bring Jesus' healing into your family circle? What could be done to encourage the healing ministry within your local church? In your care group, what can you do to encourage others to enter into Jesus' healing? What is the difference between Jesus' healing and what the media calls 'therapy'? What could you do to help convince a friend to receive Jesus' healing?

CONCLUSION

God has shown His compassionate heart towards the sick ever since the Mosaic Law. He has always been the source of healing and salvation. Salvation contains within itself God's healing, both physically and spiritually. Both old and new covenants attest to God's healing power. The anointing power of God's Spirit continues Jesus' healing ministry among us today.

LESSON 17 – FATHER UNITES US WITH JESUS CHRIST

PURPOSE

Our union with Jesus Christ carries us into death, burial, and resurrection with Jesus. Further, our identification or union with Jesus makes us alive with Him, raises us up with Him and seats us with Him in the heavenly places. In this lesson we explore the meaning of identifying with Jesus Christ and how it affects our daily work and lifestyle, both within the Church and as we work in the midst of the world system.

GLOSSARY

John 14:20

Identification/Union – in explaining the new covenant to His disciples, Jesus introduced this idea: 'You in Me and I in you.' The grace of God in justification brings us into this extraordinary blessing. The term 'union,' refers both to our **position** in Christ as well as Christ's dynamic **presence** in the believer.

Romans 6:11

To Reckon – (Greek: *logidzomai*) the term Paul uses to exhort believers to realize and act upon their union with Christ. We are 'dead to sin', and 'alive to God', in our union with Him.

Position – the status and placement given to the believer as a result of Christ's saving work.

Presence – God's Person dwells in us by the power of the Holy Spirit. His Presence validates our 'position' in Jesus Christ and makes it effective.

OUR PLACEMENT IN CHRIST AT REGENERATION

John 3:3–5

Colossians 3:1–3

Romans 8:17

Titus 3:5

Romans 6:3–5

Through the new birth – our being 'born from above' – the Father places us into the company of all those who follow Christ, the Church. In addition, the Father unites us with His Son Jesus, such that everything that the Father gives to His Son, the Father also gives to us. The Father sees us, His followers, as one with Jesus Christ. Regeneration, which the Father performs in our behalf, by the power and washing of the Word, opens the way for us to be identified as one with Jesus Christ.

Ephesians 2:5

Galatians 6:14
Galatians 2:20
Romans 6:6; Romans 6:11
Colossians 1:1–4

Our union with Jesus Christ starts at the point of our being united with Him in His death. We are baptized into His death, united with Him in the likeness of His death; our water baptism signifies this reality. The Father then 'made us alive with Christ.' As Christ was raised from the dead by the glory of the Father, we, too, were raised that we might walk in newness of life. This union with Christ in His death and Resurrection also involves putting to death our old natures, the breaking of the power of sin in our lives. From now on, we are to reckon ourselves dead to sin and alive to God in Christ. Our union with Christ carries us with Him in His Ascension and inauguration as the Ruling Sovereign. We reign with Him in life today and look forward to a future reign in glory with Christ. Our union with Christ ties our present and future life inextricably with that of Jesus Christ. We are seated with Christ in the heavenly places. And in that position, we receive every blessing of the Father conveyed to us through the Spirit. The Spirit of God makes effective this life-giving union with Christ. He joins us in Spirit with the reigning Christ.

Ephesians 2:6
Ephesians 1:20
2 Timothy 2:12
Revelation 11:15
Ephesians 1:3

SCRIPTURAL PICTURES OF THIS UNION

The Scriptures give several pictures (metaphors) to describe the vitality of our union with Jesus Christ. First, the vine and branch show us the flow of Life from Jesus to each believer. The branch is in the vine and the vine is in the branch. Fruitfulness in our lives depends on our unobstructed relationship to the vine, Jesus Christ. Next, the metaphor of a body shows the organic union with Christ, not just an organizational relationship. We are all members of Christ's Body. As individual members, we each receive appropriate placement and function, such that the Body grows into maturity. Christ Himself is the Head of His Body; we are individually members of that Body. Finally, the Scriptures picture our union with Jesus Christ like a marriage. As Christ is the Head of the Church and Savior of the Body, He is also Husband to His Bride, the Church. Christ gave Himself up for Her to sanctify and cleanse Her.

John 15

1 Corinthians 14:27
Ephesians 1:22–23
1 Corinthians 14:12
1 Corinthians 14:13–14
1 Corinthians 14:18
Ephesians 4:12–13
Colossians 1:18
Ephesians 1:22
Ephesians 5:23–32

WHAT OUR UNION WITH CHRIST PRODUCES

Our union with Christ, above all, begins to transform us into His image. The Spirit changes our personalities such that we express the life of Christ in attitudes, relationships, and lifestyles. We daily put off the old nature that we 'be renewed to a true knowledge, according to the image of the One who created' us. Our union with Christ produces a security, a profound assurance that we are His inseparably, a full assurance of understanding in knowing God's mystery . . . Christ. Our union with Christ opens the door into intimate fellowship with the Father. Eternal life is the knowledge of God. God's grace and peace causes this intimate knowledge of God to be multiplied. All our growth by the Spirit develops in us an increasing sensitivity to and awareness of the Father's Presence.

2 Corinthians 3:18
1 Corinthians 1:30

Ephesians 4:22–23
Colossians 3:10
1 Thessalonians 1:5
Romans 8:35
Colossians 2:2

Ephesians 1:17
John 17:3
2 Peter 1:2, 3
2 Peter 1:8

THE POTENTIAL OF OUR UNION WITH CHRIST

Without an understanding of our union with Jesus Christ, the Christian might think that he must live out his earthly life in his own natural strength. We learn to 'reckon' ourselves dead with Christ, alive, resurrected, ascended, and seated with Him in heavenly places. Satan confuses and deceives believers in his aggressive effort to keep them

Romans 6:1–11
Romans 6:4
Colossians 3:1
Ephesians 2:6
2 Timothy 2:12
Romans 8:17

1 Corinthians 10:13

2 Peter 1:4
1 Peter 4:1

from 'reckoning', considering it done. Our capacity to overcome temptation depends on how much we rest in Christ. For He is the One who provides the way of escape, through our union with Him. The believer who counts on the fact that he is the partaker, the sharer, of the divine nature ceases from his own struggles. The believer avails himself of the life of God that flows from that divine nature.

There are profound distinctions between Jesus Christ and ourselves, especially in regard to bodily or physical perfection. We are not yet like Christ Himself in perfection of body, soul, and mind. We await the glorified body, perfect as Christ Himself. In seeking to walk in our union with Christ, some have erroneously considered themselves caught up in Christ to the extent of losing their own identity and personality. This is expressed in losing our responsibility and accountability as people and 'becoming one with some cosmic soul.' Satan's confusion and deception aims to unbalance our union with Christ in a myriad of aspects. Our protection is our union with Jesus Christ.

APPLICATION

What are the biblical steps for learning how to identify with Christ in all aspects of life? What are the most obvious difficulties that confront us in applying this teaching? How do we 'put to death the works of the flesh'? How do we draw more and more upon God's life in us through our union with Christ?

CONCLUSION

We are identified and united with Christ from the moment of regeneration and justification. God places us in Christ; we learn how to abide there. This life-giving, mysterious, and spiritual union with Christ is a sovereign work of God's Spirit. It is the context in which our sanctification takes place. Scriptural pictures clarify our union in terms of the vine and branches, the body of Christ, and the Church as the Bride of Christ. In consequence of this union, the Spirit mediates to us security, fruitfulness, anointing for service, and fellowship with the Father. Specifically, we are identified with Christ in His death, burial, Resurrection, Ascension, inauguration, and glory. We do not yet share His glorified body, nor do we share God's attributes of omnipotence, omniscience, and omnipresence.

LESSON 18 – FATHER GRANTS US ADOPTION AS HIS CHILDREN

PURPOSE

God adopts the stranger, the non-believer, and makes him a member of His own family, when that person, drawn by the Spirit, puts his Faith in Christ. The bond between God and the new believer, created through this act of adoption, carries a sense of certainty, and confident expectation (hope). Adoption brings the Presence of God's Spirit into our hearts, so that we cry out, *'Abba, Abba'* ('Father' or 'Daddy'). Such assurance enables us to face life today with the certainty of pardon, belonging, and eternal life. Adoption has a positive flavor, as contrasted with forgiveness and remission of sins. This lesson explores the means, benefits and results of our adoption.

GLOSSARY

Adoption – the act of God's free grace whereby He takes us, estranged sinners, into His family and grants us all the rights and privileges that result from belonging to Him.

Assurance – the work of God's Spirit in conveying the certainty of confidence that we belong to Him, have been truly saved, and will live with Him forever.

Backsliding – a turning away from daily fellowship and obedience with Christ to indulge in one's own willfulness and rebellion. Usually a temporary state followed by repentance and restoration.

Apostasy – a falling away from the Living God.

THE THREE ASPECTS OF ADOPTION

Ephesians 1:5

Galatians 4:4, 5

Romans 8:15
Ephesians 1:14
2 Corinthians 1:22
2 Corinthians 5:2, 4

In the timeless counsels of God the Trinity, He predestined us, and chose us to be adopted as His children. He decided then to take us into His family as those who were not originally members. In the present sense, He adopts us into His family as we receive Christ as Lord in our lives. To confirm adoption, He sends His Spirit into our hearts so that we can call out to Him as Father (*Abba, Abba*). In a future sense, we who have the Presence of the Spirit as guarantee of our full inheritance, eagerly await our coming adoption as children, and the redemption of our bodies.

THE BENEFITS OF ADOPTION

Adoption changes our position from outsiders to members of the inner family. Regeneration changes our 'nature'. Justification changes our

Romans 8:15
Galatians 4:6

Ephesians 1:14

John 1:12

1 John 1:3

'standing'. Sanctification changes our 'character'. We receive the Spirit as a downpayment or guarantee of our present and coming inheritance. Although it seems strange to refer to 'rights' when discussing salvation, we do have Scriptural authority at this point. John says that Father gives the right to become His children to those who receive His Son. As His children, we enter into a fellowship – a communion, a sharing of life – with both the Father and the Son. Finally, our adoption conveys to us a profound sense of assurance, a confidence that we are God's. Compare this with the unspoken, assumed confidence of relationship that characterizes a small child with his parents.

1 Thessalonians 1:5

Colossians 2:22
Hebrews 6:11
Hebrews 10:22

Paul speaks of the Gospel coming and touching the Thessalonians in power, in the Holy Spirit, and in a full assurance . . . a conviction and certainty. This gift of assurance brings both hope and faith to the believer.

ADOPTION RESULTS IN ASSURANCE

1 Thessalonians 1:5

Colossians 2:22
1 John 5:14

1 John 5:13

1 John 2:3–5

1 John 2:18
1 John 3:14

1 John 3:19
1 John 3:22
1 John 4:13

Now assurance brings to God's children a conviction that we belong to Him. Assurance works into the believer a sense of hope, of faith, and understanding of the Person of Christ..and a conviction that if we ask God for something according to His purposes, He will hear us and grant the request. As happens today, in the days of John the Beloved some wondered about their status as adopted, saved children of God. John gave a series of diagnostic statements demonstrating how assurance works in our lives. As we keep (practice) His commandments and Word, we have confident assurance that we are in Him. We know we live in a late hour because many antichrists have arisen. We know we have passed from death to life, because we love the brethren. We know we are of the truth, because our hearts do not condemn us. Thereby, we have confidence. We know that we abide in God, because He has given us His Spirit. This entire book of First John addresses the issue of our daily confidence and assurance in God's Presence and provision.

Ephesians 2:1–3

Ephesians 4:30
Mark 3:5

1 John 5:13

Romans 8:16

The gradual lessening or apparent absence of confidence or assurance may derive from the believer's taking back his self-centered lifestyle, the habits and activities that he left when he first met Christ. Neglect of God's Word promotes a lack of assurance, as will also the quenching or grieving of the Holy Spirit. In Western societies, the plague of over-work or 'busy-ness' will contribute directly to the lessening of our awareness of God's Presence. John the Beloved writes to us specifically that we might know that we have eternal life. The Spirit witnesses to our hearts that we are the children of God. We learn to discern the fact of salvation, based on God's promises. We grow in faith that we are saved, the belief that God's promises work. We come to enjoy the feelings that we are indeed saved.

APPLICATION

Ask members of your care group about their certainty of belonging to God, of forgiveness, and of eternal life. Describe the last time you felt that God had abandoned you? How can you lead your children (natural or spiritual) into confidence and full assurance of their salvation in Jesus Christ? What is the best way of training new believers into full confidence in all that God has accomplished for them?

CONCLUSION

As we recognize that God has adopted us into His family, the Spirit begins to build in us a strong sense of assurance and confidence. As we walk in the Spirit, this certainly grows stronger. We come to realize that God gave us the 'right' to belong to Him, through our faith, in Christ. We find within ourselves hope, faith and assurance that God will answer our prayers. The Book of First John gives the gamut of signals by which we know God's salvation is at work in us. Neglect and disobedience of God's Word lessens our sense of 'belonging'. Quenching or grieving the Spirit affects our inner awareness that indeed He has sealed and guaranteed Christ's salvation in us. But assurance or confidence permeates our witness and proclamation in daily life, giving to the non-believer a plain indication of God's righteousness and coming judgement.

SECTION 3:

CHRIST'S KINGDOM IN ME

LESSON 1 – THE GOSPEL OF THE KINGDOM OF GOD

The biblical view of the world clearly depicts the existence of two domains or kingdoms. The kingdom of God is revealed as the realm of God's authority and government, manifested by all that is 'good'. The other domain is ruled by Satan and the forces of wickedness and is characterized by all that is evil.

It is by God's great salvation, through Jesus Christ, that we are delivered from the bondage of Satan's kingdom and established in the glorious kingdom of God ruled and governed by Jesus Christ. This lesson will explore the nature and reality of these two kingdoms.

GLOSSARY

Kingdom – the territory subject to a king; the inhabitants or population subject to a king.

King – the sovereign of a nation; a man invested with supreme authority over a nation.

Domain – territory governed or under the government of a sovereign.

THE GOSPEL OF THE KINGDOM OF GOD

Romans 14:9
1 Corinthians 15:1–4
1 Corinthians 15:22–28

Matthew 4:23

Matthew 24:14
Mark 1:14; Luke 4:43

Ephesians 1:20–23
Romans 14:17

Philippians 2:5–11
Isaiah 9:6–7
Romans 10:9–13

John 10:3; John 14:27
1 Corinthians 8:3
John 1:48

The Good News is that Jesus Christ is the incarnate Son of God who lived a sinless life, died as substitutionary sacrifice for our sins, rose again the third day and ascended to the Father's right hand where He reigns as Lord of all.

This Good News is about the existence of a Kingdom where God's good government may be known by all who turn to Him.

The kingdom of God is God's government established under the rulership of His Son, Jesus Christ. His reign produces order, righteousness, peace, and joy in the Holy Spirit.

The Scriptures reveal Jesus Christ to be a Sovereign Ruler over a Kingdom having definite character.

Christ's Kingdom has a definite constituency through which His will and authority are made known.

THE KINGDOM OF GOD HAS PRESENT IMPLICATIONS

Psalm 27:13; Acts 2:40
Romans 5:17
Hebrews 13:8; Luke 17:21
Colossians 1:18–24
Ephesians 1:18–23

Jesus taught that the kingdom of God not only has to do with future destiny but also has immediate application to present circumstances.

The kingdom of God is personally revealed within the lives of all who acknowledge that Jesus is the Christ.

Matthew 5:14–16
Acts 2:40; Acts 4:32–37
1 Peter 2:9–12

The kingdom of God demonstrated through those who obey Him becomes a visible society and a light to the nations.

THE DOMAIN OF SATAN ALSO HAS PRESENT IMPLICATIONS

Acts 26:18

2 Thessalonians 2:9

Luke 9:42
1 Peter 5:8

Ephesians 6:12

Satan's realm is marked by darkness and wickedness. The atmosphere of Satan's realm is full of lies and deception. His activity is designed to bring about death and destruction.

Satan's specific goal is to contend with those who make up Christ's Kingdom by hindering God's purpose in their lives.

APPLICATION

Evaluate how your thinking about the order of universe may have been influenced by modern secular education. In your own words, describe how you see Jesus Christ as a King ruling over His Kingdom. How do you see yourself as a citizen in Christ's Kingdom and how do you live as one of His subjects? How would you explain the way into Christ's Kingdom?

CONCLUSION

We have examined what the Scriptures teach about the Gospel of the kingdom of God. Considering the consequences of those teachings for our own lives, it is now time to decide our personal relationship to God and His government expressed through His King, Jesus Christ. The next lesson will consider the steps we must take.

LESSON 2 – ENTERING THE KINGDOM OF GOD: REPENTANCE

PURPOSE

The act of repentance is the first step toward entering the kingdom of God. God's salvation initiative secures for us the privilege of entrance into His Kingdom. Our response, through repentance, is the necessary action we must take in order to enjoy His benefits.

This lesson will consider the importance of repentance as taught by Christ and the benefits that result from obedience to His command.

GLOSSARY

Sin – to miss the mark, a condition which describes the state of all men apart from God's forgiveness.

Conviction – to expose, convince, or reprove.

Repentance – (Greek: *matanoeo*) – to have a change of heart after consideration and regret.

Revelation – God's self-disclosure to man concerning Himself and His Truth.

REPENTANCE IS THE FIRST ACT OF OBEDIENCE

Matthew 3:2
Luke 13:2–3; Acts 17:30

Ezra 18:31

Joel 2:12

Matthew 4:17
Mark 1:15; Acts 2:37–38
Acts 3:19; Acts 5:31
Acts 11:18
2 Timothy 2:24–25

The Gospel of Jesus Christ calls us to turn from a life of sin and self-centered living to enter Christ's Kingdom.

Repentance is the act of turning from our own ways to seek Christ and His Kingdom. It involves a change of heart, as well as a change in direction.

Repentance is commanded by Christ and is an essential part of our obedience to Christ as Lord and King. It is a gift from God, indicating His willingness to forgive. Without this enabling gift, we could not respond to His Love and Mercy.

CONDITIONS ACCOMPANY REPENTANCE

Romans 3:23
Psalm 53:3; Isaiah 53:6

Romans 6:23
Hebrews 2:2
2 Peter 2:12–13

2 Corinthians 7:8–11
Joel 2:13

A necessary condition that must exist before repentance can occur is conviction of sin. This involves an awareness that our disobedience to God's commands has separated us from God.

The Bible reveals that the wage or penalty for our sin is death. This death is eternal separation from the living God without hope or remedy.

It is through the consciousness of sin and its consequence that we are able to experience a godly sorrow which leads to the act of repentance.

Ephesians 1:18–22
2 Corinthians 4:6
1 Peter 2:9

1 John 1:9; Romans 10:9
Proverbs 28:13; 1 John 1:9

Psalm 34:18
Psalm 51:16–17
Isaiah 66:2

Acts 2:27–28
Psalm 119:58–60
2 Corinthians 7:8–11

Colossians 3:5–17
Romans 8:29
2 Corinthians 3:18

Colossians 2:11–14
Psalm 78:38
Mark 2:5
Ephesians 2:7
1 John 1:9

Ephesians 1:18–23
Ephesians 2:14–21
2 Corinthians 5:17

Ephesians 2:1–5
Ephesians 2:8–10
Ephesians 5:5–10
2 Corinthians 5:9

The Gospel of Jesus Christ brings us the glorious Good News of God's provision through Christ's redemption. The revelation of this Good News is another essential part of true repentance.

Confession – of our sin and the need for Christ's redemption – is also a vital condition accompanying true repentance.

EVIDENCE OF REPENTANCE

A broken and contrite heart is a characteristic of someone who is experiencing a repentant attitude.

The renouncing of our former way of life, lived in disobedience to God's commands, is additional evidence that repentance has occurred.

Embracing a new life in Christ and walking in obedience to His ways indicates that we have truly repented.

THE RESULTS OF REPENTANCE

When we turn to God with a repentant heart, His power and authority provide us with forgiveness.

The forgiveness which God extends to us in Christ brings us into the riches of God's grace and speaks to us of God's faithfulness.

Through this forgiveness, we receive new focus and direction in life. We are no longer bound by the things and ways of this present age, but are able to turn our attention toward Christ, His Kingdom, and the goal to do God's will.

We receive a new faith which trusts completely in Christ's death, burial, and Resurrection for our salvation. It is through this faith, not our own efforts, that we are able to live a life which is pleasing to God.

APPLICATION

Explain what it means to be 'under conviction' for sin. Describe how repentance requires a radical break from a former way of living. Have you personally had such an encounter with God? What role does the Holy Spirit have in helping others to see the reality of their sin and their need to turn to God in repentance?

CONCLUSION

Repentance is acknowledging that our ways are wrong and lead to death. Faith in God enables us to establish a relationship of trust with God. This relationship in turn enables us to learn new ways which lead to life in Christ. Repentance is the first step through the 'Open Door' (Jesus Christ) to this new life in the kingdom of God. The next lesson will further examine the issue of trusting in and believing on God's provisions.

LESSON 3 – THE NECESSITY OF FAITH

PURPOSE

This lesson will examine the vital role of faith for entering the kingdom of God. By means of repentance, we turn from our former manner of life to demonstrate faith in God's provisions through Christ. We will consider the biblical nature of faith at work in this process.

GLOSSARY

Believe – to have firm conviction as to the reality or goodness of something (*Webster*).

Faith – (Greek: *pistis*) – confident trust and persuasion based upon testimony received.

Trust – assured reliance on the character, ability, strength, or truth of someone (*Webster*).

FAITH IS UNSHAKEABLE CONFIDENCE IN AN UNSHAKEABLE KINGDOM

Hebrews 11:1–7

Faith is in evidence when we are sure of those things which God has promised ... those things in which we place our hope. Faith is also evident when we are certain about things that we can not see with the natural eye.

Romans 4:17
Romans 5:1
Hebrews 11:8

Biblical faith goes beyond 'believing in God' to 'believing God'. Abraham is an example of someone who believed God, trusting what God had promised, and acted accordingly.

Romans 10:8–11
Hebrews 11:5–6

The Scriptures reveal that it is necessary to demonstrate this kind of confident trust in God and His provisions if we are going to be pleasing to Him.

FAITH HAS CLEARLY DEFINED ORIGINS

Romans 10:17
Hebrews 12:2
Colossians 1:28
Ephesians 1:13
Ephesians 3:6
Colossians 1:3–6

We receive faith from outside of ourselves as a gift from God. We do not have the ability to generate faith apart from God's help.

The Bible declares Jesus Christ to be the Author and Perfecter of our faith. It is the work of Christ in our hearts that produces the initial ability to trust Him. His ongoing work in our lives, through the Holy Spirit, matures and perfects our faith.

Faith is made available to us in the proclamation of the kingdom of God. When we respond to the 'Good News' of Christ and His Kingdom, we are quickened in faith to believe His promise.

Romans 10:17
Luke 8:15; Proverbs 8:34

Faith comes by means of hearing God's Word. As we receive the word of God into our lives, faith is strengthened and increased.

FAITH IS DIRECTED TOWARDS GOD AND HIS WORD

Mark 11:22

Our initial response of faith is directed toward God Himself. It is in His Person that we place our trust and confidence.

John 17:6–8

Our faith in God is also demonstrated through trusting in His Word. Who God is and what God says are inseparably linked together in a holy relationship.

Hebrews 11

Our faith is exercised with assurance that God is completely faithful to fulfill His covenant promises. God steadfastly stands behind all that He has said He would do.

FAITH ACCOMPLISHES SPECIFIC PURPOSES IN OUR LIVES

1 Peter 1:3
1 Peter 1:23–25
Hebrews 6:18–20

It is through faith that we are born again to a living hope. We are considered as dead in our sin and without hope apart from Christ. But through faith in Christ, we are made alive and given an eternal hope built upon God's faithfulness.

John 3:16
John 3:36
John 6:40
John 17:3

It is through faith that we are able to receive eternal life as promised by God. We are not only quickened with a new life for this present world but are assured of spending eternity in God's presence.

Romans 8:1–17
Galatians 5:16–25

It is by the exercise of faith that we are able to live our lives on earth in the power of the Holy Spirit. It is by living our lives in faith that we are able to be pleasing to our heavenly Father.

Romans 10:8–11

2 Corinthians 10:3–5
Ephesians 1:18–23
Revelation 12:10–11

The exercise of faith gives us power over Satan and the works of the kingdom of darkness. Where Satan has evil designs and plans for destruction, those who trust in Christ are able to use their faith to overcome these evil works.

John 14:12
1 Corinthians 12:4–13

It is through faith at work in our lives that we are able to do the very works of Jesus. He has promised that if we would believe in Him, we would do the same works that He did through His ministry on earth.

Galatians 5:2–25
2 Peter 1:5–11

Through the working of faith we are able to demonstrate the fruit of the Holy Spirit in our lives.

APPLICATION

Review the time in your own life when you turned to God and first exercised faith toward His promises for you. Describe some of the benefits you have realized in your life as a result of placing your confidence in God. In what areas of your life (family, friends, finances, and other areas) do you recognize the need for a greater measure of trust in God's provision?

CONCLUSION

Repentance is acknowledging that our ways are wrong in the sight of God, and turning away from them to the ways of the Lord. Faith is trusting God so that a relationship with Him is established. It is this living relationship based upon confident trust in His faithfulness that we learn His ways which lead to life.

It is Satan's ability to deceive us that makes self-will unreliable. By repenting of self-will and trusting God, we are freed from Satan's dominion. Faith is the positive step towards God's government and a new life of trusting God's provisions for our lives in His Kingdom.

LESSON 4 – RESPONDING IN WATER BAPTISM

PURPOSE

The act of water baptism is an essential part of our response in faith to the Gospel of the kingdom of God. This lesson will consider the importance of our obedience to Christ's command to be baptized and the results of that obedience in our walk.

GLOSSARY

Baptize – (Greek: *baptidzo*) – to immerse or submerge.

Immerse – to plunge into something that entirely surrounds or covers.

Submerge – to put under water.

ANALOGIES OF BAPTISM IN THE OLD TESTAMENT

Noah and the Ark

Genesis 6:14–18

Genesis 6:18–22

Genesis 6:17
Genesis 7:1–7

Genesis 7:17–24

Matthew 24:37–39

God commanded Noah to build an ark of great proportions into which he would lead his family as well as representative members of the animal kingdoms. The purpose of this ark was to provide a means of escape from the impending judgement of God that would come upon the earth.

God's judgement came upon the earth in the form of flood waters which covered the face of the earth, destroying all living creatures. The ark into which Noah entered through faith, in obedience to God, preserved Noah and all with him. The ark passed through the waters of God's judgement.

Genesis 8

Genesis 9:1–17

The old order of life with its evil was cut off under the judgement of God. Those who had been obedient to God were delivered from the judgement and emerged to a new life under God's leadership.

Moses and the Red Sea Crossing

Exodus 8:1

Exodus 14:21

God commanded Moses to lead His people out of the bondage of Egypt. In the course of their journey, they were pursued to the edge of the Red Sea by the armies of Pharaoh. Supernaturally, the Red Sea was opened by the power of God so that the children of Israel could pass through the water and cross over on dry land.

Exodus 14:26–31

Hebrews 11:29

The waters closed over the armies of Egypt and cut off their ability to pursue and dominate God's people. The waters were a form of God's judgement against a sinful order, delivering the Israelites from its access and control.

Exodus 15:26

After the Israelites had passed through the waters, they were free to pursue God's purpose under His direction by following His ways.

INSTANCES OF WATER BAPTISM IN THE NEW TESTAMENT

John the Baptist proclaimed a message of repentance to prepare the way for Jesus. He baptized those who had a repentant heart.

Jesus Himself, was baptized in water in order that He might fulfill all righteousness and that which was foretold concerning His life.

Those who responded to Peter's preaching on the day of Pentecost submitted themselves to the waters of baptism as they were commanded.

Those who responded to the message of Philip as he proclaimed Jesus Christ and His Kingdom were baptized.

Paul the apostle responded in obedience through baptism when he was converted to faith in Jesus Christ.

The Gentiles at the house of Cornelius were baptized when they heard the message of Christ and His Kingdom. It was through the obvious work of the Holy Spirit that the Gentiles were admitted into the new covenant through the waters of baptism, even as the Jews had been.

PAUL DEFINES BAPTISM AND ITS SIGNIFICANCE

Through water baptism, we are able to visibly identify with Jesus Christ in His death for our sins.

When we are submerged in water baptism, it is our identification with Christ in His death and burial. We are buried with Him in death by means of baptism.

Water baptism is a picture of our being united with Him by faith, and a statement that our old life has been crucified ... it's now dead and buried with Christ in His death.

When we are raised from the waters of baptism, we are declaring that as Jesus was raised from the dead by the power of God, so are we being raised to walk in a new life with Christ.

We no longer live by the standards and conduct of our former manner of living, but through God's power, we are able to crucify those deeds and live according to the will of God.

CONDITIONS WHICH MUST PRECEDE WATER BAPTISM

Before being baptized, we must hear the Gospel of the kingdom of God and recognize its demands.

We must obey the requirements of the Gospel through repenting of our sins and turn to God for the cleansing of our guilty conscience.

We must place our confidence and trust in the finished work of Jesus Christ, and the fact that His sacrifice was for each one of us as individuals.

GOD INTENDS CERTAIN RESULTS FROM WATER BAPTISM

Baptism shows that we have been transferred from the kingdom of Satan and his evil works into the glorious kingdom of God's Son.

Matthew 3:6

Mark 1:4

Joel 1:21
Matthew 3:13–17
Luke 3:21

Acts 2:41

Acts 8:12

Acts 9:17–18

Acts 10:48

Romans 6:3–5

Acts 2:14–36

Acts 2:37–38

1 Peter 3:21
Mark 16:15–16

Romans 6:3–13
Colossians 1:13

Romans 6:2
Romans 6:11

Colossians 1:9–14
Galatians 3:27

Deuteronomy 6:5
Mark 12:29–31

Colossians 2:11–15

Colossians 1:18–25
Matthew 28:18–20

Our lives are to reflect that we are now dead to the power of sin and are made alive to God to do His will and walk in His ways.

Our governmental allegiance changes as we yield our lives to Jesus Christ as Lord. He becomes our model for living. 'Clothing ourselves with Christ' becomes our goal.

Being freed from the power of self-centered living, we now set our affections upon God, loving Him with our heart, soul, mind, and strength.

Through public declaration through baptism of our conversion to Jesus Christ, we clearly identify our lives with Him. We are also identified with His Body, the Church, and His mission in the world.

APPLICATION

Study and discuss the Old Testament analogies given in this lesson. How do they speak to you of the results of obeying God in water baptism? Explain the spiritual transaction of 'changing governments'. How is water baptism an abiding sign to the believer of his or her change in kingdoms?

CONCLUSION

Water baptism is a clear declaration and testimony of our having yielded allegiance to Jesus Christ as Savior and Lord. It is an act of obedience, bringing the assurance of cleansing from an evil conscience through identification with the death, burial and resurrection of Jesus. It is the most basic step we must take as we rise to our new life in Christ.

LESSON 5 – BAPTISM IN THE HOLY SPIRIT: POWER FOR LIVING

PURPOSE

The same power of the Holy Spirit that revealed Christ to us and delivered us from sin is available to empower us for godly living.

This lesson will consider God's provision for us through the Holy Spirit, how to receive the infilling of the Holy Spirit, and what He will accomplish in the lives of those who receive this power.

GLOSSARY

Empower – to give official authority or legal power.

Filled – having received a full supply.

Promise – a declaration that one will do a specific task to the extent that it becomes the grounds of expectation.

GOD HAS GIVEN A SURE PROMISE

Isaiah 59:21
Ezra 39:29
Joel 2:28

John 16:7–15
Acts 1:8

Acts 2:1–39

Through the Old Testament prophets, God made a promise that He would send an outpouring of the Holy Spirit in the latter days. This visitation was to be a powerful manifestation of God's Spirit upon all who believed.

Jesus Christ, before He ascended to the right hand of God, promised to send forth the power of the Holy Spirit upon the disciples.

The promise was fulfilled on the day of Pentecost. The apostle Peter declared to all who witnessed this event that if they repented and were baptized, they too would receive the Holy Spirit.

Acts 19:1–7

God further used the apostle Paul to proclaim the promise of the Holy Spirit to the Gentile community.

RECEIVING THE BAPTISM IN THE HOLY SPIRIT

John 17:3–8
Acts 16:31

Acts 2:38

A most basic requirement in receiving the Holy Spirit is believing the Good News that God loves us and has demonstrated this love by giving His only begotten Son for our sake. It is through receiving Christ that we are able to have a right relationship with God.

Believing the Gospel, we are to repent of our sins and turn toward God, seeking His Kingdom in our lives.

The first command we have from Christ is to be baptized in water as a testimony of our identification with His death and burial for our sake. From water baptism, we rise to live a new life in Christ by the power of the Holy Spirit.

Acts 19:1–6

Romans 6:3–13
John 7:37–39

Through faith, we can expect to be filled with the Holy Spirit and power, just as He promised. In repentance, we turn from our old way of living to seek the Lord. Through the indwelling power of the Holy Spirit, we are able to live a new life in Christ.

SCRIPTURAL EVIDENCE OF HOLY SPIRIT BAPTISM

Acts 2:4

Acts 10:46
Romans 8:26
Acts 19:6

Acts 2:15–17

Speaking with 'other tongues' was normally present when individuals were baptized in the Holy Spirit in the Early Church. They offered praise and prayers to God in languages that they had not learned. This same evidence is regularly experienced by Christians today who are baptized in the Holy Spirit.

Prophesying by the Holy Spirit was also evident in the New Testament Church when the power of the Holy Spirit moved upon them. This was a supernatural speaking forth by the function of the Spirit in a known language.

Acts 1:8
Acts 4:29–31
Acts 9:22; Acts 14:3

Acts 13:52
Romans 14:17

A power to witness and proclaim the Gospel of the kingdom of God beyond normal human abilities was another manifestation of the Holy Spirit's power at work in the life of the Early Church.

A great sense of joy came upon all those who received the Holy Spirit. Wherever the Holy Spirit is at work, peace, joy, and righteousness are the resulting evidences.

THE HOLY SPIRIT WORKS IN AND THROUGH US

Acts 1:8
Acts 4:31–33
1 Corinthians 2:4
John 16:14
Galatians 5:18–23

1 Corinthians 12:4–11

John 16:14–15

John 14:16
John 14:26

Romans 8:26
Ephesians 6:18
John 15:7–8; John 16:26–27

Matthew 3:16–17
Ephesians 1:13–14

The Holy Spirit empowers us to be witnesses for Jesus Christ. Through His power we are able to bring glory to His Name and proclaim the kingdom of God.

The Holy Spirit will work in our lives to bring forth the fruit of a godly life.

The Holy Spirit will give gifts and tools which are necessary for the Church to accomplish God's purpose in the earth. By giving us the things that belong to Christ, we are able to be ambassadors for His ministry.

The Holy Spirit is a constant companion who faithfully guides us into truth.

The Holy Spirit assists and deepens our prayer life. He enables us to ask and receive from the Father those things that are necessary to fulfill His will.

The Holy Spirit is a seal and guaranty that we belong to the Lord and is a token of greater things yet to come.

APPLICATION

From the evidence in Scripture of baptism in the Holy Spirit, do you believe that you have had this experience? Identify several reasons you believe that it is important that every Christian be filled with the Holy Spirit. How will the 'fruit of the Spirit', as outlined in Galatians 5:18–23, change your relationships at home, church, and in the world?

CONCLUSION

The infilling of the Holy Spirit is a dynamic and distinct event in the life of the believer. By this means, God empowers us to become His witnesses. Through the Holy Spirit we are enabled to function in the spiritual realm, to be conformed to the image of Jesus and to extend His ministry in the earth.

LESSON 6 – THE NEW COVENANT FOUNDATION OF CHRIST'S KINGDOM

PURPOSE

It is essential for us to understand that the basic nature of our relationship to God is covenant. Our hope and security depends exclusively upon God's faithfulness to His promise in the new covenant of our Lord Jesus Christ. The ability to appropriate and enjoy the benefits of God's covenant is determined by our response of repentance, faith, and obedience.

His promise followed by our faith results in a covenant bond. We will examine the unique bond as the foundation for living life in the kingdom of God.

GLOSSARY

Covenant – (Hebrew: *berith*) – to bind or fetter.

Faithfulness – a firm adherence to promises (*Webster*).

Relationship – kinship, the state of being related.

TWO FORMS OF COVENANT IN SCRIPTURE

Genesis 21:22–34

Genesis 31:43–55

1 Samuel 11:1–4

Genesis 8:20
Genesis 15:1–21
Exodus 12:1–13
2 Samuel 23:5
Luke 22:14–20

Covenants may be established between men or equals with each being bound by an oath. Examples of this type of covenant bond can be seen in solemn arrangements between Abraham and Abimelech, Laban and Jacob, and David and Jonathan.

The biblical picture of God's covenant relationship between Himself and men is always a matter of the superior party extending covenant to the inferior party. Examples of this understanding of covenant are evident in God's relationship with Noah, Abraham, Moses, David and Jesus.

God originates His covenants and prescribes both the conditions and the rewards of His covenant promises. His covenant is effective in an individual's life only as that person agrees to the covenant and embraces the conditions established by God.

Jeremiah 31:31–40
Luke 22:14–20
Ephesians 2:11–18

The ultimate fulfillment of all of God's covenants is the new covenant of Jesus Christ and the Church.

COVENANT IS A BINDING TOGETHER INTO ONE LIFE AND ONE WILL

1 John 3:16
Deuteronomy 7:7–9

Hebrews 11:24–26
Revelation 12:11

The very heart and life of a covenant relationship is covenant love. God demonstrates this kind of love by seeking our highest good and benefit at His greatest expense. Covenant love is a love for others that is greater than the love of self.

Luke 5:1–11

The strength of covenant relationship is commitment. This quality of commitment comes in response to realizing the will of God. When Peter saw Jesus, he was able to see himself in proper perspective and, subsequently, to see the will of God. When Peter saw the God's will as the ultimate issue, he left all to do God's will.

John 6:37–40; John 7:16–17
John 17:10–11
Ephesians 2:14–16

Commitment to other members of Christ's Body, the Church, is the result of God's will and His direction.

2 Timothy 2:11–13

Leviticus 7:11–21

Sacrifice is always associated with covenant relationships revealed in Scripture. Because independent wills are the cause of separation, they must be put to death. Sacrifice indicates one's willingness to die in order to remain faithful and to preserve the overseeing value. It is also symbolic that life is being given to benefit the other covenant member.

OUR RESPONSIBILITY IN THE NEW COVENANT IS PERSONAL OBEDIENCE TO JESUS CHRIST

Exodus 19:3–6

Joshua 1:1–8

Romans 6:11–18

Jeremiah 31:31–34

Every covenant in Scripture contains responsibilities associated with promised blessings. It is necessary to walk in obedience to those responsibilities if one is to realize the covenant promises.

Receiving a covenant necessarily means that we are agreeing to the responsibilities associated with that covenant.

Commitment to God is demonstrated by commitment to His covenant and the demands He has defined in that covenant.

APPLICATION

Define the difference between a covenant and a contract.

Describe the role a man or woman fulfills in the course of establishing a covenant bond with God.

How can one apply the New Covenant of Jesus Christ in their daily life?

CONCLUSION

Covenant thought and living are no longer prominent factors in modern culture. For the Church of Jesus Christ to understand her foundations and mission, covenant thought and life must be restored to proper perspective. Covenant bonds are the cohesive factors that bind the individual to God's provisions and the members of His Church to one another.

LESSON 7 – OBEDIENCE TO CHRIST THE KING

PURPOSE

Our purpose in this lesson will be to examine the importance of obedience to Jesus Christ as Lord and King. By the act of repentance and exercising faith towards God, we turn from the kingdom of darkness ruled by Satan and enter the kingdom of God. Jesus Christ has been established by God our Father as the Lord and Ruler in His Kingdom.

Entering the kingdom of God now means that we have a new King Whom we serve, and obedience to His commands is the guiding standard for living our daily lives under His reign.

GLOSSARY

Example – someone or something that serves as a pattern.

Imitator – one who follows a pattern, model or example.

Obedience – the act of conforming to the wishes, commands or standards of another.

OBEDIENCE TO GOD IS OUR STANDARD FOR LIVING

Genesis 2:15–17

Exodus 20:12

Deuteronomy 6:1–9
Deuteronomy 13:4

Genesis 2:15–17

God, as Sovereign Creator, has the right and ability to say how we should live. After He created Adam, He required obedience to His commands as the means of receiving life and blessing.

The Law or Ten Commandments were given by God through Moses in order to benefit and bless His people. Obedience to these commands were necessary to secure His blessings.

The result of failing to follow His command in preference for self-will was separation from God and death.

OBEDIENCE TO JESUS CHRIST IS THE NEW TESTAMENT STANDARD FOR LIVING

Matthew 6:33

Matthew 5:17
Romans 10:4
Galatians 6:2

Matthew 17:1–5

Matthew 28:16–20

Jesus instructed the disciples that their foremost need in life was to seek first the kingdom of God and right standing before His presence.

Jesus Christ is the fulfillment of the Old Testament Law, and it is now the 'Law of Christ' which governs our lives in the kingdom of God.

When Jesus was transfigured before the disciples, God revealed Jesus to be the fulfillment of the Law and prophets under the Old Covenant. Now God calls for obedience to Christ as His new order.

Jesus concluded His earthly ministry by calling for obedience to His commands as the basis for extending His mission into all the world.

OBEDIENCE TO CHRIST IS MOTIVATED BY LOVE

John 14:15

John 15:10

John 15:10
1 John 5:2–3

Ephesians 5:1–2

Jesus emphasized that the only appropriate response of love for Him was obedience to His words.

The love which Jesus had for the Father was demonstrated through His obedience to the Father's will.

Our love for Jesus and our desire to abide in His love will be demonstrated through obedience to His commands.

Imitating the example we have in Jesus' obedience to the Father is our guiding rule for obeying the commands He has given to us.

GODLY LEADERS PROVIDE GOOD EXAMPLES

1 Corinthians 10:31–33

1 Corinthians 4:15–16

Hebrews 13:7, 17

The apostle Paul called attention to his own life and ministry as an example for younger disciples to follow in their desire to obey Jesus.

Our heavenly Father has provided earthly examples who can assist us in more clearly following Christ's own example.

These earthly examples do not replace Christ as our model, but serve to point us to His example as our guiding standard.

APPLICATION

Identify ways you can fulfill the commands of Jesus in your daily life during the days ahead.

Can you identify an earthly example that has helped you to more clearly follow the Lord Jesus?

Write out, in a few words, areas in which you believe that Christ is speaking to you about obedience to His commands in your life.

CONCLUSION

The evidence that we truly love God is reflected in our obedience to His commands. Jesus is our foremost example of what it means to love God with all of our heart, soul, mind, and strength. We are to follow His example as the guiding rule for daily life and conduct. We have also been given earthly leaders whose lives we can model in our efforts to more clearly follow in the steps of Jesus.

LESSON 8 – WORSHIPPING THROUGH CHRIST THE KING

PURPOSE

The most fundamental need of the human heart is to draw near to God in adoration and worship. Sin and rebellion created a separation from God which made true worship impossible. It is through the shed blood of Christ and His sacrifice for us that we are restored to right relationship with God. With this new relationship, the ability to enter the presence of God with worship and adoration was restored.

It is the purpose of this lesson to consider our place in worship and some of the important aspects of offering praise and thanksgiving to God.

GLOSSARY

Adoration – the act of regarding with reverent admiration and devotion.

Praise – to glorify or exalt.

Worship – to regard with extravagant respect, honor and devotion; attributing worth.

GOD DESIRES WHOLEHEARTED WORSHIP

Exodus 20:1–6

Deuteronomy 6:5

Genesis 35:2–3
Exodus 20:24–26
Exodus 25:8

Proverbs 11:19
Ezekiel 18:4
Romans 5:12

Leviticus 4:20
Leviticus 8:34
Leviticus 10:17
Leviticus 14:21

Leviticus 17:11
Romans 5:9–11

When God gave the Law to Israel through Moses, He set forth guidelines for life and conduct. The first of these commandments indicate His interest in preserving a proper relationship of worship with His people.

God made provision for a place of worship for those whose hearts were turned towards Him in adoration.

Sin and rebellion resulted in separation from the presence of a holy God. The penalty for sin against God was death.

In His covenant love, God made provision for a substitutionary sacrifice to make it possible for sinful man to approach Him. The spotless sacrifice was offered in the place of the guilty party.

The shedding of the blood of the sacrifice satisfied God's righteous demands. Through the substitutionary sacrifice for the guilty party, fellowship was restored and the ability to approach God in worship was recovered.

JESUS WAS THE ULTIMATE SACRIFICE

Hebrews 10:1–12

Hebrews 9:11–14

Hebrews 7:23–25

Through the shedding of His own blood for our sake, Jesus Christ forever satisfied the requirements of a Holy God.

Jesus, having been raised from the dead by God's power, precedes us into God's eternal presence and there functions as our High Priest and Advocate.

1 Peter 2:4–10

The perfect sacrifice of Jesus has opened the way for us to approach the presence of the living God and to function as priests unto God by offering Him our praise and worship.

WE ENTER GOD'S PRESENCE WITH THANKSGIVING

Colossians 1:12–14

Psalm 100
Psalm 107:1, 15

When we exercise an attitude of thanksgiving, our minds will become focused upon God and His provisions in Christ.

Thanksgiving for Who God is and what He has done is the context and atmosphere of all true worship.

An attitude of thanksgiving opens our minds and hearts to be filled with the light of His presence.

PRAISE IS RECOGNITION OF GOD'S ATTRIBUTES

Psalm 150
Psalm 95
Hebrews 13:15
Psalm 29
Psalm 136

2 Chronicles 20
Acts 16:16–34

Scripture reveals praise as being demonstrated through physical acts of adoration.

Verbalizing the divine characteristics of God is also an integral part of offering praise to God.

God's power is released when God's people outwardly extol Him and magnify the divine attributes of God in their worship.

WORSHIP ASCRIBES VALUE AND GREATNESS TO GOD

Psalm 95:1–6
Ezra 44:16

Ezra 44:15–19

1 Peter 4:10–11

Hebrews 10:8–14

1 Peter 2:5

Worship moves from focusing on the deeds and attributes of the Lord to devotion towards the Lord Himself in a priestly function.

We have been called to replace the ministry of the high priest in the inner court under the old covenant. We are called to this role of priestly ministry under the new covenant.

We no longer offer animal sacrifices, as this has forever been settled by the blood of Christ. We do stand in the presence of God to present spiritual sacrifices of worship that are pleasing to Him and which offer Him a sweet smelling savor.

APPLICATION

Describe what you can bring to the Lord that would minster to Him and be a source of refreshment to Him.

It is awesome to think we have been created with the capacity to bless God. How can you do this in the practical areas of daily living?

Describe the similarities between the high priest in the old covenant and our role as priest under the new covenant.

CONCLUSION

Our ultimate calling in this life and in the next is to be worshippers of God. Learning those things which go to make up our priestly roles in praise and worship is one of our most important responsibilities in the kingdom of God. The skills of gratitude, praise, and worship should be progressively developing in every area of our lives and characterize our daily walk in devotion to Jesus.

LESSON 9 – PRAYER THROUGH CHRIST THE KING

PURPOSE

The great salvation of God revealed in Jesus Christ has opened the way for us to be regenerated into a right relationship with God. By repentance, obedience through water baptism, and placing our trust in Him, we enter the kingdom of God. The foundation for life in His Kingdom is a living relationship with God through Christ.

Personal communion and fellowship with God in prayer is both a privilege and a responsibility as heirs of His Kingdom. We will examine the importance of this role in our daily walk.

GLOSSARY

Devotion – an act of prayer or supplication.

Intercession – to meet with, to come between.

Meditation – to reflect, contemplate or ponder.

SEEKING HIS FACE

Jeremiah 29:12–13
Deuteronomy 4:29
Isaiah 55:6

2 Chronicles 7:14
Luke 11:10

1 Chronicles 16:11, 35
Psalm 34:15–17

God has promised that He would draw near and reveal Himself to those who would call upon Him and seek Him with all their hearts.

God has promised that He would intervene in our behalf if we would approach Him with an attitude of humility and repentance.

We should seek the Lord as the source of our strength for living and deliverance from our enemies.

JESUS PROMISED THAT GOD WOULD HEAR AND ANSWER

Matthew 7:7
Mark 11:24
Luke 18:1

Matthew 18:19–20

John 14:13–14

John 15:7
John 15:16
John 16:24
Luke 11:9

Jesus, by His own example and teaching, called for diligence in prayer.

Jesus assured His followers that our heavenly Father will give His attention and respond to those who would gather and agree in His name.

Jesus promised that He would grant what was asked in His own name . . . those things which are in accord with His will.

Jesus taught that vital relationship with Him was a key to seeing answered prayer. Abiding in Him, and His Word abiding in us, is the foundation for effective prayer. This is the basis for confidence that our Heavenly Father hears and answers.

Luke 22:39–41
Mark 6:46; Luke 11:1
Matthew 14:23
Matthew 26:36–44

John 17

Matthew 6:9

Matthew 6:10
Matthew 6:33

Matthew 6:11
Matthew 7:7–11

Matthew 6:12
Luke 17:4
Ephesians 4:32

Matthew 6:13
Proverbs 3:5–6
Ephesians 6:10–18

Matthew 6:13

Psalm 57:7–11

JESUS IS OUR ULTIMATE EXAMPLE IN PRAYER

Throughout His life and ministry, Jesus was seen to be in continual prayer. When Jesus prayed, it was with intensity and prevailing requests. Jesus is our ultimate example in intercessory prayer.

JESUS INSTRUCTED THE DISCIPLES HOW TO PRAY

Hallowing or revering the Lord's name in worship is our appropriate first response in prayer.

Seeking His Kingdom and His will on earth should be our primary motivation in prayer.

Inquiring of the Lord for our daily bread reflects our dependence upon Him to meet our practical and spiritual needs in everyday living.

Receiving and extending forgiveness should be the natural outgrowth of our awareness of how much God has provided for us in His great salvation.

Trusting the Lord for guidance that will deliver us from the works of Satan is the basis of our confidence and the armor which He provides gives us the protection we need.

Our prayers should conclude with thanksgiving, recognition, and praise to God for His great name and His faithfulness to meet all our needs.

APPLICATION

Use the guidelines which Jesus established in His model prayer to direct a time of daily prayer for you.

What opportunities do you have to gather with other Christians to 'agree together' in the Lord's name?

Recognize specific answers to prayers and look for an occasion to give public testimony to God's faithfulness in meeting your needs.

CONCLUSION

Jesus Christ has opened the way for us to have a living relationship with God as our heavenly Father. He has promised that He would personally abide within us and has now sent forth the person of the Holy Spirit to empower us for our daily lives. It is the privilege and responsibility of prayer that enables us to enjoy the benefits of this relationship with God and the provisions of His Kingdom.

LESSON 10 – LEARNING TO HEAR HIS VOICE

PURPOSE

Life in the kingdom of God involves right relationship with God and the active pursuit of His will in our daily lives. Guidance is the link between the King and His people. He has promised to direct our steps if we would trust in Him. This lesson will consider the important subject of recognizing His voice and following His guidance as we seek to fulfill God's will.

GLOSSARY

Direction – instructions about where to go.

Guidance – the act of giving direction, counsel, or supervision.

Leading – going before those who follow; Jesus not only advises, He goes before us.

GOD'S COVENANT COMMITMENT TO OUR WELFARE

Genesis 2:15–17

Deuteronomy 29:9
2 Chronicles 31:21
Psalm 1:1–3

Joel 1:7–8
Genesis 39:1–3

In the beginning, God prescribed guidelines for living that were designed for the welfare of those He had created.

The purpose of the Law under the old covenant was intended to lead to prosperity and life under His government.

God desires to bring His people into the place of blessing and success. His means of accomplishing this is obedience to His standards and guidelines.

GOD'S COVENANT COMMITMENT TO DIRECT OUR STEPS

Genesis 12:1

Exodus 13:21–22

Psalm 5:8
Psalm 27:11
Psalm 25:5–9

Proverbs 3:5–6
Psalm 23:2

God not only calls His people, but is committed to show them where to go.

God led Israel by becoming personally involved in directing their steps.

When David placed his trust in God through an attitude of dependence, God directed his steps.

Our confidence for today and the future is based upon God's faithfulness to direct our steps. As we place our trust in Him, we can be confident of His leadership.

THE HOLY SPIRIT LEADS UNDER THE NEW COVENANT

John 14:26
John 16:13

Acts 13:2; Acts 13:4
Acts 11:5–12

Jesus assured the disciples that after His departure, the Holy Spirit would be sent as a guide to them.

The book of Acts gives accounts of the many ways the Holy Spirit gave specific and personal direction to the Early Church.

Romans 14:17
Galatians 5:5
Galatians 5:16–18
Galatians 5:22–25

Romans 8

The apostle Paul taught that the kingdom of God can only be realized through the work of the Holy Spirit. It is 'by' the Spirit that we are able to 'see' the Kingdom ... and it is 'in' the Spirit that we are able to experience the Kingdom.

It is clear in Scripture that the normal Christian life involved being filled with and led by the Holy Spirit.

THE BIBLE CONFIRMS THE HOLY SPIRIT'S DIRECTION

2 Timothy 3:16–17
Acts 1:16

2 Peter 1:21
Jeremiah 36:2
Ezekiel 1:3

Revelation 2:7
1 Corinthians 2:13

Hebrews 3:7–8
Hebrews 4:12

The same Holy Spirit that leads us today is the One Who inspired the Scriptures in the beginning.

It is the Holy Spirit that moved upon the ancient prophets, giving to them God's Word and showing them things yet to come.

This same Holy Spirit is at work today in the Church of Jesus Christ, delivering God's Word through His servants and through direct revelation.

The Holy Spirit and the Word of God as contained in the Scriptures are in complete harmony concerning the will of God.

APPLICATION

Describe how you believe the Word of God is used in our lives to determine God's will. In what ways have you experienced the leading of the Holy Spirit in your life in recent days.

Identify areas in your life where you need personal direction and specifically commit them to God in prayer. Consider what Scripture says about these areas and look for the Holy Spirit's direction.

CONCLUSION

God our heavenly Father is committed to give us personal direction and establish standards by which we may know His will. Entrance into the kingdom of God through repentance, water baptism, and faith paves the way for a new life under the Lordship of Jesus Christ. The clear guidance of the inspired Word of God as contained in the Scriptures and the leading of the Holy Spirit are the normal means that God uses to direct our steps into His will.

LESSON 11 – DISCOVERING OUR PLACE IN THE KINGDOM OF GOD

PURPOSE

The kingdom of God is made up of all those who have recognized God's Sovereignty through Jesus Christ. The citizens of the Kingdom have been called by Christ to relate and function together in the Church, which is His Body, in the earth. We are, therefore, called to be Church people and function together to fulfill His purpose in the earth.

Part of the work of the Holy Spirit is to lead us into the local church and place us there in functional ministry for the building up of the Church. The Church then becomes an expression of Kingdom life in a community and the setting where Christians find placement.

GLOSSARY

Ability – competence in doing or performing.

Calling – urging or bidding to a particular course of action.

Church – those who are called out of the world to be together under Christ's headship and to fulfill His purpose in a locality as well as the world.

Kingdom – those who relate to Christ's Sovereignty and reign.

Purpose – an object or end to be attained.

THE HOLY SPIRIT SETS US INTO CHRIST'S BODY

1 Corinthians 12:13

When we believe in Christ and repent of our sins, it is the work of the Holy Spirit that baptizes us into the Church of Jesus Christ.

1 Corinthians 12:12

There is diversity and variety regarding placement in Christ's Kingdom.

1 Corinthians 12:14–17

Each part of God's Kingdom is vital and necessary to the purposes of God in the earth.

THE HOLY SPIRIT IMPARTS GIFTS FOR SERVICE

1 Corinthians 12:7

God gives gifts of the Spirit to individuals for the good of all.

1 Corinthians 12:11, 18

It is the Holy Spirit who determines, according to His wisdom, how the gifts are distributed.

1 Corinthians 12:4–6

The gifts which are apportioned to us in the Holy Spirit are supernatural in nature and not to be attributed to natural abilities.

1 Corinthians 14:1

We should earnestly seek the gifts of the Spirit, especially those areas that we believe that God has called us to steward.

GOD'S PLACEMENT AND GIFTS ARE FOR SERVICE

Ephesians 4:16
Romans 12:5

Ephesians 4:12
1 Corinthians 14:3

1 Corinthians 13

The successful function of each member is essential to the success of all other members of Christ's Body.

Every Christian is being prepared by the Holy Spirit for works of service which will build up the whole Church.

The proper motivation for the development of our place in Christ's Kingdom is the love of God at work in our hearts.

GOD PROVIDES LEADERS TO HELP US WITH OUR CALL

Ephesians 4:11–16

The governmental gifts which Jesus appoints in the Church are established to prepare God's people for effective service and ministry.

The end result of effective service is the building up of the entire Church towards the unity of the faith and the knowledge of the Son of God.

Through the exercise of godly leadership, we are able to discover more clearly our place and role in God's economy.

APPLICATION

What areas of gifting do you recognize in your own life as the work of the Holy Spirit?

Are there areas in your life that are recognized and affirmed by those around you?

How would you describe the long range purpose of God in your life?

CONCLUSION

Being born again into a new life in Christ involves the practical implication of how we will now live. The work of the Holy Spirit is to place us into the body of Christ and to equip us for works of service. Our responsibility as heirs to His Kingdom is to seek out His will and the gifts He has given to us for fulfilling His calling upon our lives. As each believer finds his place within the Church, the Church in turn is to equip and strengthen the believers as they function out in the world. Much more will be said about this in later sections of this book.

LESSON 12 – THE CALL TO STEWARDSHIP

PURPOSE

Entrance into the kingdom of God involves both privileges and responsibilities. We have been given the privilege of being 'joint-heirs' with Christ in the kingdom of God, and the blessing of a living relationship with God as our heavenly Father.

The Holy Spirit also has placed us within the Church and equipped us for works of service. We have been entrusted with God's resources to utilize in our personal lives and for the extension of the kingdom of God in the earth. This lesson will examine the need to be responsible stewards of that which has been entrusted to us by the Lord.

GLOSSARY

Authority – power to influence or command thought, opinion, or behavior (*Webster*).

Faithful – steadfast in affection or loyalty; firm in adherence to promises.

Steward – one appointed to manage the affairs and belongings of another.

Stewardship – a sphere of responsibility for which one must give account.

MANKIND WAS CREATED TO STEWARD

Genesis 1:26–31

When God created the heavens and the earth, He gave man the authority to rule over every aspect of creation.

Genesis 2:19–20

When God delegated Adam and Eve with authority to oversee His resources, they became stewards of His works.

Genesis 2:15–17

God established definite boundaries and guidelines for responsible usage of all that had been provided for mankind.

Genesis 1:1
Psalm 24:1

Stewardship is based upon the realization that God owns all things.

Good stewardship is dependent upon a proper understanding of our responsibility toward all of the resources God has intrusted to us.

Psalm 24:1

We have been entrusted with the resources of our earthly environment. Abuse of natural resources will have consequences for which we will give account.

Romans 5:17

The righteousness of God has been given to us to steward. We are to guard the gift of righteousness which has been imparted to us through Christ.

Ephesians 2:1–10

The grace of God has been poured into our lives for us to channel or direct toward others. We have not received God's grace merely for our consumption but also to extend to those around us.

1 Corinthians 12:7–11

The gifts of the Holy Spirit have been given to God's people for service. These gifts are given to us for the purpose of edifying others.

Colossians 3:17

The name of Jesus has been given to God's people to represent His authority. We are to properly use His Name to extend His Kingdom.

Acts 4:32–34
1 Peter 4:10

Personal possessions and wealth have been provided to extend His Kingdom. God's prosperity in our lives is to abound in the extension of His Kingdom.

STEWARDSHIP REQUIRES GODLY CHARACTER

Psalm 100:3
John 17:2–4

It is essential for a steward to recognize the owner and His rights concerning those things He has entrusted to the steward.

Matthew 21:33–41
Genesis 3:1–13

A good steward must develop the quality of loyalty. When Adam was disobedient to God's commands, his unfaithfulness demonstrated disloyalty to the One Who had entrusted him with His works.

Philippians 2:8
2 Kings 5

A good steward must learn discipline if he is to properly manage the things of another. Gehazi is an example of what occurs when one forsakes self-discipline, yields to greed, and loses his opportunity.

A good steward must learn obedience expressed in the form of careful hearing and attention to detail concerning the things of another.

Matthew 21:33–41

Productivity is a quality which must be developed in the life of a steward. This involves wisely using what has been provided to yield greater fruitfulness.

1 Samuel 17:34–36
1 Timothy 6:20

A good steward must properly care for and protect what has been entrusted to him.

GOOD STEWARDSHIP WILL BE PRODUCTIVE

Matthew 25:14–30
John 15:1–2

Our heavenly Father intends that we bear much fruit for His Kingdom. It is His nature to produce and increase.

John 15:3

God sends His Word to us as a means of pruning our lives in order that we may bear fruit.

John 15:5–7

It is through an abiding relationship with Jesus that we can realize the kind of fruit that God requires. It does not depend upon our initiative but upon Him as our life source.

John 15:8
Romans 7:4
Philippians 1:11

God is glorified through our lives when we bear fruit in His name. It is evidence of His grace and life at work in us.

John 15:8

Through faithfulness to His Word, we are able to demonstrate that we are the disciples of Jesus Christ.

GOOD STEWARDSHIP WILL BE PROMOTED

Luke 19:17

When we show ourselves to be trustworthy in small matters, it is pleasing to God.

Luke 19:11–19

When we are faithful in the management of His resources, God is able to cause us to increase.

Luke 19:20–25

A dishonoring attitude towards God and mismanagement of resources will provoke God's displeasure and discipline.

Luke 19:26

The reward of faithful stewardship is both an increase in capacity for responsibility and the enlargement of His blessing.

APPLICATION

Describe areas of your life, besides finance, that you believe are part of good stewardship.

In what areas of your life do you need to review priorities in order to be a better steward?

Identify gifts which you believe have been deposited in your life by the Holy Spirit and how you can envision being a good steward over those areas.

CONCLUSION

The subject of stewardship most often is seen related to the area of financial responsibility. The issue of good stewardship covers the entire spectrum of what has been entrusted to us by God. This includes time, talents, family, material, resources, spiritual giftings, finances, and everything else we might identify as belonging to our personal lives. Managing those things in a manner that glorifies God and extends His Kingdom will require fruitfulness.

LESSON 13 – STEWARDSHIP AND FINANCIAL RESPONSIBILITY

PURPOSE

We are called to a life of fruitfulness and productivity in the kingdom of God. Being faithful stewards of God's resources, gifts, and callings is essential to the success of our role in His Kingdom.

The proper management of finances and material resources is a vital expression of good stewardship. It is also an essential requirement for the ongoing support of the ministries in the church which are extending the kingdom of God. This lesson will consider the important role of financial faithfulness to God with what He has entrusted to us.

GLOSSARY

Honor – the act of esteeming attributes or recognizing worth.

Firstfruits – the first portion or gain.

Responsibility – moral, legal, or mental accountability.

Tithe – one tenth of one's income which is due to God, the owner of all things.

HONORING GOD WITH OUR 'FIRSTFRUITS'

Genesis 1:1

Genesis 4:4

When we bring our tithes before the Lord, it is an act of recognition that He is the Author and Owner of all things.

Abel offered up some of the first portions of his flock to God as an expression of worship and honor.

Genesis 14:18–21

Abram gave a tenth of everything to the Lord's representative, demonstrating his gratitude and worship to God for His faithfulness.

Genesis 28:20–22

Jacob recognized that his success depended upon God's favor. He acknowledged God as the source of his provision by vowing to give a tenth of all his increase to God.

The spirit of the tithe was evident in these acts of giving prior to the requirement of a tithe under the Law.

THE TITHE SUSTAINED THE LEVITICAL PRIESTHOOD

Leviticus 27:30–34

Numbers 18:21–26

The requirement of the tithe was established under Moses as an act of sanctifying God's portion of all their increase.

The tribe of Levi, serving as priests under the Old Testament order, received the tithe offerings as their inheritance and provision.

Numbers 18:21

The tithe was the means of sustaining the living ministries which were dedicated to the service of the sanctuary.

1 Timothy 5:17–18

Those who were committed to the teaching of God's Word and His ways were cared for from the tithes of the people.

1 Chronicles 9:26–29
Numbers 18:26

The Levites were appointed as custodians and administrators of the tithes and offerings.

TITHING SERVES AS A GUIDE FOR CHRISTIAN GIVING

Matthew 5:17

Jesus said that He did not come to do away with the Law, but rather to fulfill it. The Law was perfectly fulfilled as He lived His life and ministry in obedience to the Father.

Jeremiah 31:33

Hebrews 8:10

Those who receive Christ and His perfect sacrifice have Christ living in them. The Law of God is now written on their hearts by the Holy Spirit. The Christian's motive for obedience to God's ways is the love of God, not a legal requirement.

Romans 8:2–4
Hebrews 8:6

Under the new and better covenant established in Christ, the law of love and generosity supersedes the requirements of the Old Testament Law.

Matthew 5:16–20

2 Corinthians 9:7–8

The spirit of giving under the new covenant should at least fulfill the legal requirement of the Law and go beyond to reflect grateful hearts who seek financial responsibility towards the kingdom of God.

Hebrews 7:5

Matthew 23:23

Tithes and offerings under the new covenant provide support for the church's ministries as it did for Levites under the old. The local church is the place where tithes and offering are received under the new covenant.

APPLICATION

Explain the relationship between support of the Levitical priesthood in the Old Testament and how we support people in ministry today.

Consider what percentage of your income is given in the form of tithes and offerings. Is this in keeping with what you believe to be revealed in the Scriptures concerning financial responsibility?

How is Old Testament understanding of the tithe applicable to the New Testament Church?

CONCLUSION

Finances and material resources are necessary for the support of the Church and related ministries which are actively extending the kingdom of God in the earth. It is through financial faithfulness on the part of God's people that these ministries are able to function and fulfill their mission.

LESSON 14 – WE ARE AMBASSADORS OF THE KING

PURPOSE

Our citizenship in the kingdom of God involves the responsibility of properly representing Christ and His interest to the world around us. In that sense, we are ambassadors of Jesus Christ and His Kingdom.

This lesson will examine the origins and character of this role and how it serves to extend Christ's Kingdom in the earth.

GLOSSARY

Ambassador – an authorized representative or messenger.

Representative – one who is delegated to speak or act in behalf of another.

GOD DELEGATED HIS REPRESENTATIVES IN THE EARTH

Genesis 1:28–31

Genesis 2:19

After God created Adam, He commissioned him to rule in His stead over all aspects of creation.

Adam was 'involved' as God's ambassador to creation when he named the living creatures. God gave Adam the ability to exercise initiative in ruling the earth.

Genesis 1:28

Adam was also invested with the authority to rule under God's direction and commands.

Genesis 2:20–24

When God gave Eve as a 'helpmeet' to assist Adam, order and structure were established in order to extend His rule and purpose.

REBELLION RESULTED IN THE LOSS OF POSITION

Genesis 3

When Adam and Eve disobeyed God's command, it produced a separation from the presence of God and estrangement with His holy nature.

Genesis 3:17–19

The effects of this 'fall' were revealed in a limited ability to rule on behalf of God's interests.

Galatians 3:19–24

The Law was given to show mankind where he fell short and point men to Christ the Messiah who would come as God's faithful representative in the earth.

GOD'S ORIGINAL PLAN WAS RESTORED IN CHRIST

John 17:1–8

Jesus Christ lived without sin and disobedience in this life and was therefore perfectly qualified to be God's representative.

John 8:28–29

He taught that His purpose and mission in life was to do the Father's will and, consequently, represent Him in the earth.

John 5:19–27

The only things which Jesus did during His earthly ministry were what He could see the Father 'doing'. As a result, He proved to be a faithful ambassador of God's government.

John 20:21

In the kingdom of God, we are called to be God's representatives in the same way that Jesus demonstrated by His example.

2 Peter 3:18

Our ability to stand as God's ambassadors in the earth can only be accomplished by God's grace revealed in Christ.

WE ARE COMMISSIONED AS CHRIST'S AMBASSADORS

We have been sent in His name to represent all that His name implies.

Matthew 28:19–20

We have been given His authority to execute His interests throughout the earth.

Matthew 28:18–20

Mark 16:15–20

We have been given His power to effect His work and ministry.

John 14:26
John 15:26

We have been given His Spirit in order to reflect His character and attitude to all with whom we come in contact.

APPLICATION

Consider practical ways by which you can serve as an ambassador of Jesus Christ in your work or school environment.

Describe a recent occasion where you had opportunity to function as Christ's representative.

What area of your daily life do you feel most challenged to develop your testimony as an ambassador of Christ's Kingdom?

CONCLUSION

Citizenship in the kingdom of God includes the wondrous and awesome fact that God has given to each of us the ability to be His personal representative in the earth. Functioning as His ambassadors in all spheres of life is one of the primary roles we must seek to fulfill as we pursue the will of God. We have not only been given the call to be His representatives, but also the authority of His name and the power of His Spirit to fulfill the task. Seeking first the kingdom of God will mean establishing the Lordship of Jesus in our own personal lives and then properly representing Him to those spheres of life where we have been directed by the Holy Spirit.

LESSON 15 – WE ARE AMBASSADORS OF CHRIST'S CHARACTER

PURPOSE

We are ambassadors or representatives of Jesus Christ. This means that we must reflect His character if we are going to carry His message. His reputation in the world is directly affected by our lives and conduct. This lesson will examine the qualities of Christ's own character that are produced in our lives by the Holy Spirit.

GLOSSARY

Character – qualities impressed by nature or habit on someone that distinguishes them from others.

Flesh – (Greek: *sarx*) – can mean the state of the unrenewed or unregenerate mind.

JESUS IS THE MODEL OF DIVINE CHARACTER

John 14:5–11

Jesus demonstrated integrity, a quality of being undivided or complete. His life was consistent with His words.

John 17:4

Jesus was loyal, the quality of being faithful to one's government, cause, or mission. Jesus was loyal to His Father, His Father's will, and His Father's mission.

John 17:4

Jesus was faithful. He was steadfast in affection and allegiance. He demonstrated faithfulness by completing the task assigned to Him at the expense of His own life.

Matthew 11:29

Jesus was gentle in His dealings with those under heavy burdens. He was full of compassion and lacking in harshness.

Matthew 19:17

Jesus reflected goodness. This was evident in that all He accomplished was characterized by excellence and virtue.

Luke 10:33–34

Jesus acted in kindness, a quality of compassion and a forbearing nature. He pointed to the need for this quality in His reference to the Good Samaritan.

Mark 8:17–21

Jesus was patient, a quality of steadfastness in the face of opposition, difficulty, or adversity. Jesus was patient and longsuffering in His dealings with the disciples.

Matthew 4:3–11

Jesus exercised self-control. This involves restraint over one's impulses, desires, and emotions. Jesus demonstrated self-control in the face of temptation.

John 13:1
John 15:9
John 15:13

Jesus revealed God's divine love – *agape* love. The nature of God moved Jesus to have compassion without selfish motives. Jesus demonstrated this ultimate expression of love by laying down His life for our sake. He sought our good at His expense.

THE HOLY SPIRIT IMPARTS CHRIST'S CHARACTER

John 16:13

The Holy Spirit was sent into the world to guide the followers of Christ into all truth.

John 16:13

It is the mission of the Holy Spirit to faithfully take those things pertaining to Christ and reveal them to His disciples.

John 16:14

Those things which are Christ's are brought into the lives of those who are joined to Christ.

Galatians 5:22–25

The result of this revealing work of the Holy Spirit is the manifestation of Christ's character in our lives. This is seen in the form of the fruit of the Spirit.

WE ARE TO PUT TO DEATH OUR FLESHLY NATURE

Matthew 16:24

Jesus taught that if any one would be His follower, they must be prepared to deny the natural inclinations of the flesh.

Romans 8

The apostle Paul, by the inspiration of the Holy Spirit, commanded that we put to death the works of sinful flesh.

Galatians 5:13–26

The power of the Holy Spirit enables us to deny the deeds of fleshly works in order that the fruit of the Holy Spirit might be released in our lives.

WE ARE CALLED TO REPRESENT CHRIST'S CHARACTER

John 17

The foundation of Christ's earthly ministry was His character. The life He lived, in keeping with God's will, was the basis of His credibility.

John 17:18

Jesus sent us into the world in the same manner and by the same standard that He was sent into the world by the Father.

John 17:21–26

The revelation of Christ's character in us is a primary means for the world to see Jesus today.

APPLICATION

Consider ways that you can better represent Christ's character in your response to your neighbors.

What areas do you sense that the Holy Spirit is at work in your life to manifest the character of Jesus more fully?

Describe someone you believe is a true ambassador of Christ in that they reflect the character of Jesus. In what ways?

CONCLUSION

Being an ambassador of Jesus Christ and His Kingdom on the earth involves being a good representative of not just Who Jesus is by virtue of position, but also Who He is as a person. His character reflects the very nature of God and it was for the revelation of God's nature that He came on earth as our example. It is our responsibility to follow the model of Jesus and seek to emulate His own example before the world around us. In so doing, we become ambassadors to this present generation.

LESSON 16 – WE ARE AMBASSADORS OF CHRIST'S LOVE

PURPOSE

We are called to represent Christ in all that He is – His character, His love, and His power. Christ is holy but He is also compassionate. Were it not for His compassion, His holy nature would only judge us. Jesus, however, loves us and all creation.

His divine love caused Him to become our Redeemer. His love in us will cause us to represent Him to the world in a redemptive way and reveal Christ's love through us.

GLOSSARY

Love – (Greek: *phileo*) tender affection realized in fellowship or common bonds – as in brotherly affections. (Greek: *agape*) a self-sacrificing, self-forgetting form of love which originates in God. This form of love is a more costly and higher expression of love. It is this form of love that we see demonstrated in the life of Christ and which we are called to emulate.

LOVE WAS GOD'S MOTIVE IN SENDING CHRIST

Romans 5:8

John 3:16

John 15:13

Romans 5:8

John 15:10

God was interested in our welfare even when we were not seeking Him or His will. He had compassion on our lostness and ignorance.

God's love and commitment to our welfare was demonstrated by seeking our good at His expense.

There is no greater expression of love manifested in the earth than Jesus laying down His life for our sake, even though we were yet in our sins.

The commitment of Jesus to the Father's commands was an integral part of abiding in His Father's love and fulfilling the Father's purpose in the earth.

CHRIST HAS BECOME THE STANDARD OF LOVE

John 15:10–11

1 John 4:20–21
John 15:12
John 15:17
John 15:10

John 13:34–35

Jesus referred to Himself as the example and pattern we are to follow.

Jesus has commanded us, as joint heirs in His new covenant, to love one another.

Obedience to Christ the King is an integral part of abiding in His love in the same way that Christ's own obedience enabled him to abide in the Father's love.

Following Jesus' own example by laying down our lives for one another is the means by which the world will know that we are His followers and representatives.

CHRIST'S LOVE IS OUR SUPREME MOTIVE

1 Corinthians 13

Colossians 3:14

1 John 4:16

Ephesians 5:2

Ephesians 3:19

Galatians 5:6

1 Corinthians 13:13

It is the divine love that gives meaning to every other virtue and gift.

Love is that virtue of God in our lives that holds all other virtues in proper relationship to God.

It is through living a life of love that we can know that we are abiding in God.

We are commanded to live a life of love in the same manner that Christ loved us.

It is the revelation of the love of God in our lives that enables us to receive a fuller measure of God in our lives.

We are rooted and established in God's love as the vehicle through which true faith is expressed.

Love is set forth as the one virtue and fruit above all other attributes that Christians should pursue in this life.

APPLICATION

Discuss why the absence of love changes an otherwise good deed into a futile effort.

Identify an act of service you could render to someone where the complete object of your concern would be their welfare.

Describe areas in your life where you can sense the Holy Spirit expanding your capacity to love others.

Describe the fulfillment you have experienced as a result of acting with selfless love towards someone.

CONCLUSION

Representing Jesus Christ in the world setting will involve reflecting His character as the standard of Christian living. Where character is the foundation for ministering to others, love is the vehicle through which true faith is delivered in the interest of others. If we are to be faithful ambassadors of Jesus Christ, representing Him in His love for the world will be our foremost assignment as citizens of His Kingdom.

LESSON 17 – LIVING IN CHRIST'S VICTORY

PURPOSE

We have been established in the glorious Kingdom of our Lord Jesus Christ and equipped for effective service to extend His interests in all the earth. We have also been given the ability to stand in victory against the warfare of Satan who hates God and resists the purposes of God in the earth.

This lesson will examine the warfare and the victory which is assured us in Christ.

GLOSSARY

Success – a favorable termination of a venture (*Webster*).

Victorious – conquering, having won a victory.

Warfare – military operations between enemies.

GOD IS COMMITTED TO OUR VICTORY AND SUCCESS

Deuteronomy 28:1–14

Joshua 1:6–18

God has assured success and prosperity to all who walk in obedience to His covenant.

The fact that success is assured does not mean there will be no conflict. It is the guarantee of a victorious outcome.

Romans 8:37–38

Our greatest assurance of success is Christ's own commitment to our victory.

GOD HAS PROVIDED THE MEANS TO VICTORY

Isaiah 61:1–3
John 1:1–4
John 1:11–13

He has provided His divine nature to attain victory. When His nature is at work in us, we are assured of conquest.

Isaiah 10:27
2 Corinthians 10:3–4

God has provided the anointing of the Holy Spirit to assist in warfare.

Ephesians 6:17

He has provided His Word to work as a sword in coming against the enemy.

Mark 16:17–18

He has given us His name and the authority of that name to do exploits.

Revelation 12:10–13

We have received the power of the blood of Jesus which has dealt with sin and secured victory over Satan.

Revelation 12:11

We have acquired the word of our own testimony to establish our victory in Christ and to overcome the devil and his works.

WE ARE BEING LED IN A TRIUMPHANT PROCESSION

2 Corinthians 2:14–17

There is a victory procession now in progress, led by Jesus Christ as the conquering King. Those who are joined to Him are a part of this victory celebration.

Colossians 2:14–15

Romans 8:37–39

Ephesians 3:9–12

Jesus disarmed and spoiled principalities and powers through His finished work on the cross.

Our present position in this life is one of sharing in His triumph as conquerors over sin and over ourselves.

Our present responsibility is to manifest His wisdom and extend His victory to powers and principalities.

WE ARE EQUIPPED WITH ARMOR FOR WARFARE

Ephesians 6:14

We receive a belt of truth, speaking of the foundation of our walk in Christ as truth and light. We are protected by a breastplate of righteousness. Our position of right standing before God enables us to stand firm.

Ephesians 6:15

Our feet are covered with the preparation of the Gospel of peace. Wherever we step, the readiness of the Gospel puts us on a sure footing as we go in His name.

Ephesians 6:16

The shield of faith is a moveable weapon that we utilize to deflect the flaming missiles of the enemy that are directed toward us.

Ephesians 6:17

The helmet of salvation speaks of protection to our minds. Our knowledge of the great salvation of God in Christ protects our minds from Satan's attack. The sword of the Spirit is an attacking weapon, used to come against Satanic plans and strongholds that are set for our destruction.

APPLICATION

Identify areas of your life where you believe that you have come under attack by Satan's schemes.

What specific pieces of God's armor are needed to deal with those areas?

Discuss the role that you personally must play in standing against the powers of darkness.

What difference does it make if you do your part?

CONCLUSION

We have been called to share in the victory of Jesus Christ in both heaven and on earth. We are also called to the continuing process of Christ's enemies being made His footstool. All that is required to fulfill this mission has been provided for us. It is our responsibility as citizens of the Kingdom to put on the armor of God and go forth with His authorization to the warfare. In so doing, we will displace the works of Satan in Christ's name and extend His victory in all areas of life throughout the earth.

SECTION 4:

CHRIST'S KINGDOM IN THE FAMILY

LESSON 1 – HEAVEN ON EARTH

PURPOSE

God is the Author and Architect of all creation. He designed the family, as the crowning act of creation, and as the earthly expression of His heavenly Kingdom. The Scriptures describe the family as the basic social unit created by God to extend His Covenant promise and Kingdom reign throughout the earth. In this lesson, we examine the biblical foundations for productive family living as a bulwark against the many destructive humanistic theories of modern society.

GLOSSARY

Mandate – an authoritative command.

Family – the basic unit of society, ideally and historically comprised of a man, his wife, and their children. Many families today have experienced brokenness, but are assured of God's care, guidance, and provision as they place their trust in Him.

Lineage – descent in line from a common progenitor (*Webster*).

Dominion – supreme authority; absolute ownership.

Microcosm – an entity or unit that is the smaller version of a larger unit.

GOD GIVES THE DOMINION MANDATE TO THE FAMILY

Genesis 1:1
John 1:1–3
Colossians 1:15–17

Genesis 1:27–28

When Scripture says, 'In the beginning,' this denotes the outset of all natural and biblical history. Prior to that, we have the existence and presence of the Living God.

God crowned His creative activity by preparing a man, a woman, and the capacity for family. He blessed them with His covenant, that they would be fruitful and multiply, and that they would fill the earth and subdue it.

Genesis 1:28
Genesis 2:15

God placed within the family unit both the order and the government through which He wanted them to manage His creation. They were to subdue and rule over the creation He placed at their disposal.

Genesis 1:28–31
Psalm 115:16
Psalm 8:6–8

God gave to Adam and his family the responsibility to govern for God throughout His entire creation. God blessed His creation with fruitfulness. Adam's family had the privilege and opportunity to manage for God all human, plant, and animal life.

Genesis 4:1–2

As children of Adam and Eve, Cain and Abel expressed the governing mandate that God had given. Cain worked in agriculture; Abel in livestock.

GOD ESTABLISHED THE FAMILY AS A FOUNTAINHEAD

Genesis 1:28

God designed the family unit to serve as the source of social development, as well as custodians of truth for successive generations. Within God's covenantal instructions to that first family, we find several principles that govern life on earth:

(1) **Productional and Reproduction** – God instructed them to be 'fruitful'.

(2) **Expansion and Growth** – God commanded them to 'multiply and populate the earth'.

(3) **Occupation** – God desired that the whole earth be 'filled' with the righteous seed of Adam and Eve's family.

Genesis 2:19

(4) **Subduing** – God gave the first family the responsibility of mastering and training the whole creation. They not only named all livestock, birds, and beasts, but they also cultivated the Paradise Garden where God placed them.

(5) **Ruling** – God entrusted to Adam's family – and all future generations – dominion and authority over His created masterpiece.

The pattern for family, from the beginning of creation, is the microcosm and blueprint for all social relationships. The social principles that govern all people and societies have their roots in the family.

The structure for the earthly family has its prototype in the Persons of the Triune God.

GOD'S COVENANT FAITHFULNESS IN THE FAMILY

God revealed and demonstrated His own covenant faithfulness in the old covenant within the setting of earthly families, especially His chosen people, Israel.

Genesis 7:11

2 Peter 2:5

God demonstrated His covenant faithfulness to Noah and his family at the time of impending judgement. Noah's sons, their wives, and their children entered the ark together. God expressed His grief and love for all families on earth with ample time and warning before He sent the flood.

Genesis 12:3
Genesis 18:19

Genesis 12:2–3

God gave His covenantal promise to Abraham and the descendants of his household. Individually and collectively, God blessed them that they should become a great nation with a great name, and carry blessing to **all families on earth**.

Genesis 12:1–11

Genesis 26:1–5
Genesis 26:23–25
Genesis 28:10–15

God expressed and confirmed His covenant faithfulness through the heirs of Abraham and his descendants, Isaac and Jacob. And God personally encountered their descendants to assure them of His faithfulness to their families.

Genesis 12:1; Exodus 1:1–7
Exodus 19:1–6
Galatians 3:14–17

God developed Israel as a family before releasing them to become a nation. Of the seventy leaders who went into Egypt with their families, God produced 600,000 men plus families.

Galatians 3:14

God conveyed His covenant promises through Abraham's lineage, and extended His grace to us through His 'Seed' Jesus Christ.

Galatians 3:8–9

Galatians 3:26–29

God transmitted His covenant promise to all the Gentile nations of the earth through Abraham's descendants. To belong to Abraham's family means that we belong to Christ.

THE NEW COVENANT AND THE FAMILY

Matthew 19:1–12

1 Corinthians 7:7–9

Romans 5:17–18
2 Corinthians 5:17

2 Corinthians 5:16–21

2 Corinthians 5:17

1 Corinthians 15:17–49

Ephesians 5:22–33

Ephesians 1:9–10

God reaffirmed and fulfilled His original purposes for the family in the new covenant. Jesus explained that the authentic pattern for the family would be found in its fulfillment in the kingdom of God.

Jesus Christ, as 'the last Adam,' atoned and paid for the sin of Adam and his descendants. God, in Christ, reconciled all people and all families on earth to Himself. He established a new order in which all that He revealed to Abraham and his descendants is brought to completion in God's family of believers.

Through Christ's sacrifice, God not only reconciled all people to Himself, but He also restored the defaced image of God in all those who would receive Him and the new covenant.

The apostle Paul reaffirmed God's original pattern for the family in his epistles. He shows the full extent of God's intention for the purpose and function of family within His Church.

More will be said throughout this section concerning God's grace and redemption for families who have experienced brokenness. We will also discuss what it means to be a part of God's spiritual family, the Church.

The family – redeemed and yielded to Christ and obedient to His ways – demonstrates God's original intention for the family He created. The family is God's model for the redeemed families of the earth.

APPLICATION

Name five factors which contribute toward the building of a biblical family unit. Identify five forces in modern society which work against healthy family life. What forces can you identify as having had the greatest impact on your family? How can God's provisions in Christ and His Word meet specific needs within your family?

CONCLUSION

No aspect of contemporary life will have a more dramatic effect on our society than the condition of the family. The most critical issues of our day and the future will revolve around the differences between families shaped by current ideas and those formed by the classic foundations of God's Word. His Word clearly outlines the nature and purpose built by the Creator into the respective roles for men and women. Heeding these guidelines leads God's people to experience life as He intended it. And by living in terms of the biblical standards for family, God's people demonstrate on earth the heavenly design for God's Kingdom on earth.

LESSON 2 – THE NATURE OF MANHOOD

PURPOSE

God, by His own creative act, formed humanity and established people in the earth. From the outset of creation, God called people to rule over all His works and to be His representatives in creation. God designed people to be stewards in His Kingdom. Modern society, from a variety of perspectives, tries to devise and define what constitutes male and female. God clearly sets forth in Scripture the purpose for manhood and womanhood. We will examine here the nature of manhood and how man's role applies in the kingdom of God. It is critical that man's purpose be understood by both men and women.

GLOSSARY

Mankind – the human race including men and women.

Male – that which relates to the distinction of man in God's creation.

Female – that which relates to the distinctions of women in God's creation.

GOD IN CHRIST DEFINED MANHOOD

Genesis 1:26–27
Genesis 2:4–7
Isaiah 42:5
John 4:24

Genesis 3:9–24

God determined the nature of manhood from the beginning to be in Christ. God created man in His own Triune image. Man derives his identity from God, Who is Spirit.

A right relationship with God forms the basis for maintaining godly manhood. This relationship depends upon a yielded heart followed by a lifestyle of seeking to please God. Satan vigorously challenges this commitment . . . as in the Garden of Eden, so also now in contemporary society.

Genesis 2:18–24

1 Corinthians 11:7

Man's existence and design preceded that of woman in the order of creation. This infers neither superiority or inferiority for man or woman. Rather, in God's creative act, He formed each uniquely in His own image, for His own unique purposes.

Genesis 1:28
Psalm 8:6–8

Genesis 2:15

God originally designed man to be His governmental representative over His Kingdom on earth. He gave Adam and his descendants dominion over all the works of His own hands. In the midst of the Garden of Eden, God placed Adam with the instruction to 'work it and take care of it.'

GOD DESIGNED MAN TO SERVE HIM AND HIS KINGDOM

In His creative act, God fashioned man to fulfill certain functions in God's Kingdom, as well as in God's family. Let us examine these functions:

Genesis 1:28–31

Genesis 2:15
Ephesians 5:22–31

Luke 12:48

Genesis 2:19–20
1 Peter 3:7

Genesis 2:15

Ephesians 5:25–31

Genesis 2:16–17

Matthew 22:21
Hebrews 13:17

Deuteronomy 6:1–2

1 Timothy 3:12

Matthew 28:19–20

2 Timothy 2:2

Genesis 1:28

John 15:16

Genesis 1:26
Genesis 9:1–3
Psalm 8:6–8

Matthew 5:14–16
Matthew 9:8

Ephesians 5:18–23

Proverbs 25:26

1 Samuel 2:22–25
1 Samuel 2:30–36

Isaiah 2:1–5
Ephesians 5:31–32
Colossians 3:12–17

God designed man to **govern** for Him. Adam expressed his stewardship role by working the Garden and cultivating it. He named all animal life according to what he felt matched the animal's nature.

God designed man to **initiate his own plans** and work. God gave man a sphere of responsibility and expected him to carry out the work within the limits God set. God rewards man for the initiative he takes.

God designed man to **render decisions** in carrying out God's purposes. Whether in his home, work, or leisure, man's capacity and willingness to make decisions reflect God's image in him.

God designed man to **provide** for his family and for others under his care. God grants the grace – both the ability and resources – for man to engage his sphere productively.

God designed man to **protect** the sphere of responsibility granted to him – his family, extended family, and business interests. God then sets the limits of protection within the rest of His revealed Word.

God designed man to **be accountable** for his family and other responsibilities. Since God created, anointed, and entrusted man with these spheres, then man is primarily responsible to God. However, God also provides earthly leadership within the Church and society to whom man must give account.

God designed man to **train and equip** others. Under the old covenant, God instructed man to train and equip his own children, and those of his household. In the new covenant, a man's success in training his children qualifies him for serving within the household of God. Christ's instruction at Ascension places the work of training upon His followers.

God designed man to be productive – to bear fruit. When a man carries out his responsibility with godly motive and methods, then God Himself intervenes to bless his work.

GOD REVEALS HIMSELF

God so fashioned the nature of man that His own image would be on display in man's attitudes and actions, revealing His own nature. Man's capacity to be productive, teach, protect, provide, decide, initiate, and govern reflects facets of God's own nature.

As man fulfills his appointed role within his sphere of God's Kingdom, then his family and society see the display of God's nature. Through the lifestyle and attitudes of a godly man, people are drawn to praise and glorify God.

As man abdicates his appointed role within the kingdom of God, his family struggles under the lack of grace – the vital example of God's nature and role in their lives is missing or defaced. Society also suffers from the lack of a living illustration of God's grace and provision. The fate of Eli's sons demonstrates the result of a father honoring his sons more than honoring God.

God's plan of salvation not only means forgiveness for sin, but also God intends to restore man's ability to reveal His Person and nature in the midst of his family and society.

THE NEW COVENANT FULFILLS THE OLD

In the new covenant, God subordinates man to Jesus Christ as his head. The yoke of submission to Christ releases in man the grace and purpose of God, as well as protecting him from Satan's deception.

In the new covenant, God places the man as the one responsible for decisions made within and on behalf of his household.

In the new covenant, God gives the man grace to be both the natural and spiritual provider for his family unit. Success within his family and business qualifies man then for responsibility within the local church. (Following lessons will address those men who may be called to the single life and other special services for God.)

In the new covenant, God calls man to account for the grace, direction, and provision given to him for use within his family, business, and society. Further, the man gives account to his church leaders in reference to his doctrine and lifestyle.

APPLICATION

Identify those role models in your life that have been examples of godly manhood. In what ways do current models of manhood seen in public media contradict the biblical pattern of man? Contrast the concept of 'macho' in contemporary society with what we can observe about godly manhood from Scriptures. What about the image of the weak, 'bumbling' male? If you are a man, what areas of your own life do you believe need to conform more fully to God's design as indicated in the Bible?

CONCLUSION

A successful society depends upon its understanding of the roles of man and female as well as how those roles are worked out in the family. What a nation would become will be determined by the health of its families and their descendants. As followers of Jesus Christ, we must commit ourselves to biblical patterns and role models both for success in our own families as well as for the purpose of being lights in the midst of the world's darkness.

LESSON 3 – THE NATURE OF WOMAN

PURPOSE

The humanism of Western culture has deeply challenged the biblical role and identity for woman. It is vital that Christian women and men understand the biblical perspective for woman's identity. We will consider here some of the distinctiveness for which God designed women. As women fulfill the purpose and place for which their Creator designed for them, they enjoy God and experience the blessings of Christ's Kingdom. (Following lessons will address those women who may be called to the single life and other special services for God.)

GLOSSARY

Nurture – that which promotes growth, feeds, or nourishes.

Respond – to answer or reply; to correspond to; to be answerable.

Procreate – to beget; to generate or produce; to engender.

GOD IN CHRIST CREATED WOMAN IN HIS IMAGE

Genesis 1:27
Genesis 5:2

God in Christ determined the nature of womanhood at the beginning of creation. God created woman, along with man, in His own image. She derives her identity from God who is Spirit. And she enjoys a uniqueness from God, as does man.

Genesis 2:25–3:24
1 Peter 3:4
Genesis 3:1–8

A right relationship with God forms the basis for experiencing godly womanhood. This relationship with God depends upon a 'quiet and gentle spirit,' yielded to God's Person and ways. Satan, as in the Garden of Eden, moves aggressively against woman in her identity and purpose.

Genesis 2:21–23

God created woman from the substance of man. Chronologically, she follows man in his creation. The particular creative activity God decreed in fashioning woman speaks of her special identity and fulfillment in God.

Genesis 2:21
Genesis 2:18, 20–23

God created woman to fill the lack God saw in Adam. God saw her as one with Adam in created substance. Further, God fitted the woman to the man in order to form a completed work. He made the woman 'suitable' to the man – one who corresponds to and fills the need God recognized in man.

Genesis 2:23–25
Proverbs 31:10–31

The distinctions God built into woman are sourced in His ingenuity and in His image. They equip the woman in nature and work for irreplaceable family and social roles.

GOD DESIGNED WOMAN TO SERVE HIM AND HIS KINGDOM

Genesis 2:13

1 Corinthians 11:9

Ephesians 5:32
Proverbs 31:12

Genesis 3:20

Proverbs 31:28

Proverbs 31:13–22

God fashioned the very nature of woman to fulfill specific work and roles in His Kingdom and family. As a 'helper', companion, and wife to Adam, the woman fulfilled particular facets of God's nature not present in man. She brings him good, not harm.

God fashioned the woman to be a nurturer, one who would bear children and bring them through their growth stages.

God fashioned the woman to be a manager. God had in mind more than administrating the raising of her children. The writer of Proverbs mentions the abilities of a godly woman in the areas of real estate, fabric, trading, adorning her household, and helping the poor, among many other skills.

Ephesians 5:22–23
Genesis 2:18
Proverbs 31:11
1 Corinthians 11:9
Acts 18:1–26
2 John 1:13
Romans 16:12

1 Timothy 5:10
Luke 8:3
Acts 9:36
Acts 16:14

Titus 2:3–5
Proverbs 31:26
Proverbs 1:8
Proverbs 6:20

God fashioned the woman with the capacity to be a supporter – one who comes alongside and enables another. This unique capacity, or grace, both nurtures her children and sustains her husband.

God fashioned the woman to walk in His Spirit and exercise the gifts of the Spirit granted to her. (See especially Priscilla's work in Acts chapter 18.)

God fashioned the woman to minister good deeds. Some ladies travelled with Jesus and helped support Him. God used others in miraculous ways to witness to His power and to aid in the establishing of new churches.

God fashioned the woman to equip and train other women for their roles in family and society. God gave her a special capacity for wisdom and instruction, to be a sensitive and loving counselor. Her teaching focuses on detailed application rather than the more 'principle-orientation' of her husband.

Ephesians 5:22
Ephesians 5:32
Genesis 3:16
1 Corinthians 11:3

1 Peter 3:5–6
1 Peter 3:1–5

Ephesians 5:25
1 Peter 3:7

God fashioned the woman to be a godly example of the Church's relationship to Jesus Christ Himself. For the woman, in her lifelong yielding and deference to her husband, mirrors the attitude of the Church to Her Lord, Jesus Christ.

God fashioned the woman with the grace to give godly respect for worthy leadership. God exhorts the husbands to live with them in love, respect, and consideration so that nothing will hinder their prayer life together.

GOD CREATED WOMAN TO COMPLEMENT MANHOOD

Genesis 2:18
1 Corinthians 11:11–12

Genesis 3:16
1 Corinthians 11:3
Ephesians 5:22–23

Ephesians 5:25–30

God created the nature of woman in such a way to complete all that He invested in man. For without the woman, man remains incomplete. She, through God's unique endowment, provides the complementary aspect lacking in man's nature.

From the beginning of biblical history in Eden through the New Testament, the Scriptures exhort wives to be accountable to their husbands' leadership. This grace of yieldedness reflects that of the Church to Christ.

Christ then exhorts the husbands to love their own wives as they would love their own bodies. This relational bond forms the basis for

Ephesians 5:22–33

establishing and maintaining all ties – family and social – within local cultures.

Christ and His relationship to His Church is most clearly displayed in the husband-wife bond. When this bond weakens, so also all other social ties begin to fray and disintegrate.

Therefore, God has so fashioned women to model the Church itself . . . to display the true condition and attitudes of the members of the body of Christ to the Church of Jesus Christ. By virtue of this grace upon women, they become a barometer of:

(1) The condition of any society on earth

(2) A society's attitudes towards God, the Church, and spiritual leadership

(3) A society's choice to be selfless or selfish; cohesive or fragmenting

The Holy Spirit exhorts wives, due to the unique significance of the female role, to honor their husbands' leadership. On the other hand, God exhorts the husband to love, cherish, and lay down his life for his wife. The future of any society depends upon women receiving this grace to give themselves to their husbands and children. Respect for and yieldedness to husbands, family needs, and a larger social purpose displays to the world the Church's submission to Her Lord and His new covenant.

APPLICATION

What do you view as the primary cause of the controversy over woman's role in Western culture? Whom do you recognize as a public example of womanhood as revealed in Scripture? If you are a woman, who or what has most influenced your attitudes about womanhood? Identify areas you believe should conform more to a biblical pattern.

CONCLUSION

Modern society views men and women as competitive and adversarial in nature and activity. The Scriptures view each of them as unique but complementary to one another. This revealed truth, unavailable to people from any source but God, has become one of the most relevant areas for ministry within the Church of Jesus Christ today. The inability of men and women to live successfully with the God-ordained roles in marriage relates directly to the increased number of dysfunctional families and divorces.

LESSON 4 – THE SINGLE PERSON AND GOD'S KINGDOM

PURPOSE

Throughout biblical history and tradition, the single life occupies a place of godly respect, based on God's purpose and calling in a person's life. Whether a temporary state or vocation, the single person's role in Christ's Kingdom has special significance in contemporary society. We will examine here the biblical background and calling for the single person's lifestyle.

GLOSSARY

Vocation – calling; a summon to a specific work, lifestyle, or course of action.

Eunuch – under the old covenant, a man rendered incapable of producing children, for the sake of giving his life to a particular service. Under the new covenant, a person chooses to live a single life and not produce children, for the sake of giving his life, his time, his energies and his resources, to God's service in His Kingdom.

THE SINGLE LIFE AS A CALLING FROM GOD

God calls some of His followers to the single life. God summons them to His purposes, to accomplish those good works for which they were created in Christ Jesus. His grace, specifically matched to the single life, enables such a believer to live productively in Christ's Kingdom, without a spouse or children.

When God calls His follower to experience the single life, He usually has in mind some particular career or vocation. Whether to government, as Daniel, or to ministry, as Paul, the focus is on God's eternal Kingdom and the individual's investment of his life and energy into it.

Scriptures set forth many examples of godly, productive persons who were called to serve God in the midst of the single life:

(1) **Elijah** and **Elisha** apparently lived and worked throughout Israel as single men.

(2) God instructed **Jeremiah** to remain single because of His purposes for him and because of war's devastation, which was to overwhelm those in Israel.

(3) **Daniel** and his friends, when taken into the service of the ruler of Babylon, were probably made eunuchs. (The Hebrew word for 'official' carried the requirement of the eunuch's life.)

Daniel 1:3

Matthew 19:11–12

Ephesians 2:10
2 Timothy 1:9

Daniel 1:3
1 Corinthians 7:7, 8, 17

1 Kings 19

Jeremiah 16:1–4

Daniel 1:3

Matthew 3:4

(4) **John the Baptist**, with his itinerant lifestyle, his dwelling in uninhabited places, and shortened ministry, was probably a single man.

1 Corinthians 7:8–9

(5) The apostle **Paul** lived and ministered either as a single man or a widower. His missionary trips and imprisonments left no room for maintaining the married life.

Acts 21:8–9

(6) **Philip** the Evangelist maintained his own household with four single daughters, all of whom functioned in the gifting of prophecy.

Ephesians 5:23–32

(7) **Jesus** of Nazareth remained a single man during His days as carpenter and His three-and-a-half years of ministry in Galilee and Judah. By later revelation, we come to understand His position . . . He is the Bridegroom to His Church.

Matthew 19:11–12

The single life can only be lived by God's specific calling and grace. Given the tenor of contemporary society, with its demand for unrestrained self-fulfillment, God's gifting must take hold in the single person's life to train and enable him. The single life cannot be viewed as an expression of personal ego, or the desire to avoid the responsibilities of married life.

Ephesians 2:11–13
Ephesians 2:19–22

God calls all those in the single life to live within His household – His family. And within the Church, Jesus makes provision for the single or widow by joining them in faith and lifestyle with the rest of His congregation. This grace flows especially well to the single person when they join with a small group of believers within the Church for worship, teaching, counsel, and service.

Romans 1:24–26
Ephesians 2:3
Galatians 5:19–24

The issue is to give one's self wholly to God, unrestricted by the opportunities represented in marriage. The sexual act is laid on God's altar as a sacrifice to Him. Profligate, wanton living as heterosexual or homosexual has no place in God's Kingdom and will only draw God's displeasure in a person's life.

Isaiah 56:4–5

God grants special blessings to those who live before Him in the single life. The promises phrased by Isaiah find their fulfillment through Christ and His Church, in the Holy Spirit.

Special conditions:
(1) Bind themselves to God
(2) Love the name of the Lord
(3) Worship before God
(4) A lifestyle of obedience to God
(5) Bind themselves to the new covenant in Christ

Special blessings:
(1) A place within the household of God
(2) A name and a memorial
(3) Access to God's holy mountain
(4) Joy in the house of prayer

THE SINGLE LIFE AS DEVOTION TO GOD

1 Corinthians 7:32–40
Psalm 27:4
Psalm 73:25–28

A follower of Jesus may choose, within God's will, to live the single life for a season of undistracted devotion to God. David, the Psalmist, cried out to God to be able to spend his life and energies in devotion to Him.

Psalm 119:9–10

1 Corinthians 7:32–35

2 Timothy 2:15
1 John 2:15–17

The single life gives the opportunity to devote one's self to the Word of God. The time otherwise given to the opportunities within married life, or the time used in pursuing the affairs of business or the world system – all this time becomes a sacrifice to devotion to God. This unrestricted commitment to the Spirit and contents of the Scriptures prepares the person for future stages in God's purpose.

Galatians 6:10
James 1:27
Romans 12:9–13
Romans 16:1, 2
2 Thessalonians 3:10–13
1 Timothy 5:11–13
1 Timothy 5:5
1 Corinthians 7:32, 34

The single life allows one's time to be filled with service to God, His people, and the needy. The entire Missionary Movement in the nineteenth and twentieth centuries would have floundered were it not for the sixty-percent membership rate of non-married personnel.

The single life allows more time to be given to prayer and intercession. It is time-consuming to endeavor to enter into the lives and needs of the poor and afflicted and so bear them in the name and situation before the throne of grace.

Ruth 1:16–17

Acts 16:13–15

The single life, in God's timing and purposes, may result in a lifelong commitment to God's service. Ruth's lifetime commitment to God was restructured for her to serve Boaz. Lydia, the business woman, devoted her time and her home to the apostles and the Church.

CHRISTIAN WIDOWHOOD AS SERVANTHOOD

Exodus 22:22–23
Isaiah 1:17
Luke 2:36–38
1 Timothy 5:9–10
Acts 9:36
Luke 2:36–38
1 Timothy 5:5
1 Timothy 5:10
1 Timothy 5:16
1 Timothy 5:10
1 Timothy 5:3–5

God's special call and protection of widows in the Old Testament and in the Early Church shows the esteem He places on them, especially as examples of servanthood:

(1) A reputation for good works
(2) A hope fixed on God alone
(3) A life given to prayer
(4) A commitment to hospitality
(5) A servant of the believers
(6) A friend to the afflicted and distressed
(7) A life above reproach, not given to self-gratification

THE SINGLE LIFE: BIBLICAL ADVANTAGES

The Scriptures point out three main advantages to the single life:

1 Corinthians 7:32–40

(1) The single person has undistracted or prolonged time available in the worship and service to God

Revelation 14:4
Ruth 1:16–17

(2) The single person has mobility concerning residence, work, or country. God can take freely of their time, energies, and resources

2 Timothy 2:4
1 Timothy 6:6–10

(3) The single person has a financial simplicity, unencumbered by the responsibilities of spouses and children

APPLICATION

What provision can be made for the single adult in the contemporary church life other than matchmaking? Review your personal attitudes towards those who believe that God has called them to a single life-style. What are some of the special needs of those who are single either by choice or by circumstance? How may the local church supply those needs? If you are single, what are some of the ways that you believe God is calling you in service?

LESSON 5 – THE MARRIAGE COVENANT: GOD'S DESIGN FOR FAMILY STABILITY

PURPOSE

The stability of the family unit is dependent upon the solid foundations of the marriage covenant. This covenant provides the moral and social fiber in terms of which the Church of Jesus Christ and His Kingdom will grow and mature. We will examine here the covenant nature of the marriage relationship and how its structure provides permanence in this age of growing instability.

GLOSSARY

Covenant – a coming together; a binding together; a permanent bond based on self-sacrifice for the common good.

Contract – an agreement between two parties in which each party binds himself to perform or forbear certain acts.

Bond – union, connection; a binding.

Technological Society – a society which provides necessities for human sustenance and comfort based on laws of science as expressed through applied science.

THE NATURE OF BIBLICAL COVENANT

Genesis 2:21–25
Matthew 19:4–6

Ephesians 5:31
Ephesians 2:10

In a biblical covenant, God brings together two parties as husband and wife and joins them for life as one person. This divine arrangement reflects God's purposes in the couple's life and work. Through this commitment structure, God pours His blessings, as given in the new covenant.

Genesis 2:22–23
Ephesians 5:22–33

God creates and sustains a revelatory mystery in the union of a man and woman. This mystery is the vehicle through which God reveals His own character, works, and purposes on earth. In the midst of this biblical marriage, God discloses His very nature and attitudes for all people on earth to observe.

Ephesians 5:31–33
1 Corinthians 11:2–12

Through the biblical nature of earthly marriage, God symbolizes the covenant relationship between Christ and His Church. Christ's Headship, His love, and His lifestyle of laying down His life for others – all this God builds into the committed relationship that binds the husband and wife.

BIBLICAL MARRIAGE AS COVENANT, NOT CONTRACT

People make contracts because of mutual distrust, thereby, making provision for legal security. A biblical covenant reflects a divine arrangement which ensures mutual trust and commitment. The bonding

Galatians 2:15
Galatians 2:18
John 15:12–14
Galatians 2:15
Genesis 15:9–21
Galatians 2:17–18

Genesis 17:1–22
John 15:9–17

Matthew 19:1–12
Ephesians 5:25, 32–33

Romans 7:1–3

Matthew 19:4
Matthew 19:8–9

Deuteronomy 24:1–4
Matthew 19:4–8
Deuteronomy 22
Leviticus 20

inherent in covenant leads the parties to mutual personal sacrifice for its fulfillment.

Earthly contracts may be altered, if the circumstances surrounding the contract become changed. Biblical covenants endure in the face of altered events and situations. They are unconditional; that is, God fulfills His promises irrespective of human failings or earthly conditions.

Contracts focus on the 'rights' of parties in an effort to forestall or circumvent potential hurt or loss. Biblical covenants focus on the commitment, loyalty, fidelity, and responsibility inherent in the divine arrangement.

Lawyers structure earthly contracts to be impersonal, such that the terms and fulfillment do not depend on momentary, emotional whims. Biblical covenants, by contrast, depend on the functional reality of personal relationship between the two parties.

Contracts reflect the 'meeting of minds' worked out through mutual dialogue in the face of anticipated difficulties. Biblical covenants always involve the joining of lives in a specified lifestyle. The bond established by 'cutting covenant' emerges clearly as the most important aspect of the agreement.

Contracts seek cooperation in the face of self-seeking parties. The details of the contract must protect the alleged 'rights' of each one. Biblical covenants join two parties in terms of self-sacrifice. That is, each party agrees to lay down his life for the other to ensure that the covenant will be fulfilled.

Earthly contracts are always open for renegotiation. By contrast, biblical covenants have their source in God Himself Who structures terms of the covenant He has offered. In Christ, the marriage covenant is not only made between husband and wife, but also between them and God.

BIBLICAL MARRIAGE ENDURES FOR LIFE

God has designed the marriage bond, or covenant, to endure for one's earthly life. In structuring the marriage bond, God sets forth the fundamental aspect of Christ's relationship to His Church – covenant, loyalty, and faithfulness.

God has designed the bond of marriage to endure as long as the other partner is alive. His design includes all the grace, the resources, and the appropriate Word to handle abundantly any situation.

Jesus referred to the beginning of creation as the time when God established the guiding rule for marriage bonds. The creation ordinance did not anticipate or provide for the divorce, or the breakdown sin causes through self-seeking instead of self-giving.

God released to Moses, under the old covenant the provision for divorce, as a result of sin in the human soul and subsequent hardening towards God's will and purposes. In the Mosaic Law, a writ of divorce was granted only for offenses that were punishable by death, thereby releasing the other party.

Matthew 19:4–8
1 Corinthians 7:13–15

In the New Testament, Jesus acknowledged sexual offenses (fornication) as grounds for divorce. The apostle Paul adds 'desertion' as grounds for divorce in the situation of a believer married to an unbeliever.

PLAGUE OF DIVORCE IN CONTEMPORARY SOCIETY

The Family Research Council makes the following comments about the effect of divorce on the American society:

(1) As of 1990, twenty-five percent of all American households are headed by single parents

(2) Appoximately ninety percent of single parent households have no father involved

(3) Approximately 1.6 million couples choose to live together without biblical marriage vows

(4) Approximately seventy-one percent of teenage suicides are the children of divorced parents

(5) Divorce and illegitimacy are the primary causes of poverty

BIBLICAL MARRIAGE IN A TECHNOLOGICAL SOCIETY

Contemporary society chooses to root itself in principles and attitudes derived from applied science. The great 'shift' from Judeo-Christian values came to light during the 1960s. This slide into value-chaos cannot be reversed apart from God's merciful intervention.

Even while our technology has improved, our morals have degenerated. Kinship ties and supportive neighborhood groups have been weakened by lifestyles that:

(1) Disregard and despise Judeo-Christian values

(2) Encourage two-career families

(3) Establish 'alternative' models for family

(4) Requiring work-mobility that removes employees from their homes, families, and relatives

(5) Pressuring Christians to live and work as though biblical values were irrelevant

The effect of contemporary values and lifestyles is to:

(1) Reduce the size of families

(2) Replace family functions with institutions

(3) Coax mothers to work outside the home and turn the raising of children to an outside institution

(4) Use school systems to totally replace parental involvement in children's education

(5) Replace family relationships with peer relationships in institutional environments such as school or work

Luke 14:25–35

In the midst of the present secular environment, God calls us as Christians to make a radical commitment to the original designs for the respective roles of male and female, as well as marriage itself. God's revelation through Jesus Christ, as set forth in the Scriptures, summons us to a thorough surrender to Him and a daily appropriation of the values and lifestyle inherent in that revelation.

The relationship between Jesus and His Church provides a beautiful model of how husbands and wives ought to relate. It has been said that a husband needs to ask, 'Am I willing to die for her?' And wives might ask, 'Am I willing to live for him?' It is this attitude of submission to one another and to Christ that helps a marriage to not only survive but serve as a 'light' to others.

Colossians 2:14–16
Matthew 5:13–16

The family established on Christ's values stands as a light and preservative in the midst of a darkened, decaying society. Marital fidelity and stability, so derided by contemporary society, represent the basic foundations for a healthy society.

APPLICATION

Describe the practical consequences of viewing marriage in the light of biblical covenants. Reflect upon the application of the phrase, 'for better or for worse', as it appears in the traditional wedding vows. Why is that phrase used? Why would that phrase not appear in a contract? What areas of your life and attitudes do you sense in presently being adjusted by God's Word in regard to biblical marriage?

CONCLUSION

The marriage covenant between a man and his wife is the most fundamental component of the family. The health of the family – and consequently the Church and society – is dependent upon the health and stability of the marriage relationship. The appeal of Jesus Christ in Matthew 19 clearly reflects the original pattern in contrast to the contemporary models of His time. In like manner, the Church of Jesus Christ appeals to the original patterns of Scripture for the marriage bond. We look to God and His Scriptures, not contemporary society, in order to receive the stability and blessing that God intends.

LESSON 6 – THE MARRIAGE RELATIONSHIP: THE NATURE OF LOVE

PURPOSE

The love relationship between husband and wife is the life of a marriage covenant. The bond of affection enables the marriage covenant to mature and more clearly exemplify the relationship between Christ and His Church. We will consider here how this relationship functions and what contributes to its success.

GLOSSARY

Helpmeet – one who is suited and equipped to assist another.

Love – (Greek: *agape*) the self-sacrificing compassion of God evidenced in seeking another's welfare at the expense of personal interest.

Complement – to supply fullness or completion.

WHOLENESS AND COMPLETENESS IN MARRIAGE

Genesis 2:21–24
1 Corinthians 11:11–12

God designed the marriage union to provide wholeness and completeness for husband and wife. At creation, God determined that 'it was not good for man to live alone.' He had fashioned man in such a way that he was incomplete apart from the woman. From that time until now, neither the man nor the woman are complete simply in themselves.

(As Christians, we also affirm that God calls some to carry the **grace** of the single life. For them, fulfillment or completeness is found in Christ Himself.)

Genesis 2:24
Ephesians 5:31

God designed the marriage union to create 'one flesh', or one person. That is, the two when joined in covenant become a completed person. Each one brings to the marriage union the uniqueness that the other lacks.

Romans 12:5

1 Corinthians 10:17
1 Corinthians 12:4–6

Only in the union of complementary parts can wholeness or oneness be achieved. Completeness depends upon the grace each one carries for fulfilling God's design in the other partner. The ability to provide a complementary nature depends upon the partners yieldedness to Christ and willingness to find fulfillment in the other person.

God provides the biblical pattern for marriage as a complementary union for fulfilling His own purposes in the couple's lives.

CHRIST AND HIS CHURCH: HUSBAND AND WIFE

Ephesians 5:22–33

Ephesians 5:22
1 Corinthians 11:3, 11–12

God has modeled the relationship of a husband to his wife on Christ's relationship to His Church. In the same way that Christ provides Headship for His Church, the husband carries the task of providing leadership for his wife.

Ephesians 5:25
John 15:9–14

In the same way that Christ loves His Bride and lays down His life for Her, so also the husband learns to give himself to his wife to meet her needs. Sacrificial love means using one's own time, resources, and energies to meet the needs of another.

Ephesians 5:26–27

Christ 'washes' His Bride with His Words with the intent of making Her radiant. In the same way, the husband learns to so use his own words and the Word of God to bring his wife to her own radiance.

Ephesians 5:29

Christ nurtures and cares for His Bride, the Church, as He would His own body. So also the husband learns to cultivate and sustain his bride as he would his own body.

Ephesians 5:31
1 John 2:15–17
Proverbs 2:16–19

Christ demonstrates His own covenant faithfulness to His Bride, the Church, through loyal commitment and enduring, loving devotion. A husband learns to give his trust and loyalty to his wife, resisting all efforts by the world system to deceive him into unfaithfulness.

Ephesians 5:32

Christ's compassion and insight draws His Bride to Himself, allowing the Holy Spirit to work in Her heart. In the same way, the husband learns a lifestyle of insightful compassion for his wife, and so he draws her to himself and to the work that God's Spirit would accomplish in her.

THE CHURCH WITH CHRIST: THE WIFE WITH HER HUSBAND

Ephesians 5:22

God designed the relationship of a wife towards her husband to match that of the Bride, the Church, towards the Bridegroom, Jesus Christ. Even as the Church yields to the Lordship and leadership of Her Lord, so also the wife acknowledges and yields to the leadership her husband provides.

Ephesians 5:22
2 Corinthians 1:4
Colossians 3:18–19

As the Church trusts God's leadership as provided through Jesus Christ and His Word, so also the wife trusts God's leadership as furnished through her husband. And even as the Lord listens with insight and compassion to the members of His Body and Bride, so also the husband learns to listen, with a hearing heart, to the insights and concerns of his bride.

Philippians 4:19
Psalm 23:1
2 Corinthians 9:8

As the Church relies upon the covenantal provision that Christ makes for His Bride, so also the wife learns to rest in the covenant that binds her husband to her. For in and through that bond, God supplies the provision she needs and cannot produce for herself.

Genesis 2:20
Matthew 28:19–20

As the Church serves Jesus Christ to fulfill His God-given mission of a worldwide evangelization, so also the wife assists and facilitates her husband in the fulfillment of the calling God has placed upon their lives together. As the Church is suited, or gifted, to assist in Christ's mission, so also the wife receives God's gifting to fulfill her mission as joined to her husband.

Ephesians 5:33
1 Peter 3:1–6

As the Church honors Her Lord and Master in attitude and conduct, so also the wife learns to respect her own husband in her attitudes and lifestyle. The godly lifestyle of the wife exemplifies the wisdom of God released into the ordinary events of life.

LOVE AS THE LIFE OF MARRIAGE

John 15:12
John 13:34

'*Agape*' love attracts one person towards another and motivates them to promote the other's welfare at their own expense. Further, the quality inherent in this love leads to sharing lives, resources, energies, and time.

Ephesians 5:25
1 Peter 3:7
Song of Songs 2:8–13

God designed the Church to respond to Christ's love-initiative. So also, in the marriage bond, God equips the wife to respond to her husband's initiative in love.

1 John 4:19

The insight and tenderness of Christ's love for us releases us to mature and grow in love for God. In the same way, as the husband learns to love his wife with tender insight, he releases her to growth in her own maturity in the image of God.

1 Peter 3:7

As Jesus Christ demonstrates His love for His Church through godly leadership, love, and care, we respond to that kind of love. In the same way, the godly wife responds to her husband's prudent leadership and insightful, loving care.

1 Peter 3:1–6
Ruth 1:1–18

God has filled His Scriptures with instruction in lifestyle through the lives of His children. Their obedience, or lack of it, leads us in the establishing and maintaining of a godly marriage relationship.

By walking in the biblical pattern of mutual giving and support, we engender, cultivate, and enhance tender feelings for one another. The love relationship flourishes in this climate.

Ephesians 5:25

Christ commands the husband to love his wife. The Greek word is '*agape*', and characterizes the marital love as self-giving. Divine, sacrificial love always draws the husband to give of himself to meet the needs of his wife. 'As God loved the world' . . . 'as Christ loves the Church' . . . this is the pathway the husband learns to walk in loving his own wife.

APPLICATION

Contrast the biblical picture of marriage as reflected in Scripture with the contemporary ideals of love and marriage. Identify those areas of your life and attitudes that have been influenced by the ideals of contemporary love and marriage. Describe the place of romantic feelings as they relate to the bonds of marriage. What are the causes of romantic feelings or the lack of them? How does understanding marriage as a covenant affect your confidence in the durability of your marriage relationship?

CONCLUSION

Current attitudes of romance and marriage are usually understood only in terms of physical desires and superficial attractions. Contemporary marriages rise and fall in direct relationship to the changes, fluctuations, and whims inherent in human emotions and self-serving desires. God builds biblical marriages upon the covenantal reality of commitment, faithfulness, and trust. The romance of marriage will experience challenges and testings. But when based on biblical covenant, the bonds hold, even when momentary emotions and circumstances prove very trying.

LESSON 7 – FATHERHOOD: GOD'S PLAN FOR LEADERSHIP

PURPOSE

By God's design and appointment, fatherhood is the fundamental and essential component of society. This very truth is under incredibly severe attack today. As contemporary society becomes increasingly secular, it will distort and confuse the biblical roles for the father. Many secular role models for fathers litter the current scene today. None of them approaches the strength and productivity of the biblical role. We will examine here the Scriptural model for fatherhood and some biblical patterns which exemplify godly leadership and responsibility.

GLOSSARY

Father – one who accepts the responsibilities for procreation; caring, providing, and protecting children.

Secular – behavior, thought, and culture patterns controlled by the world system and dominated by the spirit of disobedience; that which is against spirituality and holiness.

Provider – one who furnishes or supplies.

GOD IS OUR FATHER AND THE ORIGINATOR OF FATHERHOOD

Psalm 2:7; Isaiah 9:6
Psalm 89:26–29
John 1:1–2
Isaiah 41:25–26
Deuteronomy 32:6
Isaiah 64:8; Isaiah 63:16
Ephesians 3:14

Psalm 68:5
Psalm 10:14
Matthew 2:10

Acts 17:24–25

Romans 8:14–15

Ephesians 1:5
1 Corinthians 8:6
Ephesians 4:6
Hebrews 12:9
Acts 17:26

Matthew 3:5–6

According to the biblical revelation, God is a Father and the One from whom all fatherhood arises. God is eternally Father. Therefore, the Son is eternal, like His Father.

Moses speaks of God as the Father Who formed us. God's role in reference to creation is that of Builder, the One Who fashions. In reference to people, He is Father. Isaiah reveals God as 'our Father' and the One Who fashions us.

David declares God to be the Father to the fatherless. He Fathers those who have come into a place of having no resources and no hope. Malachi acknowledges God as the one and only Father of all covenant people. Paul proclaims to the Athenians God's creatorship and that He gives all people their life and breath.

Paul represents the Holy Spirit as enabling us to call upon God as 'Abba' (Father or 'Daddy'). Paul tells the Ephesians that God predestined us to be adopted as His own children. For Paul perceives God as Father, the One upon Whom we totally depend for all things. From one person, God has made all people on earth.

God's call comes to us to enter into fellowship with Him as Father, through faith in Jesus Christ. Since He is eternally Father, we can learn from Him what it means to be earthly fathers. For God warns earthly societies of the curse that arises from broken father-children relation-ships. He also tells us of His provision to rescue societies from impend-ing curses by the restoration of father-children relationships.

GOD IS THE PATTERN FOR FATHERHOOD

As the Scripture affirms, God the Father is the Source, the ultimate Provider of all life and resources throughout the universe He created. The universe is not in a self-developing mode; it starts and stops at our Father's word.

Since God is the Source – the ultimate Provider of life and resources – then all accountability ultimately belongs to Him. He rules His creation on His own terms and calls all people to give an account to Him in His own timing.

In the same way that God provides for His children, so also earthly fathers should make provision for their families. And as God calls all things to account to Him, so also He calls fathers to account. He holds them accountable for their family provision – even if the wife works to help pay the bills.

God manages His universe in such a way that fathers must give account to Him for their leadership and provision. Therefore, in an ideal situation, family members give account to the father of the family.

Even as God disciplines and trains His own children to bring them to maturity, so also He calls fathers to take the responsibility for train-ing and forming their own children.

GOD GIVES LEADERSHIP TO FATHERS

God calls fathers to represent godly leadership before their wives and children. He delegates them as family leaders in the kingdom of God. God appoints the father, along with his wife and children, to a place of representing Christ's interests before the people of the world system.

The basis of authority for the father lies in the authority that God has granted His Son, Jesus Christ. And as the Father sets the para-meters for instruction and discipline with His children, so also earthly fathers define the structure within which they form the maturation process of their children.

Successful family leadership prepares fathers to participate in the leadership for the Church. The father learns leadership skills within his own family structure. He practices leadership by delegating respons-ibilities within his family and calling each one to account for his work.

BIBLICAL EXAMPLES OF POOR FATHERHOOD

The Scriptures do not hide the failures of the men and women who took part in the drama of redemption over the ages. God held Adam responsible for the sin of listening to Satan. And the effect of that sin still touches all of us.

Ephesians 3:14–15
1 Peter 1:3–5
2 Peter 1:3
Genesis 1:1
Psalm 102:25

Psalm 66:7
Psalm 103:19
Psalm 24:1
Romans 14:12
Hebrews 4:13

Romans 14:10, 14
2 Corinthians 5:10

1 Timothy 5:8

Hebrews 12:7

Isaiah 64:8
Ephesians 6:4
Hebrews 12:5–11

1 Corinthians 11:3

Ephesians 5:22–24

1 Corinthians 11:3
Deuteronomy 21:19
Deuteronomy 6:20
Proverbs 22:6
Ephesians 6:4

1 Timothy 3
Titus 2

Matthew 18:23
1 Peter 4:5

Genesis 3:9–12
Genesis 4:1–15
Romans 5:12

Genesis 3:17

Leviticus 10:1–11

1 Samuel 3:10–14
1 Samuel 2:22–25

1 Kings 1:5–6
2 Samuel 15:1–12
2 Samuel 18:1–18

Aaron's sons rejected their father's leadership by ignoring his instructions to follow the Word of God precisely as stated. They offered 'strange fire' before the Lord and thereby forfeited their lives. Eli also failed with his sons. Eli refused to restrain his sons when they made themselves contemptible before the Lord. They also paid with their lives.

David's son, Adonijah, led rebellion against his father to take the throne of Jerusalem. Another son of David, Absalom, also led rebellion against his father. Both were killed by troops loyal to David.

In nineteenth and twentieth century world history, we find many examples of powerful leaders, who by their own testimony, rejected the ways of their earthly fathers and brought disaster upon entire cultures and populations. Some of the more prominent: Adolf Hitler, Joseph Stalin, Mao, and Sigmund Freud.

APPLICATION

What has most influenced you in your thoughts regarding what it means to be a father? What observations can you make regarding the examples of fatherhood as portrayed through the media? State the relevance of Scriptures which are thousands of years old regarding fatherhood to the conditions of contemporary society. What would you say is most needed in the area of fatherhood within the Church today? Some adults today suffered under poor fathers when they were young. If you are in that condition, how can a godly understanding of true fatherhood bring healing into your life and hope for your own children?

CONCLUSION

No society is any stronger than the families that comprise that society. Few families can be stronger than the quality of fatherhood demonstrated in that family. The confusion which surrounds male and female roles in contemporary society can only be remedied by re-affirming the essential role served by fathers in God's Kingdom. The strength of the Church of Jesus Christ and the hope for current society depends upon righteous men who will commit to Jesus Christ and to assume their roles before God as leaders in their homes and productive contributors within Christ's Kingdom.

LESSON 8 – MOTHERHOOD: GOD'S PLAN FOR FAMILY NURTURE

PURPOSE

During this past century, our society passed through several profound changes in reference to the biblical role of motherhood. In the agricultural era, mothers functioned in the home as an integral part of the family life for the entire family. Industrial society increasingly replaced the older agricultural society. The newer role for woman in the marketplace displaced the previous role of the wife and mother at home with domestic responsibilities. Current Western society, founded on applied science, continues the thrust of devaluing the biblical role of women as wives and mothers. While the Scriptures teach God's call for some women to the single life and service, we will examine here the guidelines Scripture sets forth for the vital and revered place of a mother with her family.

GLOSSARY

Role – a function assigned with a position.

Sacrifice – to surrender or suffer loss for the sake of obtaining something deemed more valuable.

GOD CREATED WOMAN TO RESPOND TO HUSBAND AND FAMILY

Genesis 2:3
Genesis 3:16
Titus 2:4

According to Scripture, God fashioned the woman in such a way that she would respond primarily to her husband and family. Her immediate motivation moves her in love towards those whom she cares for and serves.

Titus 2:5

Her heart-felt standard guides her to carry out her responsibilities with self-sacrificing energies. The purity and sensitivity of heart enables her to reflect special facets of God's nature given to no other of God's creatures on earth.

Titus 2:5
1 Timothy 5:10
Proverbs 31:20

The godly woman focuses her insight and concerns on her household, for which God has graced her with appropriate abilities. Her capacity in love-care overflows in hospitality for guests and the needy.

Titus 2:5

1 Peter 3:1–6

The role of the godly woman within the home extends her husband's authority into each sphere of child care and home arrangement. The town leaders respect her husband when he takes his place among them, due to his wife's grace and diligence. Her yieldedness before her husband speaks broadly into the marketplace of non-believers.

GOD CREATED WOMAN FOR OTHER PRODUCTIVE ACTIVITIES

Proverbs 31:10–31

God has so fashioned the woman that her call to family care does not preclude her involvement in other productive activities. The Proverbs 31 woman has stood for some 3,000 years in testimony to the extensive gifts God bestows upon His daughters. He gives her abilities – in real estate, fabrics, training, and home decoration, and in many other areas.

1 Timothy 5:10
Acts 9:36

The Scriptures call women to good works as one of the best demonstrations of their relationship to God and their husbands. Their God-given sensitivity to details and situations permits them to hear the voice of the Lord in meeting the needs of others. Their benevolence and compassion to others outside their own household exemplifies the mercy of God at its finest.

THE WIFE'S AUTHORITY DERIVES FROM HER HUSBAND

1 Timothy 5:14

God gives to the wife responsibility and accountability as an extension of that which He gives to the husband. Her managerial role within the household expresses her husband's authority. The Greek word *oido-despotein* literally means 'house-rule'. She applies in practical ways the Word of God, with sensitivity to detail and situation, such that her household vibrates with the grace and *shalom* peace of God.

1 Corinthians 11:1–3
1 Peter 3:1–6

The wife's role is a governmental one with her husband's headship in focus. Chrysostom, one of the early Church Fathers, describes the wife's role as that of a 'second authority'. Her yieldedness to her husband enables her to transmit the authority of Christ as represented in her husband.

GOD CREATED WOMAN TO SACRIFICE AND NURTURE

John 3:16
1 John 3:16
1 John 4:7–11
Philippians 4:19
2 Corinthians 9:8

A mother's care for her family exemplifies that of God's love and care for His children. 'Agape' love focuses on sacrificial, protective care. God demonstrated this supremely in and through His own Son, Jesus of Nazareth. God continues to express His unique love for us within the context of our daily lifestyle. He protects our pathway and affairs; His sacrificial love pours out His own resources in our behalf.

Exodus 2:3

Genesis 21:10

The Scriptures show us various godly women who sacrificed for and protected their families. Moses' mother released him to God's keeping through a simple basket in the river Nile. She abandoned all hope of ever seeing him again. Abraham's wife, Sarah, perceived the awkward situation of her own doing, between Isaac and Ishmael. Her husband heard her advice as a word of God and sent Ishmael and his mother away.

1 Kings 3:16–28

John 19:25

Solomon used the quality of a mother's love and willingness to sacrifice personal rights to discern the true mother from the imposter. Mary, the mother of our Lord, constantly expressed her concern for Jesus' welfare right up the very hour of His Crucifixion.

GODLY MOTHERHOOD INFLUENCES BOTH GOD AND CHILDREN

Luke 1:38

Proverbs 31:30

As a wife yields to and obeys God, He then uses her as a vessel for His own purposes. Her obedience enables her husband in his sphere and releases her children to the grace of God in their lives. Her godly example draws praise and esteem from her family as well as the society where she lives.

1 Samuel 1:22–28
Luke 1:38
Judges 13:1–5

Matthew 7:26

A godly mother expresses her commitment to God by dedicating her own children to Him and His plans for their lives. She uses all her grace-gifts then to train and prepare them to honor God in their lives. As women of faith approached Jesus of Nazareth and He honored their requests, so faithful wives and others, through intercession, have influence with God in the lives of their husbands and children.

APPLICATION

Identify particular areas where you were especially blessed by your own mother's care. Make a special effort to communicate your gratitude to her whenever possible. Describe ways by which the role of motherhood could be more revered in contemporary society. What specific areas of education do you see as tied to the mother's role during the formative years of child development? If you are a mother, what do you believe should be your primary guide or resource in raising your children?

CONCLUSION

Current social and economic pressures devalue the godly role of mothers at home with their children. Alternate child care structures abound outside the home environment. Families need to evaluate carefully the impact of giving the mother's role to alternative people during the children's formative years. We in the Christian community need to embrace the challenge of supporting the entire family and specifically the role of the mothers. When mothers must be absent from their own children, then the community needs to learn how to become a resource for mothers in the care and training of their children.

LESSON 9 – PARENTING: NURTURE, TRAINING, AND DISCIPLINE

PURPOSE

The combined roles of the father and mother provide the dynamic for parenting skills within the family environment. Given the variety of options currently offered in secular society, only the Scriptures themselves actually present **God's design** for parenting skills. We will examine here the training of parenting skills based on covenantal relationships and Kingdom authority and goals.

GLOSSARY

Father – a man who procreates a child, or functions in a paternal capacity.

Mother – a woman who procreates a child, or functions in a maternal capacity.

Parent – a father or mother who assumes the duties of loving, maintaining, educating and training children.

GOD GIVES CHILDREN: PARENTS STEWARD THEM

Psalm 127:3–5

God grants children to couples and asks these parents to steward their children in His ways. Children represent both gifts and heritage from the Lord.

Psalm 128:1–5
Deuteronomy 28:1–4
Genesis 15:1–5
1 Samuel 1:1–28

Children express the blessing of God, which He chooses to bestow for His purposes. God withholds or releases children to parents depending upon His immediate plans for them as they serve Him in His Kingdom.

Psalm 112:1–2

Luke 2:49–52

Proverbs 1:8–19

God intends that the children of covenant families become mighty in His ways and purposes. Their 'might' results from parental training in the ways of God. God's on-going blessing on Dad's and Mom's parenting skills produces young people who are mighty before God, effective in character, and productive in society.

Proverbs 22:6

Romans 12:4–6

1 Corinthians 12:4–11

God imparts to the children of covenant parents a variety of giftings. He then enables the parents to recognize and develop these giftings. God anoints the parents to start their children in the skills and pathways which find their greatest fulfillment in God's own Kingdom.

COVENANT LOVE: GOD'S CHOICE FOR CHILDREN

Proverbs 22:6

Genesis 16:9–12
Genesis 17:15–22

God's original plan shows that children proceed from the covenant love of their parents. God eventually blessed Abraham's offspring Ishmael. However, He reserved His covenantal blessing for the child produced through the love of Abraham and Sarah. Covenant love represents not simply human desire, but a commitment from the parents to receive God's blessing in children.

Hebrews 12:4–11

Colossians 3:1–17
Ephesians 4:17–32

Covenant love involves discipline – the training of children to walk in God's ways, contrary to natural desire and cultural pressures. God designs His path of discipline to impart a self-identity to the child, as well as release him from the tyranny of living only to fulfill selfish cravings. Maturity means to live relationally by the Scriptures for the good of the whole community or society. (Note the relationship between the words 'discipline' and 'disciple'. Discipline is for training purposes, not a release for parental frustration.)

Proverbs 22:6–15

Proverbs 13:24

God anoints parents with unity of purpose and methods for the maturation process. Prayer and fasting produces a willingness in the parents to present to their children a godly and united purpose. Disagreement produces double-mindedness in the discipline process. This robs the child of security of relationship and his own self-identity. He encounters the persistent temptation to manipulate his parents, one against the other, to obtain his own way.

TRAINING CHILDREN IN THE MIDST OF LIFE

Psalm 68:6

Deuteronomy 4:9
Exodus 10:1–2

Deuteronomy 6:7–9
John 7:1–5

Deuteronomy 6:20–25

Isaiah 28:9–10
Proverbs 1:8
Proverbs 6:20

God has so arranged family life that training children takes place in the midst of the daily routine. God places individuals within the family context because issues encountered there provide the very training that best prepares children for life in God's Kingdom. God placed Jesus of Nazareth within a family context to learn not only godly principles but understand how to handle the conflicts of life.

The daily routine of family life provides the setting for a 'class in session'. In this context, parents talk about God's Word and principles while their children are 'seated, walking, lying down, or getting up'. The mother especially has the teaching gifting for the repetition and explanation necessary to form the child's thinking. The father's instruction of principles balances out what the child receives.

Ephesians 6:4
1 Timothy 3:4
1 Timothy 5:10

The father, with his emphasis on biblical principles, takes the leadership in demonstrating effective training and discipline. On the other hand, the mother takes the lead in nurturing her children through application of the biblical principles. Her 'hands on' approach permits the children to experience the practical, not just theoretical, aspects of godly living.

CHARACTER GOALS IN CHILD TRAINING

Proverbs 1:1–5
Proverbs 2:1–28

Ecclesiastes 12:9–14
Proverbs 1:7
Exodus 20:20

1 Timothy 1:5

Titus 1:6

Proverbs 3:22

Parental nurture and training includes specific character goals. Biblical character sets the limits in terms of which wise behavior is best expressed. God's blessing unambiguously attends wise behavior. Wise behavior is based on the fear of the Lord; the fear of the Lord is the beginning of wisdom.

Paul instructs Timothy in the care of Ephesian leaders and people to focus on 'agape' love, a pure (clear) heart and a good (forgiven) conscience. These qualities provide the basis for practical and enduring faith in Jesus Christ. Sound judgment and discernment, so prized

Luke 2:41–52

Hebrews 6:7–10

1 Timothy 3:4

by the Proverbs writer, grace the person who pursues them. He finds life for his very soul in them.

God gave His Son, Jesus of Nazareth, the opportunity for testing in the area of yieldedness. He acquired 'reverent submission' through his family environment. And although He was the Son of God, He learned obedience through trials. If Jesus learned His character qualities through His family's lifestyle, our own children must also.

APPLICATION

What is your own vision for your children? How does it reflect God's covenant priorities? Which Bible characters suffered because of a lack of parental training? Write down several ways by which you can build biblical training into your routine of family life.

CONCLUSION

In our generation, we have seen the dispersion of the extended family and the dissolution of biblical roles for parents. God considers these vital and determining factors for the moral and spiritual preparation of children. The perverted models of parenting that dominate our society magnify the dissolution process. God appoints covenant parents to follow biblical guidelines and models as the primary means through which they train their children. God entrusts to parents the opportunity to steward the lives of those He commits to their care. Parents, and biblical parenting, are under tremendous attack in today's society. So-called 'experts' have duped many parents into believing that they don't have what it takes to raise their own children. But the same God who gave your children to you will also provide you with the wisdom, strength, and resources that you need to successfully raise them. 'I will contend with those who contend with you, and your children I will save,' God promises.

Isaiah 49:25

LESSON 10 – DISCIPLINE: MEANS FOR MATURITY

PURPOSE

The subject of training and discipline within the home has received much attention from various sectors of contemporary society. We hear the case made for children's 'rights', parents' 'rights', and the ever present issue of how much government regulation should be involved in the domestic life of the family. God's Word addresses the confusion of current society. We will examine here a biblical basis for discipline, and the guidelines the Scriptures afford us in the application of discipline within the home.

GLOSSARY

Secular Humanism – a philosophy or religion that rejects Judeo-Christian values of a Sovereign God, absolute standards, Man's sinful (selfish) nature, and the essentiality of biblical discipline.

Training – the act or process of educating to produce consistent behavior.

Discipline – the oversight, instruction, and correction necessary to protect and produce maturity.

Chastise – the act or process of correcting or punishing with a view toward reclaiming the child from his self-destructive behavior and broken relationships.

'Rod' – an instrument for correction or punishment.

GOD DESIGNED DISCIPLINE TO PRODUCE MATURITY

Hebrews 12:4–11
Job 5:17
Proverbs 3:11
Proverbs 4:13
Proverbs 23:12
Proverbs 4:10–28
Proverbs 1:28–33
Proverbs 5:23,32
Proverbs 6:20–23

Proverbs 13:24
Proverbs 1:7
Proverbs 13:18

Proverbs 8:32–36
Proverbs 13:18
Proverbs 19:18
Proverbs 10:17
Proverbs 15:5

Acts 2:38

God trains His children through the use of discipline; He makes it a pathway to maturity. Instruction provides the necessary information to produce wise and good behavior. To ignore instruction invites disaster in morality, in family life, and in business.

Discipline calls children to account for their behavior. The godly standard set before them feeds back into positive self-identity. The warnings for rebellious behavior provide guidelines to prevent self-destruction, foolishness, and poverty.

Correction calls children to learn self-discipline. God asks children to learn how to guide their own behavior. To set the reality of parental correction constantly before the child leads him in the pathway of biblical wisdom.

Biblical punishment or correction exacts a price in the life of the child for unacceptable behavior. Parents relate the punishment to the seriousness of the offense. God sees discipline as His means for bringing about repentance and restoration. A child's rebellion breaks

Hebrews 12:5–7, 11
Job 5:17
Psalm 94:12
Proverbs 23:13

relationships with their parents, siblings, or friends. Discipline promotes repentance and the re-establishment of broken relationships.

God uses discipline to affirm His profound love and care for His children. Lack of discipline confirms that God has no covenant relationship with that person. God also uses discipline to produce a righteous lifestyle and maturity in the pathways of God.

GOD'S DISCIPLINE THROUGH PARENTAL DISCIPLINE

1 Samuel 3:13

1 Kings 1:6
Proverbs 11:20

Romans 12:4–6

Proverbs 3:11–12
Proverbs 13:24

Proverbs 2:15

God extends His own ways of discipline through those which the parents employ. God requires that parents assume the responsibility for the conduct and level of maturity of their children. God provides daily grace-gifts to discern and evaluate the level of discipline necessary. The Word of God itself also provides specific pathways for correction.

From God's perspective, the motivation for discipline lies in the desire to obey God and love one's children. Unchallenged, persistent willfulness in the child prepares him to encounter the sterner aspects of God's judgement upon earth. God designs parental discipline to remove the foolishness (selfishness) and evil (rebellion) from a child's life.

Proverbs 29:15
Proverbs 15:5
Proverbs 10:1
Proverbs 15:20
Proverbs 17:25
Proverbs 19:13

God's perspective on a child includes the obvious need for correction and discipline. Parental failure to provide opportune training and discipline sets the stage for the child's lack of self-worth. Far worse for the child is the resulting inability to handle the giving and receiving of forgiveness, as well as the coping with the standards and prohibitions of life, schooling, business, and society. The tragedy touches both the parents and children.

DISCIPLINE AS VERBAL INSTRUCTION AND UNDERSTANDING

Deuteronomy 6:4–6

The normal process of discipline includes verbal instruction that the child comprehends. Instruction needs to touch the child in ways that are practical and related to normal life's situations.

Genesis 2:15–17
Proverbs 6:23
Proverbs 15:31–32

Proverbs 23:13–14

Parents must be sure that children understand the biblical instruction and the consequences for ignoring or disobeying it. God expects that our correction or discipline fall within appropriate guidelines:

(1) That it be administered promptly when required

(2) That it be consistently and fairly applied

(3) That it be lovingly administered (not in anger) with the goal of restoring relationships

GOD AND 'THE ROD'

Proverbs 13:24

Proverbs 22:15
Proverbs 23:13–14

God commands the use of the 'rod', or corporal discipline as a normal part of training children. Scriptures state clearly that, among other methods, some form of physical discipline is a necessary part of child-training.

Proverbs 19:2
Proverbs 22:15
Proverbs 10:8
Proverbs 12:15
Proverbs 23:13–14
Ephesians 6:10–17
James 1:22

God considers the rod of authority as a way to open the child's ears to hear His wisdom. For the rod of authority delivers the child from the evil of selfishness and willfulness. The act of corporal discipline, as love in action, stands between one's children and the evil bent of his old nature and the world system.

Corporal discipline is administered within the overall framework of godly goals and methods of discipline. It is administered in love, not in anger, so that the end of the matter is greater understanding and respect, rather than a provoking of wrath and rebellion.

GOALS OF FAITHFUL DISCIPLINE

Proverbs 29:14

Proverbs 1:7

2 Peter 1:5–11

Hebrews 12:10

Hebrews 12:11

Proverbs 1:23, 33
Proverbs 3:2–3
Proverbs 4:1–19

God designs certain goals for our children to be realized through the faithful application of discipline. Wisdom, as a lifestyle, leads first to the fear (reverence, awe) of God and then the knowledge of God. Individual maturity – the ability to respond to God appropriately in lifestyle and work – derives from a life that is disciplined biblically.

Consistent, biblical discipline produces a harvest of peace and righteousness for those who have been trained by it. One who lives in safety, comes to know the thoughts of God, prolongs his life, brings prosperity, and finds health for the body.

MISUSE OF PARENTAL AUTHORITY

Genesis 1:17

God cautions parents about the mis-application of discipline. Since God made children in His own image, as He did parents, then they learn to discern and respect that image of God, however faint they may consider it.

Scriptures suggest the following:

Matthew 18:15

(1) Discipline in private preserves the dignity of the child. Public ridicule for offenses only encourages broken relationships within and outside the family.

John 17:17; Genesis 18:19
Ephesians 6:4
Colossians 3:21

(2) God bases discipline upon His Word and the conditions of His covenant. Mood swings and convenience provide an unstable base for deciding the conditions for discipline.

Hebrews 10:24–25

(3) To encourage, instead of scolding or humiliation, moves the child toward personal integrity and the desire to accomplish good works before God.

Ephesians 6:4
Colossians 3:21

Proverbs 19:2
Proverbs 18:13
Proverbs 25:2

2 Corinthians 1:17–20

Proverbs 22:6
Colossians 3:21

2 Corinthians 5:18–20

Scriptures warn parents to avoid provoking their children to anger and bitterness. It demonstrates wisdom from God to gather facts carefully (without prejudice) and to move in a deliberate and measured pace to accomplish the discipline.

The child learns most easily from consistent and unwavering discipline. This provides stability in his life from which he learns to respect parental ideas and words. Discipline that proceeds from an angry, offended, and vengeful spirit serves only to produce an angry, offended, and vengeful spirit in the child. Confrontative love that seeks to mend and reconcile surges from the heart of our loving Father who reconciled all mankind to Himself – in the awful cost of His Son. He calls us to learn how to confront lovingly – to restore what has been offended and broken – often at the expense of our own time, convenience, and cultural upbringing.

APPLICATION

How do you respond to those who would say that physical discipline is emotionally harmful? What do you believe to be the results of the lack of physical discipline? Describe here what you believe would be an orderly and sound approach in applying physical discipline to a child. Describe other means of discipline which may be observed in Scripture and which God has used with His own children.

CONCLUSION

Genesis 18:19

Proverbs 22:6

The current legal climate concerning the issue of child abuse has heightened and confused the issue of physical discipline within the home. Western society places great value on a person's 'rights' irrespective of age. This leaves Christian parents in need of a clear and defensible philosophy for training and discipline within the family. God's Word presents an unchanging standard that has endured for thousands of years. It sets forth the ultimate guidelines for raising children toward productive adulthood. God's formula for successful parenting: instruction in righteousness through biblical guidelines of consistent discipline. The Lord gave Isaac to Abraham because Abraham would 'command his children' and train them in rightousness. In doing so, he gave them a legacy of blessing. Parents today are told not to shape their children – to let them grow and develop 'naturally' on their own. But this is contrary to God's Word and has produced a harvest of heartbreak. If you are afraid to shape or train your children, you must be warned that there is a multibillion dollar secular education and entertainment empire 'out there' that is more than eager to do it for you. Who will shape your children?

LESSON 11 – A TRAINING GROUND FOR STEWARDSHIP

PURPOSE

The atmosphere of the family is the first environment in which the individual learns values and standards for living. The quality of life experienced within the home and in relationship with parents has proven historically to be the predominant influence which shapes the child. Further, their attitudes and perspectives for living as mature adults are formed in this setting. Here we shall examine the family in the light of Scripture as the training ground for righteous living in the kingdom of God.

GLOSSARY

Stewardship – a sphere of responsibility to be worked for another, for which one must give account.

Responsibility – the state of being accountable or answerable as for a trust, or office or for a debt (*Webster*, 1829).

GOD'S DESIGN FOR THE FAMILY

Genesis 2:18–25

Genesis 2:15–17
Genesis 2:1–7
Genesis 3:1–24

Genesis 1:28
Genesis 9:1–17

Deuteronomy 4:9–10
Deuteronomy 6:4–9
Proverbs 22:6
Proverbs 1:8

Psalm 68:5–6

Hebrews 13:2
Deuteronomy 15:7–11

God fashioned Adam and Eve in His image. He designed the family structure to receive each child, and develop His image in them through nurture and training. God revealed His own nature and ways to the first family within the sphere of their family.

Through the setting of the first family, God planned to extend His own rule throughout the earth. He entrusted the management of family and work assignment to them.

God commanded the parents to instruct, develop, and release their children in the ways of God. He designed the family context as the best possible environment in which child training could take place. The Book of Proverbs represents those principles which unerringly prepare children to serve God.

God also structured the family context to receive those who are alone (solitary) in life. Whether widow, single, dysfunctional, or disadvantaged, God designed His grace-gifts to flow to them within the family setting.

LEARNING TO HONOR GOD AS SOVEREIGN

Deuteronomy 5:7–8
Exodus 20:3–4

Deuteronomy 6:1–9

God instructed parents to focus primarily on training their children to recognize and honor God as the Sovereign Creator-Possessor of all things on earth and in heaven. God reveals Himself as the Sovereign Creator of all things. We recognize and worship nothing in the entire

Deuteronomy 5:8–10

Proverbs 1:7
Proverbs 9:10
Proverbs 15:33

Deuteronomy 5:11
Genesis 2:15–17
Matthew 25:14–30
1 Timothy 3:4–5
1 Timothy 3:12

Deuteronomy 5:6–21
Matthew 5, 6, 7

Ephesians 2:1–3

Colossians 3:1–14

Matthew 25:14–30

universe that could remotely be imagined as standing more above the Person of God in Jesus Christ.

To fear (reverence in awe) the Living God is the beginning of knowledge, of wisdom, and of understanding. All orientation to life begins here: to know the Holy One, the Lord.

God enables the parents, in the context of the home, to train their children in the appropriate exercise of authority or responsibility. Whether the management of a child's sphere, or the respect for the spheres of others, God designed the home environment for imparting these values.

God asks the parents to develop in their own children the capacity to revere and steward the ways of God as revealed in the Scriptures. The world system places the 'rights' of the individual above honoring God. The setting of the home provides the most practical environment for working into children's lives the capacity to honor God above their own natural desires and the demands of local culture.

Within the home, God asks parents to teach their children how to assume responsibility for their own actions. In this context, children learn either to see themselves as victims of circumstances or as accountable to God for their choices and actions.

LEARNING TO HONOR PARENTS

Exodus 20:12
Leviticus 19:3
Deuteronomy 27:16

Deuteronomy 5:16
Ephesians 6:1–3

Proverbs 3:11–12
Ephesians 6:4
Proverbs 4:22
Proverbs 3:8

Ephesians 6:1–3
Exodus 20:12
Jeremiah 9:23–24

Through parental instruction at home, children learn respect and reverence for parents and the authority they exercise under God. After God Himself, parents are the first expressions of authority in the earth.

In honoring one's father and mother, the child encounters the first occasion in which he learns to defer to the preferences of another. As the child learns to honor his parents and follow their leading, he builds the links within himself for physical and emotional well-being. In following the wisdom of God, the child places himself in the pathway of God's on-going blessing in life.

As the child learns to submit to his parents' authority, as God's, he begins to enter the authority of God's Kingdom on earth. He opens his spirit and mind to know not simply God's deeds on earth, but to know the Lord Himself.

LEARNING TO HONOR FAMILY MEMBERS

Deuteronomy 5:17
Romans 13:9–10
Deuteronomy 5:17
Leviticus 24:17
Romans 12:10
1 Timothy 5:21

Deuteronomy 5:18–21

Philippians 2:3
1 Corinthians 10:24

Deuteronomy 5:20
Exodus 23:1
Leviticus 19:11
Leviticus 6:2

The family context provides the first opportunities for the child to develop the capacity to defer to another. Parents impart understanding of the value of human life in teaching their children how to lay down their own lives for others. The concept of self-sacrifice runs counter to the current scene of self-fulfillment.

Children within the context of the home observe, emulate, and learn to respect the covenant commitments represented within the family ... that of parents to each other, of children to their parents, and to one another.

The parent's example shows the children how to steward the reputation of others, either in avoiding hyper-critical speech and 'putting down', or in promoting honor and sensitivity. To honor one another as those who bear the image of God, children learn this most of all in the home and among their peers.

LEARNING TO HANDLE MATERIAL POSSESSIONS

Proverbs 3:9–10
Proverbs 10:2
Proverbs 13:11
Proverbs 22:7, 9, 26

Through example, parents impart biblical attitudes towards material possessions. They live before their children the principles of God's Word concerning stewardship and accountability. Parents display how to handle money wisely: earning, tithing, giving, spending, and saving. These activities will either confirm or contradict what you have taught them with your words.

Proverbs 13:20
Proverbs 4:20–22
Proverbs 3:13–15

Parents provide for their children a fountain of life and health as they channel God's wisdom in the daily affairs of life. Their authority – as an extension of God's – validates their practices.

Psalm 119:9–11
Ephesians 6:1
Ephesians 5:21
Proverbs 4:3–4
Proverbs 4:10–17

Children first recognize God's perspective on individual integrity in the human interplay within the family. They may learn to despise life through media violence, abortions, guns, drugs, and gang mayhem. Or, they learn to appreciate the image of God in other people.

Proverbs 10:4–5
Proverbs 6:6–11
Proverbs 13:4
Proverbs 18:9
Proverbs 21:5
Proverbs 22:29

In the home, the children absorb parental attitudes towards work, its value and its function in life. The alternate views sourced in the world system give value to work either as replacing God in priority or as despising it. God establishes the home as training ground to see work as God's gift, as responsibility, and as the place for exercising grace-gifts on behalf of others.

1 Corinthians 12:4–7

APPLICATION

Identify several areas in your attitudes toward material possessions which were shaped by parents and family. Identify ways by which training in the family will positively influence the work ethic in the marketplace. What areas of your life do you believe God is addressing concerning personal stewardship of those resources entrusted to you? What role does tithing and giving serve in your life toward fulfilling responsible stewardship?

CONCLUSION

The trauma and confusion experienced in the marketplace today originates with the inadequate training by parents in the home. Our society more and more expects schools and other social institutions to impart to children what parents never did. The child's work ethic and responsible management of material resources grow out of the formative years of development, as children observe how their parents, handle life in the context of the home. God gives to the parents, and to the Church in appropriate grace-gifting, the responsibility for instructing the next generation regarding the proper management of values, character, morals and wealth. The blessing of God's ways for the next generation depends upon the diligence of parents and the local church today.

LESSON 12 – THE EXTENDED FAMILY: GOD'S DESIGN FOR FAMILY SUPPORT

PURPOSE

In our society, the departure from Judeo-Christian values has severely damaged the structure of the immediate family and almost neutralized the existence of the extended family. The Scriptures speak clearly about the value God places on extended families and the purpose they fulfill in His design for society and His Kingdom. We will examine here the family relationships beyond those of husband-wife and parent-child.

GLOSSARY

Nuclear Family – the family unit composed of a father, a mother, and all of their children.

Extended Family – the family unit composed of a father, a mother, and their children, as well as grandparents, aunts, uncles, cousins and in-laws.

GOD EXTENDS HIS COVENANT PROMISE THROUGH FAMILY

Genesis 6:18
Genesis 9:8
Genesis 12:1–3

Genesis 48:1–21
Exodus 1:1–5
Numbers 26:4–51
Exodus 1:5
Numbers 26:51

Genesis 12:1–3

Galatians 3:6–9
Galatians 3:26–29

God created the family as the basic social unit through which He extends His covenant promise and Kingdom reign on earth. God dealt with both Noah and Abraham in terms of family units.

The sons of Jacob became the tribes of Israel, the extended families whose ancestry lay in Jacob's offspring. The seventy descendants of Jacob who entered Egypt emerged 430 years later as 600,000 men in twelve tribal groupings. Genesis Chapter 49 carries the characteristics of each of the twelve tribal heads.

God purposed through the extended family of Abraham – people of faith – to convey His covenantal blessing to every family group on the face of the earth. Abraham's natural family was used by God to generate the nation of Israel. He also used Abraham's family to produce all people of the faith on earth.

GOD ESTABLISHES TRANS-GENERATIONAL IDENTITY

Genesis 12:2–3

Genesis 8:16–22

God established extended families so that through them He might grant generational identity and blessing. Extended families share some genetic traits in common. The offspring recognize common characteristics and understand themselves as part of the larger family. God extended His blessing beyond Noah to his related family members.

Genesis 17:3–8
1 Timothy 1:5
2 Timothy 2:2

God extended His covenant promise through Abraham's natural family, to his descendants and all the generations that would follow – as they walked in obedience to the covenant. Abraham imparted his faith to Isaac; then Isaac to Jacob; then Jacob to his descendants. The apostle Paul uses this trans-generational principle in showing Timothy the source of his faith. Paul then uses the same principle in the training of spiritual descendants.

GOD ESTABLISHES FAMILY HERITAGE

Matthew 1:1–17

God conveys distinctive family heritage through the members of the larger family units as they work and fellowship with each other. These extended families bear God's trans-generational purposes on earth. Scripture recognizes and emphasizes the linkage of generations preceding the birth of Jesus of Nazareth.

Genesis 28:3–14
Genesis 26:2–6
Genesis 22:17; Psalm 78

Jeremiah 1:4–5
Galatians 1:15
Ephesians 3:21

Matthew 28:18–20

God promises salvation to succeeding generations and transmits that promise through the heritage of extended family. God also transmits the memory of His covenant and His deeds generationally.

God uses human ancestry to communicate His purposes and plans for the Gentile nations. The Early Church, through their spiritual offspring, began the transmission of Christ's glory to their generation and those to follow. The Church today continues to convey and relay the Good News about Jesus – in obedience to His covenant and commands.

Exodus 34:7
Exodus 20:5
Jeremiah 32:18

God warns extended families that spiritual problems may be passed down through subsequent generations. Trans-generational blessing, through disobedience, turns into generational plague, curse, or punishment.

GOD HONORS THE WISDOM OF PRECEDING GENERATIONS

Exodus 20:12
Deuteronomy 21:18–21

Proverbs 1:8
Proverbs 2:1
Ephesians 6:1–3
Deuteronomy 5:16

God requires that today we learn to honor the preceding generations so that we can receive their wisdom and heritage. The old covenant required that the children learn to honor their parents. To dishonor one's parents means to cut one's self off from receiving or inheriting all that they had learned and experienced from God.

The new covenant validated by Christ's blood, also calls for children to honor their parents. For this pleases God and opens the way for blessing to attend the life of the children. Children learn to honor their parents within the home. They also learn, by extension, to honor their family's heritage and ancestry.

To honor the members within the basic family sets the precedence for honoring members of the extended family, both blood and marriage relationships. For honor of one generation toward another creates appreciation for heritage as well as truth from the preceding generations.

Leviticus 19:32

1 Kings 12:8
1 Timothy 5:1
Hebrews 13:17
Romans 13:1–5

1 Timothy 5:8

GOD GIVES HEALTH AND CHARACTER TO EXTENDED FAMILY

The health and character which God builds into the extended family is essential to the future of the Church and society. Honor and care toward the aged determine the blessing of God upon future generations. Honor toward parents and relatives gives a foundation for honor toward all those in authority in the Church and throughout local society.

Parental care exercised towards children now establishes a pattern in the children to demonstrate similar care towards succeeding generations. The practice of love, honor, and nurture in the basic family unit will be conveyed to the extended family, and from this to the larger community of the society itself.

APPLICATION

Describe the attitudes you encountered during childhood in regard to extended family relationships. What areas do you recognize in your life that ought to conform more fully to a biblical approach to family in the future? Review your sense of heritage and how God has used your extended family to instill values of importance to your life. What impact will the trend toward fewer children have on society?

CONCLUSION

God works in society primarily through family units. Contemporary society – secular and humanistic – places far more value on individualism and personal fulfillment. The Bible clearly teaches us that our heritage, as a gift from God, forms a vital part of who we are and enables us to fulfill our mission as servants to those around us. One primary mission of the Church of Jesus Christ is to establish strong families ordered upon biblical principles. The hope of current society lies in God's truth embodied in Christian families as they demonstrate righteous management and compassionate care of children.

LESSON 13 – THE ALTERED FAMILY: THE OBJECT OF GOD'S SPECIAL CONCERN

PURPOSE

Due to the alternative views of family within society, the Church finds itself challenged to minister to the exceptional or dysfunctional family situations. The increased incidence of divorce and divided homes seriously impact the domestic atmosphere and society in general. Jesus calls His Church to follow His own example of upholding the Father's original standards, while loving and working with those in the exceptional family situations. We will explore here how to extend the kingdom of God into altered families and to impart God's special provision to those not living within the biblical standard or ideal.

GLOSSARY

Altered Family – a family unit in which either the mother, the father, or both, are absent and not supporting their family.

Nuclear Family – a family unit composed of a father and mother with all of their children.

GOD'S LOVE FOR ALTERED FAMILIES

Genesis 1:27

Genesis 2:24

Genesis 2:18–24

Psalm 68:5
Psalm 82:3

Psalm 68:5
Deuteronomy 10:18
Psalm 146:9
Psalm 68:5

Deuteronomy 24:1–4
Ezra 10:3
Jeremiah 3:1
Matthew 5:31
Matthew 19:7
Luke 16:18
1 Corinthians 7:27

God has demonstrated His concern for those in altered families, especially in the Mosaic Law and the new covenant. Since He Himself lives in the complexity of a Divine Company – the Trinity – He desires that no one should live all alone in life.

He completed His creation of Adam by giving Eve to him. He considered it not good for Adam to live alone. God reveals Himself as a Father to the fatherless, making provision for them in His Law.

God, as Father, makes provision in the old covenant for the widow, the orphan, and the stranger (the non-covenant worker or guest). Also, He set the lonely and the single people in families.

While God reveals His own hatred for divorce and all its effects, He acknowledges the sinfulness (selfishness) of people by making provision for divorce in the Mosaic Law. The relational and emotional havoc created in divorce neutralizes the very covenantal bond through which God deals with all people on earth. God calls us to relate to the fragmented members of altered families with the same grace and love our Heavenly Father extends to us.

GOD ASKS HIS PEOPLE TO LOVE ALTERED FAMILIES

Some 3,000 years ago God, began to call His people to demonstrate loving concern for those in altered families. The Law of Moses in the

Deuteronomy 10:18
Psalm 10:14
Proverbs 15:25
Jeremiah 49:10
Hosea 14:3

James 1:27
Deuteronomy 14:29

Acts 6:1–6

old covenant provides for the protection of the widow, the fatherless, and the alien (non-covenant worker or guest) in Israel.

In the same way today, God calls His people of the new covenant to care for widows, orphans, and strangers. God's concern for the altered families in the Early Church prompted the first administrative efforts within the Church to address those needs.

SERVING GOD BY SERVING ALTERED FAMILIES

Romans 8:15
Galatians 4:3–6
Ephesians 1:5

We grow in understanding that God, by His grace, included all of us who believe within His family. As members of His redeemed family, He granted us the full rights and privileges of His only begotten Son – our Brother – Jesus Christ.

Since we have received the spirit of adoption from God, we need to learn to exercise the same spirit toward one another. Whenever we can, we look for ways to include the members of altered families in our own spiritual families – in our natural families, too, when appropriate. Here are some biblical examples:

Ruth 1–5
1 Kings 17
Matthew 1

(1) Boaz, Ruth, and Naomi
(2) Elijah, the widow, and her son
(3) Joseph and Jesus
(4) Paul and Timothy

Proverbs 18:24
Deuteronomy 26:12
Isaiah 1:17

Isaiah 1:15–25

God delights in making provision for those who are suffering from daily wants due to of their altered family situation. He indicts Israel many times for their failure to represent His compassionate faithfulness. Their unwillingness to follow God in this respect contributed to their captivity as a nation and subsequent dissolution.

APPLICATION

Identify specific opportunities available for you to extend care to individuals impacted by altered family conditions. Why do you believe that God reflects special interest towards the orphan and widow? Name several specific qualities that should be present in a woman's life for her to qualify for recognition within the Church as a true widow. If you are in an altered family situation, have you found a local church family that will care for and bring healing into your life?

CONCLUSION

God closely identifies with the members of altered families. He calls His people to serve them by enabling them to find their place in God and His Church family. God set the example for fatherhood for us by sending His only begotten Son, Jesus Christ, to meet our needs. Jesus became our Brother and restored us to the Father. God wants us to learn how to impart this great salvation, the acceptance, and nurture to single people, single parents, widows, and the fatherless. The

Church's effectiveness in the local society will be measured by its ability to demonstrate care and show mercy to those who are already objects of God's special care. Those who show mercy are the ones who receive mercy.

LESSON 14 – THE REDEEMED FAMILY AND SOCIETY

PURPOSE

In several lessons we have reviewed the original model for family and society, as God Himself stipulated through the Adamic, Noahic, Abrahamic and Mosaic covenants. Beginning with the Davidic covenant, we see God's shift from stating the original model to that of restoring the damage brought to mankind when sin passed into all people. The Scriptures show that the world system hates and repudiates the original model for family and society. If they already despise the original model, how then can they be expected to take seriously God's redemptive goal and process for the family? In this lesson we will look carefully at God's goals and healing process for the family and society.

GLOSSARY

Redeemed – the salvation and sanctification process, based on conformity to the image of Christ, which the Holy Spirit undertakes in all Christ's followers, in their families, their societies, and nations. The completion awaits the return of Christ, our resurrected bodies and the fullness of God's Kingdom on earth.

Original Model of Family – the family as initially revealed in Eden and defined through the Mosaic Law.

Redeemed Model for Family – the family as seen through Jesus' perspective; the family structure and purpose as seen at the high point of God's revelation in Jesus and His apostles.

GOD'S PROVISION FOR REDEEMING THE FAMILY

Romans 5:12–21

Genesis 6:5–8

After Adam and Eve's failure in the Garden, sin passed upon all mankind, as demonstrated in death. The rebellion-selfishness infection grew progressively worse. Broken relationship with God heads the list, followed by tangled relationships within the family. Notice how soon murder appears in the post-Edenic society. Gradually, every attitude, intention, and act fell victim to the person's rebellion and selfishness. God stated that He could stand it no longer and sent the Noahic flood in judgement and cleansing.

Exodus 19–24

Galatians 3:19–25

Galatians 3:26–29

Galatians 3:17

God structured and communicated the Mosaic Law to show people just how far they had gone into sin. The Law functioned to reveal the dimensions of sin. It carried no inherent power to give life or righteousness, or to save or change people. The Law held us as prisoners, locked up to an awareness of sin. In effect, it leads us to Christ. The Law did not nullify the Abrahamic covenant, which placed one's relationship to God on the basis of faith, rather than fulfilling a law.

2 Samuel 7:4–16
2 Samuel 7:14
Psalm 89:30–37
Proverbs 3:11–12

Jeremiah 31:31–34
Ezra 36:22–32
Matthew 5:17

As God progressively revealed His covenant with David, we see a distinct shift in attitude. God now deals with David in terms of redemption and restoration – not obedience or disobedience. God will correct him when he sins, as any earthly father would correct his own children.

The new covenant now comes into focus through the Prophets, especially Ezekiel's description of the restoration and redemption which God will bring about. Jesus came as the fulfillment of this covenant and every promise and type in the entire Old Testament, through His obedience and death on the cross, His outpouring of the Spirit, and the abiding gifts.

We want to draw three conclusions from this quick survey of man's sin and God's redemption: First, the original family model, given in the Garden of Eden, has suffered along with all of creation as rebellion and selfishness progressively infected its very core. Second, the original family model finds its redemption and completeness – structure, identity, and fulfillment – in Jesus Christ. Third, Jesus' victory at the cross enables us to build our families around the Word and Spirit of God as revealed and fulfilled in Jesus of Nazareth.

BALANCING THE ORIGINAL AND REDEEMED FAMILY MODEL

Genesis 2:18–25

Ephesians 5:21–33

Hebrews 7:18–19

Hebrews 8:7

Hebrews 8:13

Ephesians 5:21–33

The original family model from Eden to Moses contains the 'bare bones' outline of all that God intended for mankind. The true dimensions and fullness of that family model can be found only in Jesus Christ. We must avoid thinking that the original model is sufficient for His Church today. The Scripture labels the Law, or the old covenant, as having inherent 'weakness and uselessness,' as being 'set aside,' as not being 'faultless,' as 'becoming obsolete, growing old and ready to disappear.'

The redeemed family model finds its meaning in Jesus Christ, not self-fulfillment. The 'rebuilt' model takes the 'bare bones' of Adam's revelation and transforms it within the framework of Jesus' lifestyle and attitudes. The apostles heard deeply the Living Word with whom they worked for some three years. They re-worked the original model of the family (and all things), to express all they heard from the Creator-Architect whose lifestyle affected them so profoundly.

THE NEW TESTAMENT CHURCH AND THE REDEEMED FAMILY

Jesus takes the original family model and transmutes it into a family motivated by the Holy Spirit, structured by the Word of God, and focused on fulfilling God's plan for their lives. This redeemed family is built by the guidelines of the Spirit, not an earthly society. The original family model aimed at producing an earthly society (Israel) which was to find its fulfillment in Jesus Christ and His re-definition and redemption of the family.

Hebrews 11:9–16
Romans 12:1–2
Galatians 6:14
Colossians 3:1–3

The redeemed family looks for a city with eternal foundations, whose Maker and Builder is God; they present themselves daily to God as a living sacrifice. They glory in the cross and consider themselves crucified to the world system and the world system to them. They fix their eyes – their life's perspective and purpose – on Jesus Christ. Individually and corporately, they learn to reflect Jesus' own perspective.

Luke 18:18–30
Luke 14:25–33

Within the redeemed family, the parents see themselves in terms of Jesus' plans for them and their children. The husband labors to lead and provide for all members of his family. He cultivates his love relationship with his wife. He recognizes the Spirit's giftings upon her and provides opportunity and resources for godly development. He enables her to grow into her place of radiance in God.

Ephesians 5:25–33

She develops a quiet, gracious, and yielding spirit before God so that her husband, children, and society receive the full measure of witness her life expresses. Her uniquely enabling support releases her husband into the fullness of God's purpose for him so that he can sit with the leaders in Church, business, and society.

Hebrews 12:3–11
Proverbs 3:11–12

Ephesians 6:1–4

They work with each child, as a specific and unique gift from God, training and equipping each one for his privileged placement in God's Kingdom. The children learn to fear the Living God to yield, to obey, to develop control of mind, body, soul and old-nature. As they emulate their parents' lifestyle, by serving and protecting their brothers and sisters, their witness permeates their life in the school, church, and neighborhood.

THE CHURCH AND THE FRACTURED FAMILY MEMBERS

The local church, by the Word and Spirit, should exemplify in its members the reality of the family redeemed by the grace of God. As adult members learn to handle the pressures of life within their own spheres, God will use them as a family to reach into the local society and communicate His own grace, mercy, and wisdom. God permits the testing of the well-ordered Christian family to rid them of any hints of self-righteousness or arrogance in attitude.

Luke 4:18–19
Isaiah 61:1–4

Jesus, in the synagogue of Nazareth, declared Himself as the fulfillment of Isaiah's Messianic prophecy. In Isaiah's statement, we see that this Messiah comes to heal the 'afflicted and broken-hearted' or 'shattered in heart.' The New Testament Epistles abound in godly principles and power for addressing all the needs included in the 'shatteredness' of Isaiah and Luke. Let us look at the 'shattered' in our churches and society.

Ephesians 5:21–33

More than fifty percent of marriages in America end in divorce. God has revealed His own attitude towards divorce: He hates it. The reason lies in the relational and emotional havoc created in divorce, effectively neutralizing the very covenantal bond through which God deals with people on earth. More than that, the earthly marriage expresses the mystery of Christ's relationship with His Church. A superficial attitude towards commitment in marriage reflects a similar attitude of commitment to Christ. Millions have been shattered by this experience, and need the healing that only Christ can bring.

Let us enumerate here the various types of brokenness affecting families:

1 Timothy & 2 Timothy
Titus 1–3
1 Corinthians 7:39

(1) **The widowed** – specifically mentioned by the Lord as a special object of His love and concern. In the Pastoral Epistles, we see them as a special responsibility for the elders and community. They are eligible for marriage.

1 Corinthians 7:10–16

(2) **Divorced, but 'still single'** – Paul specifically states that if the unbelieving spouse abandons them, they are free. Some interpret this 'freedom' as eligibility for re-marriage; others do not. Paul encourages them to remain as he is.

Matthew 19:9
1 Corinthians 6:18
1 Thessalonians 4:3

1 Corinthians 6:18
Proverbs 2:12–19
Proverbs 5:1–23
Proverbs 9:13–18
Proverbs 7:1–27

(3) **Divorced, but 'living together'** – Paul addresses 'immorality' as a general category of sexual relationships outside of biblical guidelines. Our society encourages and approves the practice of sexual relations for teens and adults, asserting that this benefits the person's mind, soul, and body. Paul states categorically that immorality injures the one who indulges in it. The Book of Proverbs details the consequences of sexual relationships outside of the biblical guidelines. In fact, one major purpose of developing wisdom is to avoid relating to the 'strange (non-covenant) woman.' The writer states explicitly that God's judgement upon a person who directs his life without God's wisdom permits him to walk into immorality.

(4) **Divorced and re-married as Christians** – So many 'disenchanted' believers fall into this category, numbering some 15 million in our society. For whatever reason, their first marriage ended in disaster. Without condoning the reasons for the fractured marriage, they enter into another relationship and seek the Lord's and the Church's blessing. And within that new relationship, they bear the consequences of breaking their first covenant, as well as the opportunity for grace and redemption.

(5) **'Dead beat' parents** – Those who procreate and then abandon their families in order to live in the fantasy of self-fulfillment. God calls His Church to step in with emotional and family support for those abandoned. Often, the one leaving has been the father, but it is occurring with rising frequency among women.

(6) **The homosexual who is celibate** – Some Christians recognize these tendencies within their bodies and souls. They resist their old natures, bringing them to the cross and the grace of God. Pledged to Christ alone, they live 'in the Spirit,' and turn their backs on the standards and attitudes of society.

(7) **The homosexual who is promiscuous** – The demand of our society that individuals be allowed to practice freely their inner desires stems from the principle of self-fulfillment. Jesus operates in terms of self-denial. Jesus expects self-denial from the promiscuous, to cease his promiscuity, whether it be homosexual or heterosexual. Jesus' pathway of grace includes and covers the disasters and repeated attempts for 'holy' living.

(8) **The dysfunctional or abusive marriage** – God gives His own ministry giftings to address and cover the needs represented for the abused spouse and children.

(9) **The addictive lifestyle** – Again, God showers His Church and followers with all the ministries necessary to work with these 'shattered' people.

There are many more areas of brokenness in homes. Jesus knows the need; Jesus paid the penalty for the sin at the cross; Jesus broke the power of sin through the Resurrection. Jesus provided the giftings and grace at Pentecost to bring all these expressions of 'shatteredness' to Him and His healing grace through His gifts upon the Church.

APPLICATION

How would you handle a 'stranger' in your church service? Would it make a difference to you if they were divorced, dysfunctional, or shattered in some other way? How would you express the grace and compassion to them? Do you sense within yourself a tendency to withdraw from them because they are not like you? What concrete steps could you take to restore with gentleness a 'shattered' person? Have you ever experienced a shattering? What steps are you taking to receive healing?

CONCLUSION

The grace of God has come to earth, first in Jesus and now in His Church. Jesus, long ago, committed to address the needs of the shattered through His death on the cross and gifts of His Spirit. Today He calls His followers to express His grace and mercy by recognizing the kinds of brokenness that devastates lives. More than that, Jesus gives His grace gifts to some of His followers to engage the healing process with the community of believers. And Jesus constantly tests His Church to expose the self-righteousness that isolates His followers from the very people who most need His provision. The redeemed model of the family encompasses the fullness of God Almighty on earth; the redeemed family builds itself into the redeemed local church.

LESSON 15 – MANAGING FAMILY FINANCES

PURPOSE

God has revealed in His Scriptures all things that pertain to life and godliness, including His principles for financial freedom. Scripture speaks directly to the issues of financial stewardship, of earning and spending money. God has designed the family to exemplify basic stewardship in finances. We will examine here some of those biblical guidelines.

GLOSSARY

Economics – (Greek: *oikonomikos*) pertaining to the management of the household; the study of the management of production, distribution, and consumption of goods.

Surplus – that which remains when need is satisfied; an excess of earnings over expenses, designed to result in savings.

Debt – that which is due from one person to another; frequently the result of not generating a consistent family financial surplus.

Family Economics – the study of the management of household finances in accordance with God's will and principles as set forth in His Word.

BIBLICAL GUIDELINES FOR FINANCES

Matthew 6:33

God designed the human family as the primary witness to the grace of God for individuals, families, and societies. Therefore, His Word sets forth clear guidelines for attitudes towards finances and material possessions. The fundamental attitude: seek first the kingdom of God.

1 Timothy 6:6–8

Philippians 4:19

Philippians 4:10–13

The Holy Spirit produces contentment in a believer through his soul and spirit. This contentment, or peace, depends not upon food, supplies, or other resources; rather, on the capacity of a believer to trust God in all circumstances.

1 Timothy 6:10
Proverbs 13:11
Proverbs 28:20
Hebrews 13:5
1 Timothy 3:3

The temptation to become rich easily and quickly, enslaves the one who follows it. Slavery to the love of money effectively neutralizes one's trust factor in God. Accumulation of resources depends on the attitude of 'gathering money little by little' to make it grow.

Proverbs 22:1
Proverbs 10:22
Deuteronomy 8:18
Proverbs 23:5

The Scriptures set forth a 'good name' as far more desirable than great riches. God's blessing produces wealth and He adds no sorrow to it. But riches acquired through haste or deceit 'take wings and fly away . . .'

BIBLICAL QUALITIES FOR PRODUCTIVITY

The Scriptures delineate clearly the attitudes that please God and result in His blessing for producing income. We mention several here:

Diligence – the steady application of time, energies, and skill to the work. As contrasted with laziness, which is equated with robbery or destruction.

Faithfulness – loyalty and constancy in carrying out assignment or responsibilities. As contrasted with inattentive, sloppy work habits, which result in poverty.

Wisdom – application of biblical attitudes and principles to one's family, work, and lifestyle. As contrasted with foolishness: emptiness in the heart, no reservoir of biblical attitudes and principles, resulting in self-destructive, poverty-prone behavior. Biblical wisdom produces riches and honor.

Skill – the developed ability or aptitude to use one's knowledge effectively. Skills represent God's gifting to people for the development of society. Note the skills God gave for the tabernacle and Solomon's temple. To ignore or leave them untrained insures poverty for the individual or family.

Education/training/job knowledge – gradual acquisition of tools through deliberate study or apprenticeship. Given the constant changes in job markets, one's knowledge gained twenty years ago leaves him vulnerable in understanding and retaining his job.

Work heartily – With zest, gusto, sincerity, we purpose to please God, primarily – not simply our bosses. That perspective assures us that we also please our earthly managers. To serve God with the skills and placement He designs brings joy to the worker's heart.

BIBLICAL GUIDELINES FOR GIVING

The Scriptures present to us various guidelines to help us in our giving to God. The concept of the 'tithe' predates the Mosaic Law by several hundred years. Abraham tithed to Melchizedek, priest of the Most High God. Offerings to God date back to the time just after expulsion from the Garden of Eden.

The Mosaic Law, or old covenant, details for the worshipping faithful just how to please God with tithes and offerings. The failure to share with God their firstfruits led Israel into captivity. But God promises restoration based on resumption of tithes and offerings.

The Scriptures exhort us to give generously, because God has given generously to us. God's dictum: 'Whoever sows generously will also reap generously.' The opposite is also true. Scriptures outline for us in great detail the attitudes and process that should underly giving, especially giving generously.

Proverbs 19:17
Proverbs 22:9
Deuteronomy 24:10–15
Galatians 2:10; Acts 11:29

Luke 20:25
Matthew 17:24–27
Romans 13:6–7

Proverbs 23:23
Proverbs 4:7

Proverbs 21:17–20

Proverbs 22:7
Proverbs 22:27

Proverbs 11:15

Philippians 4:16

Proverbs 22:26–27
Proverbs 6:1–5

Proverbs 10:4
Proverbs 6:6–8
Proverbs 28:20–21

God especially encourages us to share our portion in life with the poor. To share with the poor is the same thing as sharing with God. And God keeps track of those who share or do not share with the poor.

BIBLICAL GUIDELINES FOR SPENDING

From the teachings of Jesus of Nazareth, we see the biblical necessity of paying our taxes. Paul the apostle adds the injunction that with paying our taxes or revenue, we should also pay honor and respect.

Spending habits sourced in weakness – compulsive, impulsive and without regard for consequences – lead the individual and family into back-breaking debt. In this scenario, provision cannot be made for the family's future or next generations. The entire media industry seeks to separate the viewer from as much money as possible. One of the gods of Western culture devotes itself to satisfying the indulgences and wastes of the society.

Financial planners who have an appreciation for Judeo-Christian values suggest the '10–10–80 program' to guide family spending ... ten percent for tithes and offerings; ten percent to savings; eighty percent for all necessities, (taxes, food, clothing, shelter, insurance, and so forth).

Since spending habits reflect heart attitudes, we must ask God to reveal destructive spending to us. Destructive spending means one buys what one wants, when one wants it, without regard to the value represented in the price paid. In this scenario, poverty lies waiting at the door.

DANGERS AND CONSEQUENCES FOR DEBT

The Scriptures place limits around us to guide us especially in avoiding debt, or the need for discharging debt. Since debt is cast in such a favorable light by the credit card industry, we need to face the jolting reality from the Scripture: Debt makes me a slave to the lender. The interest paid on debt robs the worker of his financial future.

To borrow today what I cannot afford presumes on the grace of God that He will in fact provide for my indulgence. Indulgence means that I cannot pay for what I just bought. God will indeed provide our every need as seen within our covenantal relationship. God does not lead us to borrow money for which we have no collateral or means of repaying.

To co-sign obligates the signer to the debt incurred by the original borrower. Scripture warns us on this subject.

GUIDELINES FOR GENERATING SURPLUSES

We save for the future through diligence. We learn wisdom from the ants because of their genetic habits of gathering and storing. The Scriptures guide us to store what God gives us beyond our immediate

Proverbs 27:23–27

Proverbs 13:11

Proverbs 22:3
1 Timothy 5:8
Galatians 6:10

Romans 12:8

2 Corinthians 9:5–15

Philippians 4:10–17

2 Corinthians 9:1–5

Matthew 6:19–21

Proverbs 13:22
Proverbs 19:14
2 Corinthians 12:14

needs. This way He provides for our future needs; He provides for others in need through our generosity; He provides for our future generations . . . or He may do all three.

The Scriptures direct our savings in terms of gathering money little by little to make it grow. To save money in small increments reflects this biblical wisdom, instead of waiting until we have a large sum of money we don't need for other commitments. That rarely, if ever, happens.

The interest earned from various types of savings accounts, if left in the account, earns interest on the savings plus the interest. This compounding of savings, especially if left for 25 years or more, will generate surpluses for generosity towards the work of God's Kingdom, for retirement, or the next generation.

Prudence means planning for the future. Scripture mandates that we provide for our own families. Scripture also instructs those who are rich (who have more than enough for their own needs) to become rich in good deeds. Paul mentions the gifting from God that enables a person to become a 'giver'.

GUIDELINES FOR INVESTING SURPLUSES

We give generously because God gives generously to us. We invest our giving when we share it with others who labor in God's Kingdom, the local Church, outreach to the poor, evangelism, missions, biblical teaching, and other ministry. Paul the apostle taught the new Gentile Churches to distinguish themselves in giving to the needs of others.

We store treasure in heaven for ourselves when we give our resources or invest them in people and projects that further the kingdom of God. Scripture also leads us to store our resources in the form of an inheritance for our children's children.

APPLICATION

Take inventory of the many ways that God has blessed you and your family in material things. List three areas in your own life that you need to address in order to be a better steward of that which God has entrusted to you. Seek the assistance of a Christian financial planner to establish sound budget for prudent stewardship. Have you studied Scripture concerning the tithe and in giving? How do you apply this understanding to your own finances?

CONCLUSION

Managing household finances in accordance with God's revealed will brings us both challenges and rewards. Appropriate biblical attitudes form the foundation for financial freedom. God reveals His ideas for maximizing earnings, enjoying giving, and minimizing financial dangers. His Word shows us how to generate consistent savings and avoid the slavery of debt. God gives both financial liberty and peace of mind as we follow His ways in finances. Scriptures make it abundantly clear that wealth and prosperity are a result of obedience to God and His Word. Teaching your children this principle will bring them a lifetime of blessing.

LESSON 16 – FAMILY AND EVANGELISTIC FRUITFULNESS: GOD'S STRATEGY FOR REPLENISHING THE EARTH

PURPOSE

Beyond the individual, the Kingdom of God expresses itself most immediately in the human family. God blesses the family with righteous seed, or offspring, for spreading the knowledge of Himself worldwide and replenishing the human race. Within the context of the family, God supplies the resources for procreation, productivity, and evangelism for His purposes throughout the earth. We will examine here God's purposes and plans for covering the earth with His people.

GLOSSARY

Procreate – produce offspring; beget, engender or generate descendants.

Fruit – *Agriculture:* the harvest of labor; *Family:* children, descendants.

Benevolence – the disposition to accomplish good works; charitableness.

Seed – progeny, offspring, children and descendants.

THE FAMILY, PROCREATION, AND THE HUMAN RACE

Genesis 2:24
Matthew 2:15
Genesis 1:11, 20
Genesis 1:24–25
Psalm 22:30–31
Genesis 1:28
Genesis 17:1–8

Genesis 1:22
Isaiah 6:3
Genesis 1:26–28
1 Timothy 5:10–14
Titus 1:6
Romans 4:13–16
Psalm 25:12–13
Isaiah 61:9

Isaiah 11:9

God designed the family for procreation of the human race. Healthy procreation proceeds from family nurture, covenant, and government. Fruitfulness expresses the nature of God. He commanded the multiplication of animal, bird, and fish in the original creation. Then He instructed Adam and Eve to be fruitful and increase in number.

God purposed to fill the earth through procreation within the family. He wanted the parents to raise the children to inherit and manage the earth. Nurturing within the family context provides the training for the children to walk in the ways of the Lord. Spiritual nurture, the goal of the new covenant, has its reflections in the old covenant and its emphasis on human procreation. The earth will be filled with the knowledge of God as the offspring of godly parents fill the earth.

There are some couples who do not conceive children of their own who are nonetheless called and graced by God to bear spiritual offspring. Whether through adoption or service within the body of Christ, they extend the love and Good News of Christ's Kingdom into new fields, bringing forth a rich harvest of righteousness and blessing.

THE FAMILY, BENEVOLENCE, AND GOOD WORKS

Genesis 1:28
Genesis 7:16–20
Philippians 2:1–4

Colossians 3:23–25

Genesis 12:1–3
Deuteronomy 15:7–11
Mark 7:9–14
1 Timothy 5:4–16

God designed social life on earth such that the family express its faith-relationship with God by becoming the primary source of benevolence and good works. Generosity and good works normally overflow from a biblically-oriented and productive family.

God called us, through Abraham and Christ, to be a blessing to all the world. Family productivity means that God's blessing flows beyond the family, especially towards the relatives. Care for one's family and relatives equates with practicing one's faith in Jesus Christ. Also, to care for one's believing relatives relieves the local church of meeting that need.

Acts 11:19
Galatians 6:10
2 Corinthians 9:1–3

1 John 3:16

3 John 5–8

God designed family blessing to extend beyond the family and touch the believer in Christ. Whether local or trans-local believers, the family reaches out with God's blessing to help address their needs. Benevolence and good works need to walk in step with evangelistic and church planting efforts to help demonstrate the practicality of Christ's life and teachings.

Leviticus 19:33–34
Psalm 146:9
Psalm 112:9
Proverbs 19:17
1 Timothy 5:10
Hebrews 13:2

God designed family blessing to reach beyond the known believers and touch the strangers and the poor. God permeated the Mosaic Law with His own attitudes about social justice for people without family structures. God reaches out to include them within His love-care. The non-covenant workman, the traveler, the wanderer (homeless), the foreign guest, the abused – all these God includes within the responsibility of His Israel, now His Church. Christian families who reach out to involve dysfunctional individuals and families will find significant opportunities for evangelism and extending the knowledge and blessing of God.

THE FAMILY, EVANGELISM, AND CHURCH PLANTING

Genesis 1:11

Psalm 1:2–3

Psalm 92:12–15

God built this principle into creation: fruit reproduces after its own kind, whether animal, bird, fish, trees, or agricultural sowing. We see the principle most fully displayed in the human family. From righteous parents and family spring God's life and blessing. God's life reproduced in the children reaches out through them and touches the neighborhood, town, and world.

Genesis 1:28

Isaiah 11:9
Psalm 98:2, 3
John 15:2–8, 16

God designed us to reproduce after our kind. This means that we will also reproduce our spiritual life in others. To reproduce the graces of the Holy Spirit in our children, and then in extended family and neighbors, spreads the glory of God over the face of the earth. Jesus sends us forth to bear much permanent fruit in the lives of new believers.

THE FAMILY OF JESUS CHRIST BLESSES THE NATIONS

Genesis 12:1–3
Genesis 22:15–18
Acts 3:24–25
Galatians 3:6–9
Genesis 3:15

God sent His own Son, Jesus Christ, into a family within a local society, and as the Righteous Seed, God reaches through Him into all the families of the earth. Jesus fulfilled the ancient Word of God as the Seed of the woman (Eve) who would bruise the serpent's (Satan)

Genesis 17:2
Galatians 3:29

Isaiah 6:13
Isaiah 6:7, 8
Genesis 17:3–6
2 Samuel 7:12–13

John 12:23–24
1 Peter 1:23

head. Jesus Christ, as offspring of Abraham, fulfilled the Word concerning the promised Covenant Seed.

God conveys His plans and purposes through 'holy seed', or offspring. Not only did God use Abraham to fulfill His purposes, He also chose David and his descendants to establish the kingdom of God on earth. Jesus, as the descendant of David, proclaimed and epitomized this mission. Jesus of Nazareth is the glorified Seed that John saw and proclaimed. Peter refers to believers in Christ as those who have been born of 'incorruptible' seed, the Word of God. God has designed the family so that it produces abundant fruit, after its kind. This fruit forms the future leadership of the Church of Jesus Christ as well as local society.

APPLICATION

Describe how productive families can produce a generation triumphant in the ways of God. Identify some creative ways for families to live evangelistic lives in their local communities. Can you identify how God has used your natural family to convey spiritual reality? What goals would you set for your household that would enable you to conform more fully to the biblical model of the family? Identify some of the costs of family failure. In what ways can couples without natural children bear Spiritual children?

CONCLUSION

The family fulfills a vital role in the kingdom of God as the fountainhead of productivity and fruitfulness. The basic unit of the immediate family finds its identity and purpose beyond itself in the larger context of worldwide evangelism and the kingdom of God. The multiplication of righteous offspring in the context of godly families provides the resources for the spread of the Church and God's Kingdom throughout the earth.

LESSON 17 – THE FAMILY AND THE CHURCH

PURPOSE

The principles of the natural family extend to the Church. They provide the structure and atmosphere in which we work as part of the household of God and functioning members of His Church. The spiritual health of the local church matches the condition of the families which form its membership. The Scriptures set forth the Church as the family of God and the body of Christ in the earth. In this final lesson of this section, we address the family as the basic unit – beyond the individual – which comprises the Church.

GLOSSARY

Church – the committed Christian community worldwide; the local gathering of the followers of Jesus Christ.

Household – those who live under the same roof and form part of the same family.

Community – a society of people who enjoy common bonds, privileges, interests, and goals.

Integrity – wholeness, entireness, completeness; unbroken state which comprehends the character of an entity; internal soundness.

THE FAMILY IS THE CHURCH IN MINIATURE

Ephesians 3:15
Ephesians 5:21–33

Ephesians 6:4

Matthew 6:9
Philippians 4:19

Ephesians 5:22–6:4

Colossians 3:18–21
1 Peter 3:1–7
Ephesians 5:21
Hebrews 13:17
1 Peter 5:1–5

Proverbs 22:6
Ephesians 6:4
Hebrews 12:4–11

Both the Church and the family related to fatherhood as the source of authority and guidance. For the family is a miniature expression of the Church. The father in his own home leads and guides his family. The Church looks to God as Eternal Father, the one source of all authority and provision.

Appropriate subordination with the natural family conveys the truth of yieldedness to godly authority within Christ's Church. God requires subordination with the natural family. The capacity to defer appropriately within the family forms the training ground for yieldedness with Christ's Kingdom as expressed through His Church.

The experience of training and discipline within the family context sets the stage for equipping and oversight through the leadership of the Church. As children learn to respond to and value their family instruction and reproof, they sensitize themselves to the guidance, the reproofs, and impartation of God's Spirit.

THE CHURCH IS A FAMILY

Psalm 103:13

Ephesians 3:18

Hosea 1:1–2:23

Isaiah 49:15–16
1 Thessalonians 2:7–11

Matthew 6:9–13
Matthew 7:7–11
1 John 3:1,16
John 3:16

Romans 8:15

Galatians 4:5, 6

Matthew 3:17
Psalm 2:7
2 Samuel 7:14
1 Chronicles 17:13
Matthew 3:17
Matthew 9:14–15
John 3:27–30

Ephesians 5:21–6:4

Ephesians 4:11–16

Acts 2:44–45
Acts 4:34–35

1 Peter 2:4–10

God reveals Himself, without excuse, in terms of family roles and identity. In the Scriptures, God characterizes Himself as Eternal Father, the only God who deals with followers in terms of fatherly compassion. He depicts Himself as a devoted and faithful Husband, dedicated to the love of His life. He also portrays Himself as a nursing mother, giving sensitive care and attention to His children.

Jesus instructs us to approach God as our Father – not simply as a generalized, abstract personage – but the God, Who as Father, loves and cares for us with a faithfulness beyond human comprehension. The apostle Paul shows us the meaning and closeness of the fatherly relationship in the Spirit's prompting us to call Him 'Abba', the equivalent of 'Daddy'.

God the Father speaks of Jesus, very simply, as His Son. From the mystery of Psalm 2 ... to the Davidic declaration of Samuel ... to the Heavenly declaration at Jesus's Baptism ... the Scriptures recognize Him as God's own and only Son. The Scriptures also recognize Jesus as a Bridegroom, Who sees His Church relationally as His Bride.

Relationally, the husband-wife bond symbolizes the mystery of just how Christ relates to His Church. God looks at the Church as a spiritual unit, His family, nurtured through the headship of Christ to become like Christ. And this Church, God's own family, practices love-care for one another and for those in the world. The Spirit of God builds Christ's Church as God's family into a spiritual household, a dwelling place for the Living God.

CONSISTENCY IN FAMILY ORDER AND CHURCH ORDER

Numbers 1:5–16
Numbers 7:2
1 Timothy 3:1–5
1 Corinthians 14:34–35

The ability of the Church to experience and practice order presupposes the same quality of order within the home and family. God designated the man, as the head of his household, to represent his family before God and the Church. Likewise, he represents God and the Church before his family. Under the new covenant in Jesus Christ, spiritual realities inhabit and permeate that which under the old covenant was only natural. Therefore, the headship and the resulting order expresses itself most clearly in the effect the local family has upon the Church and the kingdom of God.

Acts 6:3
1 Timothy 3:1–13

1 Timothy 2:11–15
1 Corinthians 11:3

The functional roles of man and woman extend beyond the family into the Church. The dynamics resident within family roles overflow into Church life, leadership, and mission. God assigns men the responsibility of roles having to do with ministry, leadership, and authority. God also assigns appropriate roles to women within the Church, such as ministry, and service as expressing and serving the roles that men exercise as leaders.

FAMILY: SUPPORTING THE CHURCH

God assigned the family the fundamental role of resourcing the Church and Her mission on earth. Parachurch groups or service organizations

Romans 12:13
Romans 13:8
1 Peter 4:9–11

Romans 16:1–2

1 Timothy 1:5
Titus 2:1–8
1 Timothy 5:8–10

Hebrews 13:1–4
Acts 18:18–19
Acts 18:24–26
Romans 16:3–5
John 13:34–35
Matthew 5:13–16

can never replace the godly family as the source for carrying out Christ's mission on earth. God, by His giftings, enables the family to extend love-care in ways that no organization could hope to match.

The complementary roles represented in godly fathers and mothers provide nurture as well as teaching. God graces the godly family for benevolence, hospitality, and service which no institution can provide. The Good News of Jesus's Gospel spreads naturally and appropriately from the platform of the family within the local church. For the Gospel, lived out in daily lifestyle, exemplifies much more accurately its inherent truth and power. However, any unresolved family problems soon find their way into the arena of the Church family.

CHURCH MINISTRY MAKES FAMILIES SUCCESSFUL

1 Timothy 3:12
1 Timothy 5:14
Hebrews 13:4
Exodus 20:12
Ephesians 5:25
1 Peter 3:7

God fashioned the family and the Church as mutually supportive in His Kingdom's work. God designs the gift-ministries, especially the five 'Ascension' gifts, to impact the family and impart truth, power, and godly structure into families. The Church leadership, enabled by its 'Ascension' giftings, helps define and support the integrity of family relationships.

As the Church leadership faithfully stewards and conveys the counsels of God regarding men, women, and children, then godly families support and extend the Church. Family health and stability will decline to the extent that Church leadership withholds biblical instruction from Church families. Likewise, a decline in the quality and health of the family produces a corresponding decline in the health of the Church.

APPLICATION

Describe some of the relational activity of a healthy family atmosphere. Show how this activity depicts life within normal Church life. How would you describe the difference between family government and Church government? Identify the place of the individual conscience within the setting of the family, as well as in the Church as the larger family of God. How can your family best support the Church and its mission?

CONCLUSION

The future health of the Church depends directly upon the teaching and training of healthy family life. Within the setting of the family, the individual first learns how to respond to godly authority, the delegation of responsibility, and the skills of service to others. Many alternate models for the family in local culture challenge the biblical home and family. Such challenges work directly against the structural integrity of the Church of Jesus Christ and hinder the fulfillment of its mission.

God designed His Kingdom to be revealed and expressed in the context of the godly family. And from the family His Kingdom extends into the life of the local church, society, and into the world.

CHRIST'S KINGDOM AND THE CHURCH

LESSON 1 – THE KINGDOM OF GOD IN THE OLD COVENANT

PURPOSE

Genesis 1:26–28

Psalm 8

Psalm 105:8–10

Exodus 2:24

God's purpose in creating mankind was to have a fellowship with us whereby He would delegate to us rule over creation. In other words, we must have a vital relationship with God in order to manage the creation that has been entrusted to us.

God is a covenant-making and covenant-keeping God. He gives His Word to establish a bond of security. That bond or covenant defines how we govern what has been entrusted to us. Our relationship to God, and His will working through us to steward creation, is His Kingdom in the earth.

GLOSSARY

Eternal – without beginning or ending ... outside of the time space realm.

Covenant – a bond established between two or more parties which produces one will and purpose. Biblical covenants were usually established in blood signifying the pledge of life to keep the terms of the covenant.

COVENANT, THE BASIS OF GOVERNMENT

Genesis 1:1–3

Jeremiah 33:20

The opening verses of the Bible establish a covenant with day and night according to Jeremiah the prophet. The certainty of day and night, guaranteed by God's Word, provides a secure framework in which creation can function. All of the activities of creation in plant and animal life, as well as in the life of mankind, are based upon the certainty of God's Word and covenant. If day and night should become unpredictable and chaotic, all ability to govern would be lost.

Genesis 2:15, 17

God's Word to Adam was a 'word bond' that established Adam's power to govern the Garden. The terms of Adam's government were established in God's covenant with him. Breaking the terms, namely eating of the forbidden tree, caused him to lose his rule over the Garden and brought adversity to creation.

Genesis 3:21

Genesis 3:15

You will notice that there is no shedding of blood in establishing this covenant, because man had not yet sinned. But after Adam and Eve sinned, blood was shed to cover their nakedness. And blood was shed thereafter in making covenants. It became understood that God's covenants are a life and death issue. Later in history, Jesus' blood was shed to keep God's promise to redeem mankind.

Genesis 8:20–9:17

Hundreds of years after Adam, when the inhabitants of earth grew wicked, God chose Noah, a 'preacher of righteousness', to build an ark for the salvation of his family and animal life. After the flood, God made a covenant with Noah that re-confirmed day and night and the seasons, and He re-confirmed mankind's rule over creation. Then, He gave His word that He would not destroy the earth by water ever again, and confirmed this covenant with the rainbow. Later, Noah offered a sacrifice.

Genesis 10:32–11:9

The Scriptures tell us that as time passed, the descendants of Noah lost their covenant relationship with God and began to act upon their own desires, finally attempting to build a tower to reach heaven. This ended in confusion and dispersions.

Genesis 12:1–8
Genesis 14:17–15:21
Genesis 17:1–21
Genesis 18:17–19

God called Abraham out of the city of Ur, near Babel, to a land that he did not know. God promised to bless all nations through Abraham and to give him a son and descendants. Once again, God had established a covenant with a chosen person and had given a spiritual blessing that would make him a leader and a blessing to others. Abraham's ability to govern God's blessings of prosperity came directly from God's covenant that was made with him.

Genesis 17:21
Genesis 28:10–17
Luke 26:42

Genesis 2:23–25

As promised, God gave Abraham and Sarah a son whom they named Isaac. God confirmed the covenant to Isaac and to his son Jacob. God's covenant included descendants, land, and blessing. But later Jacob and his family were led to Egypt and eventually their descendants were made slaves. When they cried unto the Lord, He heard them because of the covenant that He had made with Abraham, Isaac, and Jacob.

Exodus 12:1–14
1 Corinthians 10:1–2

Exodus 19:5–6

When God delivered Israel out of slavery, He brought them out by the shedding of blood, through baptism in the Red Sea, and through the cloud of the Holy Spirit. He then brought them into the wilderness where He made another covenant with them. For the first time, God's covenant was with a nation. The covenant promised that if they kept His Law, they would be His unique and holy nation. Moses' government and all of Israel's leaders after him were to be based upon the covenant revealed in the wilderness. The Law covenant was the basis for God's Kingdom being revealed to the nations of the world.

2 Samuel 7:5–16
Psalm 89:1–4
2 Samuel 28:1–7
Jeremiah 33:21
2 Chronicles 7:18
2 Chronicles 21:7

Centuries after God's covenant in the wilderness with Israel, God made a covenant with David that his Seed would rule over Israel forever. This covenant was confirmed with Solomon and given as the basis for God's preservation of Israel. Again there is a vital connection between God's covenant and man's rule. We rule by His faithfulness to His Word and His steadfast grace.

THE NEW COVENANT, THE BASIS OF CHRIST'S GOVERNMENT

Matthew 1:1, 17
Matthew 9:27
Luke 2:11

Approximately 1,000 years after David received a covenant from God that his descendants would rule, Jesus was born of David's lineage. Those who accepted Him as the Messiah, or God's anointed One, recognized that He was the fulfillment of God's promise to David; they called Him 'Son of David.'

Galatians 3:16

Jesus is also referred to as the 'Seed of Abraham' signifying that He is the fulfillment of God's promise to bless all nations. In both cases

Genesis 17
2 Chronicles 7:17–18
Luke 1:54–55
Luke 2:67–79

Matthew 26:26–29
Luke 22:14–20

Genesis 3:15
Genesis 12:1–3
Galatians 3:16

2 Samuel 7:13–16
1 Peter 2:22

Hebrews 9:1–28

Acts 1:3

Acts 1:9
Hebrews 4:14
Hebrews 5:6
Hebrews 7:1–9:28

– David and Abraham – Jesus' birth is the result of God's covenants. The previous covenants were the basis for Jesus' coming to redeem and rule mankind. The new covenant established a new manifestation of the kingdom of God – in Christ.

At the close of His earthly ministry and just prior to His crucifixion, He established a new covenant with His disciples in His own blood. That is, He pledged to give His own life to fulfill God's promise that the 'Seed of Woman' would bruise Satan's head. He gave His life to fulfill God's promise to Abraham that His seed would bless all nations. He gave His own life to fulfill the promise that David's seed would forever rule God's people. Jesus is also the fulfillment of the Law covenant in that He kept the Law without sin.

So, in Jesus Christ is the fulfillment of Old Testament covenants and promises of God. In Jesus is the establishment of a new and superior covenant which shall be discussed in the next lesson.

When Jesus died on the cross to ratify the new covenant and arose again to confirm its power, He spent 40 days with the disciples teaching them concerning the kingdom of God. After the new covenant was established, the first matter of business was the kingdom of God, or how to administrate the new covenant constitution.

Jesus ascended back to the Father to take up His High Priestly and Kingly duties, and He sent the Holy Spirit to the disciples on the day of Pentecost. The Eternal Kingdom, or government of God, was now functioning in the hearts of those who had received the new covenant and the Holy Spirit.

APPLICATION

Genesis 15–17
Exodus 19:5–6

Psalm 89:1–4

In what ways do God's covenants affect us? What was the main promise in the Abrahamic covenant? What was the main promise in the covenant with Moses and Israel? What was the main promise in the Davidic covenant? Compare the relationship between the president of a nation and its constitution, to the relationship of Jesus to the new covenant.

CONCLUSION

God is the Supreme or Sovereign Ruler over all things. He has revealed Himself and His will to mankind through covenants and given to man authority to rule within the framework of those covenants. Each covenant has given to us a revelation of God and His purpose. In each of the covenants that He has given, He gave the power to administrate that covenant to a person, a nation, or a lineage.

Ephesians 2:12–13

The entire old covenant is given to prepare us for the new covenant in Christ and to see God's Eternal Kingdom in Christ. The new covenant makes us the recipients of God's promises to the patriarchs and prophets and makes us partakers of Christ's Kingdom. Gentiles who were once 'far off' from God's covenants and promises have now been brought into the inheritance through the new covenant in Christ's blood.

LESSON 2 – THE KINGDOM IN THE GOSPELS

PURPOSE

The Gospels (Matthew, Mark, Luke and John) are the first-hand accounts of Jesus' life, teaching, and activities, as He expressed the Father's words and works on earth. These Gospels, along with the other God-breathed letters of the New Testament, show Jesus to be the fulfillment of the old covenant prophecies and types of the Messiah. The Gospels also reveal Jesus as the perfect fulfillment of the Torah, the Mosaic Law, and the priestly system carried by the Levites. In this lesson, we will discuss how Jesus fulfills the previous requirements of the old covenant, and how He establishes a new and more perfect basis for relating to God, His Kingdom, and His purposes on earth.

GLOSSARY

Dominion – supreme authority, the power to control or direct.

Sovereign – one who possesses the highest authority.

Deliverance – release from captivity, slavery or oppresion.

Mediator – 'One who interposes between parties at variance for the purpose of reconciling them' (*Webster*).

Type – a symbolic representation of something yet to come.

Covenant – (Hebrew: *berith*), a personal and corporate arrangement between God (the Great King) and His people that establishes an unbreakable relational bond and spells out mutual responsibilities.

THE OLD COVENANTS WERE INCOMPLETE

Luke 1:2–3

Jeremiah 31:31–34
Jeremiah 33:12–26
Hebrews 9–10:26

Hebrews 9–10:26

Exodus 32:15–16

Romans 3:23

Romans 7:12–8:4
Hebrews 10:3

Ephesians 2:11–12

Isaiah 60:1–22

The former covenants given to Adam, Noah, Abraham, Moses, and David all pointed to a later fulfillment: a 'seed', a blessing, a Son or Messiah who was to come. They all pointed to a future fulfillment; they were incomplete.

Another limitation of these former covenants was that they dealt with natural things: earthly tabernacles and sacrifices which were only a shadow of heavenly things. The Law itself was written in stone. The provision of the Law rested upon mankind as a cold and heavy responsibility – a responsibility which no one has ever successfully completed. And while the Law served to judge us in our failure, it could never save us. It pointed mankind to his need for salvation.

A limitation that seriously affected all who were Gentiles (Non-Jews) is that the old covenants applied primarily to Israel. While prophets like Isaiah foretold that the Gentiles would come to God through His coming Kingdom, under the old covenants they came to

Israel to get to God. For the most part, it was believed that Gentiles had to become Jewish proselytes in order to be in covenant with God. So, under the old covenants, God's Kingdom was viewed as mainly Jewish and governed by Jewish kings and priests.

THE NEW COVENANT IS SPIRITUAL

Romans 14:17
Romans 8:5–8

Hebrews 10:3
2 Corinthians 3:2–18

Matthew 27:50
Matthew 5:7

Luke 10:9
Matthew 14:13–21

Matthew 6:32–33

God's Kingdom has always proceeded from the eternal or spiritual realm. But the old covenants taught mankind spiritual lessons through natural things. The new covenant removed the physical 'props' and shadows and laid bare spiritual reality in Christ. The new covenant dealt more with attitudes or 'Law of Christ' rather than rules and regulations. It dealt with motives rather than ceremonies.

In the Gospels, we see Jesus demonstrating the power of His spiritual government over physical things such as disease, hunger, and nature. Jesus taught His followers that seeking the Kingdom first would solve the other problems. The kingdom of God in our lives (Christ's government) removes anxiety about clothes, food, and other things, because we know that if we obey Him, He will give supply for our needs.

Galatians 4:1–11
Matthew 23:1–24

Galatians 3:1–9

Galatians 5:1–6:18

While God's Kingdom has always been spiritual, the new covenant brings mankind to a more mature realization that ultimate power is in the spiritual realm, not in laws and ceremonies. The supreme message of the new covenant is that salvation is through faith in Jesus Christ, not through any works of the flesh which we might do.

THE NEW COVENANT IS SUPERIOR

Matthew 19:7–8
Matthew 22:24
John 6:32
Colossians 3:1–4

Hebrews 7:22
(Note: Entire book of Hebrews)

Philippians 3:20

Hebrews 10:1–25

1 Peter 2:5–10

Jesus often contrasted or compared His covenant with the Law covenant of Moses. The New Testament picks up this theme both in the Gospels and the successive books, particularly the book of Hebrews. Here are a few of the ways that the new covenant or bond with God through Christ's blood, is superior:

- The new covenant deals with eternal things versus natural and temporal things
- Written on the heart versus stone
- Ratified by the blood of Christ instead of the blood of animals
- Mediated by Christ the High Priest versus priests that sinned and died
- Administrated by the Holy Spirit versus earthly rulers
- The 'House' Christ built versus the one Moses built
- The old covenant was administered through Israel, a nation established on earth; the new covenant is administered through Christ's Kingdom and the Church, His body, whose names are written in heaven.

Matthew 5:17, 19
Colossians 1:9–10

To say that the new covenant is superior is not in any way degrading or diminishing the old covenant. They were part of God's purpose to point out the need for the new covenant and to prepare mankind for it. Our Lord Himself quoted from and testified to the inspiration of the old covenant. He saw Himself as the fulfillment of the old covenant promises. In Him, the old covenants are complete, and in Him we are also complete.

THE NEW COVENANT IS UNIVERSAL

Exodus 19:6

The first 'covenant of day and night' affected all of the earth. God's covenant with Adam affected all of the earth, as did the ones with Noah, Abraham, and Moses. The Law Covenant with Moses and Israel was God's choice of a nation (Israel) to be a light to all of the other nations. In it, God stressed that all of the earth was His. But Israel became obsessed with themselves and failed to reach out to the nations with the Light that they had.

Isaiah 6:3
Isaiah 9:1–7
Isaiah 42:1–4
Isaiah 60

Matthew 8:5–13
John 3:16
Matthew 28:18–20

Revelation 1:15–17
1 Corinthians 1:15–20

Prophets like Isaiah saw God's glory in all the world. But they also saw that it would come after the Messiah (Christ) came and established His Kingdom. When Jesus Christ finally did come according to the prophecies, He taught a universal salvation by faith and faith alone – allowing 'whosoever will' to enter. He chided the Jews for their lack of faith and told them that Gentiles and sinners would enter before them. Preparing to ascend, He sent His disciples into all the world to preach the Good News that Jesus Christ, God's Son lived, died, and arose again according to the Scriptures. He conquered sin and death, and all who believe in Him will have everlasting life.

We can have an eternal bond with God through accepting Jesus Christ and confessing Him as Lord. That bond, which we call the new covenant, is open to all men and women everywhere who will receive it. Upon receiving Christ, we receive His Word as the guarantee of our salvation and His Spirit as the seal and administrator of His Kingdom in our hearts.

APPLICATION

Name several covenants mentioned in the Old Testament. How do they differ? How does the new covenant differ with them? Compare Genesis 1:28 with Matthew 28:18.

CONCLUSION

Romans 8:16–17
Romans 8:31–39

The Gospels are the eyewitness accounts of Jesus' life. They bring the Good News to us and all mankind ... that God has given man the opportunity to reunite with Him and receive all of the inheritance that was lost because of sin. Through faith in Jesus Christ, we are brought into His covenant family and made joint heirs with Christ. What a promise!

LESSON 3 – THE NEW COVENANT AND THE KINGDOM OF GOD

PURPOSE

Mark 14:22
2 Peter 1:10

Hebrews 13:20

Romans 14:17

Jesus Christ established the new covenant, by His own blood sacrifice at the cross, and provided the basis of our entrance into the kingdom of God. This new covenant is the eternal bond which God established between Himself and His people. The kingdom of God is His governmental reign over both His people and all creation, as well as the means by which He produces righteousness, peace, and joy in the Holy Spirit. The covenant and the Kingdom are two separate, yet interrelated, aspects of God's great plan of redemption. We become rightly related with God through receiving Christ and His Covenant, and then become participants in His Kingdom.

GLOSSARY

Covenant – an eternal, relational bond initiated and established by God's grace with His people through the work of Jesus Christ at the cross. The new covenant, fulfillment of all previous covenants, stands as the constitution for God's people. It describes how God relates to His people and what He expects of them.

Kingdom – the eternal realm of God's sovereign, active and authoritative reign over all things in the universe.

Ephesians 3:10

Church – Christ's Bride, the chosen instrument of God, under the new covenant, through which the kingdom of God is proclaimed and revealed.

Supreme – highest in authority.

Sovereign – highest Lord or Ruler.

Lordship – dominion; power and authority.

THE NEW COVENANT THROUGH CHRIST

Romans 1:4; 8:11

Hebrews 10:1

Romans 8:10

1 Corinthians 15:20

Ephesians 1:20
Hebrews 1:1–4, 21
Philippians 2:9

Hebrews 7:22

Ephesians 1:10

When God, by His own power, raised Jesus from the dead, He brought to completion all that the previous covenants had foreseen and embodied in shadow form. The Law, the prophets, and the writings all found their intended fulfillment in Christ. His Resurrection broke all powers of Satan and released the frustration (futility) to which God had subjected mankind and the creation.

The Father seated His Son, Jesus Christ, at His own right hand. Thereby, He exalted His Son through the Resurrection from the dead to a supreme position to which no created being could attain. The Father placed the resurrected Christ far above all authority, power, or dominion in heaven or earth. Christ, by His supreme position, guarantees the

Colossians 1:16–18
1 Corinthians 15:24

operation of the new covenant, from the newest believer to the greatest nation and to the managements of the ages.

The Father then placed all things under the feet of Christ the King as the ultimate Ruler in this age as well as the age to come. He transferred all believers out from under the authority of Satan and into the authority of His own Son. Christ exercises this Kingdom authority or dominion now and until the end of the age, when He will return it to His Father.

Ephesians 1:22
Ephesians 1:10
Colossians 1:16–18

Finally, the Father appointed His Son to be Head over everything for the Church. With Christ as the Head over the Church, the Father purposes to bring all things in heaven and earth together under the Headship of His Son, Jesus Christ.

Philippians 2:9–10
Ephesians 3:10

Therefore, both in the Church and the world, the Father has established Jesus Christ as the Sovereign Ruler over creation and history. In this way, through the Church, the manifold wisdom of God will be made known to all rulers and authorities. This is the Father's eternal purpose which He accomplished in Christ Jesus our Lord.

THE NEW COVENANT ENABLES US TO ENTER HIS KINGDOM

Ephesians 2:19
Philippians 3:20

1 Thessalonians 2:12
Romans 8:28
Colossians 1:30
Acts 3:19
Acts 2:38

John 3:20
Romans 12:1–2
Acts 1:8

To receive Christ into our lives means that we agree to the terms included in the new covenant. Jesus becomes Lord over all things in our lives. His life-giving sacrifice covers our sins. Our citizenship is transferred eternally from earth to God's Kingdom.

God Himself has called us into His Kingdom based on the covenantal work of Christ. We are seen by Scripture to be 'in Christ.' And as Christ is rightly related to His Father, and we belong to Christ, then we also walk into the same relationship. Our right standing with the Father prepares us now to enter His Kingdom. That is, we come fully under His authority and purposes. And we begin to exercise the spiritual authority He has so graciously bequeathed to us.

WE SEEK HIS KINGDOM AS PRIORITY

John 3:3, 5
1 Peter 1:3–5

To see the kingdom of God, or to enter into it, depends upon being born 'from above'. One's right relationship with God arises from the experience of being born 'of the Spirit'. This new birth qualifies the repentant sinner to be received by God, cleared of his sin, and enter into Christ's eternal Kingdom. The full provision of the new covenant becomes the inheritance of the new believer.

Matthew 6:33
Matthew 6:25
Romans 12:1–2

Matthew 6:25

Matthew 6:34

However, Jesus exhorts us to place His Kingdom as priority over all things in life. We yield ourselves to Him as an appropriate daily sacrifice. Our daily concern is how to serve Jesus as Master in our lives. Concerns about what we eat or drink, how we clothe our bodies, or our appearance – these must not take priority over Jesus' plans and purposes for us. Our very future itself lies within Jesus' plan, not ours.

Luke 4:44
Acts 28:31

Jesus considered His primary mission on earth as focusing on proclaiming this Good News of the kingdom of God. This is the message Jesus delivered to His disciples and they, in turn, spread it around the Mediterranean world within a few decades.

ALL MANKIND WILL RECOGNIZE CHRIST'S KINGDOM

Philippians 2:5–11
Hebrews 1:1–4
Philippians 2:9
Ephesians 1:22

God has established His Christ as Supreme Ruler over the universe. The extent to which He yielded Himself to the Father's will through the cross is matched by the degree to which the Father exalted Him, bestowing upon Him an unmatched name, position, authority, and inheritance. Whenever non-believers – individuals or nations – attempt to 'break His chains', 'throw off His fetters', or 'take their stand against His Anointed', the Lord will rebuke and terrify them in His wrath. For He has already installed His King as Sovereign over all things.

Philippians 2:10–11
Titus 2:14
2 Thessalonians 1:7–10

Every person shall bow before Christ's Kingdom; everyone shall confess that He indeed is Lord. At the return of our Lord, Jesus Christ, all mankind will realize the majesty of His Person and the absoluteness of His power.

THE KINGDOM AND THE CHURCH

Ephesians 2:19–21
Acts 1:7–8

Matthew 28:19–20
Galatians 3:7–9

Genesis 12:3; 18:18

Citizenship in Christ's Kingdom includes membership in His Church. Jesus Christ is Head over all things for the Church. When Jesus ascended to the Father's right hand, He established a new government by the power of His Holy Spirit. Just before ascending, Jesus stipulated the mission of His Church. His disciples are to 'go and make disciples', taking to all the nations (Gentiles) of the earth the Abrahamic blessing. This 'Gospel' fulfills the covenant graciously given to Abraham.

Matthew 28:19–20

Acts 1:8
Ephesians 3:10

Christ, at His Resurrection, provided both the power and mission for His Church. Thus, the Church becomes the instrument through which the rule (Kingdom) of Christ is proclaimed in all the earth. God has purposed to make known His wisdom through the Church to all rulers and authorities.

2 Corinthians 5:16–21

The Church is now the earthly embassy of Christ's heavenly government. Believers are now appointed as ambassadors to all nations, to carry the message of reconciliation accomplished through Christ at the cross.

APPLICATION

If you are a participant in the new covenant, how did this come about in your life? How would you describe the new covenant or the kingdom of God? How do they relate to each other? Describe the relationship between the new covenant of Jesus Christ and the Church of which He is Head.

246 THE COVENANT AND THE KINGDOM

CONCLUSION

The Kingdom is the eternal realm in which the Father actively reigns through Christ. The Church is a society of people. The Kingdom creates the context in which the Church is birthed and thrives. The Church witnesses to the reality of God's Kingdom. The Church is the instrument through which the Kingdom grows and expands. It is through the new covenant, ratified by Christ's blood sacrifice, that right relationship with God becomes possible. Those who place their trust and faith in Christ's finished work on the cross are delivered from darkness and transferred into the kingdom of God, where Christ rules as Lord. Acknowledgement of Christ's Lordship and obedience to His commands causes His will to be done and His Kingdom manifested in the earth. Those who exercise obedience to Christ's commands are also members of His Church, the instrument He has chosen to reveal His Kingdom rule to all creation. The new covenant, the Kingdom, and the Church are three vital aspects of God's eternal purpose.

LESSON 4 – THE NATURE OF THE CHURCH

PURPOSE

Ephesians 1:23
Ephesians 3:10

Ephesians 3:6

The Church of Jesus Christ is revealed in Scripture as His Body and the instrument of His choosing to manifest His wisdom and rule to principalities and powers. The Church results from the proclamation of the kingdom of God. As we preach Jesus and His Kingship, those who respond are placed as His Body and members of His Church.

GLOSSARY

Body – the biblical figure used to depict the relationship and connectedness of the members of the Church to Jesus Christ as its Head and to one another.

Church – the assembly (Greek: *ekklesia*) of God's people over which Jesus Christ rules as Sovereign Head, and the instrument of Christ's choosing to reveal Himself and His will.

Gospel – the Good News of Christ's life, death on the cross, His Resurrection and reign to save us from our sins, death, and judgment.

Priority – precedence in place or work.

Repentance – to turn around, change direction, and pursue a different course.

THE CHURCH CONSISTS OF THOSE WHO RECEIVE THE GOSPEL

Matthew 24:14
Matthew 28:18–20

Jesus told His disciples to teach this Gospel to all people and to all nations on earth. He further instructed them to go into every nation on earth and make disciples of those who would respond. The commission is to baptize them in the triune name and to teach them to obey everything Jesus had commanded His original followers.

Romans 10:17

Romans 10:14–15

Acts 2:36–8
Matthew 16:17–19
John 1:12
Ephesians 2:19–21

To proclaim the message of Jesus stirs faith in those who would respond. For faith comes from hearing God's message. God's message is heard through the Word about Jesus Christ. Those who respond in faith to Christ's message receive salvation. and citizenship in Christ's Kingdom. Those who believe the Good News that Jesus Christ is the Son of God become the building materials for the Church.

THE CHURCH CONSISTS OF THOSE WHO REPENT

Matthew 10:38; 16:24

Acts 2:38; 3:19
John 3:36
Matthew 5:3–10
Psalm 51:17

Jesus taught His disciples that to acknowledge Him as Lord means to follow His leadership and lifestyle. The first step is to repent of one's sins, to recognize that one's actions and lifestyle are rebellion against the living God and worthy of just retribution. Jesus receives to Himself the humble in heart and broken in spirit.

Acts 2:47

All those who have repented for their sins and yielded to Christ's Headship are counted as members of His Church.

Colossians 3:1–3
Galatians 2:20; 6:14

Luke 14:25–27
2 Corinthians 4:77–12

As the believer seeks to please his Lord, he learns to deny his own self-centered, personal, and cultural inclinations and replace them with Christ's interest. The cross symbolized this denial, as it were – a dying to self-interest and self-will. The path of repentance gradually works in the believer the capacity to lay down his own life to fulfill all that Jesus has for him.

Matthew 6:33

Matthew 6:24

Matthew 6:28–34
Matthew 7:24–27

Jesus also taught that the believers's priority in life is to seek first God's Kingdom, His rulership in their lives. This leadership applies to all aspects of life. In response, God assures us that all other things will be cared for. By following this pathway, God's Kingdom gradually becomes the cornerstone for the believer's life.

THE CHURCH CONSISTS OF THOSE WHO RECEIVE CHRIST'S HEADSHIP OR GOVERNMENT

Ephesians 1:22; 5:23–24

Hebrews 10:7
Psalm 40:6–8

God the Father has divinely appointed Jesus to the position as Head of the Church. He Who loved the Church and gave His own life for her walks as undisputed Leader over all believers. All who claim to be part of the Church walk in submission to their Lord as Supreme Leader. Even as Jesus delighted to accomplish the will of His Father, so also His followers delight to walk in obedience to Him and His purposes.

Colossians 1:18
Colossians 2:10

John 15:16
2 Thessalonians 1:8

Christ's Headship means that He has been given the position of supreme command and importance. Christ's current dominion applies to all situations, nations, and individuals. Christ's oversight impinges on the affairs of governments, economies, armies, and politics, as well as individuals. Those who walk in joyful obedience to the Head of the Church become productive servants within Christ's purpose. Those who reject His Headship will suffer the consequences of His wrath.

Colossians 2:19
Colossians 3:12–17
Ephesians 4:15–16

A right and personal relationship to the Head releases believers to health and growth within His Body, the Church. The bond which the Spirit of God creates between the believer and His Lord permits the flow of Jesus' power and purpose for each individual believer. Jesus as the Head of the Church is the standard and final goal for all the members. Through our linking with Jesus Christ, we mature into the person and productivity that He has planned for us.

THE CHURCH CONSISTS OF THOSE WHO BECOME JOINED IN CHRIST

1 Corinthians 12:13

Galatians 3:26–29

John 17:21
1 Corinthians 12:12

Those who have received the Gospel and repented of their ways are placed by the Holy Spirit into Christ's Body, the Church. Within His Body no merely human distinctions prevail. All of us become 'one in Christ Jesus'.

The Church is one unit made of different parts comprising the whole. The diversity of the parts reflects Christ's love and gifts for all believers. As each section within the symphony orchestra, under the

Ephesians 3:6
Ephesians 4:15–16

leader's baton, produces the author's music, so also each part of the body of Christ, under His direction, brings into reality His plans and purposes.

Those who are members of the Body of Christ share a common inheritance and mutual relationship. The bond of the Spirit unites us and leads us to share our lives with all those who walk under Christ's headship.

Ephesians 4:15–16
Colossians 3:15

Our common commitment to Christ as Head of the Body and our common placement within His Body carry relational responsibilities that must be embraced by each member. Christ the Head gives specific gifts to each person in His Church. The gifts differ by divine arrangement. We serve Christ's Body by sharing generously our gifting, and we receive from other members the giftings we do not ourselves possess.

THE CHURCH IS GOD'S TEMPLE, GOD'S DWELLING PLACE

1 Corinthians 3:16
1 Corinthians 6:19

The physical bodies of believers are to be the temples of God's presence on earth. Wherever the believer lives or works, there God also lives and works – in His temple, the believer.

2 Corinthians 6:16
Ephesians 2:20–22

The corporate Church is viewed as the temple of God's living presence on earth. God's living presence in and through the Church qualifies her to become the source and conduit of God's blessings to the entire world population.

1 Peter 2:5–6

Hebrews 8:5; 10:1

The Church is being built into a spiritual building or temple that supersedes the temple of the old covenant. The old covenant represents the 'shadow' of God's real purposes. And in Christ we receive the 'substance' of all that God planned for His Church. God's household of believers is the Church of the Living God . . . the spiritual house . . . the holy temple.

APPLICATION

Ephesians 3:10–11

Describe how you see the Church in relationship to Christ's Kingdom. How is God's wisdom revealed through the Church to spiritual powers and principalities? Do you view yourself as the indwelling place of God's Spirit and part of the corporate habitation of God's presence in the earth? Describe how division in the Church affects Christ's Kingdom.

CONCLUSION

The Church of Jesus Christ is a unique and distinct expression of God's purposes. The Church universal is the fulfillment of what racial Israel was destined to portray. The natural expressions of physical Israel have given way to the more glorious Church for which they served as a sign. Christ is building a temple in the earth from 'living stones', representing those who have earnestly repented of their own ways to seek Christ's Kingdom and rule. This holy habitation is the dwelling place of God's Holy Spirit. It is through this spiritual temple, the Church, that the Holy Spirit is at work revealing the character, purposes, gifts, and ministries of Jesus Christ.

LESSON 5 – THE CHURCH IS CHRIST'S BODY

PURPOSE

It is through the Apostle Paul that we receive the inspired view of the Church as the body and bride of Christ. The harmonious functions of the human body provide Christians with a practical model for understanding how the Church should work together in a manner that fulfills God's purpose.

GLOSSARY

Body – frame, stature; assembly or confederation.

Diversity – difference, variety, distinctiveness.

Harmony – a setting or working together, agreement.

THE CHURCH IS CHRIST'S BODY ON EARTH

1 Corinthians 12:12–26
Colossians 1:24

The Apostle Paul specifically defines the Church throughout the earth as Christ's Body. Individual members, living or dead, constitute His Church, irrespective of nation, blood lines, or social status.

1 Corinthians 11:23–28
Ephesians 4:16

The Church is joined to Christ by covenant, by the new covenant which He ratified in His own blood at the cross. All the terms of the covenant become the inheritance of each believer. This covenant, common to all Church members, joins each member to the other. The covenant proceeds from Christ, the Head, and completely envelopes the believer's life.

Ephesians 3:10

Church members function together under Christ's Headship to express and fulfill His purposes, wisdom, and blessings to all people.

CHRIST IS THE HEAD AND LIFE SOURCE OF THE CHURCH

Ephesians 5:21–24

Ephesians 4:15
Ephesians 4:16

The Church is subject to her Head and Source, Jesus Christ. Even as the natural body submits to the commands which proceed from our natural heads, so also the Church receives identity and nourishment from her Leader, Jesus Christ. He, as the Head and life source of the Church, is the example for all growth toward maturity. Christ's Headship provides for us structural stability and harmony.

Colossians 1:19

Ephesians 4:10–12

Ephesians 4:16

As we are connected appropriately to the Head, we receive all that is necessary for our health and growth. All His giftings and ministries pour into our lives through the Spirit. And thereby all the members and systems within the Body mature and find appropriate development and productivity.

John 6:48–58

Jesus characterizes Himself as the 'Bread of Life'. He places Himself as the source of life flow, even as bread gives life to the natural body. As we feed on Him individually and as His Body, we enjoy a life-giving impartation that gives us growth and productivity.

THE BODY IS A PICTURE OF UNITY COMPRISED OF DIVERSITY

John 17:21

1 Corinthians 12:13
Ephesians 4:3–4
Romans 12:4–8

1 Corinthians 12:13

Ephesians 4:4–16
1 Peter 2:9–10

Oneness in identity, purpose, and activity – this distinguishes us in the eyes of the world as those who follow Jesus Christ. This unity finds its source in the covenant which Christ initiated and sustains. Through His Headship, Christ infuses His Body with unity. Unity sets the foundation for the diversity of function which Christ has granted to the individual members of His Body. The harmony of the internal structure of His Body is preserved as the diverse members subordinate their individual functions to the Head.

Unity in the body of Christ is expressed through common purpose. As believers commit to Christ's character, methods, and purposes, not only does harmony develop within His Body, but the Church becomes a force within the world scene for God's goals.

RELATIONSHIP TO CHRIST UNITES THE MEMBERS OF HIS BODY TO ONE ANOTHER

Ephesians 2:14–16; 3:6
Galatians 3:26

Revelation 5:9; 11:9

1 Corinthians 10:16–17

John 6:51

Ephesians 4:29–32

1 Corinthians 12:27

Romans 12:4–5

Common citizenship in Christ's Kingdom and Body removes any barriers or partitions which separate member from member. No distinctions, such as Jews or Greeks ... slave or free ... male or female. We are all one in Christ Jesus. Around the throne of God we will see every tribe, tongue, and nation praising His glory.

The entire Body with all its members is nourished by the one true 'Bread' which is Christ's life in the Spirit. As we share the bread and wine of communion, we witness to the reality of our common source in Jesus Christ. He is the Living Bread, come down from heaven, that we may partake of His Life and live eternally.

Submission to Christ as Head of the Church enables members to nourish and feed one another under His direction. Our covenant bond to our Head nourishes and feeds us. So also the common bonding with all other members of His Body permits His life to flow throughout all of His Body.

Each member of Christ's Body makes his own distinctive contribution through recognizing Christ's Headship. Commitment to Christ as Head of the Body causes each member to inherit the benefit of all the other members.

APPLICATION

Identify various examples of our bodily systems which work in harmony together for the good of the whole body. Consider the consequences of any given member of the body moving into self-determined action without an effective relationship with the other parts.

CONCLUSION

1 Corinthians 12:12–27

The human body presents a valuable lesson regarding the importance of internal integrity within our physical being. The inter-relationship among the various members and the essential relationship of each member to the head as the command center convey a vivid picture of the Church of Jesus Christ. The Body effectively portrays how dependent we are on right relationship to Jesus as the Head and the need of interdependence among the members who are being built together by Christ.

LESSON 6 – THE CHURCH IS CHRIST'S BRIDE

PURPOSE

The teaching that God's people constitute His 'Bride' is portrayed throughout biblical history. The Bride description most fully displays the love relationship between Christ and His people. The Old Testament concept of God as Father, Shepherd, Deliverer, and Redeemer gives only partial description of God's relationship to His people. The greatest fulfillment is this image of God's people as the Bride.

GLOSSARY

Analogy – a likeness or similarity between different things.

Bride – a woman espoused to be married. The term is applied also in the preparation of the marriage festival prior to the actual ceremony.

Reverence – to regard with fear mingled with respect and affection (*Webster*).

THE BRIDE IN THE OLD COVENANT

Isaiah 62:5
Psalm 45

The old covenant portrays God's relationship to His people as being like that of husband and wife. God describes Himself as One Who rejoices over His Bride. The Psalmist gives an exalted picture of the bride leaving her father's house to join with her husband.

Isaiah 54:5–8

Hosea 2:2–20

Jeremiah 2:2–3
Jeremiah 3:1–11

Jeremiah 3:14

Perhaps most significant is that God uses the marital relationship to depict His dealings with Israel. He has rejected and abandoned her for her infidelities, but will receive her back with kindness and compassion. The Lord remembers her youthful devotion and commitment, as one holy to the Lord. But, after receiving the Lord's inheritance, she exchanged her glory and followed worthless idols. God exhorts her to return to Him as her husband.

Song of Songs 4–5

The Song of Solomon is the richest picture in the old covenant of God's love relationship with His people. God calls them repeatedly to Himself. The picture is painted of a wife, vacillating in her commitment. Hebrew custom used the Song of Solomon as part of the Passover celebration to depict God's betrothal to Israel. Betrothal, however, actually involved vows (commitment) and represented a much stronger concept than the Western idea of 'engagement.' Under the new covenant, the Song of Solomon has been observed by Christians as a picture of Christ's love for His Bride, the Church.

CHRIST THE BRIDEGROOM IN THE GOSPELS

John 3:28–29

Jesus is pictured as the Bridegroom throughout the Gospels. John the Baptist clearly declares Jesus to be the Bridegroom. John, full of joy, waits and listens for the voice of the Bridegroom. He hears the voice and says, 'The joy is mine and it is now complete.' For John is not the Christ, but has been sent to announce the Bridegroom.

Matthew 9:15
Mark 2:19; Luke 5:34

Jesus compares Himself with a bridegroom. He asks how people can fast while the bridegroom is still present. Fasting is for the time when he is no longer present.

Matthew 25:1–3

Jesus compares the culmination of the ages to a wedding feast. He teaches us to anticipate the consummation of God's purposes on earth. Some will be ready – by the oil of the Holy Spirit. Others will miss the midnight cry of the Bridegroom because they had no oil for their lamps. The door to the wedding banquet is shut.

THE APOSTLE PAUL AND HIS ANALOGY OF MARRIAGE

2 Corinthians 11:2

Paul uses the picture of marital purity to characterize the relationship between Christ and His Church. Paul sees the local Church as a pure virgin, promised to one husband – Christ. Paul wants her to walk in sincerity and pure devotion to Jesus, for deceiving spirits aggressively undertake to confuse and compromise her commitment to her Lord.

Ephesians 5:22–33

Paul discusses the mystery of marital union with Christ and the Church. As husband and wife each walks in their assigned roles with joy and respect, the bond between them grows in a dimension energized by the Holy Spirit. This bond exceeds all humanistic explanations. So also the bond between the believer and the Lord matures in ways only the Holy Spirit can generate. The bond between Christ and His Bride simply goes beyond all attempted human description.

The picture of marriage in the earthly realm assists in recognizing the eternal truths which exist in the relationship between Christ and His Church, as we see in Paul's letter to the Ephesians. The earthly marriage bond reflects the profound mystery of just how Christ loves and has given Himself for His Bride, the Church. His care for the Church includes:

(1) Leadership initiative to provide for her.

(2) Self-sacrificing love to care for her.

(3) A desire to present His Bride holy and blameless.

(4) Cleansing her with the washing of His Word.

(5) Seeking to make her radiant, as the essential expression of her own identity and purpose.

The portrayal of the wife's response to her husband is a picture of the Church's response to Christ. Such responses include:

(1) The Bride is called upon to submit to the authority of the Bridegroom.

(2) The Bride is to respect and properly reverence the place given to the Bridegroom.

(3) Jesus, as Savior of the Church, is to be acknowledged by the Church as her Head, submitting to His Lordship in everything.

THE CULMINATION OF HISTORY, THE GREAT WEDDING FEAST

Revelation 19:7–9

Revelation 19:9

'The Bride of the Lamb' is clearly identified in Scripture as the congregation of all the believers. At Christ's return and the subduing of all His enemies, the wedding is prepared. The Bride readies herself for her Lord. And blessed are all those invited to the wedding supper of the Lamb.

Revelation 21:9–11
Revelation 21:22

Further, the Bride is identified as God's city – the Holy City, the New Jerusalem – as a Bride beautifully dressed for her Husband. And an angel carries John to a high mountain to see this Holy City, this Bride, the Wife of the Lamb. Not a physical city or temple, for the Lord God Almighty and the Lamb are its temple ... and the people of God, the City.

Revelation 22:17

The Bride, in unison with the Holy Spirit, extends an invitation to come to this feast at the culmination of all spiritual and secular history. The body of Christ, from all nations and peoples, comes together dressed in the holiness of Christ Himself to take part in this cosmic marriage of Christ and His Bride.

APPLICATION

What additional observations can you make regarding the similarities between marriage and the bonds which exist between Christ and His Church? In what ways does the relationship between Christ and His Church speak to you concerning your own home or marriage environment? How does your view of marriage affect your view of the Church? How does society's current view of marriage affect your relationship to the Church?

CONCLUSION

The relationship between a bridegroom and his bride provides a vivid picture of love, care, reverence, and submission. Through this earthly example, the Church of Jesus Christ is able to better understand how to respond functionally to the living Lord of glory and to prepare herself for His arrival. The Church should be actively engaged in the process of adorning herself through the help of the Holy Spirit as she anticipates a glorious wedding celebration.

LESSON 7 – GOVERNMENT OR HEADSHIP IN THE JERUSALEM CHURCH

PURPOSE

Hebrews 5:8
Romans 1:4
Acts 1:8

Jesus' life is the 'seed' of Church life. He was not a 'wild seed', but the Son of God who learned obedience and received His Father's trust by His complete obedience. Having conquered sin and death, He ascended to the Father's right hand to receive the administration of the Father's Kingdom. The Church He left on earth had His same Spirit and quality of obedience. To this Church He gave His authority. The emergence of Jesus' government in the Church had its earliest beginning in Jerusalem. Thus, the Jerusalem Church is the 'seed Church' for all subsequent Churches. This original seed Church provides the pattern for government, leadership, and activities.

GLOSSARY

Apostle – those disciples the Lord **originally** appointed and sent forth to establish His Church, as well as those He **later** sent forth to establish His Church.

Elder – describes the same office as pastor, but focuses on their maturity and a governing role, and almost always refers to the corporate council of pastoral leaders. Remember that each Jewish community had an eldership or presbytery. The Church followed the same pattern.

Deacon – a servant by definition. Deacons care for the temporal needs of the flocks so that the apostles and elders can give themselves more to prayer and the ministry of the Word.

Eternal – the timeless realm of God's throne.

CHURCH GOVERNMENT BEGAN WITH APOSTOLIC GOVERNMENT

Matthew 10:1–5
Mark 3:13–15

Mark 6:7
Luke 9:1

Jesus called together twelve disciples that He wanted and appointed them, designated them apostles. He wanted them to walk with Him in a special way. To them He gave power and authority to proclaim the kingdom of God, to cure diseases and to cast out demonic forces. These original twelve – who had been with Jesus – became the authorities, not only among Jesus' earthly disciples, but also in the developing Church after Pentecost.

Acts 1:15–26
Acts 2:14

Acts 3:1–10

The Apostles, after Jesus' Ascension, took the responsibility for setting in order the local body of believers. Peter assumed the role of spokesman for his Lord, his fellow Apostles, and the Word of God. Peter and John ministered healing to one crippled from birth. Jewish

Matthew 28:19–20
Acts 2:42

Acts 5:28

Acts 13:12

Ephesians 2:19

leaders considered them as leaders of this new 'teaching,' and held them liable for public disturbance.

The Apostles were entrusted with building the Church on sound doctrine. They devoted themselves to teaching, fellowship, breaking of bread, and prayer. Jewish leaders felt they would bring the guilt of Jesus down on them. The Apostles teaching drew the power of God for healing and miracles. Paul considered Apostles to be the foundation of the Church, but taught that Jesus Christ is the 'Chief Cornerstone.'

1 Timothy 1:3, 10
2 Timothy 4:3

Titus 1:9; 2:1

1 Corinthians 12:28–29

They developed 'sound' teaching which became the norm for the Church. Jesus used His Apostles to develop the type of teaching that would feed and protect the believers. And by it, false prophets and teachers were evaluated.

Apostles were recognized as having the ministry for laying the foundation of the Church. Three basic points substantiate their placement:

Mark 3:14
Matthew 28:19–20

Acts 2:5–13

(1) **They had been with Jesus.**

(2) **Jesus gave them the authority.**

(3) **Jesus used them to bring faith to the growing numbers of believers in the early Church.**

Acts 6:2
Acts 15:6

Acts 15:24

The Apostles were the original elders in the Jerusalem Church. Their authority was recognized and heeded. Their authorization was considered essential for legitimate ministry within the churches.

GROWTH OF THE CHURCH REQUIRED ADDITIONAL ELDERS

Matthew 28:19–20

Acts 9

Acts 11

The Apostles had ministry beyond Jerusalem. The very term itself means 'send forth.' Jesus commissioned them to go to every nation. Soon they helped established Churches that grew beyond Jerusalem and beyond strictly Jewish believers. Persecution following Stephen's death forced Jerusalem believers to flee for their lives. They carried the witness about Jesus and brought many into His Kingdom. The Antioch Church became the first and greatest of the 'Gentile' churches for a season. Eventually all of the original Apostles died for their Lord outside of their native land.

Acts 15

Since they carried Jesus' specific appointment, the Apostles were called on to define some of the theological issues for the churches through Judea, as well as for Gentile churches.

Acts 11:30

Galatians 2:11

Acts 15:22

The Apostles appointed additional local elders in Jerusalem in order to cope with increasing converts and Church issues. The Jerusalem Church evaluated the dispute between Peter and Paul concerning Gentile believers. They sent out teachers, prophets, and evangelists.

Acts 1:15
Acts 12:17

Acts 21:18

Apparently, Peter served as chief apostle and James served as the leading elder or pastor in Jerusalem. Other leaders deferred to them for judgement and decision. When Paul returned to Jerusalem to report on the phenomenal growth among Gentile churches, he reported to James and all the elders.

GROWTH OF THE CHURCH REQUIRED APPOINTMENT OF DEACONS.

Acts 6:1–6

Problems developed within the Early Church that required practical assistance. Certain widows failed to receive their quotas in the daily distribution of food to the needy. These supplies had been slated to help them in their poverty. The potential for dispute also lay in the racial distinction between these Grecian (Gentile) and Hebrew widows.

Acts 6:3

The Apostles asked the Church to select those among them who were filled with the Spirit and wisdom. The exercise of Apostolic authority is clearly seen from the fact that they asked the entire Church to make choices for servants to handle the task. Note the requirements for service: full of the Holy Spirit and wisdom.

Acts 6:5

The Apostles appointed seven who met their qualifications for practical administration. The Church chose them; the apostles appointed them and turned the responsibility over to them. For they were convinced that such practical administration caused them to neglect their God-given work of the ministry of the Word of God.

1 Timothy 3:8–13

Philippians 1:1
Acts 20:28

Scripture shows that these two local offices – elders and deacons – continued. They were reproduced in churches in Judea and in Gentile lands wherever local churches were born. Note that the term bishop means overseer and describes the same function as elder. As Paul writes to the elders in Corinth, he reminds them that it is the Holy Spirit who made them overseers of the Church.

APPLICATION

Why do you think that Jerusalem is uniquely important? Why is government within the Church important? Can you identify New Testament government within your own church? Name three functions of an elder, a pastor, or a bishop.

CONCLUSION

From the early days of the Church, our Lord has been faithful to establish government or headship in the local body. He has given various ministries to ensure both order and growth. Since the Church is part of His Kingdom, it receives government from the King and His appointed leadership, rather than from democratic processes. The Church, therefore, is based on eternal rather than changing, temporal values, and has survived the winds of popular movements. Through its government in the Spirit, it has grown towards the fulfillment of God's eternal and universal purposes.

LESSON 8 – MEMBERSHIP IN THE CHURCH OF JESUS CHRIST

PURPOSE

Repentance from one's sins and the confession of Jesus Christ as Lord results in salvation or the 'new birth'. The Scriptures then command water baptism as the outward sign of obedience and the initiation into Church life. The new covenant qualifications for membership in the Church and the practical responsibilities that accompany this God-given privilege have not changed since the days of the Early Church.

GLOSSARY

Command – to exercise supreme authority (*Webster*).

Repentance – (Greek: *Metonoia*) – to turn around in response to godly sorrow; a change of mind resulting in a change of direction and conduct.

Prerequisite – something that is previously required or necessary to the end proposed (*Webster*).

Sin – to miss the mark; to come short; a voluntary transgression of Divine Law.

MEMBERSHIP IN THE CHURCH

Acts 2:29–33
John 13:13

1 Corinthians 12:3

To recognize Jesus as both Lord and Christ (Messiah) is essential for one to come into His Church. This was the message of the Early Church: 'Jesus Christ is Lord.' For no one can make this declaration except by the power of the Holy Spirit.

Romans 10:8–10

Philippians 2:9

1 Corinthians 15:12–19

Belief in the risen Christ and confession of Him as Lord is prerequisite for entrance into the Church. The Resurrection of Jesus Christ from the dead and the declaration of His Lordship has always been indispensable to Christianity. Apart from His Resurrection and Lordship, the individual believer has no hope for forgiveness or eternal life.

Acts 2:40–41

Acts 17:30–31

Those who received the Gospel responded with repentance and obeyed Christ's command to be baptized – these were added daily to the Church. Repentance is urged upon us precisely because Jesus was raised from the dead. For God has set a day in which He will judge the world through the One who He raised from the dead. To follow our Lord in baptism demonstrates that we are one with Him – in faith and conduct.

REPENTANCE FROM DEAD WORKS

Repentance from our own works is necessary to walk in life under Christ's Lordship. Repentance from our purposes is necessary for

Hebrews 6:1

Ephesians 2:1–3
Romans 8:6–14

Acts 2:38–39

Hebrews 9:14

fulfilling His purposes. The purposes and goals imposed upon us by our old natures and societies twist our lives and draw the wrath of God. For the mindset of our old nature is hostile to God and cannot submit to His purposes.

Peter, in response to those who inquired about salvation, specifically directed the inquirers to 'repent.' For repentance opens the door to be identified with Christ in baptism, to receive both forgiveness and the gift of the Holy Spirit ... only the blood of Christ can cleanse our consciences from our works that lead to death. Repentance humbles our hearts before God. It prepares us for forgiveness and cleansing and participation in the Church of Jesus Christ.

WATER BAPTISM IN THE CHURCH

Matthew 28:18

Jesus commanded His disciples to go forth and make disciples of all nations, teaching them to walk in His ways and to be baptized. The triune name used in baptism carries all power and authority to bring into daily living all that God has given to us in the new covenant.

Acts 2:38; Acts 8:19

Acts 16:31–33

The Apostles instructed all those who repented to be baptized in water, in obedience to Christ. In the evangelization of Samaria, as well as Gentile nations, baptism in water was urged for all new converts.

Acts 2:41
Acts 8:14–17

Acts 19:5–6

Those who received the Gospel, repented of their sins, and obeyed the command to be baptized were added to the Church. The great anointing that fell at Ephesus began when the believers were baptized into the name of Jesus. Any previous baptisms were inadequate to accomplish all that God had for His people.

THE PROMISED POWER OF THE HOLY SPIRIT.

Acts 1:4–5

Matthew 3:11

The promised gift and provision of the Holy Spirit comes to all those who turn to God and become members of His Church. John the Baptist specifically pointed out Jesus as the One who would baptize with the Holy Spirit. The power and fire of the Holy Spirit, said John, comes with the baptism that Jesus gives.

Luke 24:49

Acts 1:5–9

Jesus commanded His disciples not to leave Jerusalem until they received the promised Holy Spirit, poured into their lives as empowerment for their conduct and work. To be clothed with the Holy Spirit releases believers to live holy and productive lives in Jesus' Kingdom.

Acts 2:1–38

Acts 4:31
Acts 6:3–6
Acts 6:7

Acts 8:17

Acts 9:31

The Holy Spirit's power from the Presence of the Father enabled early Christians to function as the Church. They spoke boldly the Word of God. They served the physical needs of Church members. Faith in Jesus Christ spread almost uncontrollably – even among Jewish priests. The Holy Spirit was released into lives by the laying on of hands. Believers received encouragement and strength from the Spirit and lived in the fear of God – while the Church grew in numbers. The gift of the Spirit poured out upon the Gentiles.

Acts 2:39
Acts 19:1–6
Acts 19:10

God promises the gift of the Holy Spirit to all who come to Christ in repentance and obedience to His command to be baptized. The Ephesian leaders were baptized into the name of Lord Jesus and the Holy

Spirit came upon them. Thereby the Church was birthed and the evangelization of the entire Asian province began.

CHRIST'S APPOINTED LEADERSHIP IN THE CHURCH

Ephesians 4:7–13

1 Corinthians 12:7

Hebrews 13:7–17

Acts 20:28

Christ has called, appointed and endowed some of His followers with various ministry gifts. These leadership gifts bring order to the Church and guide God's people, preparing them for His work. God gives the manifestation of the Spirit in giftings for the common good.

Christ authorizes the appointment of Church leaders by the Holy Spirit and enables them to provide watchful care over members of His Church. We are exhorted to consider their way of life, imitate their faith, and joyfully cooperate with them in God's work. Obedience to Church leaders encourages them and enables them to fulfill their work joyfully. Our New Testament Scriptures teach respect for authority, orderliness, and discipline as normal Christian living.

HARMONIOUS AND PRODUCTIVE CHURCH LIFE

Ephesians 5:21

Galatians 6:14

1 Corinthians 12:12–31
John 10:11
John 15:13
1 John 3:16
Romans 12:3–8

Ephesians 1:18

Ephesians 1:18–20

Matthew 5:14–16

Ephesians 2:10
Ephesians 3:10

Ephesians 4:12–16

Our relationship to Christ as Head of the Church causes us to be in submission to the other members of His Church. In fact, out of our reverence for Christ, we submit to one another. The Western ideal of independence and self-sufficiency must be placed on the cross for mutual submission to become a reality within the Church.

As members of Christ's Church, we share a common covenant and a mutual responsibility to one another. As Christ laid down His life for us, so also we lay down our lives for one another. The dynamic of the new covenant works in us a willingness to give of ourselves to serve the needs of others. And the gifts of the Spirit provide the enabling.

As members of the Church, we share a glorious and common inheritance in Christ. Paul's prayers focus on enabling each other to know the hope to which He had called us and to experience the power to attain the same.

The recognition of fellow members of His Church is necessary for cooperation and success in fulfilling our mission. As we let our light of mission shine, others will see our good works and glorify our Father in heaven. God has prepared in advance certain good works for us to accomplish. We depend upon one another's gifts and service to reach unity in faith and the knowledge of the Son of God. Our maturity depends upon the flow of God's Spirit through those we count as fellow members in the body of Christ, for the Body grows in terms of the ligaments that support it; the Body builds itself up in love, as each part does its work.

APPLICATION

Does personal salvation bring about a desire for local Church membership? Why? Just how does your membership in a local congregation reflect your commitment to the larger Church of Jesus Christ in the earth? Identify practical ways that you are able to demonstrate your commitment to other members of His Church.

CONCLUSION

Repentance from sin and receiving Jesus Christ as Lord turns us from a life submitted to self to a life submitted to Jesus Christ. When an individual receives Jesus Christ, the Spirit leads him into obedience and to participate in His Body, the Church. This change of heart and direction enables us to function under godly leadership. Further, we learn, with other regenerated members of His Body, to build up one another and assist the Church in fulfilling her God-given purpose.

LESSON 9 – THE ORDINANCES OF CHRIST'S CHURCH

PURPOSE

The old covenant contained a multitude of ordinances and practices to be observed by the priesthood and the congregation of Israel. In contrast, the Church of Jesus Christ has been given the two primary ordinances of water baptism and communion as a matter of regular practice. Let us examine the importance of these ordinances and their meaning for the Church.

GLOSSARY

Baptize – (Greek: *Baptidzo*) – to immerse or submerge.

Circumcision – the act of cutting away the flesh of the foreskin, indicating consecration to God's covenant.

Communion – partaking of the new covenant meal in remembrance of Christ and His new covenant with us, also referred to as 'The Lord's Supper' and the 'Eucharist'.

Repent – a change of mind after consideration and regret; a change of direction or action as a result of a change of mind.

WATER BAPTISM, INITIATION INTO HIS BODY AND CHURCH

Matthew 28:19–20

Christ Himself has commanded water baptism. The Scriptures represent baptism as our initiation into His Body, the Church. Through baptism we identify with Christ in three main ways:

A. Through baptism, we identify with Christ as Redeemer and Lord

Romans 6:5

Luke 3:21–22

(1) Baptism is our initial step of obedience to the purpose of God in Jesus Christ. Jesus, in His experience of Baptism, received the Holy Spirit, His Father's approbation, and He committed Himself to His Father's purposes. So also, in our baptism, we identify with Christ and His purposes – His Kingdom reign and in His Church.

Acts 8:18–38

(2) Baptism is a physical response to the Good News about Christ and His Kingdom. Thereby we demonstrate to all observers that our commitment has changed from selfishness and the world system to Jesus Christ and His purposes.

Romans 6:1–5

Romans 6:5

Romans 6:8–10

(3) Baptism represents our death to self and Satan's kingdom, and resurrection into Christ's Kingdom. We unite, in baptism, with Christ both in His death and His Resurrection. We commit to the putting off of the old nature and its self-centeredness. At this point of death to our old nature, He raises us to walk with Him in His Resurrection power.

Romans 6:11, 22
Romans 6:14

(4) Baptism portrays Christ's ability to free us from our sins by forgiving us and releasing us from the power of sin within our own lives. Sin is no longer our master because we live by the ongoing grace of God.

Colossians 2:11–15
Romans 6:14
Romans 6:7

(5) Baptism demonstrates our faith in Christ's complete provision for our salvation over our sin, our selfish nature, the Law, and evil powers. Christ sets us free from sin; we are released into righteous living, because anyone who has died has been freed from sin.

B. In baptism, we are identified with Christ's Death and Resurrection

Romans 6:3–11

(1) Baptism is a physical symbol for death and resurrection. Our entrance into the water speaks of a dying to self and the world system. His Resurrection then infuses us with His life and purposes.

1 Peter 3:20–22

(2) Baptism is a symbol for judgement and calls to mind God's judgement on evil people in the days of Noah. Christ is our 'ark' to carry us safely through God's judgement upon sin.

(3) Baptism is a boundary, and it reminds us of how God delivered Israel through the Red Sea and the Jordan River into His Promised Land. Baptism separates us from the past and identifies us with God's ongoing purposes.

Romans 6:13

Romans 6:22

(4) Baptism is a beginning of righteousness. From baptism we are raised up to yield our members as instruments of righteousness in service to God. Our slavery to sin and death is replaced by joyful servanthood to a righteous and gracious God.

Colossians 3:1–3
Colossians 3:12–14
Galatians 5:13–14

(5) Baptism is a beginning of service. From baptism we are raised up into a new life of service to others. The focus of life becomes not self-fulfillment, but rather enabling others to find their place and work in God.

Philippians 3:10–14

Galatians 2:20
Galatians 6:14

(6) Baptism is a continual reminder of our need to grow in knowing Christ. We constantly identify with His death and Resurrection power throughout our entire lives. Dying to our old life, through baptism, also speaks of being crucified with Christ, both to our old natures and the world system.

C. In baptism, we are identified with Christ's Church

Philippians 2:15
Acts 2:40
Ephesians 5:8
Ephesians 2:1–3
Ephesians 5:6–7

(1) Before baptism, we were identified with a self-centered and perverse generation. Now we shine like light – like stars. We stand out in bold contrast to the immorality and lawlessness of the non-believer. God's wrath awaits those who live in disobedience.

Ephesians 2:12

Ephesians 2:19–20

(2) When we are baptized, we are 'added' or joined to a new group of people. Formerly we were separated from Christ, excluded from citizenship in Israel, foreigners to the covenants, without hope and without God. Now we are fellow citizens with God's people and members of His household.

1 Corinthians 12:13

Galatians 3:26–29

(3) When we are baptized, we are placed into one Body with all those who also follow Christ, irrespective of background. For we were all baptized by one Spirit, and we all drink of one Spirit. Before Christ, there are no slave or free, Jew or Greek, male or female.

1 Peter 2:9–10
Ephesians 1:4
Colossians 1:22
Deuteronomy 10:15
Exodus 19:6

(4) In baptism, we become identified with a 'chosen generation'; the people of God who are called to live in His light. We have been chosen to become holy and blameless. As God chose Old Testament Israel, He chose us to become a royal priesthood, a holy nation, a people who belong to God.

D. In baptism, we identify with Christ's mission in the world

Matthew 28:19–20
Luke 24:46–49

Galatians 3:8–9

(1) The mission that the Father committed to Jesus, He then passed on to us. God first proclaimed the Gospel to Abraham, then expanded it through Jesus of Nazareth, the Early Church and 2,000 years of church expansion.

E. In baptism, we are identifying with Christ's Kingdom government as opposed to our former government under Satan's darkness

Colossians 1:13

Acts 26:27–18
Romans 6:6
Ephesians 1:19–22

(1) Our slavery to Satan's power and reign in our lives gives way to Christ's sovereignty and active reign in our lives.

HOLY COMMUNION, THE COVENANT MEAL AS REMEMBRANCE

A. In Ancient Times, eating together had a special significance as an expression of covenant ties

Exodus 24:9–11

Exodus 12:1–28

(1) Moses and the Elders of Israel ate a meal together in the presence of God, at the very time of ratifying the old covenant by the sprinkling of blood. God's Presence attended them, like sapphire, clear as the sky.

(2) Israel ate together the Passover Meal, each family in his home; each household sacrificed one lamb. They ate it in haste, roasted meat, bitter herbs, and bread without yeast. They waited indoors while God struck down their captors and delivered them out from under the authority of Egypt.

B. Jesus instituted the new covenant meal on the same day as Passover

Matthew 26:26–27

Mark 14:22–25

(1) The new covenant meal signified that the old covenant had been fulfilled and replaced.

Luke 22:19–20
1 Corinthians 11:23–26
Hebrews 9:12
Hebrews 9:25–28

Hebrews 10:8–10, 14
1 Corinthians 5:7
Hebrews 10:12–13
1 Peter 1:19
Hebrews 9:26–28

Hebrews 10:18

Luke 22:14–22
1 Corinthians 11:23–26

John 6:53–58

John 15:5–7

Isaiah 55:1
Jeremiah 2:13

1 Corinthians 11:23–32

1 Corinthians 11:28–31

(2) Jesus Himself established the new covenant by His Own body and blood. His body – broken on the cross – and His blood poured out there together signify the ratification of the new covenant, effectively and permanently replacing the old covenant.

(3) Jesus Christ Himself was the Passover Lamb, without spot or blemish, sacrificed just once to cover all sin, for all people, for all time. When forgiveness is granted there is no longer a sacrifice needed for sin.

C. Jesus instructed His disciples to share the covenant meal as regular practice

(1) To remember Him in this covenant meal is to proclaim both the significance of His death and resurrection, as well as His second coming. They were to practice the covenant meal as often as they came together.

(2) Jesus had taught the disciples that it was necessary for them to eat of His Body and drink of His blood. Without it, they would have no life from God. He who 'eats and drinks' of Jesus regularly continues abiding in Christ.

(3) To eat and drink of Him means to continue feeding on His Word and Spirit. This is the real food and real drink that endures to eternal life. The Scriptures speak of God's life as a spring of living water.

(4) By faith, through receiving the covenant meal, we recognize Christ's Presence among us. Therefore, to eat this meal without appropriate self-scrutiny draws judgement. For His Presence requires that we examine ourselves and receive Him in awe.

(5) To eat this meal in irreverent fashion can result in serious discipline from Christ, such as such weakness, sickness, and even death. Yet God's discipline is always redemptive among His people. He disciplines us lest we be judged by those in the world system.

D. Regular participation in this meal stirs up the Church in three ways

(1) We are stirred to remember Christ as the unique source of our salvation from sin and judgement.

(2) We are stirred to remember His lifeflow through other members of His Body.

(3) We are stirred to remember the basis for our living hope about the future in God.

APPLICATION

Have you received baptism? If so, in what ways has it affected you? Describe how your identification with Christ has joined you with other believers. What is your responsibility to the people of God with whom

He has joined you in covenant? Explain why communion is more than just remembering Jesus.

CONCLUSION

The two ordinances of baptism and Communion keep before the Church of Jesus Christ the eternal truths of the new covenant. They serve to remind us of the love of God, Christ's death and resurrection on our behalf and our commitment to follow Him until He returns.

The new covenant meal reminds us of His Presence, faithfulness and the many promises that He has given to help us fulfill our mission. An honest and sincere response to these ordinances on our part enables us to appropriate anew the great salvation that is ours in Christ and renews us in the life of the Church.

LESSON 10 – WORSHIP IN THE CHURCH

PURPOSE

The Church receives her life from Jesus Christ. Therefore, the Church reflects His glory and holds Him in highest honor and esteem. The New Testament reveals a Church that is grateful for Her salvation, praising Jesus Christ for His attributes and worshipping Him with the sacrifice of self-denial and devotion. The New Testament culminates in a heavenly scene where all creation worships Him. In previous lessons, we have discussed worship and the individual. We will examine here the true nature of worship and how the Church can express herself to God as He originally intended.

GLOSSARY

Thanksgiving – the act of expressing gratitude to God for His blessings in Christ Jesus.

Praise – ascribing to God the attributes of greatness due His name.

Worship – The act of bowing down before Him who sits on the throne, assuming this posture so that His will can be revealed to waiting hearts.

ATTITUDE AND ACTS OF THANKSGIVING

Psalm 100:4
Psalm 95–100
Philippians 4:6–7

Psalm 95:1–11

Worship begins here: the attitude and act of thanksgiving to God for all His grace. The underlying attitude of being thankful – this focuses on God, not circumstances.

Thanksgiving expresses one's deep appreciation for God, who He is, and what He has done. What God does for us grows out of who He really is in His nature. Our gratefulness to God for His character and His attributes prepares our hearts to enter further into His Presence.

Leviticus 7:11–14
Psalm 100:4
Ephesians 5:20

Thanksgiving causes the 'gates' of His court, or His Presence, to open to us. Fellowship (peace) offerings under the old covenant expressed to God thankfulness. They opened the way for God to respond favorably to the worshipper. So we give thanks without ceasing to God the Father for everything.

John 6:11
John 11:41

Thanksgiving releases the Father's supernatural power to us and opens the way for His response to our requests. Jesus' custom was to give thanks to His Father before asking Him for provision or healing. This He did verbally and publicly.

Philippians 4:6–7

Thanksgiving releases to us God's gracious provision of peace or 'shalom'. In the action of praise, anxiety finds itself replaced by peace.

GRATITUDE OVERFLOWS INTO PRAISE

Hebrews 13:15
1 Peter 2:5

Psalm 9:1

Psalm 26:7
Psalm 47:7
Psalm 63:4
Psalm 101:1
Psalm 103:1
Psalm 147:1

Ephesians 1:6, 12
Ephesians 1:14

Hebrews 13:1, 5

Ephesians 5:19

Psalm 150

Exodus 15:1; 20–21

Psalm 47:1
Psalm 63:3–4

As thanksgiving increases, worship moves into the dimension of praise. Gratitude starts us on the path into God's Presence. Gradually praise overtakes and fills the worshipper. For in praise, we verbally and overtly exalt the Lord.

We ascribe to Him the greatness that is appropriate to His Person and deeds. We recognize His character; we acknowledge His attributes. We join all other creatures and creation in declaring praise to Him Who alone deserves it. The chief purpose of the Bible's longest book, Psalms, is that of declaring and teaching the praise of the Lord God.

The Scriptures, as well as the life of Jesus, show us the pathway for praising the Living God. Our lifestyles shout aloud the praise of God as we walk in obedience. Our mouths, our spirits, our minds continually offer to God the sacrifice of praise.

With hymns and spiritual songs we fill our lives to counter the pernicious influences of the world system. We sing and make music to the Lord, always praising Him by giving thanks to Him for everything that impinges on our lives.

With instruments of music, we fill the air around us with praises to our God. The Spirit within us moves us to dancing with joy, much like Miriam who led Israel in praise to the Lord for deliverance from the Egyptian armies.

With clapping, with shouting for joy, with lifting our hands, we follow our God as taught by the Psalmist. We find that Christian worship is rooted in the Hebrew expression of praise. Our bodies, not only our minds and voices, become vehicles for the holy expression of love and praise to our God.

BOWING BEFORE GOD TO RECEIVE HIS WILL AND PURPOSE

Mark 14:36
Matthew 26:39
Psalm 95:6
John 4:21–24

Isaiah 6

Romans 12:1–2

Matthew 4:9

Luke 4:8
Matthew 4:10

Revelation 4:1–11

Romans 12:1–2

Worship culminates in bowing before our loving Father to receive from Him that which is pleasing to Him. It is the glory of God's Spirit to accomplish in us and enable us to move in worship. For worship is not tied to a certain place on earth, but to the work of the Holy Spirit.

Worship is the attitude and act of prostrating one's self, one's will and life purpose, before the Living God – yielding ourselves to His purposes. Worship is the presentation of one's self as a daily sacrifice to Him and His ways. Satan's great desire in tempting Jesus was to bring Him to the act of worship to himself instead of to the Father. Jesus' magnificent response turned all worship back towards His Father, thus ending the discussion once and for all.

Worship brings us to the One Who sits on the throne of all sovereignty. To worship God in His sovereignty releases us to our appropriate place in His creation, destined to live for His glory.

Worship is based on the true realization that Christ is worthy of any and all sacrifice that we can make. Our very lives and lifestyle, then,

1 Peter 4:1–2

John 5:19–20
Matthew 26:39
Hebrews 10:7

Acts 2:14
2 Chronicles 5:11–14
Revelation 5:8–13

become on-going worship to Him. For we commit to live for and serve Him, not the self-centered lifestyle demanded by the world system.

The ultimate evidence of a truly worshipping people is their obedience to His will, as well as dedication to His purposes throughout the earth. As Jesus came to accomplish the will of His Father, His very lifestyle became constant worship to Him. To live to accomplish the Father's purposes draws us into the lifestyle of worship.

The highest expression of corporate worship is that of His people and instruments making 'one sound'. Worship in the Spirit produces a harmony like a choir – focused on the Person of God Himself ... the opposite is a cacophony or babbling produced by those seeking self-expression as a substitute for true worship.

APPLICATION

What do you consider major hindrances to real worship? How can we as Christians, following John 4:23, move effectively in worship? Can worship become dangerous? If so, how? (See Psalm 135:20; Revelation 19:5; Luke 9:34.)

CONCLUSION

Worship begins with a grateful heart, overflows in ascribing greatness, and ends in bowing down to receive His will. The Church is God's instrument for reflecting His glory, giving glory through worship, and leading creation to know how to worship Him. Worship is the atmosphere in which God reveals His Word and His will. The Scriptures make it clear that the Church at the end of this age will not only be a glorious Church, but a Church that is glorious in worship.

LESSON 11 – DAILY LIFE WITHIN THE EARLY CHURCH

PURPOSE

The book of Acts provides us with a trustworthy account of the first days of the Church in action. Acts also establishes a model for the Church in today's society. This model contains four basic spiritual elements which infuse Church life today by the power of God's Spirit.

GLOSSARY

Devoted – solemnly set apart or dedicated.

Prayer – the act of communicating with God, or requesting with earnestness and zeal.

Fellowship – (Greek: *Koinonia*) – sharing life together.

Fervent – ardent; earnest; excited.

DEVOTION TO THE APOSTLES' TEACHING

Acts 4:33

Acts 5:30–32

Acts 10:39–43

The Early Church applied itself to the apostles' teaching since they had been with Jesus in His ministry. Jesus had called them to bear witness to His Resurrection as well as the Good News of the kingdom of God. In the act of receiving the apostles' message, salvation became a reality among the early Christians.

Titus 1:9

Acts 2:1–4
Titus 1:9
Titus 2:1

The apostles had spent up to three years with Jesus. They had received the first outpouring of the Spirit at Pentecost. This qualified them to teach the ways of Jesus to the first converts. Their teaching eventually became known as 'sound doctrine'. Proper understanding of the apostolic message was therefore essential for healthy Church life.

Ephesians 3:4–5

John 14:26; John 15:36
Colossians 2:8–10
Judges 3
Acts 5:12

Christ committed His message to His apostles. He gave them His Spirit for ongoing detail and clarification. They were the authority for sound doctrine and provided a proper understanding for living the Christian life as God intended. God authenticated His message through them with signs and wonders.

DEVOTION TO FELLOWSHIP

Acts 2:44–47

Acts 8:1–3

The Early Church devoted itself to fellowship. The Holy Spirit's intense Presence mixed with the apostolic teaching worked in these early believers a desire for fellowship. They devoted themselves to fellowshipping with each other in order to explore and learn the Spirit's Presence in each other. These wholesome relationships formed the basis for the intense and persistent evangelism, signs, and wonders of the Spirit.

Philippians 1:3–5

Acts 2:42

These early Christians had a common partnership in the same Gospel shared by all believers. Their common experience at the hands of their Savior issued in their common activity of evangelism and church planting.

Ephesians 2:19
John 3:3,5
Philippians 3:20

These early Christians had a common source in Jesus and a citizenship which identified them with one another. Their national origin had been replaced with a heavenly focus.

Ephesians 3:15
John 13:34
John 15:12

These early Christians had a common family wherein they related with a kindred spirit. Even the human ties of natural generations came second to those of their birth in the Spirit.

1 John 1:7

1 John 1:8–10
1 John 1:3–4

These early Christians experienced the flow of Christ's life through their Christian fellowship. They walked in the light of God's Spirit and God's truth. Therefore they came to know deep fellowship with each other because of the cleansing blood of Christ.

MEETING FROM HOUSE TO HOUSE

Acts 2:46–47

The Early Church was in continuous session since they met from house to house. These early Christians would break bread in their homes in the true spirit of fellowship. The Church in the home was the norm.

DEVOTION TO PRAYER

Acts 12:5–17

Acts 1:14

Mark 1:35
Mark 6:46–47

Luke 6:12
Matthew 6:9–13

Acts 1:14
Acts 2:1

Acts 2:42
Acts 4:24–31

Acts 12:5

James 5:16

Matthew 7:7–8

The Early Church gave itself to prayer and intercession for God's purposes. They joined constantly in prayer to touch God's Person and His will for their lives and Church.

These early Christians took Jesus' model of fervent prayer to His Father. Morning or night, at home, in the workplace, or in the fields, they followed Jesus in how to approach the Father and what to say.

For these early Christians, their Church was born in a prayer meeting. The presence, power, and gifts of the Holy Spirit poured forth in response to their waiting on God in fervent prayer.

As a continuing activity, they called on God in prayer for Him to intervene to accomplish His own purposes through their lives. God responded in a variety of supernatural ways.

They walked in sound doctrine, in right fellowship with God and each other, and in an environment of grateful praise. These factors show their ability to pray effectively according to the will of the Father. They learned how to 'ask, seek, and to knock' in prayer.

APPLICATION

What do you believe is the central message of the apostles' teaching and its application for today's Church? What distinguishes fellowship in the Church from 'fellowship' in secular society? Why do you need to be involved in fellowship of praise, thanksgiving, and prayer?

CONCLUSION

One of the challenges of modern society is the complexity of daily life and the many activities that confront the individual believer. Jesus Christ, as Head of His Church, has built into the fabric of Church life four simple guidelines that provide a framework for Christian practice. Devotion to sound instruction, meaningful fellowship, sharing on a personal or small group level, and earnest prayer, constitute the basic elements which make up daily Christian living. Maintaining these things in the face of other social demands will establish believers and assist the Church to grow and mature.

LESSON 12 – DISCIPLINE WITHIN THE CHURCH

PURPOSE

The governing leaders of the Church (pastors and elders) are responsible for maintaining order and godly standards of conduct within the Christian community. Godly conduct glorifies God in the larger society and gives the Church a foundation for evangelism. We will consider here how responsibilities of Church discipline are carried out in local congregational life.

GLOSSARY

Discipline – to instruct, govern, and correct with a view to bring someone to repentance and reformation of life.

Oversee – to superintend, overlook, implying care (*Webster*).

DUTIES IN GOVERNING THE CHURCH

Pastors and elders are required by Scripture to administrate the following specific duties in the governing of the Church:

Ephesians 20:20–35

2 Timothy 1:13

(1) Pastors and elders instruct the Church regarding sound doctrine and behavior. In Paul's farewell address to the Ephesian elders, he tells how he taught them publicly and house-to-house. He instructed them in 'sound doctrine', including repentance, faith, and the whole counsel of God. Second Timothy is a leadership manual with more than 20 commands of how Timothy is to pastor the flock of God in Ephesus.

Matthew 28:19–20

1 Corinthians 1:16–17
1 Corinthians 11:23–28
1 Corinthians 12:28

1 Peter 5:2–3

1 Timothy 5:17; 3:5

(2) Leaders are to administrate the ordinances of the Church. Jesus specifically told His disciples to baptize and teach. Further, He instructed them to commemorate His death in the communion meal of the new covenant.

(3) They are to oversee and govern local church gatherings. For that purpose, the Holy Spirit deposits His gifts on those whom He chooses. As shepherds who will give account, they are to oversee the Church. As family men, they are able to respond to various needs of God's family.

2 Timothy 4:2

(4) Pastors and elders call God's people to heed sound biblical standards. Their lives are to be models of conduct to which they call the flock of God.

Titus 2:15
1 Corinthians 11:28–34

1 Corinthians 14:1–40

(5) These leaders are to exercise discipline in situations where believers' lives are in contradiction to biblical standards of conduct.

(6) Pastors and elders oversee the exercise of spiritual gifts. They are to lead and protect God's people from the self-centered, self-exalting misuse of spiritual gifts.

DISCIPLINE AS NECESSARY FUNCTION OF LEADERSHIP

1 Samuel 2:12–3:14
1 Corinthians 5:1–7
1 Timothy 1:19–20
1 Corinthians 11:31–32
Titus 3:9–10

John 7:8–13

Romans 16:17–18

The responsibility for maintaining biblical order and conduct falls directly upon the pastors and elders. To neglect discipline leads to serious consequences for the individual as well as the corporate body of Christ. For if we do not judge ourselves within the Church, we will fall into judgement at the hands of the world system.

The whole community of believers suffers when their leaders neglect their responsibility to exercise love and care through discipline. Unchallenged lawless behavior or doctrine soon works through the Body like poison.

Revelation 2:19–20

Revelation 2:5

God Himself reveals His role in directly judging Church leadership and churches which tolerate obvious sin within their churches. For it is Jesus Himself who walks among His churches to evaluate their faith, their teaching, and lifestyle.

1 Corinthians 5:2–13

1 Corinthians 5:6–7

Biblically applied discipline will purge the Church of corrupting influences or evils. Self-directed teachers or believers who major on fulfilling their own cravings soon spread their pernicious influence throughout a healthy Body.

Revelation 2:5–18
Revelation 3:3

Numbers 25:1–12
1 Corinthians 11:28–32
Psalm 106:28–30
Hebrews 10:26–31

Biblically applied discipline will turn away God's anger and impending judgement. To ignore God's standards of lifestyle while claiming to live as a Christian is to invite corrective discipline. Weakness, sickness, and death are mentioned as some of God's ways of cleansing His Church.

1 Samuel 15:23

Biblically applied discipline continuously reminds God's people of how He feels about sin and rebellion. Rebellion in whatever form quickly grows into witchcraft and idolatry.

BIBLICAL GUIDELINES FOR DISCIPLINE

A. Discipline over private offenses

Matthew 5:23–24

Jesus tells those who have offended others to seek reconciliation before trying to offer their sacrificial gifts to the Lord. Restitution is very much part of this process.

Matthew 18:15–17

Jesus tells those who have been offended to seek restoration with an estranged brother or sister in Christ. Either way, offending or being offended, the command is to seek reconciliation by working with our brothers and sisters within the body of Christ.

Ephesians 4:25–32

The standard for inter-personal relationships set by the new covenant focuses on restoration of fellowship. Long term grudges (unforgiveness) invite the Lord's discipline.

B. Discipline over public offenses

1 Corinthians 5:3–13

The pastors and elders may bring before the entire congregation those who have severe violations. Especially when such believers refuse to respond to instruction, exhortation, reproof, or effective discipline.

2 Timothy 3:6–15

2 Timothy 4:1–5

Scriptures require leaders to discipline publicly an individual for activity which contradicts the Word of God. Part of the effectiveness of public discipline lies in the exposure of sin to the entire Body of believers.

C. Discipline of the Church leadership itself

1 Timothy 5:20

Galatians 2:11–14

1 Timothy 5:21
Deuteronomy 16:19
2 Chronicles 19:7
James 2:1–9

Those who stand in positions of leadership are subject to public correction as an example to others. Paul's public rebuke of Peter for discrimination between Jews and non-Jews set an example for the apostolic church to follow.

Church leaders are charged with the responsibility of executing faithful instruction and discipline without favoritism. For partiality contravenes the teaching 'to love your neighbor as yourself'.

APPLICATION

Identify from Scripture situations that would require discipline from Church leaders. What do you see to be results of effective discipline within the Church of Jesus Christ? Identify in your own life those areas that you believe would have benefited from caring discipline.

CONCLUSION

Hebrews 12:6–7

The Scriptures are clear that we should not despise the discipline of the Lord, since it is profitable for the members of God's family. In these days many have focused attention on the abuses of authority or on the weaknesses of those in positions of leadership. This points out the need for Christians to pray that God will grant to His Church both righteous government and effective discipline.

LESSON 13 – ECONOMICS OF THE CHURCH

PURPOSE

The work of God in the earth has been consistently supported by faithful stewardship among His people. All the earth belongs to the Lord. God's entrustment of His resources requires responsible stewardship of those resources towards the fulfillment of His purposes. God has revealed His principles of good stewardship in both the old and new covenants. In earlier lessons, we discussed stewardship and the individual believer. Now, let us examine the issue of church finances.

GLOSSARY

Firstfruits – the first profits of anything.

Steward – one called to manage faithfully the provisions of another.

Tithe – a tenth portion or part (10%); the act of tithing. The tithe is to be given to the local Church, or to the place where the believer receives care and feeding.

TITHING THE FIRSTFRUITS

Genesis 4:4

The principle of honoring God with 'firstfruits' reaches back through biblical history to the very beginning. Abel offered up to God the fat portions from some of his firstborn of the flock. God received his offering of faith; Cain's was rejected.

Genesis 14:20

Abraham offered a tenth of everything he possessed to Melchizedek, priest of God Most High. Abraham did this at least 450 years before God gave the tithing law to Israel in the old covenant.

Leviticus 2:12, 14
Exodus 34:22

God ordained under the old covenant that His people should bring an offering of 'firstfruits' from their flocks and fields. Thus, the worshipper honored God for His faithfulness in giving productivity.

Leviticus 27:30

2 Chronicles 31:5

The tithe from fields and flocks demonstrated in a practical way to all observers (covenant or non-covenant) the bond of allegiance, trust, and obedience between God and His people. Tithing was considered an act of worship which set forth God's Truth. This act of tithing, in keeping with God's covenant, opened the way for God's abundance to flow to His people.

Numbers 18:8–13
Numbers 18:21–24

Malachi 3:10

The tithe and the 'firstfruits' honored God as Creator-Provider of everything. Further, these tithes provided the food supply to sustain God's designated priesthood. For the priesthood received no inheritance in Israel; the people supplied their livelihood through their tithing.

Malachi 3:6–10

The Old Testament viewed withholding of tithes as tantamount to robbing God. To tithe recognized and honored God as Creator-Provider. Failing to tithe placed the worker in the position of trusting his own strength and wisdom for provision in life. Bringing the whole tithe into the storehouse releases the floodgates of heaven to pour out blessing.

Malachi 3:11–13
Exodus 26:23
Deuteronomy 28:15

Under the terms of the old covenant, God initiated blessings and curses to accompany the exercise of faithful stewardship. To ignore appropriate stewardship was to imperil the person's life, his family, and work.

FAITHFUL STEWARDSHIP AND LIBERALITY

Luke 11:42
Matthew 5:17–20

Jesus fulfilled and affirmed the Law, the covenants, and their tithing provision. He went beyond the tithing of the old covenant to teach faithful stewardship and liberality.

Matthew 6:20
Matthew 19:21
Luke 12:33

Jesus introduced the idea of treasure in heaven as His ideal, not just amassing wealth for one's own use. Self-sacrificing in order to meet the needs of others far exceeded the old covenant injunction of helping the poor. To give sacrificially at one's own expense to meet the needs of others (even non-covenant people) was a standard that Jesus introduced early in His ministry.

Matthew 6:1–4
Colossians 3:23–24

Matthew 23:5

Jesus taught that giving should be structured in such a way that God Himself would be pleased. Many times, such giving would be done in secret. To gain the attention of people in giving brought severe condemnation from Jesus.

Luke 21:1–4

2 Corinthians 8:2

2 Corinthians 8:12

Mark 12:43–44

Jesus used the giving of a poor widow to show His perspective. One's actual giving is measured by one's ability to give. That is, God views the percentage of one's total assets as the standard, under the new covenant, for measuring giving. This widow, as well as some of the Corinthian believers, gave out of their poverty. Such generosity is a more accurate measure of the heart of God toward His people.

GENEROUS GIVING AT THE NEW TESTAMENT STANDARD

Acts 4:32–35

The New Testament Church was marked by generous giving, based on the recognition that everything was the Lord's. These early believers considered all that they had to be the Lord's Therefore they shared generously with those in need.

Acts 11:29
2 Corinthians 8:2
2 Corinthians 8:3–7
Philippians 4:16

2 Corinthians 8:1–15

The standard for the early disciples was to give to those in need each according to his ability. Paul taught and exercised the same standard among the Gentile churches he founded.

The Apostle Paul left the following instructions concerning giving among the churches. He used the Macedonian churches as examples:

1 Corinthians 16:2
2 Corinthians 9:4–5

(1) Christians should regularly set aside a sum of money in accordance with their income for the support of the ministry.

2 Corinthians 9:7

2 Corinthians 9:5

(2) Christians should exercise their giving with a cheerful attitude, not reluctantly, or as those under compulsion. Forced generosity is a contradiction in terms.

2 Corinthians 8:12

(3) A Christian's attitude of heart is under the scrutiny of God. For He looks for the giving of the willing heart, based on one's capacity to give. This is what pleases the Lord.

Romans 12:8

2 Corinthians 9:6
Isaiah 58:7

(4) To some Christians God grants the grace or gift of giving. The Scriptures exhort these givers to give with liberality or generosity.

(5) The Scriptures outline for us the direct relationship between a person's generosity and God's response in bestowing blessing upon them. Whether old covenant or new, generosity expresses the heart of God towards His people. Isaiah equates fasting with generosity towards the needy.

TITHES AND OFFERINGS TODAY

Matthew 23:23
Luke 11:42
Genesis 14:18–20

Genesis 28:22

The Church today still operates by these time-tested and biblical principles of tithes and offerings. Tithing is affirmed in the new covenant. For its origin is not the old covenant, but the general revelation of God's nature before the Abrahamic Covenant. The principle of tithing precedes and transcends the Law (old covenant). This practice honors God by recognizing Him as Creator-Provider of all things.

Malachi 3:10
1 Corinthians 10:6, 11

God's viewpoint about the practice and importance of tithing as revealed in the old covenant, serves as an example and instruction for us today. Israel's failures as a people are placed in Scripture to keep us today from setting our hearts on evil or self-indulgent lifestyles.

Matthew 5:17–20

The spirit of giving and generosity under the new covenant both fulfills and exceeds the minimum requirements under the Law (old covenant). All we have belongs to the Lord; tithing underscores just how seriously we take God's place in our lives as Creator-Provider.

APPLICATION

Examine the degree to which you practice regular giving in support of Church ministries. Does this amount to a tenth or more of your income? If a 'tithe' is used as a guideline, what do you consider to be a personal goal in giving towards the work of Christ? In what ways can you be involved in supporting the work of the Church in addition to your other financial contributions?

CONCLUSION

Throughout biblical history, it can be observed that faithful stewardship has extended God's Kingdom in the earth. The Scripture indicates God's good pleasure with a cheerful and generous heart. God's people can rest in the assurance that they demonstrate faithfulness and honor toward God through good stewardship. He will surely attend to their needs and bless them according to His riches in Christ. We do not 'give to get' – but, in giving, we are assured of His faithfulness to provide.

LESSON 14 – APOSTLES AND PROPHETS

PURPOSE

When Christ ascended into heaven, He gave what is known as 'Ascension Gifts' to the Church universal. These five gifts are ministries of Christ that He has designed for the purpose of equipping believers in every generation to learn how to do the work of ministry. Such ministry brings the Body of Christ to its stature of fullness, or maturity. Christ gave the ministries to His Church in order to continue His own work of maturing and equipping. The first two gifts are 'apostles' and 'prophets'; they represent the foundational ministries within the Church.

GLOSSARY

Apostle – (Greek: *Apostolos*) literally, 'one sent forth'.

Prophet – one who speaks forth; a proclaimer of God's messages. In the Septuagint, the Greek translation of the Old Testament, it is the Greek word 'seer' (see 1 Samuel 9:9). This indicates that the prophet is one who is gifted to receive the Word of God either by hearing or by vision. The prophet is a 'forthteller,' and a foreteller. He can reveal present truth or things to come.

OVERVIEW OF THE ASCENSION GIFTS

Ephesians 4:11–13

Ephesians 4:8

Acts 1:4

These gifts Christ gave to His Church: apostle, prophet, evangelist, pastor, and teacher. They are sourced in the work Christ accomplished in ratifying the new covenant. As He ascended to the right hand of His Father, He poured forth the Holy Spirit and these ministries.

Ephesians 4:12–13
1 Corinthians 12:27–30

Christ gives these five ministries to every generation of His Church. Each generation of believers needs the input of these ministries. For Christ has designed them to fully equip and mature His people to accomplish His work.

Ephesians 4:12

These ministries equip God's people for the work to which He has called them. Note the contrast: these ministries do not themselves accomplish the full work of God. Rather, they train God's people so they can accomplish all God has designed for them.

Ephesians 4:18
1 Corinthians 12:12–31

God has designed each of the five ministries with a unique function. Each ministry carries a different enabling. Each is indispensable in equipping and maturing God's people for their function and service in His Body.

THE APOSTLE

The New Testament refers to several men as 'apostles', in addition to the twelve originally chosen by Christ. They are Barnabas (Acts

Acts 1:13
Matthew 10:2–4
Mark 3:13–19

14:14); Andronicas and Junias (Romans 16:7); two unnamed brothers called 'apostles/messengers of the churches' (2 Corinthians 8:23); Epaphroditus (Philemon 2:25); Paul, Silas and Timothy (1 Timothy 2:6).

Ephesians 4:11–12
Ephesians 2:19–22

Among the five ministry gifts, 'apostles' are one of the two foundational ministries. Apostolic ministries establish the local Church in its nature, structure, and mission. They are 'fathers' to local congregations.

Ephesians 3:3
1 Corinthians 2:6–10

The apostle's gift carries the ability to perceive with insight the nature of Christ's Church. For Christ has placed the Church beyond the ability of unregenerate people to discern; He has shrouded her in 'mystery'.

Ephesians 5:32

1 Corinthians 3:10

The apostle's gift carries the ability of 'masterbuilder' (Greek: *Architekton*). God designates them as the principle constructors in laying the foundation of local churches.

Mark 16:20
Acts 4:29–33
Acts 5:16; 8:6
Acts 16:18; Acts 19:12

The apostle's gift carries its own validation expressed in supernatural signs. These signs point to the Presence and power of Christ as He enables His followers to break the power structures of local societies and establish more local churches.

Acts 13:1–8
1 Corinthians 4:15

Christ gives to apostles defined spheres of operation. They function and work:

Acts 14:21–23
2 Corinthians 10:13
1 Corinthians 4:17–21
1 Corinthians 5:1–8
Titus 1:5

(1) **Beyond the border of a local church**
(2) **As spiritual fathers to churches**
(3) **To raise and/or establish churches**
(4) **To maintain order within churches**

The original apostles were uniquely foundational to the New Testament Church and the flow of revelation. There is no biblical reference for the cessation of this gift-ministry. The office (gift-ministry) of apostle and its responsibilities continues to be valid today, as it was in the Early Church.

THE PROPHET

Ephesians 2:19–22
Ephesians 4:11

Ephesians 4:11

1 Corinthians 3:9–10

The prophet, together with the apostle, form the foundation of Christ's Church, Christ Himself being the Chief Cornerstone.

The gift and office of prophet mentioned in Ephesians 4 seems to indicate a person who was recognized beyond the local Church as a spokesman for God. His work, together with the apostle, was to establish and equip local churches with the Word of God.

Here are some of the prophets mentioned in the New Testament:

Acts 11:28
Acts 21:10–11

Agabus, representing Jerusalem and Judea, addressed the issue of famine for the Roman world, and Paul's pending imprisonment in Jerusalem.

Acts 15:22, 32

Silas and **Judas**, leaders among the brothers in the Jerusalem Church, carried the Council's letter banning discrimination against the Gentile believers. They did much to encourage and strengthen the brothers.

Acts 13:1

God spoke through **'certain prophets and teachers'** from the church at **Antioch of Syria** to launch Saul and Barnabas on what turned out to be their first missionary trip among Gentile populations.

Acts 15:32

The prophet's major function was to bring a specific message to churches, or to confirm a Word previously delivered by the Lord. The work of governing or directing the Church fell to the pastors and elders.

Acts 21:10–14

Within the local Church, God's Spirit does enable certain members to prophesy. Having that gift does not mean that one is a prophet in the sense of Ephesians 4:11, as was Agabus. Those who prophesy in a local Church are exercising a gift of the Holy Spirit which we all should desire for building up the local Church. The office of the prophet is recognized beyond the local assembly. The gift is the prophet himself, called and sent by Jesus Christ to His Church. In Lesson 17, we will cover prophecy among the other gifts of the Holy Spirit.

APPLICATION

Are there men whom you believe function as apostles and prophets in today's church? How does the prophet function in relationship to the apostolic ministries? For clues, study the relationship of Paul and Silas, or Paul and Agabus. Why are the ministries of the apostle and prophet considered to be the foundation ministries of the Church of Jesus Christ?

CONCLUSION

Jesus Christ gave the five-fold ministry gifts for building His Church. His ministry is the pattern for their function. That is, each gift can be seen in the life and ministry of Jesus while He was on earth. Those with apostolic or prophetic ministries can pattern their ministries after the life of Jesus. The ministry of Christ through these gifts will continue His work of establishing and maturing His Church. The fullness of the Church's calling depends upon local churches recognizing and receiving these ministries as Christ's gifts.

LESSON 15 – THE EQUIPPERS OF THE CHURCH

PURPOSE

Jesus Christ, at His Ascension, gave five ministry-gifts for enabling His Church to fulfill His purposes on earth. These ministry gifts are designed to equip God's people to carry out the work of ministry that brings the body of Christ into its fullness. Each gift is necessary for Christ's Church in any generation, in any location on earth.

GLOSSARY

Acts 21:8

Evangelist – one who brings Good News; a proclaimer of the Good News.

Acts 20:28

Pastor – (Greek: *Poimen*) a shepherd who tends herds or flocks; pastors guide, feed and protect those who belong to Jesus Christ.

Acts 20:20–21

Teacher – one who equips the Church with sound (healthy) doctrine through biblical instruction.

REVIEW THE ASCENSION GIFTS

Ephesians 4:8

When Christ ascended to the right hand of God the Father, He gave gifts to His people as part of the fulfillment of the new covenant.

Ephesians 4:13

Christ gives these gifts to His Church for its continued maturity, until the Church fulfills Christ's ultimate purpose. Every generation and every believer needs these ministries in order to be fully equipped and matured for Christ's work.

Christ designed these gifts and ministries to equip the believers for the work to which Christ has called them. These gifts are not the exclusive domain of a select few who work for God in place of the believers. They are designed to release – not replace – the followers of Christ.

Christ planned each of these ministries with a unique function so as to equip and mature all His followers in the multi-dimensional work of His Church and Kingdom.

EVANGELISTS

John 4:1–26

Isaiah 61:1–4
Luke 4:18

Jesus is our example of the evangelist. He reached out consistently to the needy, to the despised, to any and all who might be willing to receive His message. Isaiah prophesied concerning the Messiah's person and message. Jesus acknowledged His calling as being given by God and anointed by God in both message and power.

Acts 21:8
Ephesians 4:11
2 Timothy 4:5

The term 'evangelist' is used only three times in the New Testament. Yet those in the Early Church recognized and encouraged this gifting of proclaiming God's Good News in power. Many of the

Acts 4:31
Acts 8:4

Acts 8:5–8

Acts 21:8

disciples at that time walked in the anointing of evangelism without necessarily being designated an 'evangelist' by the local churches.

However, Philip was a designated evangelist among the churches. His gifting functioned with great power among the Samaritans, despised by Jews. Although he is the only one specifically mentioned as an evangelist, his placement among the original seven deacons speaks of his position in the Church in Jerusalem.

Acts 8:14

Philip's ministry as an evangelist was mobile; he traveled among the cities with the knowledge and approval of the Jerusalem Council.

Luke 4:18
Acts 8:40

The New Testament describes the biblical function of the evangelist: They carry the content and power of Christ's Good News beyond the borders of local congregations.

Acts 8:5–8
Matthew 4:23–25

They demonstrate the truth of Christ's message and Kingdom with the power of Christ's Person. As Jesus proclaimed, healed, and drew people, so also Philip proclaimed the Good News of Christ's Kingdom in great power and conviction.

PASTORS

John 10
Psalm 23

John 10:1–18
Hebrews 13:30

Jesus is our example of the pastor. The Old Testament bears ample witness to the pastoral nature expected among God's leaders. Jesus Himself fulfilled and extended the role of pastor by His self-designation as the Good Shepherd. This was to become the standard for pastors in His Church throughout the ages.

John 10:11–13

Hebrews 13:30

Pastors follow Jesus' example of feeding, guiding, and protecting His sheep. They lay down their lives for His sheep. For He is the Great Shepherd of the sheep. Jesus is the pastoral pattern given in Psalm 23. His entire life and ministry expressed His Father's compassionate heart for His people.

Pastoral functions include the following:

John 21:15, 17
1 Timothy 3:2
2 Timothy 2:24
Acts 20:28
1 Peter 5:3
1 Peter 5:2
John 10:11–15

(1) **Feeding** the flock that belongs to God
(2) **Teaching**
(3) **Guarding** the flock over which God has made you overseers
(4) Being **examples** to the flock
(5) Being **shepherds** while you serve as being **overseers**
(6) **Laying down** your life for the sheep

Ezra 34:1–18
1 Peter 5:1–4
Hebrews 13:17

Philippians 1

Colossians 16:15–16
Ephesians 5:21

Pastors must be accountable, for the Holy Spirit has made them overseers to shepherd God's people. Ultimate accountability to God Himself is balanced with accountability to fellow leaders here on earth. Fellow leaders, overseers, and bishops supply gifting and perspective beyond that of a local pastor. Paul exhorts the Corinthian leaders to submit other leaders and to everyone who joins in the work.

TEACHERS

Acts 2:42

Ezra 7:6, 10

Teachers (Aramaic 'Rabbi') instruct the people of God in the Truth revealed through Jesus Christ. An Old Testament model is Ezra, who taught and instructed the people of Israel, much like Moses. The truth they teach is a blend of words, personal example, and lifestyle.

Mark 3:14–15
Acts 4:13

Matthew 23:8
Matthew 8:19
Mark 9:5
Luke 8:24
John 8:4

Acts 2:42
1 Timothy 1:3
Acts 20:29–31
Titus 1:9

Titus 1:10–11
Titus 2:1

1 Corinthians 12:28

John 14:26
John 16:13
1 John 2:20, 27

Acts 11:22–30

Acts 15:35
Acts 14:15–41
Acts 17:22–32

Matthew 28:20

1 Timothy 4:13
2 Timothy 4:2
1 Timothy 4:6
1 Timothy 6:17–19
2 Timothy 1:13

Teachers in Jesus' time established a much more personal relationship with those they taught than is typical today. Jesus chose the Twelve primarily that they might be 'with Him.'

Often the disciples called their teacher by the title of Master. This expressed the respectful authority that the disciple gave to his teacher because of his expertise in the Scriptures and his lifestyle.

God entrusts teachers with the apostles' doctrine. Satan intrudes the teaching of 'false' doctrine with great vigor so as to deceive and destroy the faith of God's people. Apostles' doctrine promotes the health of God's people. False doctrine emerges from rebellious people, mere talkers and deceivers, who serve as wolves to destroy the flock of God.

Teaching is a prominent gift within the Church. It is listed third in importance, following the apostle and prophet. For the teacher cuts to the core of the issue, and with anointed skill discloses the real problem or truth. The Spirit within him drives him not to rest until the kernel issues stand exposed in the light of God.

Both Paul and Barnabas functioned as local teachers before their commissioning as missionaries to the Gentile churches. Throughout their travels in Gentile lands, their teaching ministry released the power of God for establishing and maturing new churches.

When Jesus released His disciples to worldwide proclamation, He specifically asked them to teach new believers to obey everything He Himself had taught them. And present day teachers have the same responsibility as their New Testament counterparts: teach contemporary Christians to observe and practice everything Christ has taught them. For the eternal truths of the Scriptures produce sound doctrine and healthy followers of Christ.

APPLICATION

In what way does the pastor benefit the contemporary Church? How should he function in the light of the New Testament model? Do you have a personal pastor whom you believe God has placed in your life for spiritual direction and counsel? Describe how you see the role of the evangelist assisting the Church today in fulfilling its mission to the nations of the earth. What person has been a major influence upon you through their teaching?

CONCLUSION

Apostles, prophets, evangelists, pastors, and teachers are gifts which Christ has given to build His Church. Each gift has its own distinctiveness and function for the purpose of equipping God's people to build His Church in the earth. The release of these ministry gifts and their proper relationship to one another is essential for Church development and expansion.

LESSON 16 – THE POWER OF THE SPIRIT IN THE CHURCH

PURPOSE

The outpouring of the Holy Spirit on the day of Pentecost empowered the Church to be a faithful witness to Christ and to the Gospel of the Kingdom. The Holy Spirit continues to work through gifts which He bestows upon the members of the Church for the common good and building up of the body of Christ. We will examine here these gifts and how they operate within the Church.

GLOSSARY

'Agape' **Love** – the quality of God's love that is unselfish and loyal.

Anointing – the act of pouring (as oil) upon; a consecration.

Unction – the act of anointing.

THE BAPTISM IN THE HOLY SPIRIT

Matthew 3:11
Luke 24:39
Acts 1:5

The normal experience of New Testament Christians included the baptism in the Holy Spirit. To be clothed with God's power enabled Christians to know God deeply and to fulfill His purposes in their lives.

Acts 1:7–8
Acts 2:1–4
Luke 24:48–49

Jesus promised the Holy Spirit to all His disciples. He instructed them to wait in Jerusalem until He came and clothed them with power. His enabling was necessary for them to reach out to all nations with Christ's message of salvation.

Acts 1:5; 2:38

Acts 4:31
Acts 5:12; 6:8
Acts 6:1, 7

The Father's promise of the Holy Spirit was for all who would repent and put their trust in Christ's finished work. Under this unction and anointing of the Spirit, the Apostles ministered, and many thousands of people responded, including Jewish priests.

Acts 8:14–18

Acts 10:44

The subsequent ministry of the apostles was to pray for others that they might also receive the Person and power of the Holy Spirit. And much to the surprise of the apostles from Jerusalem, even Gentiles who repented received the unction and anointing of the Holy Spirit.

Acts 10:44–48
Acts 19:1–9
Acts 2:1–4

The baptism in the Holy Spirit is an experience distinct from baptism in water. However, it may occur simultaneously. A normal response to being filled with the Holy Spirit is speaking in tongues, as the Spirit gives utterance.

THE GIFTS OF THE HOLY SPIRIT

1 Corinthians 1:7
Romans 1:11

1 Corinthians 12:7

The Holy Spirit dwelling in Christians manifested Himself actively through the New Testament Church. As believers walked in obedience to God and love for their neighbors, the manifestation of the Spirit for the common good became the normal lifestyle.

Acts 1:4
1 Corinthians 12:4

1 Corinthians 12:12–13

1 Corinthians 12:6

John 15:26

1 Corinthians 12:21–26

The Holy Spirit Himself is the Gift from the Father. His manifestations (gifts) are diverse. The Source is One; the streams are many. The same Spirit, Lord and God infuses His power into His people in a variety of giftings to serve His own purposes in the Church and on earth.

The Spirit operates in diversity. His own unity feeds into the varied membership of Christ's Body. Together they all serve the Head, Jesus Christ. Instrumental sections within the symphony orchestra produce the composer's desired music under the hand of the skilled conductor. In the same way, the Holy Spirit enables believers (and groups) to fulfill the Father's cosmic purposes under the mighty hand of the Church's Conductor, Jesus Christ.

1 Corinthians 12:6–7

1 Corinthians 14:22–25

God designed the diversity of spiritual gifting for the corporate good, not for competition. For the Spirit-given abilities work within the individual Christian for the benefit of other believers (and non-believers).

GOD'S EQUIPPING FOR HIS PURPOSES

1 Corinthians 12:4–6

1 Corinthians 12:12

1 Corinthians 12:21

1 Corinthians 12:12

1 Corinthians 12:25

1 Corinthians 12:21–27

1 Corinthians 12:14–31

All the gifts of the Holy Spirit are part of the necessary equipment to fulfill God's purposes in the Church and on earth. Although there are many parts within the body of Christ, each section must function by the unction and anointing of the Holy Spirit. Only in this way can the overall mission of Christ be fulfilled.

The full complement of these gifts is as necessary to Christ's Body as the functioning parts within our physical bodies is necessary to normal and healthy living. As members of His Body, we must recognize the indispensable gifts that other members of His Body have received. For without the Spirit's gifts upon all of our brothers and sisters in Christ, we will be left with inadequate equipping for fulfilling Christ's purposes in our lives.

GIFTS OF THE HOLY SPIRIT: MOTIVATION

1 Corinthians 13
1 Corinthians 14:1

1 Corinthians 12:31
Philippians 1:15–18
Philippians 2:3–4

The '*Agape*' love of God is the only appropriate motivation for exercising the gifts of the Holy Spirit. God's profound love in His believers motivates them to desire and to function in His gifts. The temptation and desire to work from power, popularity, or wealth afflicted the Early Church as it does the contemporary Church.

When motivated by God's love, the believer considers the welfare of others. He focuses not simply on his experience in exercising his gifts. Rather, he asks the questions: 'Will this gift serve the needs of others?' 'Is this the right time to express my gift?' But self-motivated use of the Spirit's gifts will be confronted by the Lord.

GIFTS OF THE HOLY SPIRIT: ORDER

1 Corinthians 14:33–40

1 Corinthians 14:22–25
1 Corinthians 14:26–33

God designed the gifts of the Holy Spirit to be used in the Church in an orderly manner under the direction of local pastor and elders. Order and harmony in the assembly is necessary for an edifying atmosphere in the Church. God is not the Author of confusion. Disorder in the use of

1 Corinthians 14:29–33

1 Corinthians 14:12

the gifts reveals either selfish motivations or influence of demonic forces.

Those exercising the gifts are to subject themselves to others, especially to the authority in the local congregation. Basically, the believer with his gift is a servant; his focus is how to serve and edify others. God designed the authority of the local congregation as a releasing environment for the exercise of His gifts.

APPLICATION

What need do you see for the gifts of the Holy Spirit in the contemporary Church? Identify what you believe to be gifts of the Holy Spirit at work in your own life. Define baptism in the Holy Spirit as contrasted with baptism in water at conversion.

CONCLUSION

The Father, through His Son, poured out the Holy Spirit upon the Early Church on the day of Pentecost. The power and manifestation which accompanied those first Christians became the enabling force which sent them into all the world doing the works of Christ and fulfilling His mission. The same Holy Spirit is at work in the Church of Jesus Christ today, filling believers and equipping them with His gifts for building the Church toward a mature expression of Christ. Recognition and proper use of the gifts of the Holy Spirit is as essential today as it was for those who received the Spirit in the opening days of the Church.

LESSON 17 – THE GIFTS OF THE SPIRIT EQUIP FOR SERVICE

PURPOSE

Romans 12
1 Corinthians 12

The gifts of the Holy Spirit provide the Church with three different categories of supernatural equipment: Revelation, Power, and Vocal gifts. It is vital that we comprehend the ways of the Holy Spirit through His gifts. His Person and gifts produce a healthy Church, able and committed to fulfilling Christ's purposes on earth.

GLOSSARY

Inspired – 'God breathed' or Holy Spirit motivated and produced.

Revelation – the act of disclosing or communicating Truth from God that is not available to mankind in any other way.

1. REVELATION GIFTS

Daniel 12:17

Revelation Gifts convey the mind of God not otherwise accessible to people. Daniel the prophet bore God's revelatory message to kings and leaders during his century. The entire prophetic ministry in Israel and Judah depended upon God's revealing His purposes through mere mortals.

A. Word of Knowledge

Mark 19:13–15

John 4:16–19

In the life and ministry of Jesus of Nazareth we see the 'word of knowledge' that the Father gave freely to Him. Jesus' perception and understanding of people came from this flow of the Spirit within Him. Note His awareness of the location of a suitable guest chamber for celebrating Passover. Jesus understood the Samaritan woman's situation to such an extent that she thought He was a prophet.

Acts 9:11–12

Acts 10:18

The word of knowledge is a supernatural revelation of facts known and given by God. Often the prophetic gift is contained within it. Ananias of Damascus received detailed revelation and instruction from the Lord concerning Paul's conversion. Peter received a 'work of knowledge' or factual message regarding three men who had come seeking him.

Acts 5:3

God gave a word of knowledge to Peter and the Church leaders, revealing deception regarding finances in the local church.

This gift in operation is not to be confused with natural knowledge, or even a profound understanding of the Scriptures, or theology. Rather, God imparts supernaturally through His Spirit the knowledge that is needed. The gift can be counterfeited by psychics or witchcraft.

B. Word of Wisdom

1 Corinthians 12:7–11

Matthew 11:25–30

A word of wisdom carries a supernatural revelation as to how God wants a situation implemented. This 'wisdom' is an application of knowledge. It reflects the divine 'mindset' regarding God's overall purposes and how the immediate situation is to be interpreted. Jesus praised His Father for giving Him the 'heavenly' perspective and hiding it from the 'wise and learned'.

1 Corinthians 1:18–31
1 Corinthians 2:6–10
1 Corinthians 1:30

Genesis 6:13–22

God has chosen to reveal His wisdom through Jesus Christ. The wisdom of men was such that they killed the Lord of Glory. Jesus Himself has become 'for us wisdom from God.' God gave Noah much more than a word of knowledge concerning impending judgement. Noah received the divine perspective, the reasons, and the outcome.

Genesis 41:16
Genesis 41:37–40

Daniel 5:11

God gave to His servant Joseph, divine wisdom to interpret Pharaoh's dream. Thereby God implemented His purposes for Egypt at that time. The rulers of Babylon recognized the godly wisdom that Daniel offered, but ignored its application, to their own destruction.

Acts 10:9–16

Acts 27:27–44

God used words of wisdom in Peter's life to break through the barriers of strict legalism – or Gentile discrimination – so that the Gospel might be released to the nations. Paul received God's wisdom at the point of shipwreck and led passengers and crew to safety.

C. Discerning of Spirits

1 Corinthians 12:7–11

Luke 8:26–38

Discerning of spirits refers to supernatural insight in the realm of the spirit world and the understanding of which spirits are operating. Jesus operated in this gift when the demon-possessed man of Gerasenes approached Him for help.

Acts 13:6–12

Acts 16:16–21

God gave Paul supernatural discernment at work in the sorcerer who tried to obstruct the word and power of God. In Philippi, Paul discerned the predictive spirit in the slave girl. He rebuked it and drove it out, much to the consternation and anger of the owners.

1 Timothy 4:1–3

2 Thessalonians 2:9

Paul, in his Church planting epistles, mentions the need for exposing 'seducing spirits', 'lying spirits', and 'doctrines of devils'. God designed this gifting to reveal the demonic sources. Further, this gift unmasks false messengers and false miracle workers.

2. POWER GIFTS

1 Corinthians 12:7–11

Power Gifts convey God's energy into a given situation, so that the result cannot be credited to the intelligence or skill of people.

A. Faith

Matthew 17:20
Matthew 21:22

Faith is a supernatural trust in God, not just personal salvation. Rather, the ability to believe God, without doubting, for the accomplishment of His purposes in miraculous ways. This faith then affects the behavior of the believer.

B. Working of Miracles

Acts 3:7; 5:5
Acts 13:11
Acts 20:10

Working of miracles is a supernatural intervention of God into the daily affairs of life. God rearranges 'natural law' for His own purposes. Note the number of times God intervened through the apostles to accomplish healings.

C. Gifts of Healings

Matthew 4:23–25

Acts 5:16
Acts 9:34
Acts 14:10
Acts 16:18

Gifts of healings are supernatural powers to accomplish healing of sicknesses. Jesus' earthly ministry was characterized by this gift, among others. The healing power of Christ poured through His disciples during the time of the Early Church, validating both the message and messenger.

3. VOCAL GIFTS

Vocal Gifts are gifts that use speech and often are the vehicle for conveying other gifts such as knowledge, wisdom, or healing.

A. Prophecy

Acts 11:28

Acts 21:11

Prophecy is an utterance inspired by the Holy Spirit in a known language. Agabus, speaking through the Holy Spirit, indicated things yet to happen on a national and regional level.

Again by the Spirit, Agabus told Paul about certain things that would happen to him if he pursued a certain course of action.

B. Tongues

1 Corinthians 14:4
1 Corinthians 14:18

1 Corinthians 14:13–17
1 Corinthians 14:27–28

1 Corinthians 14:22
1 Corinthians 14:26
Isaiah 28:11, 12

Tongues are a Holy Spirit inspired utterance in an unknown language or tongue. God releases the gift of tongues to us for personal edification.

In public assembly, the Holy Spirit releases this gift in conjunction with the gift of interpretation. The interpretation may carry an exhortation, comfort, or a prophetic word.

In the use of the gift of tongues, the Holy Spirit addresses the nonbeliever in the assembly. Paul cites Isaiah, the Old Testament prophet, concerning the existence and use of this gift.

C. Interpretation of Tongues

1 Corinthians 12:10
1 Corinthians 14:13–28

Interpretation of tongues is a Holy Spirit inspired utterance that gives the meaning of what has been spoken in an unknown language. This gift serves the Church assembly to bring forth the edifying content and value of a message in an unknown tongue.

The rendering of a message in tongues does not conform to word-for-word translations. Rather, the one who interprets communicates the same message to the assembly that the Holy Spirit inspired in the form of an unknown tongue.

APPLICATION

Explain the distinction between the working of miracles and the gifts of healing. Identify examples of the word of wisdom in operation in the Church today. Define the difference in operation between a word of wisdom and a word of knowledge.

CONCLUSION

The Early Church functioned in vital dependence upon the activity and gifts of the Holy Spirit to operate on their behalf. There are 44 direct references in the New Testament to the Holy Spirit at work in the Early Church, indicating the prominence of the Spirit's activity. The gifts of the Holy Spirit are no less needed in today's Church for the fulfillment of its mission in the world.

Let us pray earnestly that God will pour out His Spirit afresh and release the gifts of the Holy Spirit to move His Church forward into the works of Christ. It is crucial that those who manifest such gifts – as well as the use of these gifts themselves – be under the supervision of local leaders who are accountable for the validity and timing of the gifts exercised in the congregation.

LESSON 18 – THE GIFTS OF THE SPIRIT EQUIP THE CHURCH

PURPOSE

Christ has bestowed on His Church gifts and ministries through the Person and Power of His Holy Spirit. The effect of these gifts and ministries extends beyond simply satisfying the needs of Church members. God intends these gifts to prepare Christians for meaningful service and ministry to others, as well as to fulfill God's overall purposes in the earth. We will consider here just how the ministry gifts promote the expanding ministries of the Church.

GLOSSARY

Gift – (Greek: *Charis*) powers and faculties endowed by the Holy Spirit in the life of the Christian.

1. GIFTS OF THE SPIRIT FOR THE USE OF THE CHURCH

In addition to those gifts of the Spirit listed in 1 Corinthians 12, the Holy Spirit imparts other gifts for His use within the Church.

A. *Service* (Greek: *Diakonia*)

Romans 12:7

Service is a ministry of serving the needs of others. The Holy Spirit makes these people especially sensitive to the daily needs of fellow believers: physical, emotional, and spiritual.

B. *Exhortation* (Greek: *Parakaleo*)

Romans 12:8

Exhortation is a ministry of calling others to fulfill the truth they know. Those who express this gift make an appeal through encouragement, comfort, and instruction.

C. *Giving*

Romans 12:8
2 Corinthians 8:2
2 Corinthians 9:11–13

Giving is a ministry of releasing resources, given by the Holy Spirit, to help others. Such people carry the impulse of the Spirit to meet specific financial needs.

D. *Leadership* (Greek: *Proisemi*)

Romans 12:8

Leadership is given by the Holy Spirit to those to whom He entrusts the daily affairs and direction of the Church.

E. *Mercy*

Romans 12:8

Mercy is the Holy Spirit's enabling to enter into the immediate problems or sufferings of God's people. This gift ministers mercy and comfort to those in difficulty.

2. GIFTS OF THE SPIRIT TO STRENGTHEN ALL MEMBERS

Romans 12:2–6
1 Corinthians 12:4–7
Galatians 5:6

1 Corinthians 12:4

1 Corinthians 12:7–11
Romans 14:19

1 Corinthians 12:12–31
Romans 15:1, 2

1 Peter 4:7–11
Romans 12:3–5

1 Corinthians 13:1–14:1
Philippians 2:4

The Holy Spirit gives Christ's gifts so that all members of His Body may be strengthened for loving action towards others. With the variety of gifts, services, and working, we have but one singular source, the Holy Spirit.

Through the gifts, the Holy Spirit moves us toward the common good and benefit of all the members of Christ's Body. The simple goal is the strengthening and maturation of the Church.

The Holy Spirit, through the gifts, demonstrates to all members of the Church that no one member has received all the giftings. Rather, the member with a certain gift receives all he lacks through the gifts that God has given to other members.

The gifts of the Holy Spirit are instruments of God's love-care in that they are always to be used in seeking the benefit of others.

3. SERVING GOD AND OTHERS THROUGH THE GIFTS

Romans 12:1–2

Romans 12:3–8

Ephesians 4:7

2 Corinthians 10:13

John 15:16

Isaiah 11:9

The goal of the Christian life is to offer all we have in service to God and the welfare of others. As members of Christ's Church, we need to be realistic in assessing God's calling and gifting in our lives. To think too highly of ourselves invites an arrogance and self-seeking in the use of the gifts. On the other hand, to think too little of God's gifts and expected servanthood places us in the position of an unprofitable servant, one not involved in productivity.

Members of the Church are an ever-expanding expression of the Holy Spirit's activity and gifts, not only in the Church, but throughout the whole earth. As the Church grows, the Glory of God continues to increase 'to cover the earth as the water covers the sea.' Here are some of the ministries that God's Spirit uses for spreading His work throughout the earth:

A   Teaching and publishing ministries which take God's Word to the nations. They express the Word of God sent forth for the healing of the nations through Christ.

Hebrews 10:32–34
Matthew 25:42–45
Proverbs 14:31
Hebrews 13:2

John 17:20–23

Acts 13:1–3

B   Benevolent and mercy ministries that work with 'street people', the hungry, prisoners, 'AIDS' sufferers, disaster relief, and others in need. They express the goodness of God to people, irrespective of their spiritual condition.

C   Networking ministries which promote interaction among groups of churches for the spreading of the Gospel and a united witness to the unsaved.

D   Missionary agencies which assist those whom God has sent to the nations for planting and maturing new churches.

APPLICATION

What gifts do you believe have been given in your life for the benefit of Christ's Church? Identify potential hindrances to functioning in the areas for which God has called and equipped you. Identify those ministry gifts which Christ sent into your life to equip you for effective ministry. How have these gifts helped you in your ministry?

CONCLUSION

The purpose of the ministry gifts for the Church today is the same as for the Christians who lived in the First-Century Church. The members of Christ's Church are to be equipped for action and effective ministry to one another ... and to the world in which they live. From Christ's perspective, there are no spectators or bystanders in the ranks of His followers, as they seek the fulfillment of His mission in the earth. Christ has arranged His work so that each member receives the necessary preparation and equipping to release them in ministry to others.

LESSON 19 – THE MISSION AND GROWTH OF THE CHURCH

PURPOSE

Jesus, at the point of His Ascension, commissioned His Church to carry out His purposes in the earth. He endowed His Church with a distinct mission to be fulfilled through the power of His Spirit. From the Gospel first preached to Abraham, to the worship scene around the throne, we see Christ's purposes to be fulfilled by those for whom He loved and died. Here we will examine both the dimensions of the mission and how it is to be fulfilled.

GLOSSARY

Mission – task assigned; the act of sending.

Missionary – one sent from a local church to propagate the Gospel of Jesus Christ.

Witness – testimony; attestation of a fact or event.

CHRIST'S COMMAND TO HIS CHURCH

Matthew 28:19–20

Luke 24:45–52

Matthew 28:19

Acts 11:19–21

The original apostles received directly from Jesus Christ the command to fill the earth with His teaching. We, as members of His Church and heirs of His apostles, have received the same specific command.

In response to Christ's wishes, the members of His Church are to give themselves to His process of making disciples from those of all nations on earth. The Church in Jerusalem had a problem with declaring the Gospel to Gentiles. God provided such persecution that they shared Christ with those in Cyprus, Cyrene, and Antioch of Syria.

Genesis 12:3
Galatians 3:6–9

God promised Abraham that through him all nations were to be blessed. Paul established this promise as the door through which Gentile nations would come to God. Our tendency to keep the Gospel for our 'group' only is well documented in Church history. But God continues to intervene to accomplish His purposes for blessing all people groups.

Matthew 28:19
Mark 16:16

Ephesians 3:6
Galatians 3:26–29
Galatians 3:28

In response to Christ's wishes, the members of His Church are called on to baptize disciples and receive them into Christ's Body and its fellowship. To belong to Christ is to be named as Abraham's offspring, and heirs according to God's promise from approximately 1900 BC. All distinctions between people, races, money, and power are erased in Christ's Body.

Matthew 28:20

Colossians 3:16
1 Timothy 4:11

In response to Christ's wishes, the members of His Church are to teach new disciples everything that Christ has given to His original disciples. We gather the new believers and impart to them the riches of God's Presence and Word.

PROCLAIM, TEACH, AND DEMONSTRATE HIS TRUTH

Matthew 28:19–20

John 16:8–11

Jesus commanded His Church to proclaim, teach, and demonstrate His Living Truth. Through this witness the Holy Spirit works conviction and repentance into people. Thereby they turn to the Lord and walk into His Kingdom.

Acts 1:4–8

Luke 24:48
Acts 2:32–33
John 15:27

Acts 1:8

Acts 6:7

Jesus promised His disciples that He would send His power from the Presence of His Father. They were to wait until they had received His equipping power. For that power would enable them to live as His effective witnesses.

The initial witness of the Church is to the local area. For the Early Church, this was represented by Jerusalem. Here the Word of God spread rapidly, overtaking a large number of Jewish priests who then became obedient to faith in Jesus.

Acts 1:8

Acts 8:1–4

Acts 8:14

In ever spreading concentric circles, the Early Church increased their witness. Judea and Samaria represented the surrounding areas which next received a significant impact through the lives of the Church members. So great was the number of Gentiles who turned to Jesus that the Apostolic Council in Jerusalem sent Peter and John to help.

Acts 9:1–15

Galatians 1:18–24

Acts 9:15

Through Saul of Tarsus (Paul), Jesus Christ extended the witness of His Jerusalem Church. Much to the dismay of the Jerusalem Council, Paul went to visit them. Since he was such an outcast among Jews, he wanted to receive their approval authority. For God had burned it deeply into his heart: He was a chosen instrument to carry the name of Jesus to the Gentile peoples. Eventually all the original apostles died outside Judea as witnesses for their Lord and Savior, Jesus Christ.

THE EARTHLY MODEL OF HEAVENLY TRUTHS

Hebrews 9:10–14

Jesus Christ has placed His Church on earth to serve as an earthly model for heavenly realities. The Church's identity and function as Bride, family, temple, and Body prepares the Church for placement and work in heaven.

Isaiah 62:5
2 Corinthians 11:2

Revelation 19:7

The Church serves here on earth as a Bride in preparation. She openly displays the quality of love relationship between God and herself for all the world to see. Her allegiance, trust, and obedience to her Lord witnesses to her preparation process for the day of her wedding.

John 1:12; Romans 8:15
Ephesians 1:14–15
2 Corinthians 6:18

The Church lives as a family on earth to demonstrate God's Fatherhood to all people on earth. He is Father by creation; He is Father by redemption . . . for all who will receive Him.

Ephesians 2:19–22

1 Corinthians 3:16, 17
Matthew 16:18

By the work of the Holy Spirit, the Church is in the process of being brought together and built into a temple. This temple not only serves as a model for God's Truth on earth, but also becomes God's dwelling place on earth – God with His people in the midst of unbelievers.

Romans 12:5

Ephesians 1:23

Colossians 1:24

Colossians 2:19

The Church functions as Christ's Body on earth for all the nations to observe. Each part of the Body receives its own gifting and function to build up the Body. The strength and maturity that flows through its ligaments and sinews enables her to point towards the perfect harmony in Christ's Kingdom.

CHRIST'S FULLNESS IN THE EARTH

Ephesians 1:23

Matthew 16:18

1 Corinthians 15:23–28

God has ordained that the Church should grow as the expression of Christ's fullness in the earth. Christ's fullness means that He will build His Church in such a way that it will prevail over the powers of hell. Rebellious spirit forces, as well as death itself, will come under the sway of Jesus Christ through His Church.

Acts 2:41

Acts 2:47

Christ's fullness means that His Presence in the Church, through the Holy Spirit, draws people to Himself to be added to the Church. Like iron filings to a magnet, the fullness of His Presence in the Church attracts those from all the earth, irrespective of race, nation or society.

Acts 4:4
1 Corinthians 1:18

Acts 5:14

Acts 6:7

Christ's fullness means that by the proclamation of Christ's Word, in and through His Church, people believe and become His disciples. As the Church displays the glories of her Lord in teaching, lifestyle, and service, the longings of unregenerate mankind are stirred to respond to Christ.

Ephesians 4:15–16
Colossians 1:15–21

Colossians 2:9–10

Christ's fullness means that His Church is to grow and increase throughout the earth. As His Church matures worldwide, people and spiritual forces will see an ever-increasing expression of Christ's identity and works.

WISDOM OF GOD EXPRESSED TO ALL CREATION

Ephesians 3:10

Philippians 2:1–11

The growth and maturation of the Church will manifest the wisdom of God to all creation and to spiritual forces in heavenly places. Every nation, tribe, language, and people group is destined to acknowledge that Jesus Christ is the Lord over all.

Ephesians 3:10

God has chosen His Church as the instrument through which He purposes to make known His wisdom to all the principalities and powers in the heavenly places.

Revelation 21:1–4

God is building His Church as an earthly reflection of a heavenly city. This city is the habitation of God's very Presence. He Himself is its Light.

APPLICATION

Describe practical ways that Church members are able to witness effectively for Christ and His Kingdom. What can you do to encourage your fellow Church members to find their places in fulfilling the Great Commission from Jesus Christ? Describe how you view your present commitment to Christ's command for worldwide Church planting. And how is that commitment demonstrated in your involvement with the local congregation?

CONCLUSION

The Church of Jesus Christ is the unique, chosen instrument of God for revealing His purposes in the earth. Jesus Christ died for the Church. Christ Himself is committed to building this temple of living stones into His dwelling place. **It should be the desire and goal of every Christian**

to gain Christ's perspective on the Church's role on earth and in society today. There is no higher issue today than the nature of the Church of Jesus Christ and her mission of proclaiming the Kingdom of God throughout the nations of the earth.

CHRIST'S KINGDOM IN THE MARKETPLACE

LESSON 1 – THE EARTH IS THE LORD'S

PURPOSE

This lesson will be the cornerstone of the rest of this volume because one must properly view God's role in creation or nothing else really fits. It is the 'top button of the coat;' if it is in the wrong place, everything that follows will also be in the wrong place.

The Scriptures present God as Architect, Creator, and Owner of all things. Accepting this cardinal fact profoundly affects human work ethics and economics because we thus become economically accountable to Him. Section 6 will present God's claims on our productivity and this lesson will focus on His ownership of all.

GLOSSARY

Create – (Hebrew: *barah*) to make from nothing.

Economics – the science concerned with the description and analysis of the production, distribution, and consumption of goods and services (*Webster*).

Ethics – the science of moral philosophy, which teaches men their duty and the reasons of it.

Sovereign – supreme in power; possessing supreme dominion. God is the Sovereign Ruler of the universe.

Creator – the One who causes, produces, or creates.

CREATOR

Genesis 1:1

Proverbs 8:22–31

Genesis 1:1
John 1:1–14
Colossians 1:16–18

Psalm 24:1, 2
Isaiah 40:12–26
Daniel 4
Psalm 8
Psalm 104

The very first statement of Holy Scriptures is 'In the beginning God.' Before He did anything – He already was. He is eternal, pre-existent, and He is above all else. The rest of history unfolds from that reality.

God, who existed before all things, created all things. All initiative and power flowed from Him to creation. He also sustains what He created; creation does not have a life of its own.

Since God is the Creator and Sustainer of all things, He is the Owner as well. He holds all legal claims to all things. He is Sovereign by virtue of power and legal right. As Owner, He has sole rights to determine the use of all resources. These rights extend to the stars and all the heavens.

EXALTED

Exodus 15:1
Psalm 93
Romans 1:20
Psalm 95:1–6

The Lord is exalted above all else. While He is revealed in creation, He is above it all. Creation is the expression of His power, His ability, and His beauty. While we have not seen God, we can see His works which are infinite – unsearchable. No one has found the boundaries of

Psalm 19:1
Psalm 145:1–7

creation. Therefore, creation reveals an awesome God of eternal and infinite magnitude.

Proverbs 15:33
Isaiah 55:1–13
Deuteronomy 10:12
Ecclesiastes 12:13
Matthew 10:28

The fear or awe of God is the beginning of wisdom. To realize that we are placed in creation by one so unsearchable is the beginning of a right attitude and understanding of all else.

LORD

Isaiah 45
John 1:3
1 Corinthians 8:6

Colossians 1:16

Acts 17:26–27
Daniel 4

Matthew 28:18
Hebrews 1:2

The reason that it is essential to establish our understanding is because He is also Lord. That is, He did not create all things and then forsake them. He is a Father very much involved in creation and its maturation. He pursues purpose among the elements and among the nations. While mankind may learn of these things and steward the work of His hands, all things are for His eternal purpose.

The sovereignty of God goes far beyond the Church or those who acknowledge Him. He is Sovereign over the nations, having created their boundaries and seasons. All authority remains in His hands and He has created within mankind the desire to know Him.

PURPOSEFUL

Ephesians 1:9–12
Ephesians 3:11
Romans 8:28–30
2 Timothy 1:9

Romans 1:19–20
Acts 14:17
Psalm 97:6
Ephesians 1:1–23

Ephesians 1:18–23
Revelation 1:8
Revelation 22:12–13

Creation is not just a whim or an accident. The biblical view is that God is a Person of purpose and all His acts are purposeful. While His purpose is not always evident to us, it is the thread that holds the fabric of history together.

As we study creation we are taught that things have a purpose which fits into a larger order of things. This order and interaction of natural things teaches us that the mind behind all of this is orderly and purposeful. His purpose runs through all that He has done.

The purpose of God has an end or goal. God is working through Christ and those who are called to His purpose toward a certain end. And while we do not know all of the precise details of that end, we know that the end itself is in Christ. The Bible teaches us, therefore, to do all things to the glory of Christ who holds in His hands the eternal purpose of God.

PRINCIPLES

Genesis 1:2–31
Genesis 8:17
Genesis 9:1, 7
Genesis 35:11

Psalm 1:2–3
Psalm 40:8
Psalm 119
Matthew 5:17
Romans 7:12, 14, 22

The Creator, Owner, and Lord of creation has ordained a purpose for creation. Part of that purpose is that creation be fruitful or productive and glorify Him. In later lessons, we will see how a major purpose for mankind is to assist in making creation productive and thus contributing to the ultimate purpose of God.

It is important to know that God has built principles into creation by which it works. Creation is not erratic, inconsistent, or incoherent. To the unlearned, it can seem that way. But the more we learn of God and creation, the more we can understand how and why things work. There are laws and principles that govern how creation works. There are so-called natural laws and there are spiritual laws as well. The same God created both the natural and spiritual realms. The Bible

Psalm 119:5–7, 9–11, 32, 63, 98, 130, 175

should be viewed as an instruction manual for relating to God and His world.

While we tend to view law as a 'moral' word, it is a very practical word. The Law as presented in Scripture is not some arbitrary legislation voted upon by mortals. The Law consists of invisible principles such as the law of gravity, or the law of cause and effect. Laws are not restrictions upon our happiness – they are keys given by God to find the joys and secrets of creation. The more keys we discover, the more doors we can open.

APPLICATION

How does recognizing God's ownership affect your attitude toward the environment?

How does it affect your sense of possessiveness toward things?
How does this view differ from socialism? Or capitalism?
If the earth is not God's, then whose?
Therefore, does 'might make right?'

CONCLUSION

Psalm 14:1
Psalm 100

We have not invented God, unless of course we invented creation. The fool has said, 'There is no God.' Even a cursory view of the stars, some of which are incomparably larger than our sun, will tell us that creation is infinite and the One who made it is awesome. But the Bible calls upon us to go beyond accepting the obvious. It calls upon us to recognize Him as Lord, seek His purpose, and learn His principles. In doing so we can be introduced to the rewards of knowing and serving the Creator Himself and being part of His purpose.

LESSON 2 – THE DELEGATION OF THE EARTH

PURPOSE

Lesson 1 focused on God's ownership of all things based upon His creating and His sustaining of all things. This lesson will go beyond God's ownership to discuss His purpose for creation and how mankind fits into it.

While God has all authority and rights regarding creation, He is not self-centered. He has created mankind in His own image and shared the power to create and sustain with mankind. Through humanity, God has extended His nature and purpose. He has also delegated the opportunities and responsibilities of this planet earth.

GLOSSARY

Delegate – to send with power and authority to transact business.

Husband – to direct and manage with frugality in expending anything; to use or employ in a manner suited to produce the greatest effect (*Webster*).

Productivity – the activity associated with producing.

RULER

Genesis 1:26–31
Genesis 5:1
Genesis 9:6

Psalm 8:6

Hebrews 2:6–8

Mankind was created in God's image, and like God, man is a many-faceted being. One of the aspects of God's nature that has been given to mankind is that of ruling. God of course maintains ultimate authority, but has given to each of us a measure of management skills that must be developed if we are going to reflect His nature. Our original mandate was to rule, therefore this trait must be somewhere in each of us.

Isaiah 9:6
Romans 7:4
Isaiah 9:7

Colossians 1:10
Matthew 25:14–30

Good management is more than maintaining or controlling one's resources; it is multiplying or increasing one's resources. The Bible calls this fruitfulness. We normally refer to it as productivity. God apparently is infinite in creative acts and fruitfulness, overseeing His ever-increasing Kingdom. To be like Him is to exercise our abilities in such a way as to preserve and prosper.

HUSBAND

Genesis 2:15
Genesis 2:19–20
Genesis 4:1–3

Husbandry means more than the male role in marriage. It is the overall care that brings productivity. The Bible speaks of the husbandman (farmer) and modern agriculture refers to animal husbandry (care of livestock).

Mankind, collectively, was created to 'husband' life on this planet – animal and plant. We are to name, cultivate, and use as desired all forms of plant and animal life – with the exception of one tree! It is interesting that one of Adam and Eve's sons was a caretaker of plants (Cain) and the other a shepherd (Abel). Adam and Eve developed their companionship and family life around the task of sharing responsibility.

FAMILY

Genesis 2

Proverbs 31:10–31

Adam was also a husband to his wife. God gave both Adam and Eve biological family and economic roles with definition and restrictions. Man was to take care of the woman who was to help him in his task of management and productivity. Interdependence was the order from the beginning. God saw that loneliness was not good. He ordained the family so that social and economic principles could be learned which were to be employed in their world task.

Genesis 4:1–2

Adam and Eve not only functioned together in overseeing creation, but had children together and trained them to join them in the family business of managing the earth. Adam and Eve not only had a 'maintenance mentality,' they had a growth mentality and produced and trained their sons. Thus the family was not only a spiritual and relational unit, it was an educational and economic unit.

Genesis 3

Genesis 4

It should be noted (and will be in Lesson 3) that Adam and Eve's division produced later division among their sons. And that division manifested itself in two primary areas: work and worship. It seems that as children of Adam, when we begin to have problems with our relationship to God, we soon begin to develop bad attitudes toward our fellow man that will usually show up in the field-workplace. The first murder was a family-related, religion-related, and vocation-related crime.

The lesson seems to be that if the family can stay right with God, they will probably stay right with each other, and vocationally prosper together. In any case, the family was the first social unit where relationships and training had a direct effect on training and economic development.

APPLICATION

What were some of Adam and Eve's responsibilities?
    How does working together bring economic progress?
    Why is conflict costly?
    In what ways can one's family affect one's economics?

CONCLUSION

In the beginning, God did not distinguish between natural and spiritual obedience. Care for the natural resources was a spiritual issue. Productivity was also a spiritual issue. Spiritual fellowship with God was – and still is – revealed by practical obedience in natural responsibility to family and society.

While everyone will not be called to marriage and producing a natural family, we all have a serious stake in the successful functioning of families, since we live in a world either blessed or cursed by their fruit. Unless we become burdened for families, we will become increasingly burdened by the failure of families.

LESSON 3 – THE GREAT DECEPTION

PURPOSE

After God created the heavens and the earth, He delegated the oversight and development of it all to Adam and Eve. They were to remain accountable to Him; and as long as they obeyed the Lord, they enjoyed great freedom and the abundant fruit of creation.

There was one particular area that God reserved for Himself and that was the fruit of the Tree of Knowledge of Good and Evil. From the beginning, God taught mankind that freedom was not absolute and that with delegated opportunity also comes responsibility and accountability.

This lesson will show how Satan caused mankind to believe that disobedience could produce quicker and better results, but how in fact it cost them a great opportunity and lost resources.

GLOSSARY

Accountability – responsibility for a trust; the state of being liable to answer for one's conduct.

Anarchy – want or lack of government; political confusion.

Deception – the state of being deceived or misled.

Redemption – deliverance from bondage, distress, or from liability to evil (*Webster*).

GOD IS A PROVIDER OF OPPORTUNITY

Genesis 2:15

Genesis 2:17

Genesis 3

God created mankind in His own image with creative abilities and great opportunities. Mankind named the animals and enjoyed the idyllic garden – a paradise. Beyond, that, they were given the opportunity to expand paradise throughout the earth while enjoying each other's unique companionship and producing children.

The only reservation given to them was to abstain from eating the fruit of the Tree of Knowledge of Good and Evil. The Tree represented God's ownership, and the first fruits were His. This is a principle maintained throughout the Bible. The Tree also represented the necessity of obedience to some rule or government if creation was to operate successfully. In addition, God seems to be saying that moral knowledge is no substitute for faith and obedience when it comes to productivity and stewardship. In other words, being smart doesn't necessarily make one productive.

SATAN IS A FORCE FOR FAILURE

Isaiah 14:12–14
Ezra 28:17

We need to remember that Satan once occupied a lofty place in the heavenly order, was exceptionally intelligent, beautiful, and musically gifted. He was thrown out of heaven because, in his pride, he led a rebellion against God. The issues of recognition of God, delegation, and stewardship are important eternal issues that also have bearing on human history.

Proverbs 6:16–19

Satan's real problem was with God. He hated – and still hates – all authority, obedience, and faithfulness because these virtues remind him of God and his own fallen character. Wherever he sees a righteous and productive order, he will seek out a weakness in order to exploit and destroy the order. Satan destroys through sowing doubt and discord.

Genesis 3:1–6

1 Timothy 2:14

When Satan came to earth and examined creation, he discovered the one restraint on human freedom and assaulted that particular issue. Secondly, he appealed to Eve, rather than Adam, who had received the original instruction from God. He approached her with questions designed to bring doubt. His next step was to appeal to her own desire to 'know for herself' and the possibility to be 'as God.' Eve was deceived through believing her own perspective instead of the Word of God. She ate as Adam watched passively, after which he followed her lead.

Genesis 3:8–13

It is noteworthy that when God arrived in the Garden for His regular fellowship with Adam and Eve, they were hiding. They realized several things: They were naked ... (self-awareness), they were disobedient, and they were accountable. It is also noteworthy that God called for Adam ... 'Where are you?'. Adam was held responsible for both his actions and his wife's.

The process toward failure was disorder, doubt, deception, and deliberate sin on Adam's part. (The Bible doesn't say he was deceived ... his sin was willful.) The whole idea that creating one's own rules to success and ignoring God's prescribed principles was a tragic error that continues to face each successive generation.

Genesis 3:15–24

Adam and Eve's behavior brought God's disapproval. For the first time they felt separation, guilt, shame, and condemnation. For the first time, they tried to blame each other and to refuse personal accountability. Because of disobedience, paradise was lost along with innocence and relational harmony.

Not only were Adam and Eve forced to leave this idyllic Garden, but death entered their lives because of sin. In addition, their labor was increased by a rebellious creation. Disobedience had not brought more freedom – rather it had brought less.

GOD IS A FORCE FOR REDEMPTION

Romans 11:29

Genesis 3:15

God's plan for man and creation was not destroyed because of man's disobedience. Though mankind's sin brought judgement and loss of blessings, God's purpose was still in effect.

In the very midst of God's judgement on sin, He gave a promise – that the seed of woman would triumph over the enemy. It is significant that Jesus Christ was born of a woman and conceived by the Holy Spirit. Jesus is not born of Adam, nor is He the son of Adam, but He is the Seed of woman and the Son of God. So even in judgement God gives a promise that He would provide salvation.

In addition, God provided a sacrifice in the Garden to cover man and woman, to remove their sense of shame and embarrassment. This animal sacrifice was the first offering of the innocent for the guilty, and a foreshadowing of Christ's own death, and the exchange of His innocence for our guilt. By faith, our 'nakedness' (our sins) is covered with His righteousness. When God looks at us, He sees Christ's own righteousness.

While this episode tells us a lot about mankind's weakness and Satan's guile, it also tells us a lot about God's covenant love and determination to provide redemption for fallen humanity. As the apostle Paul says in Romans 5:20, 'Where sin abounded, grace abounded even more.'

APPLICATION

In what way did Adam and Eve fail?

What lessons are to be learned that might apply to our own work place?

How do 'short cuts' cause us problems in today's world?

When is creativity and personal initiative a healthy thing?

When is it not?

CONCLUSION

The Scripture is clear that we are created as stewards – not owners. God has provided us all with great opportunities, and a right relationship to Him gives us great freedom to develop these opportunities. Pride and ambition can make us vulnerable to temptation and cause us to take apparent short cuts to additional power, rather than waiting for His promotion. When we violate His place or take what is forbidden, we jeopardize our place and opportunities. Nevertheless, even if we fail, His grace is available. Jesus offers us an opportunity to be redeemed and restored if we do not blame others and accept our own responsibility. By His grace He forgives and forgets our transgressions. By faith in Him, He becomes our Overcomer of temptation and example of true faithfulness and promotion.

LESSON 4 – THE COMMISSION TO LABOR

PURPOSE

The reluctance to work – laziness – is not only a character flaw but it affects the quality of the work that we do perform. Laziness causes us to approach work as an adversary or 'evil,' and the effect is misery for both ourselves and those who depend upon us. Laziness or a negative attitude toward work not only affects us personally, but the entire economic order.

GLOSSARY

Work – management, state of labor, exertion of strength and skill to produce a desired effect.

Product – that which is formed or produced by labor or by mental application.

Management – administration of one's responsibility.

Galactical – having to do with the furthermost boundaries of the universe.

GOD IS THE ORIGINAL 'WORKER'

God explodes the notion that power is associated with not having to work or making others perform labor. God is proof that laziness is not a wise choice even if one has all power. He demonstrates that creative labor is the choice of one who has wisdom.

Genesis 1

Psalm 8:3

Psalm 104:1–30

God worked six days in creating the heavens and the earth, but that by no means implies that those six days were His first or last work days. Since all galactical creation is His – His efforts are infinite. But God is not only the God of the *macroworld*, He is the God of the *microworld*. He created the smallest of objects and life forms. God labors in the grand vista and in the greatest detail.

Genesis 6:3

Isaiah 64:8

John 5:17

God is also working with mankind. He said, 'My Spirit will not always strive with man.' Isaiah saw God as a 'Potter' who shapes His people as a potter shapes clay. Jesus said, 'I must be about My Father's business.' God has business with mankind. Jesus says, 'The Father works and I work.'

Genesis 1:28–30

God ordained that mankind should work. Mankind is created in God's image and therefore created to enjoy creative and productive labor. From the very outset, mankind was given a responsibility and a mission to oversee, manage, and bring productivity from creation. Considering the magnitude of creation and that there were only two people in the beginning, it was an incomprehensible task and opportunity.

Genesis 1:8–9

However, it is apparent that God did not intend for man to do it all alone. While man was given great freedom, God regularly visited with man in the evenings to give counsel and to receive man's accountability. It is also apparent that God was not impatient but saw man's mission as a long process. As mankind multiplied and expanded his occupation, God's delegated rule would be extended.

Genesis 1:26

We should be aware that this mission is stated before man's fall. In other words, mankind had a purpose and responsibility to labor before sin entered the world. Work is not the result of sin, it is the result of God's purpose.

Genesis 2:21–25

In addition to working on the mission to manage creation, the man had responsibility to husband his wife. The woman had the responsibility to be a wife or a companion helper to her husband. So along with responsibilities in the world, there were responsibilities in the family which seemed to take precedent even over those in the world. This mutual support was necessary to their world task.

Colossians 3:17
Ecclesiastes 9:10
Proverbs 12:24
Proverbs 13:4, 11

Since God created and commissioned mankind to work, productive work should be viewed as holy in that it is as unto the Lord. The Bible tells us that whatever we do in word or deed should be done in the name of the Lord. The Scriptures also state that whatever we do should be done with all our might. Our efforts are not simply for the approval of the boss or the market; they are for the approval of God. In our highly specialized society, labor can take many forms in contrast to the primarily physical labor of earlier days. Productive labor is any expenditure of energy that goes into providing a service or product that is useful to society. In our 'information-oriented' society, providing insight and knowledge or helping others to develop skills has become the work of many. But many others are contributing by raw physical effort. Whatever one's role, it is vital that we see ourselves as giving and taking from the social labor pool with a sense of satisfaction. This satisfaction comes from knowing that God has called us to serve in this way, and that He is pleased.

Matthew 25:23

Genesis 3:14–19

What about the curse? God speaks of the curse on the serpent, the increased difficulty of the woman, and the increased difficulty of the man because of a curse on the earth. It is important to note that neither Adam's nor Eve's role changed from what it was before they fell: Adam was responsible. Eve was his wife, companion, and helper. But after the fall, there is a new factor – sin had entered man, woman, and the earth. With sin came a whole set of problems like some disease that spawns other diseases. Because man was in charge of creation, his sin affected all earthly creation. Man brought the curse . . . not God.

Man's rebellion against God caused a loss of harmony with God, the Source of all authority. To the extent that man was separated from God, he became separated from the natural order, and rebellion entered it. Mankind now had to earn a living and produce and raise children in a hostile rather than friendly world. The curse didn't fundamentally change our task, it just made it a lot harder. And so it is with sin.

2 Corinthians 5:18–21

If separation from God makes things more difficult, then reconciliation through Jesus Christ should give us added strength and authority to accomplish our tasks.

APPLICATION

Why is work holy?
  Do you view your work as holy?
  Why is it important for you to respect the work of others?
  How can a biblical work ethic benefit society?

CONCLUSION

Genesis chapters 1–3 provide the 'seed truth' for the rest of the Bible. The law of beginnings determines the law of harvests. A proper understanding of our efforts toward God, family, and society will serve us well not only on pay day, but at the end of life. If we see work properly, we will not merely work to purchase pleasure, but we will take pleasure in our work. The product of joyful and skillful labor will endure long after our moments of pleasure have exhausted themselves and burst like mere bubbles.

LESSON 5 – THE FAMILY IS AN ECONOMIC UNIT

PURPOSE

Genesis 1:26–28 gives us mankind's mission in the earth. Genesis 2 gives us the story of God's creation: the Garden of Eden, Adam, Eve, and their responsibility to oversee plant and animal life. Genesis 3 deals with the fall of mankind and God's promise to redeem their progeny through the seed of woman. Genesis 4 is the beginning of life in the untamed world beyond the Garden.

We are told that Adam and Eve had sons, Cain and Abel, who had vocations. While we do not have a detailed account of daily life, it is evident that family life was built around 'making a living' and productive labor. It can be safely assumed that training and support for vocational life came from the family and benefits returned to the family. Though much time has passed since then, up until recent years the family was a very foundational economic unit where vocation was passed on to the next generation and training began early.

Names of families like Smith, Baker, Cook, Boatwright, Farmer, and many others actually came from their vocation. Identity and task were much the same. While that has not continued into our hi-tech and transient society, the family is still where attitudes toward work and money are first formed. Let us see from the Bible that it was intended to be so and that families face a serious task in today's pleasure-oriented society.

GLOSSARY

Progeny – offspring; children; descendants of the humankind.

Procreation – the act of begetting; the generation and producing of the young (*Webster*).

THE COMMISSION

Genesis 1:26

Genesis 2:20–23

Genesis 2

The commission to rule was given to the family. Oversight within the family was the male's responsibility, but oversight of creation was a corporate responsibility. They worked together to do their work. So the family learned team work in carrying out tasks.

Genesis 2 specifically states that loneliness in labor is not good and that Eve was created as a companion helper. It is not clear that this was a domestic help only. It was a shared sense that when one went out to work, it was on behalf of both. The task did not separate them; it brought them together. It is vital that economic needs not separate family members, but each member's activity be viewed as the family's long-term purpose. That seemed easier when all of the family worked in the family business than it is now – when many times family members work in isolation from one another. Economic and vocational isolation often become the basis for family separation. Staying involved in one another's task and each other's rewards is vital. Even when one is the primary income producer and the other a companion and homemaker, both parties must be aware of their common goals and how they function as one unit.

PASSING THE PRINCIPLE

Proverbs 22:6–15
Proverbs 23:13–24

Proverbs 29:15

Proverbs 17:6
Proverbs 31:28

Children are part of the mission for most families – 'Be fruitful and multiply.' Children greatly complicate the family, especially in our modern economy. The cost and complications to bring them into the world at an average hospital facility, care for them at home, and educating them at school represents one of life's biggest investments in love, time, and money. Parents have every right to expect that in their older years there will be real returns on those investments in love, time, and money. And there will be, if parenting is understood beyond procreation or merely producing someone to love like a 'human pet' that must be catered to.

Genesis 2

Adam and Eve focused Cain on farming and Abel was directed toward animal husbandry. They seemed to have divided up resources of plant and animal life. By the time they were born, Adam had likely developed considerable knowledge which he passed along.

Genesis 4:5–8

It is worth noting that the first murder was unresolved family rivalry gone awry. It was vocational and religious at its roots. Cain was jealous and bitter toward Abel, and God refused his sacrifice. Cain failed to heed God's warnings and killed his brother at the work place – in the field. The problem was an unresolved family problem, an unre-solved problem with God, and a problem that carried over into the work place. How often do you suppose vocation is adversely affected by relational and religious problems?

Genesis 4:17–22

The Scripture goes on to tell in Genesis 4 that Cain produced sons and daughters, and their generations are named. Jabal was the father of those who dwelt in tents and had livestock. Jubal was the father of musicians. Tubal-cain was a forger of metal. It is evident that vocation was part of identity and was passed on.

Genesis 6:10–18
Genesis 7:6–7

Noah, was a shipbuilder and was joined by his family in that serious effort lasting roughly 100 years. It would be obvious that Noah, the righteous man, both led his household and passed on his know-ledge of boats in completing a vessel 450 feet long, 75 feet wide, and 45 feet high.

The accomplishment of this task undoubtedly required a great deal of discipline, order, and quality control.

OTHER EXAMPLES

Proverbs 1:8

The principles established in Genesis are carried on throughout history. Abraham's example with Isaac or Joseph's example with Jesus can be matched today all over the world. The entire book of Proverbs is written to instruct a son in parental guidance. The book

Ecclesiastes 2:24

Nehemiah 3

Matthew 4:21–22

covers almost all areas of life and frequently deals with subjects like labor, diligence, debt, how to handle money, and how to relate to others in the work place.

Likewise, the book of Ecclesiastes was written to pass along wisdom to successive generations. The theme of the book is that the greatest thing in life is to enjoy your labors. To do so is a gift from God. The writer of Ecclesiastes also warns against bad investments, not training your heirs, work without purpose, greed, and working for pleasure rather than taking pleasure in your work.

Nehemiah provides another outstanding example of how families worked together to rebuild the walls of Jerusalem. And over 400 years later, Jesus calls men who have been trained in their father's businesses. While God's call to man takes on a different vocational path, the training itself is part of the preparation for His purpose.

APPLICATION

How can parents train children for economic development? How early should this begin?

What is the impact of family failure or economic and social development? (The Family Research Council suggests that divorce is a leading cause of poverty.)

CONCLUSION

Luke 16:10–12
Matthew 25:14–30

Not everyone will be called to marriage and of those who are, not all will have children. Nevertheless, we all have a serious investment in the attitudes of youth toward such things as responsibility, work, economics, and excellence. Irresponsible family life and academic attitudes that go contrary to proven biblical truth have cost nations their ability to contribute to the world economy and left them in poverty. Only God knows the jobs that have left nations because families forsook their responsibility to teach their children the joy of work and the rewards of productivity. The teaching of our Lord is replete with references to such rewards. Parents who love their children owe them that knowledge – that serving Christ includes productive service to humanity.

LESSON 6 – THE CALL TO EXCELLENCE

PURPOSE

Since God has called us to work as a means to fulfill our mission in creation, and since all productive labor should be done as unto the Lord, it is fitting for us to now examine the quality of our labor and why it should be excellent. We have already been reminded that the Scriptures teach that all we do should be done with our best efforts. Now let us examine why we are called to do our best in all things, and how that pays off in the long run.

GLOSSARY

Excellence – that which is highly esteemed. To excel or to surpass in good qualities or deeds or to go beyond average expectations.

EXCELLENCE IN CREATION

Genesis 1:31

Genesis 1 closes with the assessment of God's work in creation as being 'very good.' In fact, it was perfect, complete, and harmonious. Eventually what had been very good became flawed through man's mismanagement. We are reminded in this that even things created with excellence must be maintained with excellency or carelessness can diminish their quality and value.

Exodus 15:7
Deuteronomy 33:26–29

Moses found God to be excellent in battle as He destroyed the Egyptian armies in the Red Sea. In his last earthly exaltation, Moses declared that there was none like the God of Israel who rides through the skies in majesty.

Psalm 8

Romans 1:20

Hebrews 8:6

David joins Moses in ascribing majesty and excellence to God. Psalm 8 declares God's Name, His splendor, His heavens, His crowning work in mankind, and all of the animal kingdom to be excellent. Paul joins Moses and David in stating that creation declares the glory of God. And the writer of Hebrews says that Jesus has a more excellent ministry, and mediated a more excellent covenant with better promises.

The entire Bible reveals God as excellent – above expectations – excelling in honor, power, splendor, and mercy. It is right to declare that God and His work are excellent. He has done excellent things.

Isaiah 12

Revelation 4, 5

Our God is in fact King over all the earth. He owns all resources and is supremely able to produce the most exquisite results and treasurable acts. When we worship, we worship a Sovereign, a King, One who sits enthroned on high above His people. His courts and His attendants are royally arrayed.

GOD PROMOTES EXCELLENCE ON EARTH

Romans 5:6–8

There can be no question of God's love even for the lowliest of sinners or those of poorest means. But there can also be no question that because God does love the lowly, He does not want to leave them in sin or poverty.

John 14:1–15:17

His call is to Himself, His ways, His work, and His house. Those who follow on to know the ways of the Lord learn His ways of honor, majesty, excellence, and productivity, even as they continue to love the lowliest.

Philippians 3
2 Timothy 2:1–15
2 Timothy 4:1–8

1 Corinthians 3:10–17

The apostle Paul gives us a classic apostolic example of excellency of commitment, service, and ministry even until death. His testimony is honored throughout the world because he gave himself as a living sacrifice to build Christians and churches as far as he was allowed to go. His philosophy was to build wisely on proven foundatons with proven materials. He built churches so that they could stand the trial of fire in the same way he lived his own life. Paul's work and testimony stand even after nearly 2,000 years, and show no signs of passing away.

Exodus 26

Hebrews 3:5

Both testaments are replete with examples of God's favor upon work well done. Moses was faithful in building the tabernacle to the very letter, and God filled it with His glory. The writer of Hebrews declares that Moses was faithful in all his house.

2 Chronicles 5:14
1 Kings 7:13–14

Likewise, Solomon was faithful in building the temple according to the plan given to his father David. Everything about the work was regal – even the craftsmen were filled with a spirit to do excellent work to the glory of God. When Solomon had completed the dedication, God's glory filled the temple. He was pleased with the explicit obedience and excellent labors.

Daniel 1:4–20
Daniel 6:3

Genesis 39–41

There are many other examples of excellence and how God promoted those who pursued it. Daniel and his friends were outstanding among the captives and the youth of Babylon. Even as an elderly man in the courts of successive dynasties, he continued to demonstrate excellence and he was continually promoted.

Daniel and Joseph are proof that excellence can prevail even in hostile conditions.

GOD ENABLES EXCELLENCE

2 Timothy 2:15
Ephesians 6:8
Colossians 3:23–25
Matthew 25:22–28
Proverbs 22:29

We cannot all excel at everything, but we can all seek the specific service in which we can excel. We are all told to excel at understanding the Scriptures; that God will reward the good things that we do; that by using what gifts we have, they will increase; that honor comes to those who are skilled at their work.

Peter was a fisherman when Jesus discovered him, and sometimes not a very successful one. Matthew was a despised tax-collector. Paul was an arrogant, religious, and dangerous man. But through the teachings of Jesus and the power of the Holy Spirit, they not only changed; they became world-changers.

The key to excellence is to trust Jesus with your life and set about to study and know His ways. As the Holy Spirit leads and empowers you, you will learn to serve as He served, and contribute positive assistance to society as He did. Your efforts will begin to bear the marks of being discipled by the King of Glory.

APPLICATION

How can worshipping God influence us to excellence?
    Why is it important that Christians do outstanding work?
    Who are we trying to impress with our labors?
    What has good works to do with our going to heaven?

CONCLUSION

Our standards are not derived from the average efforts in society. Being God's children makes a certain impression on our attitudes, our efforts, and our goals. His 'well done' is the preeminent goal and desire of our hearts. He is the Master Craftsman. His workmanship in our lives will make a difference – and that should be the best testimony to His own excellent greatness.

LESSON 7 – THE CALL TO FAITHFULNESS IN A FEW THINGS

PURPOSE

The late Malcom Muggeridge, a well-known British writer, was very impressed by Mother Theresa's work in Calcutta, India. Watching her ministry, endlessly transporting the sick and dying from the city streets, he asked, 'Don't you ever become discouraged?' 'No,' she said. 'Why not?' he pressed. 'Because Jesus called us to be faithful, not successful.'

It could not be put more clearly. Our call is to faithfulness first – that is success. The results are left up to the Lord. Kingdom laborers are those who labor under His Lordship in a manner that pleases Him, believing that He is faithful to bring a just reward and appropriate results. This lesson tells us that faithfulness begins with just a few things.

GLOSSARY

Faithfulness – loyalty, completing what you promise.

Steward – one appointed to manage the owner's property and affairs.

Ethic – to deal with what is right or wrong, good or bad.

UNCHANGING GOD

Hebrews 13:8
Malachi 3:6
Psalm 36:5
Psalm 89:1
Lamentations 3:23

Revelation 19:11

God is spoken of as the unchanging God. This not only means that He is eternal and steadfast in His nature, but He is unswerving in His faithfulness to His Word and His promises. What He says, He does. He is faithful as a friend and faithful in His responsibilities as God. He has never been, and never will be, irresponsible.

John, the author of the book of Revelation, saw a vision of the Eternal Christ seated upon a white horse; Jesus was called 'faithful and true.' The most accurate definition of the word faithful is Jesus Himself.

TRAINING STEWARDS

Genesis 1:26–28

God, being faithful, seeks to instill that trait in humanity since it reflects His likeness and prepares them to exercise responsibility. Mankind was created to steward the earth in the very beginning and failed because of unfaithfulness. That is, they disobeyed God, the Owner. Part of man's restoration is the process of being restored to faithfulness.

1 Corinthians 4:2
Psalm 8; 2 Timothy 2:11–15
Daniel 6:4

The apostle Paul states that a steward or trustee must be found faithful. A trustee must be trustworthy or what has been entrusted will be lost. Since God the Owner, Creator of all things, has entrusted the works of His hands to us, it is necessary that He train us to be faithful and obedient to His purpose.

LEARNING FAITHFULNESS

When one accepts Jesus Christ as Lord and Savior, one does not automatically become faithful. Sometimes poor training and habits have left one irresponsible, unpredictable, and unprofitable. As the Lord Jesus begins to re-direct their thinking through the Word of God, and by established government in His Kingdom, His disciples are re-trained.

Matthew 24:45–25:46

Luke 19:11–27
Luke 20:9–26

Jesus emphasized faithfulness in Holy Spirit teaching. He warns against wastefulness, dishonesty, and non-productivity. Since His Kingdom is one of trust and delegation, it is imperative that Kingdom citizens be prepared for responsibility. The result of learning God's faithfulness will be excellence, productivity, and the increased entrustment of His resources.

Luke 16:10–13

Faithfulness does not begin in the mammoth responsibilities of overseeing cities, great ministries, or industries. It begins with taking responsibility in a few things. This is affirmed by none other than Jesus Himself. As adults begin life as children, so do great rulers begin as servants in a few things.

Matthew 14:16–19
Luke 22:10–13
Luke 19:30

Jesus not only advocated this approach to learning faithfulness, but practiced it Himself as a child and taught His disciples the same way. Long before they were preaching to multitudes, they were serving at His meetings and were handling practical mundane matters. Jesus started His disciples at the beginning in their quest for faithfulness . . . overseeing a few things.

THE PROMISE

Luke 16:10–13

Matthew 25:14–30
2 Timothy 4:7–8
1 Peter 5:2–4

There is a reason for learning faithfulness even beyond building character and excellence in skill; it is preparation for overseeing many things. The promise to those who handle a few things well is very clear; they will be made ruler over many. God's intention in His Kingdom is not that we should be permanent slaves to the mundane. Rather, He desires to make us co-regents with Him. If we are faithful in what He gives us to do, He will give us more; if we are unfaithful, we will lose what we have.

APPLICATION

Would you describe yourself as a faithful person?

How have you gone about demonstrating faithfulness?

Is there anyone in your life other than yourself to whom you are seeking to demonstrate faithfulness?

CONCLUSION

The true worshipper of Jesus Christ not only loves Him, but desires to be like Him and please Him. One of the traits which He most admires is faithfulness, or loyalty to Him, in the task.

The place to begin learning faithfulness, as Jesus teaches, is in overseeing or managing a few things – practical things that serve His larger purpose. The family, the Church, and our vocations are logical places to begin this vital process. Christian discipleship serves the overall health of the entire community and builds the character of its citizens. It prepares us for increasing growth and responsibility. Serious attention to the few things and the small things will prepare for and preserve the great things. It will reveal His Kingdom government to a world in need of a better way.

LESSON 8 – THE CALL TO FAITHFULNESS IN MONEY

PURPOSE

Money is not only part of the world system of trade, it is part of God's Kingdom. This lesson is aimed at helping us to understand money, its use, and why God teaches us to use it properly.

Genesis 14:20

The Bible says a lot about money, even though coins as we know them were not introduced until late in Old Testament times. However, gold, silver, and a wide variety of things were exchanged like money in order to obtain desired objects, give gifts, and to support God's work in the tabernacle and temples. Tithes, or tenths of earnings, were given by Abraham to Melchizedek early in Bible history and probably at the very beginning (see Genesis 4:4).

Genesis 4:4

Genesis 12:2–3

On the basis of Abraham's faithfulness with money, God gave him true eternal wealth: The covenant, a heritage, a testimony, descendants, and numerous other blessings.

Luke 16:11

As we examine the subject of faithfulness in money, keep in mind that the importance goes far beyond money itself. Learning to master this issue is essential to development as a disciple and preparation for handling even greater issues.

GLOSSARY

Mammon – material wealth or possessions.

Steward – one appointed to manage the owner's property and affairs.

Tithe – to give to God, through His representatives, ten percent of one's earnings before spending it on anything else.

WHAT IS MONEY?

Money is more than coins, bills, or certificates. Money is a value placed upon goods and services. It is also a value placed upon wages or a value placed upon one's time and energy. For instance, an item or service that sells for $100 is valued by the owner in that amount. To the wage earner, a wage per hour or per week is the value placed upon the laborer's work – his time and energy.

Luke 12:15–23

If a wage earner makes $10 per hour, his employer is telling him that his or her energy and time is worth that amount. And if the wage earner wants to purchase a $100 item, he or she must exchange 10 hours of their life and energy to purchase it. A purchase is therefore an exchange of life for goods or services.

Matthew 6:19–21

Jesus, our King, wants us to manage life wisely since we have limited days. An exchange of life for things may not be a wise exchange. But hoarding money may not be wise either, because it can be lost or stolen. Bad investments or bad money management is like throwing away one's life. In a certain sense, money represents life.

IS MONEY UNRIGHTEOUS?

Luke 16:11

Whether money is good or evil is an interesting question. In Luke 16, Jesus uses the phrase 'unrighteous mammon' because the unfaithful servant in this story stole the employer's money; therefore the money gained was unrighteous.

Matthew 25:14–30

Leviticus 6:1–6

However, in other passages the stewards are quite honest and the resulting gains are righteous. Money is neither inherently good or evil; it is a symbol of our energy and time, our lives. If evil people get unjust gain or profit, then it is evil money. If righteous people earn just wages – or wages appropriate to time, energy, and productivity – then it is righteous money.

2 Peter 2:3

1 Timothy 6:10

What is unrighteous in the loss of money or greed? Greed leads to evil means to obtain and keep money. Paul warns that the pursuit of riches can also turn one away from the purpose of God and prove to be a snare.

Matthew 21:12–13

Jesus saw this in the temple when He went there and turned over the money changers' tables. The temple officials had offered these services to Jews coming from other nations who desired to buy sacrificial animals and needed local currency. But the service became a money-making effort and many Levitical officials had lost their integrity and their true spiritual purpose.

MANAGING MONEY

Jeremiah 22:13–17

Luke 3:14

Our stewardship of money begins before we actually receive it. It begins as we earn it. If our stewardship and our money is to be righteous, we must use our energy and time in a righteous cause – one that contributes to the wellbeing of others. Gambling, for instance, may cause one to 'win money' but it creates no useful product. It takes from one person or group and gives to another without creating a benefit for the loser. Gambling is not earning or creating wealth, it only causes money to change hands – sometimes from hands that can least afford it. Taking advantage of laborers or owners, or failing to give a just exchange of goods, services, or wages is unrighteous stewardship. Therefore, righteous stewardship of money – the basis for the favor of God – begins with honest effort and honest wages. Such an exchange gives the individual and society a product. Society is better off because of the effort.

Psalm 24:1
Malachi 3:7–12
Genesis 28:22
Leviticus 27:32
Luke 11:42
Hebrews 7:5–9

Obtaining or receiving funds justly brings us to another level of management: What do we do with the profit from our effort? The Bible is clear, since both natural resources and our life itself came from God, that the first tenth belongs to Him – it's the Owner's portion. Giving it is the statement of our recognition of His government and ownership overall. Failure to give it to Him is called robbery.

Matthew 6:20–21
Luke 19:20–21

Once the tithes have been brought to the Lord in His storehouse, the citizen of the Kingdom is faced with how to use the remaining nine-tenths also under the Lord's leadership.

Luke 12:21, 33
1 Timothy 5:4, 8
Ephesians 4:28
Deuteronomy 8:18
1 Timothy 5:17–18
Philippians 4:12–13
Galatians 6:6–10

The Kingdom citizen knows that Jesus is Lord of all that He has. Therefore, His resources are subject to the teachings of the Scripture and the leadership of the Holy Spirit. The Lord and the Scriptures teach us to take care of our own families, to give to those who are in need, and to sow toward those who teach us. While the Scripture teaches us not to trust in laid-up treasure, it also teaches us to use our money in such a way that it is an investment in heaven or eternal values.

The biblical emphasis is on recognizing God's ownership through tithing, recognition of our primary responsibility for our family, and generosity toward those in need, especially our spiritual family. Beyond that, we are told to sow generously to all around us including those who have nothing, because what we send out comes back from mankind around us.

Galatians 6:10
Luke 6:38

Leviticus 23

Proper management of our money includes giving and spending wisely. It also includes saving for unforeseen eventualities and times of rest when additional resources will be necessary. Good stewardship prevents an economy from always being on the edge or in the red.

TRUE RICHES

Proverbs 13:22

Too often the Church has taught that money or wealth of any kind was the adversary of spirituality. It had to be 'one or the other.' Such teaching is not only misleading, but has caused many to reject Christianity and many others to justify poverty. It is absolutely essential that material wealth be understood as part of God's world that He entrusts to those who are good stewards. Even the wealth of the wicked will eventually belong to the righteous.

Genesis 12:1–3
Genesis 14:17–15:21

The biblical teaching is that wise use of money is a wise use of life, and the one who devotes himself to managing temporal matters shows himself capable of managing eternal matters. Jesus says this in Luke 16:11, but Abraham even demonstrates this 2,000 years earlier. In the Hebrew mind, slothfulness and mismanagement were not evidences of 'deep spirituality.'

If indeed Abraham is an example, then management of temporal matters led Abraham into God's favor. He was given the true riches of a covenant relationship with God, a friendship with God, a family and a legacy for all the families of the earth.

Luke 12:48
1 Corinthians 4:2
1 Corinthians 3:9–15

True riches are whatever God in His mercy will give to us – salvation, the gift of the Spirit, the Kingdom citizenship, power, and privileges. But whatever true riches may be, we are accountable for them. Unto whom much is given, much is required. Financial accountability is the demonstration that we understand spiritual accountability and are prepared to receive even more desirable and durable riches.

APPLICATION

Do you have a budget?

What do you pay first?

What percentages do you designate to tithes? House? Car? The needy?

What spiritual lessons have you gained from managing money?

CONCLUSION

If we are going to tithe, be generous, meet our family needs, give to the poor — to say nothing of taxes — we need to prosper financially. The well-being of others depends upon the diligent management of our time, energy, and the money entrusted to us.

If this life was all that existed, Kingdom teaching on use of money world be the superior economic system. But this life is not all, and Kingdom economics are but a door into a vast comprehension of how things work eternally under God's reign. Financial or material faithfulness can be the threshold to all kinds of opportunities to know the Lord better.

LESSON 9 – THE CALL TO FAITHFULNESS IN APPRENTICESHIP

PURPOSE

Daniel 4:17
Daniel 4:34–37

The kingdom of God is God's government over all things and proceeds out of His own nature. That is, His government reflects Him, how He thinks and acts. To be effective in His Kingdom we must be in harmony with Him by knowing His ways, knowing how He manages, and how He wants to administrate through us.

Deuteronomy 8:6
1 Samuel 8:3
Psalm 103:7
Ephesians 4:11, 12

Proverbs 22:6

Ephesians 6:4

When one comes to know Jesus Christ through being born again, there is still the need to come to know His ways. The world doesn't teach us that. We can learn God's ways through Bible study, prayer, and the action of the Holy Spirit. In addition, the Lord has sent teachers to train us in His ways. In fact, it is God's intention that parents should train us in His ways from birth.

Children not only study in an academic sense, but they watch and listen on a practical level, and learn daily from their parents. They are also learning in an environment of stewardship. That is, the home and its provisions belong to the parents. Children are given toys, then later other objects of value to steward. Eventually they are given their own freedom.

Childhood is an apprenticeship, but is not the only apprenticeship. There are many times in life that we are called to serve under someone else's leadership in an environment that is not our own. Faithful practical service will prepare us for the possibility that we may one day become the leader, supervisor, or even owner. Meanwhile, apprenticeship when understood and appreciated, trains us to be effective and successful when the time comes. This is a Kingdom principle for the family, the Church, and our vocational life.

GLOSSARY

Steward – one appointed to manage the owner's property and affairs.

Apprentice – serving another for purpose of learning a trade or work.

Ambition – strong desire to achieve a certain goal.

Parable – short story that illustrates a moral attitude or principle.

AN ETERNAL ISSUE

Luke 16:12

Isaiah 14:3–22
Ezra 28:11–17

Genesis 3:1–7

There are several ways to learn and prepare for success. One way is through one's own ambition and determination to succeed as a 'self-made person.' Another way is through the humility of being taught and trained under someone else. In the latter way, one learns both character and practical principles and can benefit from another's experience. Though ambition can be useful, it can also be the product of pride and cause one to be restless in serving another. That person may then take 'short cuts' to arrive at a desired position for which he or she is not qualified. The end result can be embarrassing. This was Satan's problem and the problems he inflicted upon mankind in the Garden: He tried to make himself God.

Luke 16:11

Bypassing apprenticeship, obedience, and training does not make one succeed; it makes one fail. Since God does not want us to fail, He encourages us to learn from those who are successful through apprenticeship.

JESUS' METHOD

Luke 5:1–11
Luke 9:1–6
Matthew 10:24
Luke 6:12–13
Luke 6:20–49

Acts 4:13

Mark 4:1–41

Jesus selected men who were hard workers and taught them how to reach people for His Kingdom. These disciples were committed learners and followers of what they heard Jesus teach and saw Him do. Theirs was a three and one-half year apprenticeship.

Those that followed Jesus – men and women – not only learned spiritual principles, but learned that natural and spiritual principles were the same. The God of physics, chemistry, biology, zoology, and engineering is the same God of spiritual character and gifts. Natural and spiritual are interchangeable because they both reflect the same God. Practicality and spirituality were not adversaries to one another in their minds.

Luke 12:16–48
Luke 16:12

The disciples heard a lot of parables, stories about natural and common life coupled with spiritual lessons. Whether it was fishing, farming, or merchandising, Jesus drew from it. The disciples' apprenticeship was a time of spiritual learning from practical truths. The result was that they were later put in positions of tremendous responsibility after Christ's Ascension. This was what He had in mind from the beginning.

JESUS' COMMISSION

Matthew 28:18–20
Acts 2:41–42
Acts 6:1–6
Acts 11:19–26
Acts 14:21–23
2 Timothy 2:2
Hebrews 13:7, 17

Jesus did not only convert the souls of men and women, He converted their minds and way of life through training. The Lord's commission to His disciples was not only to go into the world and make converts, but to make disciples (to apprentice others as He had them). It is evident from the Scriptures that the early apostles took that commission seriously and sought to teach others through apprenticeship and practical assistance as well as the Word of God.

OUR OPPORTUNITY

While we must take personal responsibility and initiative, we do not need to 're-invent' everything. We can learn from others – even submitting ourselves to their instruction and helping them while learning ourselves. This process should begin in the home and continue throughout our lives. Progressive maturity should bring us to increasing personal initiative. Whenever we want to grow into new fields of

Luke 6:36–38
Psalm 75:1–10

Luke 3:14

activity, apprenticeship is a proven door. It is not there to hold us down, but to help us up and keep us there after we are promoted.

How we respond to those teaching us will likely determine how others will later respond to us as we attempt to teach them. How we respond to our supervisors and managers will likely set the stage for others to respond to us.

The challenge of Christ is to believe He is Lord and to believe He is able to promote us if we are faithful in effort and attitude. We are challenged to be content with our wages, but not our performance. As Christian laborers and managers, we must believe that our labor is as unto Him. If we can produce more, He will reward us righteously.

APPLICATION

Can you name some of your previous experiences in apprenticeship? How have you profited?

Did you profit from the unhappy experiences, too?

Are you currently training anyone? At home? In church? On the job?

CONCLUSION

Society outside of Christ falls into the snare of rejecting Kingdom values and wanting more position and more money for less product. The resulting financial gains are sown more to one's own flesh or pleasure. The results are not good. Poor workmanship, inflated prices, incredible debt, and 'cutthroat' measures to get to the top, will be a few of the bad results. Nevertheless, the Kingdom expression will prevail amid the results of darkness, because it works, endures, and is fruitful.

LESSON 10 – THE BIBLICAL MODEL FOR PRODUCTIVITY

PURPOSE

Through the centuries, many have proposed various economic theories for productive use of the resources God has given to us to manage. It is only through seeking first God's interest in the earth through His revealed will in Scripture that we are able to experience success and productivity as God intended. This lesson will consider the starting point for the follower of Christ and some of the alternatives with which modern Christianity must reckon.

GLOSSARY

Economics – study of production, distribution and use of goods and services.

Marketplace – the world of economic activity and trade.

Matthew 6:33

Genesis 1:26
1 Corinthians 12:4–11

The kingdom of God is the starting point for all righteous productivity. When we set God's rulership in our lives and businesses as the norm for life and labor, Kingdom productivity begins to work in and through us. This constant seeking of God's Kingdom is the premise for our right relationship to material wealth. Acknowledging and committing to His Lordship precedes the ability to steward wealth. As we recognize His right to rule in creation, we also acknowledge that all we have – giftings and resources – comes from His hands. Thus, the material resources which Christ shares with us become an issue of good stewardship, not acquisition of wealth. All He commits to our care will be evaluated and judged by Christ Himself.

ECONOMICS BASED ON THE WORLD SYSTEM

Colossians 2:8

Colossians 2:16

Colossians 2:18
Colossians 2:20–23
2 Corinthians 4:4

Christians are warned to avoid embracing moral and economic systems which are not built on the kingdom of God. Such systems have their source in him who is the deceiver of all people. They make deceiving promises because they are built upon deceiving philosophical and economic principles. They are built upon the traditions of people, originating in people's thinking rather than by God's design. They proceed from base and elementary motivations, such as greed, which have human gratification as the primary goal. These secular and humanistic approaches to life and productivity view man himself to be at the center of the universe rather than Christ as Creator and King.

Two economic systems which Christians encounter in modern life are socialism and capitalism.

SOCIALISM

Socialism speaks of an economic system which advocates that the means of production of goods within a society be owned and controlled by the State. It is marked by unequal distribution of goods and pay according to the work done.

Socialism is not built upon the Lordship of Christ, and consequently, leads to certain deceptions:

(1) On the altar of 'economic security,' it sacrifices the virtues of stewardship, risk, and personal reward for creative labor.

(2) It encourages covetousness against those who succeed beyond the norm. ('I should have what you have.')

(3) It encourages envy. ('Why do you have more than I do?')

(4) It makes the prosperous 'guilty' for their material success.

(5) It promotes civil theft through taxation.

(6) It is designed to make everyone 'equal', or pull each individual down to the lowest common denominator.

CAPITALISM

Luke 12:13–21

Capitalism: 'An economic system characterized by private or corporation ownership of capital goods; by investments that are determined by private decision rather than by state control, and prices; production and distribution of goods that are determined mainly in a free market' (*Webster*).

Capitalism more closely resembles a Kingdom model as revealed in Scripture because it emphasizes individual gifting, initiative, and accountability. However, it also tends toward results contrary to the kingdom of God.

(1) It is profit-oriented (utilitarian), not people-oriented. That is, it uses people to produce goods without necessarily seeking the good of the workers.

(2) It alienates man from his labor by objectifying labor into a series of production functions that are menial and repetitive.

(3) It tends toward individual and societal self-destruction because it rewards greed, exploitation, and unhealthy competition.

KINGDOM ECONOMICS

Matthew 6:33
Luke 16:10–12
1 Corinthians 12:4–11

As biblical people, we must seek the biblical model. Seeking first the kingdom of God involves seeking God's rulership in all areas of our lives, including material resources. Both socialism and capitalism fall short of God's design without the lifestyle and purposes of Christ Himself. Seeking first the kingdom of God involves discovery of God's wisdom and thoughts, His giftings and purposes, relative to labor and economic resources. Apprehending the will of God for marketplace economics (as revealed in and through the Scriptures) is the essence of true success and prosperity.

APPLICATION

Consider the economic system in which you work. Which parts reflect God's Kingdom and which do not?

Examine to what degree you are influenced in your thinking about material wealth by the modern scene.

How have contemporary marketing techniques and modern advertisement shaped your thinking about work and finances?

CONCLUSION

The modern Christian is faced with making clear decisions as to what standard and guidelines will govern the course of daily living. There is a growing awareness that true Christianity is not limited to the four walls of church buildings, but extends to all spheres of life. This includes the very important arenas of work and economic productivity. We are called by God to raise the standard of His wisdom and demonstrate the value of His redemption through Christ to all areas of life. The more thoroughly this is examined in the light of Scripture, the more evident it is that God comprehensively addresses every aspect of life on earth.

LESSON 11 – THE DECEPTION OF DEBT

PURPOSE

Romans 13:8
Deuteronomy 28:12–13
Proverbs 22:7
Deuteronomy 15:6

In our society today, debt is seen as a normal way of life. Not only are individuals wrestling with debt, but whole nations are dependent on debt financing for the very basic provision of life. In the Scripture, the pattern of living in debt is seen as one of bondage and slavery. **This lesson will focus on the dangers and pitfalls of debt as shown in the book of Habakkuk, as well as the hope that we have in a Kingdom economy.** It is not to condemn, but to warn and exhort, and show pathways for deliverance.

GLOSSARY

Debt – that which one person is bound to pay or perform for another.

Desire – to express a wish to possess or obtain.

Extravagance – excessive, exceeding appropriate bounds.

DEBT IS PRIDE-BASED

One of the clearest examples of the destructiveness of pride-based debt is recorded by Habakkuk, an Old Testament prophet, writing to the people of God. He gives an amazingly clear picture of the destructive step in the decline of individuals and nations who have falsely built up their worth based on debt. (We are not discussing in this lesson prudent home mortgages or similar investments.)

Habakkuk 2:4–7
Deuteronomy 28:44–45
Psalm 37:21

The process starts with the Scripture declaring that we are discussing a pride-based phenomenon. Pride causes a man to go places, to do and buy things, without being satisfied with what he has, always wanting more. His tastes are extravagant and his desires are insatiable.

The contrast is given in the middle of this indictment with the oft-quoted passage describing the more godly view of life: 'the just shall live by their faith.' The implication being that the prideful man looks for ways of providing for his inflated lifestyle outside of trust in the faithfulness of God to fulfill His promises.

In Habakkuk, the prideful man continues to live extravagantly as the time of prosperity continues, moving the lifestyle higher and higher, manipulating people and funds to provide the increasing requirements. No desire is controlled and no want is disciplined. Control, power, and satisfaction become the illusive motivating goals.

ECONOMIC DECLINE QUICKLY REVEALS WEAKNESSES

Habakkuk 2:6–8

When a decline comes, the situation quickly worsens with those people who have been manipulated and controlled by the influence

Deuteronomy 28:39–40

produced by the debt. They begin to rise and point out the flaws in the proud man's quest for self-exaltation. They scorn him and despise his empty plans, revealing in embarrassing ways the fact that his plans are based on debt, not true wealth or strength. They show that there is no real substance to the exaggerated lifestyle of the proud man.

The reality is that the repayment requirements of the debt seriously impact the proud man's ability to support his appetite. New ways must be found to finance the debt-based lifestyle. The harassment of the people only serves to urge the angry, proud man on to more cunning and destructive techniques.

FRAUDULENT PLANS ARE DEVISED AS COVER-UPS

Habakkuk 2:9–11

The reactionary and defensive plans include a cover-up of the real dilemma. The plans may be untruthful about facts, exaggerations of assets, understatements of liabilities, or required payments. One of the common ways of hiding liability is to form separate organizations and show enough assets in each to justify the debt. This prevents the disclosure of the relationship between the entities that would reveal debt far outreaching the value of the total assets or projected profit.

The plans may be shameful in their presentation and fraudulent in their implementation, all in the desire to perpetuate the proud lifestyle. The Scripture promises that even the possessions will cry out against the proud man and his pretenses. The machinery will not perform due to the corners being cut on required maintenance and repairs. The fields won't produce their yield because of poor preparation and care. Shipment of needed supplies will be delayed because of late payments in the attempt to maintain inflated cash flows. The leveraged equipment and facilities will not be operating at full productivity because of reduced supplies, demand, and worker loyalty. The decline is very real and increases in intensity.

VIOLENCE IS UNLEASHED AS A COERCION TACTIC

Habakkuk 2:12
Deuteronomy 28:36–47

Violence is a terrible word! It always implies destruction and harm. It is a brutal, unsolicited violation of trust by a person driven with frustration and anger upon a victim of their demand. Violence is the next step of a desperate debtor, driven by the pride and fear of loss of his diminishing lifestyle. The violence can be used for extortion, blackmail, or worse actions in an attempt to coerce someone into giving up their assets to support the proud man's needs. In any case, it is a destructive force against a victim as the debtor's desperation mounts.

PEOPLE GROW WEARY OF THE SHAM

The people soon grow weary of the antics and destruction, the facade and the sham represented by the debtor. They can no longer endure the hollow statements and empty plans to recapture the extravagant lifestyle and false wealth of the once proud man.

Habakkuk 2:13–14

One hopeful side of the frightening development is that out of their frustration and weariness of the oppressor, the people begin to ask hard questions about what they have entertained and with what they have been willing to live. They begin to ask if there is a more godly way to live life. They begin to search for the knowledge of God ... His foundations for life and economy without the destruction of the debt-based society and slavery. The promise is that the whole earth will be filled with the knowledge of the glory of the Lord as the waters cover the sea ... the glory of His way of building, growing, and expanding; the glory of His blessing on godly pursuits of production and provision without enslaving debt; the glory of an economy based on a giving generous Father's heart and not man's greed and grasping selfishness.

DISCREDITING OTHERS WILL FOLLOW

Habakkuk 2:15–17

In the Habakkuk scenario, we see how the proud man will continue his attempt to seduce and coerce in order to recover his eroding lifestyle. The realization that he is not succeeding, however, will result in causing even more vindictive, revengeful reactions. He will attempt to discredit others around him, exposing the weaknesses of his neighbors, and making false accusations to cover his own guilt and iniquity. He shows no remorse for his actions, only intensity in pursuing his own happiness.

THE DECEPTIVE PLOT WILL BE EXPOSED AND THE GLORY OF THE LORD WILL BE REVEALED

Habakkuk 2:16–17

Thankfully, the attempts will fail and only further expose the proud man's nakedness and shame. Disgrace will come as his empty accomplishments are shown in the light of destructiveness and his possessions are taken to pay the debt owed.

Habakkuk 2:18–19

The idolatry of possessions, wealth, power, and control will be shown to be the same as a god carved from wood, molded from clay, or hammered from some metal; not able to hear, speak or perform any useful action, propped up and exalted by man. The pursuit using debt will be shown to be empty, futile, and devoid of permanent, lasting value.

Habakkuk 2:20

At the same time, the holiness of the Lord will be revealed in great and dynamic ways that will cause the whole earth to be silenced in their reverence before Him. The people become so desperate they begin to look for the knowledge of God's truth to govern the economy and provide leadership in the uncovering of the human idolatry on the earth. The Lord is gracious and merciful to those who put their trust in Him, and He is able to save and deliver.

APPLICATION

Am I responding to life with pride, living a facade and image that is beyond my provision?

Do I have a debt that exceeds my ability to pay it or the value of my assets?

Am I living a fraudulent or deceptive life to hide my debt?

If debt is a problem in my life, how can I find repentance, grace, and deliverance?

How do I respond to those who are indebted to me?

CONCLUSION

Proverbs 16:18
Proverbs 29:23

Pride-based debt is a destructive force in a person or a nation. Pride launches a cycle of fraud and deception that ends in destruction and shame.

However, conviction of any sin from the Holy Spirit offers hope of deliverance as we apply His ways to our situation and allow His restoration power to flow. As we seek first His Kingdom, rather than our own selfish ends, we will understand better the Scripture which says, 'Godliness with contentment is great gain.'

1 Timothy 6:6

When the facade of pride-based debt is torn down, people will turn to the ways of God and He will reveal His grace and glory.

LESSON 12 – THE KINGDOM MODEL IS UNIQUE IN THE EARTH

PURPOSE

Proverbs 2:6
James 1:5
Proverbs 4:5, 7
Proverbs 9:10
Proverbs 24:3

God's wisdom stands alone as the key to successful living. The reign of Christ is the eventual destiny of all nations and it is to Him that every knee will bow in acknowledgement of His glory and wisdom. The kingdom of God is being extended in the earth at present by those who hear and obey His commands. This lesson will consider the distinctives of the kingdom of God in its approach to economic order.

GLOSSARY

Unique – one of a kind, nowhere imitated.

Partnership – working together with another.

Maturation – the growth process towards full development.

Business Ethic – the moral standards which govern one's business activities.

PARTNERSHIP

1 Corinthians 3:9
2 Corinthians 6:1
Genesis 1:27–28
Ephesians 2:10
Colossians 1:29

Exodus 28:3
Exodus 31:3–6

The kingdom of God involves a partnership which each believer has with his God in running his 'business.' God's unequivocal statement is that man is created in the likeness or image of God. And God commissioned him to steward His entire creation. This commission calls every individual in Christ to be 'in business' with the Father. That is, we are called to be fruitful, productive partners with our Lord. As we steward appropriately all that God has invested in us – His partners – we will be part of extending His interests in all the earth.

GOVERNING THROUGH PARTNERSHIP

1 Corinthians 12:4–11
Daniel 2:37
Daniel 4:17
Daniel 5:21

Ephesians 6:4

The kingdom of God raises up leaders who will govern according to His own design for each sphere of life. Further, God equips individuals to govern and function in the light of God's designs and purposes. The earth is the Lord's; it belongs to no one else. Individuals and nations are expected to govern themselves under God's ultimate authority. The family, an expression of God's government, is the basic building unit of a healthy society. Next, the local church governs and serves by equipping Christians to relate properly and serve their society in all areas of life. The proper stewardship of private property also expresses God's rulership on both personal and societal levels. Such governing leads to building strong nations as local leaders exercise rulership through the application of God's wisdom in local communities.

MATURATION, NOT JUST PROFIT

Matthew 25:14–30
Luke 16:1–13

Colossians 3:23–24

Ephesians 2:10

The kingdom of God promotes maturation of individuals in contrast to mere profit as life's goal. We are to develop our gifts and callings to provide service and productivity for the benefit of all peoples. God urges us to develop the creativity which He gives us out of His own creative nature. God shows us how to work as stewards of privately held properties or goods, instead of as owners. Also, He leads us to embrace ownership or proprietorial participation in work. People tend to see themselves just as 'workers,' just doing their 'job.' They fail to see God's trust in them by 'entrusting' to them a creative involvement in their work. This capacity for individual productivity is associated with having a proper sense of self-worth before God, as well as a 'place' in God's Kingdom in the marketplace that is designed uniquely for them.

SEEKING THE KINGDOM IN THE MARKETPLACE

Ephesians 6:7–9

Colossians 3:17

To the extent that we actively seek the kingdom of God in the area of business and economics, we will experience certain measurable results. We will experience strong leadership in God's Kingdom as owners and managers see themselves as servants of others, promoting God's calling and best interests in their lives. The establishment of a strong business ethic in the daily activity of the marketplace stimulates productivity and fruitfulness. God seeks leaders who will emphasize godly ownership, the application of creative abilities, and maturation of all those who participate.

APPLICATION

Contrast the differences in motivation when the kingdom of God functions in the marketplace as compared to the world systems. What is the difference in the respective focuses?

Describe the pathway that leads from the rule of Christ's Kingdom in the individual to the building of a strong nation.

CONCLUSION

The Lord Himself is delighted to work in partnership with all His children, in terms of His gifts and callings to them. He is the worker-God. He seeks to establish this partnership as His expression of government on earth. His government extends to individuals, to families, to local churches, to the stewarding of private properties, and to the businesses He entrusts to His children. This partnership with God leads to our own maturation as we learn to walk with Him and please Him in the marketplace. We become creatively involved with the living God in the midst of our marketplace sphere. This enables us to develop into strong business leaders who look for ways to serve others and promote God's interests within our business sphere.

LESSON 13 – PROCESS AND PRODUCT

PURPOSE

As we have already seen in this volume, Jesus Christ is both Creator, Owner, and Sustainer of all that exists. One of the principles in natural laws that He has built into creation is the law of process. That is, if you want a desired result, you must go through the necessary steps to arrive at the result.

The late Ern Baxter, a noted Bible teacher, once said, 'You can make your choices, but you can't choose your consequences.' If one wants the right product, they must choose the right process.

God has ordained a process of labor or an ideal that will enable us to be productive with both quality and abundance. Let us examine that process.

GLOSSARY

Process – actions, gradual changes towards a certain goal.

Product – the result of a process.

Fruitful – abundantly productive.

Blessing – abundance in spiritual and material areas.

Curse – to bring harm or injury to someone.

OBEDIENCE

Deuteronomy 28:1–68

Deuteronomy chapter 28 is one of the most thorough chapters in the Bible that outlines the economic blessings and curses related to obedience and disobedience. The blessings include blessed children, crops, livestock, and victory over one's enemies. The curses include economic poverty, loss of family, and defeat.

It would be easy to assume that one is blessed or cursed based upon one's moral goodness. However, more is involved here. Verse 1 makes it clear that blessings are predicated upon diligent obedience to the Lord's commands. These commands are not only the Ten Commandments (which decree a certain behavior toward God, family, and neighbor) but numerous other commands regarding all of life and vocation.

The Jews were given the ways of God regarding diet, tithes, debt, forgiveness, the administration of justice, judging prophecy, how to engage enemies, how to farm, and a wide variety of other instructions. God's purpose was not only to make a better person through obedience, but a better way to a better result. Many good people are frustrated with poor results, because while they know and love God, they have never been taught His ways. His ways produce a better result.

THE HOLY SPIRIT

Exodus 31:1–6
Exodus 35:30–36:4

1 Chronicles 2:20
2 Chronicles 1:5

God selected a man named Bezalel (a grandson of Caleb) as a master-worker and as a type to lead the construction of the Tabernacle. Hundreds of years later, God selected Solomon, a 'new Bezalel,' to implement the Temple construction. Both of these were filled with the Holy Spirit in wisdom, understanding, and knowledge in all kinds of craftsmanship.

It is obvious that the tabernacle and the temple both represented God and His people. These constructions would be symbols of God's character and ways. God, therefore, chose craftsmen who were diligent, and filled them with the Holy Spirit so that the results would be glorious.

Acts 2:38
1 Corinthians 12:4–11

The Holy Spirit is a gift. The Holy Spirit also gives gifts. One may begin to assume that the Holy Spirit's main function is to give us what we do not have or whatever we may want. However, Bezalel would teach us a different side of the Holy Spirit. The Holy Spirit fills us to help us become more skilled and to produce a better result.

A stone mason, brick layer, carpenter, or other craftsman knows that structures do not simply 'appear.' They are the result of a process from gathering materials and craftsmen, to laying foundations, and all that follows.

In God's work, the plan may come from heaven, but human process is essential to a final product. The Holy Spirit is our 'Helper.' He doesn't build it for us; He helps us to carefully observe God's ways throughout the process. The result then will be excellence, abundance, and glory to God. 'Shoddiness' in process will produce a shoddy product.

THE TEMPLE

2 Chronicles 2–6

2 Chronicles 9:1–12

2 Chronicles 5

Solomon's temple was without a doubt one of the most glorious buildings ever constructed. In today's money, its cost would be in the billions. It was not costly because of its size primarily, but because of its quality. Dedicated people and laborers had given and built a building that would take away the breath of international visitors. In fact, God Himself filled it with His presence. God's pleasure and presence in His house was the direct result of His leaders and craftsmen obeying His instructions. Rather than taking the easy way or short cuts, they went through the painstaking process of building it right. The result was glorious.

APPLICATION

Cite examples of individuals you know who reflect the law of 'process and product' in their lives.

Reflect upon your own journey and those whom God has used in your life to produce fruit that has lasting value.

In what ways do the principles in this lesson affect your attitude toward the future?

CONCLUSION

Making Jesus Lord of your life is not only a religious or spiritual decision. It is a decision to do things God's way, including how we labor. When we labor as unto Him in whatever field of labor is ours, we will go through a process of growth in obedience, skill, and understanding that will result in good consequences.

Our call is not only to make Jesus Lord of the Church or our own lives, but rather to proclaim Him as Lord of the marketplace. The economic consequences will be glorious.

LESSON 14 – SOWING AND REAPING

PURPOSE

Isaiah 55:6–13

The principles of God's own thinking are incorporated into creation. When we truly know God and His ways, mankind and creation are in harmony and both are more productive. A primary principle of God's Kingdom is that of sowing and reaping.

John 12:24–27

Jesus likens His Incarnation, Crucifixion, and Resurrection to the principle of sowing and reaping. That is, He literally buried Himself in the human situations, expecting to come forth again and multiply His own life in humanity.

1 Corinthians 15:42–58

In like fashion, the apostle Paul describes our death and resurrection as sowing and reaping; that is, we sow a mortal body and by a miracle of God's power, we reap an immortal body. Our immortal body is the result of immortal life that we have received by faith in Christ.

Since sowing and reaping is a vital principle of creation and life, we can apply it in such a way as to enrich our lives and His Kingdom for His glory. This lesson will help us to participate in this spiritual and natural process of sowing and reaping amazing benefits.

GLOSSARY

Incarnation – to become flesh.

Investment – the outlay of resources in the interest of profit.

Reap – to gather or harvest.

Sow – to put something to death for a larger purpose.

THE HUMAN PROBLEM

Psalm 126:5–6

1 Corinthians 15:36

The Scriptures say that those who sow in tears shall reap in joy. Sowing is often a tearful activity because it is hard to part with the seed that is being sown. Jesus' death, our death, or putting a resource to death is difficult and must be done in faith, believing in God's faithfulness to the principle.

John 12:24–26

Sowing is a problem to humanity because fallen man is fundamentally selfish and insecure. When it comes to sowing, it is easy to come short. This is a problem that Jesus encountered as He began to teach His disciples the principle of sowing and reaping. He told them that to try to save one's life is like failing to sow a seed – it will remain alone and unproductive.

THE SEED

1 Corinthians 15:46

The natural principle and the spiritual principle must agree. God created both spheres. The natural seed teaches us about how spiritual

Galatians 6:7

Isaiah 58:1–5
James 4:3
Hebrews 11:6
2 Corinthians 9:10

Isaiah 58
Matthew 5:7
Luke 6:27–35
Proverbs 18:24

seed works to bring harvest. The truth is the same in both natural and spiritual matters: the seed determines the harvest. We reap what we sow. Natural seed brings a natural harvest. Spiritual seed brings a spiritual harvest – bad seed brings a bad harvest. In fact, bad motives can affect our harvest. All sowing must be done in faith and done as unto the Lord of the seed and harvest.

Since the seed and our motive will determine the harvest, it behoves us to select good spiritual seed. The Scriptures suggest sowing mercy, wealth, friendship, and generosity. These are good seeds that you will enjoy harvesting.

THE MEASURE

Luke 6:38

2 Corinthians 9:6–11

The divine principle is that we not only reap what we sow, but we reap in the same measure that we sow. Sow sparingly and reap sparingly. Sow bountifully and reap bountifully. Once we begin to sow, we must determine how much we will sow. When the harvest time comes, it will be too late to think about the issue of how much.

Proverbs 11:24
Matthew 25:14–30

The human problem is that we often sacrifice the future for the present. In other words, we 'eat too much of our seed.' If we have faith in the principle and the Lord of it, we will eat less and sow more. Our life will become more outward and less selfish. We will become investors – not merely consumers. The kingdom of God is a stewardship system that not only manages, but manages well enough to include wise investment, both naturally and spiritually. Jesus taught us this through the parables and through His own life.

Ephesians 4:28
Matthew 25:14–30

Wise and liberal investment creates wealth because it provides other good stewards with seed to sow. They in turn repay us bountifully and increase our ability to sow in others.

2 Timothy 2:2

2 Corinthians 9:6–13

Of course, liberal financial investing in good stewards teaches us that wise investments of other kinds also bring dividends. The apostle Paul tells Timothy to invest himself in teaching a faithful man who will teach others. The principles of generous investing has many applications. Once generosity is learned in one area, it becomes a way of life. Generous investing and giving of money indicates that we have learned the principles and are prepared to apply them in other areas. Money represents our life and energy, and generous sowing of money is a primary way to sow.

THE PLACE

Matthew 25:24

In the parable of the talents, the slothful servant charged his master with reaping where he had not sown. The master was infuriated with this accusation because it was a charge of thievery. The servant had accused his master of harshness and stealing.

The truth is that attempting to reap where we are not willing to sow goes against the natural principle. If we want a harvest in a certain place, we sow there. Charles Simpson put it this way: 'Some people are waiting for their ship to come in and they never sent one out.' Good stewards know where they expect a crop; they know good ground and they sow in that place. Anything less than that is unwise and even dishonest.

Good business people do not expect to collect the price from other companies' products and services. They sow in the places and people where they expect to reap.

Ecclesiastes 11:1–2

The writer of Ecclesiastes tells us to sow beside 'all waters.' He says to divide our seed among seven or eight. It is wise to avoid 'putting all your eggs in one basket.' Something may go wrong with one place, but several places offer us a better opportunity of reaping.

Galatians 6:8
Isaiah 58:7
Galatians 6:10

Sowing to our own flesh or selfishly is not good. But sowing in one's family is good, as is sowing to the needy. The Scriptures also teach that we should put a priority on sowing to the household of faith or other believers. In addition, we should be willing to sow toward all people.

Isaiah 60:1–9
Revelation 21:24–26
Matthew 28:18–20

The Lord is expecting a harvest among all nations, and He has sent His disciples to sow in all nations. One of the ultimate manifestations of the principle of sowing and reaping will be a good harvest of humanity at the end of this age. A major reason that we must learn to sow and reap is so we can participate in the Lord's harvest.

Matthew 9:37–38

The Lord made it clear that the harvest is ready to be reaped, but there is a labor shortage. Laborers must be supported. As one learns to sow and reap natural things, we can send forth laborers who can sow spiritual seed in all the earth.

APPLICATION

Make a list of some of the good seed you have to sow.

Make a list of places you would like to sow.

How is your sowing already developed?

What percentage of your income are you now sowing?

What ways have you benefited from the sowing of others into your life?

CONCLUSION

Proverbs 11:25

The Scripture teaches that the generous person will prosper. We have instructions from God that will show us how to multiply what we have and bless other people in the process.

Romans 14:17

We can learn what and where to sow and delight in doing it liberally, because we believe God. This is the essence of God's Kingdom: His love causes Him and us to invest in others because we want them to know the blessings of His Kingdom life.

LESSON 15 – MANAGING WEALTH

PURPOSE

Success and prosperity are part of God's plan for His people. He spoke it in the very first chapter of the Bible and the theme is seen throughout the whole of Scripture. God also knows that the heart of man is deceitful and wicked when left to its own devices. He therefore chooses to speak warnings and direction throughout the Scripture on how to handle the wealth and blessing that He will bestow on the faithful.

GLOSSARY

Perceived need – the raising of the expectation of basic sustenance of life from the basic needs of food, clothing, and shelter to a higher level of luxury. Any more than basic need is a blessing.

PROMISES WITH CAUTIONS

Deuteronomy 6:10–16

When the children of Israel were about to go in to possess the land of Canaan that the Lord had promised to their forefathers many years before, the Lord gave a great promise about what He would provide for them. He spoke of how they would receive great and splendid cities that they did not build, houses full of good things that they did not fill, wells that they did not dig, vineyards and fruit trees that they did not plant, and that they would eat and be satisfied. He immediately included a strong warning not to forget the Lord who provided all of it.

2 Chronicles 9:20–27

When a time of abundance comes in the life of men, life-styles tend to move up with increased purchases, recreation, and luxury. The availability of provision is at first seen as a great blessing and people are grateful for the excess, but soon the abundance becomes an expectation and people establish the higher standard of living as the norm. They begin to demand the fulfillment of the higher standard. It has been said that 'today's luxury becomes tomorrow's necessity.' And it is so. No longer is heat in our homes, running water, fresh fruit and vegetables, plenty to eat, and light in the darkness seen as a blessing. These are all considered basic needs of a normal modern society. These 'basic needs' have now escalated to higher levels with the satisfaction of people driven by the fulfillment or lack of fulfillment of their 'perceived needs.' With this high expectation, gratefulness for God's provision of basic needs is forgotten.

Matthew 6:31–32

Scripture is clear with its statement about not being anxious about God meeting our needs. However, the scriptural view of needs are food, drink, and clothing. Anything beyond that is the gift and blessing of a merciful God to the people of the earth.

THE GODLY VIEW OF WEALTH IS NEITHER PROSPERITY NOR SURVIVAL, BUT PREPAREDNESS

Genesis 41:14–37

Jeremiah 42:14

Joseph saw a potential disaster as he interpreted Pharaoh's dreams. He understood the changing standard of perceived needs when he spoke of the plan for the redemption of Egypt in the time of abundance and famine. His eye was not on the period of abundance nor the period of famine, but was focused on the restoration following it. His eye saw the foundation of a national attitude and customs that would allow the nation of Egypt to go through the great period of prosperity, abundance, and wealth followed by the period of loss, destruction, and famine. In fact, Egypt went on to become a nation that accomplished unparalleled progress, building and engineering, trade and world economy – a nation to which people would escape because of the fundamental attitudes that were put into the culture and nature of the population.

Matthew 2:13–15

(Even Joseph, the earthly father of Jesus, took the young Savior to the safety of Egypt to escape the political and social upheaval of the rule of a tyrant, Herod.)

There were several principles that Joseph suggested to Pharaoh that allowed the nation to enjoy the period of great prosperity, survive a period of devastating famine, and emerge a strong nation, ready for restoration and recovery.

OVERSEERS CHOSEN AS A MEANS OF ACCOUNTABILITY

Genesis 41:33–34

The first thing Joseph suggested was the establishment of a discerning and wise leadership to have authority over the handling of the wealth. Joseph knew that the great abundance would be consumed in the rising life-styles if no one was accountable for the provision. Mankind will always change quickly to a sensuous, demanding society if the effort is not directed into a meaningful way. The way must be continually held before the people by a real person. The leaders were true representatives of the higher authority's purpose.

SAVINGS AS A MEANS OF CONTROLLING DESIRE

Genesis 41:34

During the years of abundance, the savings rates were one-fifth or twenty percent (20%) of the production. The savings allowed the people to enjoy the increase of the production in the period of abundance, but limited the runaway expansion of their desires and subsequent perceived needs.

1 Chronicles 29:1–9

(King David also saved and prepared for the building of the temple, even though God had spoken to him saying that he would not be able to personally oversee its construction. His son, Solomon, followed the carefully made plans and vast reserves that David had set aside to build the glorious dwelling place for God.)

RESERVES AS A WAY OF AVOIDING REVERSALS

Genesis 41:13–36

Genesis 47:13–26
Genesis 41:56–57

Savings were stored in a location near the people that had produced it, under the protection of the overseers. Joseph saw the need for oversight to prevent the unwise use of the surplus. He knew that the location of the vast wealth must be available for future use when the time of famine required the liquidation and consumption of the reserves. This reserve allowed the people in Egypt to emerge as the strong nation that Joseph had seen, even becoming the salvation for many people from other parts of the earth.

OWNERSHIP NEVER ASSUMED, BUT SEEN AS STEWARDSHIP OF ANOTHER'S PROVISION

Genesis 39:8–9
Genesis 47:20

Mark 12:1–9

Joseph always understood that everything he managed, stewarded, and stored belonged to another. From the rejection of temptation from his first Egyptian master's wife to the receipt of payment for the stored grain during the famine, he carefully and faithfully referred to the ownership of his master and ultimately to God.

A true steward has no ownership of the wealth he is managing. Jesus used several parables to reinforce this truth. One was the parable of the unfaithful servants 'caring' for the master's vineyard . . . and attempting to withhold the produce and even to kill the heir in an attempt to steal the ownership. The Lord's response is to come and destroy the unrighteous stewards and give the property to another.

APPLICATION

How does recognizing the ownership of God affect your faithfulness in handling wealth?

Are you putting a good portion of your present provision into some form of long-term investment or reserve with several generations in mind?

What are your actual basic needs?

Are you living in gratitude of God's provision or are you demanding more and more each year to satisfy you?

To whom are you accountable for the handling of wealth and provision?

Is someone able to review with you and make suggestions to you concerning spending and savings patterns?

CONCLUSION

The Lord desires to give bountiful provision and wealth to His people. As men are faithful to respond with gratefulness, He continues to pour out His blessings. With the blessing of wealth, He speaks principles of savings and reserves to control the changing of real needs into 'perceived needs.' Reserves allow one to survive reversals and smooth the natural fluctuations of life. All wealth belongs to the Lord and a person is only the steward of his wealth, not the owner.

LESSON 16 – TURNING MONEY INTO TRUE WEALTH

PURPOSE

Faithfulness unlocks the blessing of God to man. When man responds to the responsibilities of life in a faithful manner, the Lord responds by blessing the work of his hands, the fruit of his labor, his family, his image and reputation, and his possessions and wealth. But this is the result of a faithful life, not the goal of life. If it becomes the goal, it replaces God as the center of man's affection and becomes an idol and must be destroyed. Scriptures teach principles of how to maintain a view of wealth that will allow it to be used faithfully while keeping God at the center of life.

GLOSSARY

True wealth – those possessions, attitudes and accomplishments that have not only value in life, but have an eternal value that surpasses the momentary pleasures of this short life span.

Mammon – material wealth or possessions.

TRUE WEALTH COMES FROM FAITHFULNESS

Luke 16:10–13

Jesus teaches us in Luke concerning the results of faithfulness:

> **Faithfulness in little things; you will be given much.**
>
> **Faithful with the things of another; you will be given your own.**
>
> **Faithful even with unrighteous mammon; you will be given true riches.**

The passage ends with the warning that no one can serve two masters. Either he will love one and hate the other, or he will hold to one and despise the other.

In this passage, Jesus is talking about greater wealth that surpasses simple accumulation of possessions and money. He is talking about the riches that satisfy the deepest longings of man's heart and life: the peace that comes with being received; like the gratefulness that comes from receiving the gifts coming from a father; like the contentment in knowing one has given himself to the highest purpose for life; and assurance that even when this life is over there is an eternal place of continual relationship with the God of the universe.

Psalm 92:1

1 Timothy 6:6

Philippians 3:20

GRATEFULNESS UNLOCKS THE HEART OF THE FATHER

Luke 12:48
Matthew 13:12

The Scripture teaches that unto him that much is given, much will be required. It further states that to him who has much, more will be given

Ephesians 5:20
1 Thessalonians 5:18

... and to him who has little, even that which he has will be taken away. This passage may seem confusing at first reading. It does not seem 'fair.' However, when one reads this passage with the understanding that gratefulness unlocks the heart of God, the meaning becomes clear. Having much or having little has nothing to do with the actual amount in possession.

If one perceives he has been given much by the hand of God and responds with gratefulness for all of God's blessing, the Father's heart is moved to give even more to one whom He can trust to steward His possessions well.

Matthew 6:23
Matthew 20:15
Deuteronomy 15:9–10

If, on the other hand, one continually responds with a demand for more, believing that somehow he does not have enough, the Scripture promises that even that which he has will be taken away.

It appears that the turning of wealth into true riches can be accomplished by the changing of the perception of the wealth, not by the actual amount itself. One person may see the amount as abundance and the next one may see the amount as not enough. The first will receive more from a gracious Father while the second will lose even the existing amount, let alone any additional amount.

Proverbs 15:16

Proverbs 16:8

Proverbs says, 'Better is a little with the fear of the Lord, than great treasure and turmoil with it.' And again, 'Better is a little with righteousness than great income with injustice.'

GENEROSITY PRODUCES GREAT WEALTH

Matthew 7:7–11

The heart of the heavenly Father is continually turned toward His children, looking for ways in which to pour out His blessings and mercy toward them. His desire is to give good gifts unto His children. The Scripture states that if we, being evil, know how to give good gifts unto our children, how much more shall the heavenly Father give what is good to those that ask.

Proverbs 11:24–26

As the heart of God is toward His people, He desires our heart would be toward one another. The Scripture teaches that generosity in the handling of wealth produces great increase, prosperity, and blessing. On the other hand, one who withholds only generates poverty and curses from others.

APPLICATION

We turn money into true wealth by the consistent application of these three attitudes: faithfulness, gratefulness, and generosity. Take one area of material sufficiency in your life and test yourself with these three attitudes. Then, the same now for other areas.

Do I faithfully respond to daily work and activities?

How do I see the 'little things,' the things of another, the money I handle?

How can I be more generous to those around me?

Am I generous to my spouse and family?

CONCLUSION

True wealth is measured not in possessions or money, but in the peaceable fruit of righteousness present in our lives. True riches come to those who are found faithful in little things, things of another, and even the unrighteous mammon which they handle. Out of the grateful heart comes the further increase and blessing of God. Also, much or little is not measured by the actual amount of possessions, but rather by the perception of either having much, or having little. With the perception of having much, a generous person brings great increase, prosperity and blessing – the true wealth of the heavenly Father's favor.

LESSON 17 – BALANCING REST AND WORK: SAVING FOR SABBATHS

PURPOSE

The Sabbath is not as much a day of the week as it is an attitude about rest in preparation for times of meaningful work. In our society, weekends, holidays, vacations, and retirement are all thought of as the reward for hard work. We often hear comments about making it through the work week to the weekend: 'Thank God, it's Friday!' The Scripture also has much to say about sabbaths and holidays to be shared with members of the family. However, as we study it more carefully, we begin to see a different view of this day of rest than the modern one.

GLOSSARY

Sabbath – a period of rest from labor, usually one day a week, but also can be a longer period such as a year or more. In the Old Testament, Sabbath years were every seventh year.

Jubilee – Once every forty-nine years, an extra Sabbath year was taken to celebrate the goodness of God to the people. In that year, people who had enslaved themselves to others through debt were released and properties mortgaged were released back to the original owner.

TRUE SABBATHS START IN THE EVENING

Genesis 1

In the record of God creating the world, we find an interesting passage that states . . . 'the evening and the morning were the first day . . . the evening and morning were the second day' . . . and so on throughout the week of creation. It appears that even at the beginning, God was trying to tell us something about the order of life. Days do not start in the morning as we normally think, but rather His view is that they start at sundown in the evening. His desire was to put the evening of rest into the proper perspective. Rest is not the reward or relief of a day's work, but rather rest is the preparation for the next day's work. Seen as a vital part of the next day, rest establishes the foundation for productivity and accomplishment.

SABBATHS ARE MEANT TO BE A WAY OF LIFE

Exodus 12:40–41

Exodus 5:11–13

God led the people of Israel out of the land of Egypt where they had been held hostage for the latter part of their 400-year stay. They had been forced to be the slaves of the Egyptians, made to build great and mighty monuments, care for the needs of Egyptian people, and give themselves endlessly to these efforts. There was no day of rest, no holiday, and no vacation. There only was another day of work, full of the pressure of being driven to meet ever-increasing quotas of productivity.

Exodus 16

As God delivered them and began to establish His identity on them, setting them apart as His people, He spoke of the Sabbath as a way of life. As He was bringing them out, He immediately began to establish the pattern of setting apart the seventh day of the week by telling them to gather two portions of the food, 'manna,' that He had provided for them on the sixth day of the week. On no other day of the week would the manna stay fresh overnight, but would spoil and become rotten if kept. On the sixth day, however, they were instructed to gather and keep enough for the seventh day – and the manna did not spoil.

KEEPING THE SABBATH IS A SIGN OF FREEDOM FROM BONDAGE

Exodus 31:12–17

Deuteronomy 5:12–15

With the giving of His laws and ordinances to the people, God further defined how strongly He desired the people to keep the Sabbath as a sign that they had been delivered from the yoke of bondage. When the Commandments are reviewed, the Sabbath is spoken of as a remembrance that they had been slaves in the land of Egypt, and the Lord brought them out.

Philippians 4:19

God desires for His people to always remember that they have been released from the bondage of the world. Whether it is true slavery as it was in the days of slavery in Egypt, or bondage to life's pressures of anxiety, worry, fear, or oppression, God delivers His people – and He wants them to know it by observing a Sabbath. This is the unique privilege of the believer in God, to have a day when he does not have to toil and work to obtain his sustenance and provision. He can bask in the rest that comes from his faith in the great God who provides all his needs according to His riches in glory in Christ Jesus – a privilege only given to the children of God.

It was not intended as a day of restriction (as taught by some), but rather as a day of celebration of the goodness of God, putting aside the toils and pressures of the everyday work week and entering into His rest.

GOD IS INSISTENT THAT SABBATHS ARE TAKEN

Exodus 20:8–11

From the beginning, God built the concept of Sabbath into His creation. When He further defined the use of Sabbaths with the giving of the Law, He continually warned those not to forget the Sabbath. When some forgot the Sabbath, He reacted quickly and strongly with punishment and even death. In the Ten Commandments themselves, the commandment to keep the Sabbath is spoken fourthly, only behind the commandments concerning Himself. As a reminder of the importance of keeping the Sabbath, He states that those who don't keep it will be cut off, but those that do will be refreshed.

Leviticus 25:1–7

In the tilling of the ground, He even desired that the soil be given a Sabbath year when it would be allowed to lay untilled and unplanted. When these principles were violated, the Lord would respond by submitting the people to captivity and bondage or even exile until the days of Sabbath could be extracted.

THE PROVISION IS SAVED FOR THE SABBATH

Exodus 16:22–30

Leviticus 25:20–22

Whenever the Sabbath is described, the Scripture talks of the provision for the Sabbath. When the people were gathering the manna provided by the Lord, they were instructed to put aside the portion for the Sabbath day. When the people that were farming the soil asked what they would eat in the year of the Sabbath, the promise was that in the sixth year, the fields would bring forth the crop for three years. Food would be available until the harvest of the eighth year.

Even in the time of Jesus, the day of preparation for the Sabbath was a day in which food and provision were gathered and prepared to enjoy a day of rest from work activity as a remembrance unto the Lord.

God's promise is consistent. Sabbaths are a way of life, remembering the deliverance from captivity and the Lord's promise to provide a time of refreshing.

APPLICATION

Am I taking Sabbaths as a regular way of life?

Am I willing to lay aside the pressure of work, trusting in God as the Provider of all good things?

Have I established a way of saving for the Sabbath period, preparing provision to allow time off from normal labor to celebrate the deliverance of God from bondage?

Is God having to extract the Sabbaths from me because I have been unwilling to honor Him by taking a Sabbath?

Have I been weak and sick for extended periods and unable to work?

Is God trying to tell me something about the balance of work and rest, my effort and His provisions, saving for a time of rest and not being anxious about His provision?

CONCLUSION

One of the great privileges of being a child of God is that He has ordained a day of rest for His children. While in bondage there is no rest, but when He leads us out of bondage into freedom, a Sabbath is given. It is a time of refreshing, putting aside the normal pressures of productivity, and understanding of how dependent we are on God to provide for us. In fact, if we choose not to honor the Sabbath, the Lord promises He will extract the Sabbaths from us. If we do choose to honor the Sabbath, He has shown from the Scripture that the provision will be there for the rest period. The Lord is truly the Lord of the Sabbath.

LESSON 18 – THE KEY THAT OPENS

PURPOSE

Matthew 5:16
John 12:27–28
John 16:14
Romans 15:16
1 Corinthians 6:20
1 Corinthians 10:31

In this section we have discussed some of the consequences of Kingdom labor. Kingdom labor is diligent, excellent, faithful, and productive. The consequences of such labor is the fruit of joy in one's craft and beneficial products and services. Beyond that, one enjoys the spiritual fruits of pleasing God through diligence. But there is a very important dividend that we have kept until last: the excellence of Kingdom labor causes the world to glorify God and opens their hearts to the Gospel.

Our primary purpose as Christians is to glorify God. Jesus gave Himself for that purpose, the Holy Spirit is given for that purpose, and the Church is exhorted to glorify God in all things.

GLOSSARY

Glorify – to magnify and honor, exalt.

Proclaim – to tell abroad, declare openly.

Demonstration – the act of exhibiting certain proof.

A COMMON MISTAKE

Psalm 100
1 Chronicles 15:16–25
Psalm 16:11
Isaiah 51:11
Deuteronomy 28:47
Luke 17:15

There is no doubt that God is pleased with the sincere praises of His people. We are told repeatedly to praise and exalt Him with words and songs of praise. Our joy in serving God brings joy to Him. When we do not enjoy the service and praise of God, we are in danger of losing our place in His Kingdom. He does not want joyless labor. Such service reveals our lack of understanding and produces poor workmanship.

Matthew 5:16

Giving God verbal praise and exaltation is certainly one way to glorify God. However, a common mistake is the failure to understand that God's purpose goes beyond Christians glorifying God. His desire is that they would also cause the world to glorify God. This is a greater challenge. How can we accomplish this objective? Jesus gives us the key.

THE KEY

Matthew 5:13–16

In the Sermon on the Mount, Jesus tells us that the world will behold our works. This is true when anyone makes a claim and proclaims it. Our claim is that we have come to know the King and His name is Jesus. We, therefore, proclaim Him as Lord and entreat mankind to receive Him as King. When they hear us, they not only see Jesus, they see us. What they see will determine how they respond to the message.

Philippians 2:9–11
Revelation 5:12–14

When the world looks at us, they will see our works – that is, they will see our lives and what we actually do. They will examine our works to see if what we proclaim works better than what they already have. Because humanity is often critical and negative, they may criticize and even persecute us. But if our works endure and even prosper, the result will be undeniable admiration. Jesus teaches us that as the world beholds our good works, they will actually glorify God. Indeed, the Bible teaches us the time will come when all nations will glorify God.

Ephesians 2:8–10

It is important to know that our good works will not save us. We are saved by faith. However, Ephesians goes on to say that while we are saved **by** faith, we are saved **for** works; His work in us is designed to produce good works **through** us. As a result of His grace in our lives, we will be good testimonies of His craftsmanship – something the world can see that will cause them to say, 'Praise God!'

Preaching to the world from a platform of careless works will close the hearts of the hearers, but preaching from a platform of good works will open the world to our message.

SOLOMON'S WORKS

2 Chronicles 1:10–12
Proverbs 24:3–4

2 Chronicles 2:1–18
2 Chronicles 1:15

Perhaps one of the best examples of this truth is Solomon's works. Solomon is noted for his wisdom, and with his wisdom he built a glorious temple that in today's currency would be valued in the hundreds of millions of dollars. In addition, gold and silver became so abundant that they were as plentiful as 'stones in the streets.' Solomon also built a palace and assembled servants, craftsmen, wise counselors, and all of the trappings of prosperity.

2 Chronicles 9:3–9

2 Chronicles 9:4

The evidence that Solomon's results were good was that his servants enjoyed their work and were prosperous. Solomon's work could be characterized by words like majestic, excellent, orderly, and inspiring. The Scripture says that the collective result of all of this took the Queen of Sheba's breath away.

2 Chronicles 9:6

The Queen was wealthy and powerful in her own right and served a kingdom far away – probably in Africa. She had seen a lot of great works. But though she lived far away, she had heard of Solomon and came to see if what she heard was true. Solomon's testimony was compelling and it was true. In fact, she said that what she had heard was not half as good as what really existed.

OPEN HEARTS

2 Chronicles 9:1–3

It was what the Queen of Sheba saw that made her believe what she heard. Solomon could have been wise, but without works she would never have come. Had she been passing through, without his works, she would never have believed. His Kingdom works were the key that sent the Good News out and opened her heart to the wisdom of God.

Isaiah 60:1–22
Isaiah 2

The prophet, Isaiah, said that the phenomenon would happen again, only this time entire nations world-wide would be drawn to the light of Israel. People would come from Midian, Ephah, and Sheba, and the wealth of the nations would come also. This would happen because God would glorify and restore His excellence to Israel.

Matthew 11:2–6

When John the Baptist was in prison, he sent disciples to Jesus to inquire if Jesus was really the Messiah. Jesus' reply was that the blind, the lepers, and the lame were being healed. He said to go back and tell John 'what you see and hear.' The world must not only hear, it must see evidence of God's work.

Mark 1:32–45
Acts 3:1–16

What Jesus did was the key to crowds coming from all the villages to hear with their hearts. And the same was true of the apostles. It was their works that paved the way for their message. Their works demonstrated that Jesus Christ is King and their message proclaimed it.

Whether it is the natural works of excellence or spiritual works of power, it is the ability to demonstrate the quality of the Kingdom that attracts and opens hearts to the message of the kingdom of God. This truth must not be lost if we hope to open the world to the message. It is what they see that unlocks their hearts to hear.

APPLICATION

What is it about the Church that opens the world to hear its message?

What is your church's message?

Are the demonstrations taking place primarily inside the church building, or outside where the world can see?

CONCLUSION

Matthew 6:9–13

Romans 14:17

Isaiah 2:3

God's primary purpose is to build a people that cause the world to exalt and receive Jesus Christ as King. Then they can enter into the joy of Kingdom life and enjoy righteousness, peace, and joy in the Holy Spirit. In order to realize God's purpose in our lives, we must respond to His call to steward creation and labor in it as His laborers. Kingdom labor will produce the kind of results that honor God and bless nations, causing them to ultimately say, 'Glory to God!'

Matthew 5:14

As believers comprehend God's ways and God's world purpose, they will enter the Church for equipping, worship, and inspiration. They will leave to go out into the world and be its light. The keys of the Kingdom will open the doors to nations. How the kingdom of God functions in the marketplace is one of those keys.

The next section of *The Covenant and the Kingdom* series will help position us scripturally, philosophically, and attitudinally to approach the nations. 'Christ's Kingdom and the World' will position us to speak as Solomon did to the Queen of Sheba, with God's wisdom for the world's questions.

SECTION 7:

CHRIST'S KINGDOM IN THE WORLD

LESSON 1 – THE BIBLE REVEALS GOD'S ETERNAL WORLD PURPOSE

PURPOSE

The Bible is divinely inspired, presenting a distinct view of the world, human life, and eternity. The foundation principle for this entire series is the authority of the Bible to address creation and its future.

This lesson will examine the Bible as the divinely inspired account by which God reveals Himself, His relationship to mankind, and His plan for all the Earth.

GLOSSARY

Revelation – (Greek: *apokalupsis*) – uncovering. The act of revealing or communicating divine truth (*Webster*).

Divine Inspiration – 'God-breathed,' the supernatural influence of the Holy Spirit upon divinely chosen men resulting in their writings being trustworthy and authoritative.

Eternal – the timeless realm which precedes and transcends time.

Finite – limited by space and time.

Law – the absolute and unchanging moral standard established by God for human conduct.

Standard – the scale or rule by which everything is measured and judged.

Bible – the compilation of divinely inspired writings which reveal God's thoughts, commands, and plans for mankind.

MANKIND HAS LIMITED KNOWLEDGE

Psalm 92:5
Isaiah 55:8

Ephesians 4:17–19
1 Corinthians 2:14
2 Corinthians 4:4
Ephesians 2:1–5
Psalm 19:1
Psalm 97:6
Acts 14:17
Romans 1:20
Romans 2:15
1 Corinthians 8:7

Men and women are incapable of independently understanding God, themselves, or the answers to life. As finite creatures we are unable, through our own initiative, to grasp the ultimate issues of our origins, purpose, or eternal destiny.

The testimony of the Bible reveals that the faculties given to men and women in the beginning are greatly restricted due to the effects of sin and rebellion against God.

Natural creation, however, does testify to the existence of a Creator God and gives evidence to the fact that design and purpose are built into the universe.

The Bible portrays men and women as having a conscience which bears witness to the power and presence of Almighty God in His universe.

Romans 1:19–20

Mankind is without excuse in recognizing the existence of God and the holy obligation to acknowledge Him through obedient worship.

MANKIND REQUIRES REVEALED KNOWLEDGE

Isaiah 55:8
Ecclesiastes 3:11
Romans 11:33–36
Isaiah 40:28
1 Corinthians 2:16
Genesis 3:8
Ezekiel 43:2
Matthew 17:5
Genesis 32:1
Luke 1:11–38

Isaiah 48:16
Jeremiah 25:4
Zechariah 2:1–8
Zechariah 4:9

Galatians 4:4
John 17:7
John 14:9
Hebrews 1:1–3
John 1:14–18
Romans 1:1–4
1 Corinthians 1:1
Jeremiah 23:28
Isaiah 1:1
2 Corinthians 12:1
Revelation 1:9–12

2 Timothy 3:16
2 Peter 1:21
Jeremiah 36:2
Acts 1:16
Revelation 14:13

Genesis 1, 2
Genesis 6:1–17
Genesis 12
Exodus 3
Exodus 19–20

John 1:1–5
John 1:14

Genesis 3:15
Genesis 49:10
Deuteronomy 18:15
Psalm 69:21
Isaiah 53:1–12
Matthew
Mark
Luke
John

Acts 1:1–4
Luke 4:4–12
Matthew 5:17–18

Matthew 16:18
Ephesians 1:22–23
Ephesians 2:20–22
I Timothy 3:15
Matthew 28:19–20
Acts 1:1–8

For men and women to understand God's 'thoughts' and 'ways', divine initiative is required. Mankind dwells in ignorance or darkness apart from God acting to supernaturally reveal Himself.

The Bible records that God has revealed Himself through His own audible voice.

The Bible records that God has revealed His will through angelic messengers.

The ancient prophets claimed to be sent by God and their message was given to them by God, the Holy Spirit. It was through His inspired messengers that He delivered His thoughts to those He had created.

The Bible states that God has uniquely revealed Himself and His will through the person of Jesus Christ.

The Bible teaches that the apostles are messengers which speak for God.

Dreams, visions, and revelations inspired by God's Spirit are also noted in Scripture as being vehicles for God's thoughts.

The Bible declares itself to be a compilation of divinely inspired writings which reveal the mind and the will of God. Men and women, moved upon by the Holy Spirit, spoke on God's behalf. The Bible is the record of these inspired messages and contains accounts of God speaking directly through His own voice.

The Bible also contains the historical record of God's activity and intervention in human history. It is through this sacred record, sovereignly given, that men and women may come to know God, the answers for productive living, and their eternal destiny. The Scripture also discloses the consequences for those who reject God's message as contained in the Bible.

THE CENTRAL PERSON OF THE BIBLE

Jesus Christ, God's only Son, is the central person in all of Scripture. Jesus is revealed as being co-equal with God and the Eternal Word through which creation was established.

The Old Testament, with its prophecies concerning a coming Savior, point toward the Coming or Advent of Christ.

The Scriptures of the New Testament contain the record of His life and ministry, and portray Him as the complete and full revelation of God.

Jesus Himself based His ministry upon Holy Scriptures and thus put His seal upon the authority and authenticity of the Bible.

THE CHURCH AND THE BIBLE

The writings of the New Testament reveal the Church which Jesus established as being the instrument of His eternal plan.

The mission of the Church's founding apostles is represented in Scripture as being given by Christ and divinely inspired.

Acts 1–28
1 & 2 Thessalonians

1 & 2 Timothy
Titus
Ephesians 3:10–11

The record of the New Testament contains the early history and activity of the Church. It also contains divinely inspired instruction for Church life and mission.

The will and purpose of God moves through the Church and toward the conclusion of human history. This is made known through these Holy Spirit-inspired writings. These writings are given as a covenant by God to man and represent His unalterable promises.

THE KINGDOM OF GOD IN THE BIBLE

Genesis 1:1–31
Genesis 2:1–25

Genesis 3:1–24

Genesis 3:15
John 3:16
Exodus 6:6
Exodus 15:13
Psalm 78:35
Jeremiah 31:11
Galatians 3:13
Galatians 4:5

The Scriptures reveal God to be the Almighty Being Who created the universe with design and purpose. The Bible describes the crowning moment of God's creation as the creation of man in God's image to rule in His behalf.

The tragic consequences of mankind's failure to obey God's directives for life and blessing are given in the Bible account.

The main theme of Scripture after the fall of man is God's redeeming love for a fallen creation and His actions on behalf of mankind to redeem them to Himself. This is ultimately accomplished through the life, death, and Resurrection of Jesus Christ.

Those whom He redeems, He also restores to the position of extending His rule in the earth.

THE BIBLE IS THE RULE AND STANDARD

2 Timothy 3:16
1 Peter 1:21

Isaiah 55:8–13
1 Corinthians 2:8–13

Ephesians 6:12–17
1 Thessalonians 5:14–28
Titus 2

John 3:15–16
Romans 6:22

God has sovereignly provided and protected the written record of His will and purpose for all of mankind.

Through the Scripture and the help of the Holy Spirit, the individual may discover the knowledge of God, His nature, His thoughts, and His will for human conduct.

It is through Scripture that those who trust in God are able to know how to conduct their daily lives.

It is through Scripture that all who place their trust in the covenant promises of God can be assured of their eternal life and destiny.

APPLICATION

How has reading and studying the Bible affected your life? How do you view the Bible as applying to the times in which we now live? Describe how a 'higher view' of the Bible as an inspired message from God would affect the lives of those who take it seriously.

CONCLUSION

Colossians 2:8 indicates that there are many different philosophies which attempt to explain the meaning of life and eternity. It is only the Bible that liberates us from the limitations of human intellect and reveals God's will for human life, the world, and eternity. Acceptance of the message of Scripture leads to life and prosperity in God. Rejection of its message leads to ignorance, darkness, and death.

LESSON 2 – GOD IS SOVEREIGN

PURPOSE

The Bible, as God's divinely inspired message, reveals that God, by nature, is sovereign. He is the all-powerful and all-knowing God Who created the universe. God alone has the sovereign right to rule over all that He has created, both visible and invisible.

This lesson will examine the basis of His sovereign rule and the necessity of our obedience to His Word and Covenant.

GLOSSARY

Sovereign – one who exercises supreme authority; only God is sovereign.

Absolute – the quality of authority which is completely free from other restraint.

Judgement – a divine sentence or decision.

Providence – divine guidance, the power sustaining and guiding human destiny (*Webster*).

GOD'S SOVEREIGN AUTHORITY EXISTS BECAUSE HE IS CREATOR

Psalm 24:1
Psalm 50:10

Daniel 4:35

1 Chronicles 29:11
Daniel 4:17–34

Psalm 103:19
Matthew 6:13

God has the right to rule, as the Creator. He has the right to be the absolute Ruler in the universe.

He alone has the right of possession and rule over the inhabitants of the earth and all living things.

Those whom God has created are called upon to acknowledge His sovereignty and – because He is Creator – there are no grounds to challenge His right to rule over them.

God's ultimate place of rulership is an absolute; it is non-negotiable.

GOD'S SOVEREIGN RIGHTS AS LAWGIVER

Genesis 2:16–17
Exodus 20
Matthew 22:37–40

Psalm 19:1
Psalm 97:6

Exodus 20:1–17

Genesis 1:28

As the Architect and Designer of the universe, God alone has the right and ability to establish the laws by which it will operate.

The natural laws He has established to govern the physical world are binding (the boundaries of the universe, celestial placement, and laws of physics). The Bible also contains the record of God giving the moral laws by which human life is to be conducted.

The creation purpose revealed by God at the beginning shows God's plan to have man represent Him, His Laws, and His ways in all the earth. Man's authority is derived from God's commission.

Exodus 20:1–17

The Moral Law, as given to Moses on Mount Sinai, is God's unchanging standard for man's behavior. Every major sphere of life and conduct is addressed by these ten simple commands.

Isaiah 55:7
Ezekiel 18:21

The message of the prophets was to call people back to obedience to the laws and directives of the Almighty God who had created them for His own purposes.

John 17:1–26

Jesus Christ was and is the perfect example of obedience to the Sovereign Rule of God over creation. He is the perfect example of life lived in proper relationship to God as the Sovereign Ruler.

Matthew 5:18

The Bible reveals that we are called by God to uphold and fulfill His Law through the power of the Spirit given to us by Christ.

GOD'S SOVEREIGN POWER SUSTAINS THE WORLD

God not only created all things but is the One who holds it all together.

Colossians 1:16–17

The natural laws which govern the universe have been established by God and He has set their boundaries.

Psalm 8:1–9
Acts 14:17
Acts 17:24–28

God's control of both natural and spiritual authority sustains mankind and enables us to exist in an orderly world. Even though we have fallen short of His commands and statutes, His authority continues to uphold creation.

Matthew 6:25–34

Acts 3:12–26

God's grace is continually at work to restore humanity to the place of keeping His commands and fulfilling His will. His hand mercifully sustains the world and its inhabitants until His will is accomplished.

GOD IS THE SOVEREIGN JUDGE TO WHOM ALL GIVE AN ACCOUNT

God not only creates, directs, and sustains, but He also sits in judgement over the final outcome.

Isaiah 2:12–17
Matthew 12:35–36

God, as Sovereign Judge, will hold all nations and persons accountable to Him as Creator and Lord. This judgement will be God's sentence upon evil and upon individuals who refuse to repent of it. The New Testament teaches that God has committed the authority to judge to His Son, Jesus Christ. Judgement will be God's last resort for those who have refused His grace and walked after their own ways.

Romans 2:16
Romans 14:10
2 Timothy 4:1

John 5:22
John 5:24–27
Matthew 25:32
Revelation 1:7

Through the final judgement, God will rid the earth of all evil and the effects of sin. He will separate evildoers from the righteous and create a world where the knowledge of the glory of the Lord fills the whole earth.

Matthew 13:41–43

Matthew 13:47–50
Romans 14:10
2 Corinthians 5:10

For those who have put their faith in Christ as Sovereign King, judgement will be different. It will be God's evaluation of their stewardship of life and possessions.

APPLICATION

How do you view the current emphasis on 'rights' emphasized by various groups apart from their acknowledgment of God's sovereignty?

If God sits as a 'Sovereign Ruler' over the universe, how would you explain the existence of evil and rebellion in the earth?

Do you see evidence of God's judgement at work in the earth today? Describe how you believe it is being manifested.

What is your response to the idea of a coming judgement which concludes human history as we know it?

CONCLUSION

There are, of course, those who question the relevance of God and the Bible to modern life, presuming that human wisdom can yield the answers which solve mankind's problems. The Scriptures, however, reveal God to be a Sovereign Creator, Ruler and Judge who is proceeding on His own timetable for human history. His grace, mercy, and benevolence toward mankind is presently being revealed in the earth through the ministry of the Holy Spirit. God has demonstrated His love through giving Jesus Christ and the promise of eternal life for all who would receive Him. The hour is coming when all will face the consequences of what they have done in response to the grace of God revealed in Christ. Those who have believed will enter eternal life but those who have rejected Christ will be bound in eternal judgement and destruction.

LESSON 3 – GOD IS REDEEMER

PURPOSE

The Bible records the beginnings of the earth and human history. The failure of mankind to live according to God's Word and Laws is shown to result in tragic consequences to human life and to the earth in general.

The Scriptures further reveal the fact that humanity is helpless to remedy this state of moral and physical failure. It required redemption and reconciliation by Someone who was above sin, who had the power, and whose nature was in harmony with a Holy God. Man's condition required a Savior.

This lesson will examine how God Himself took the initiative to redeem, sending His only begotten Son, Jesus Christ, to save a lost world.

GLOSSARY

Lost – astray, without direction, disoriented.

Ransom – redemption money, payment to buy back.

Redeemer – deliverer, liberator, protector.

Saved – reclaimed, rescued, freed from harm or threat.

Sin – failure to keep God's moral law, coming short and missing the mark of God's standard for life.

Salvation – deliverance, emancipation, the act of preserving and restoring.

THE NEED FOR SALVATION

Romans 5:12–21
Genesis 6:5
Isaiah 64:6
Romans 3:23

Isaiah 59:2
Romans 1:28
Ephesians 4:18
Hebrews 9:14
Genesis 3:22–24
2 Corinthians 4:4

Rebellion against God's command resulted in the entrance of sin into the world. The condition of sin resulted in a loss of right relationship with God, the perversion of human life, and many other tragedies.

The perversion of human life through sin produced a darkened state of mind – the inability to know God's thoughts concerning life.

The fallen state of mankind rendered them lost without hope and powerless to save themselves.

To experience salvation (the act of being saved from this dire condition) required great power and resources beyond themselves.

SALVATION IS ACHIEVED BY REDEMPTION

Romans 5:8

Being delivered from the helpless condition of sin requires saving action based upon God's initiative and our acceptance by faith. We cannot save ourselves.

Leviticus 25:26
Ruth 4:4
Numbers 3:51
Nehemiah 5:8

Exodus 6:6
Exodus 15:13

Psalm 78:35
Jeremiah 31:11
Jeremiah 50:33
Leviticus 17:11

The earliest understanding of redemption is indicated in Scripture by the payment of monetary value, according to the Law, to buy back something which must be delivered or rescued.

The redeeming work of God is demonstrated by His deliverance of Israel. His instructions were to offer sacrificial animals as a ransom price. In this way, God taught that disobedience put man in a condition of captivity from which he had to be 'bought out' – a bondage caused by sin. The old covenant system was a type or foreshadowing of the perfect sacrifice that would be made in Jesus Christ's death.

JESUS CHRIST IS GOD'S RANSOM PAYMENT

Mark 10:45
Matthew 20:28

1 Timothy 2:6
1 Corinthians 6:20
1 Peter 1:18

Jesus Christ became the ultimate and final ransom payment provided by God for the deliverance of mankind. The life and ministry of Jesus ended in an act of self-sacrifice which would serve as a ransom for mankind who needed it.

The ransom paid in Christ's blood forever purchased back all that was lost through sin and rebellion for those who received Him. It provided complete and full redemption from the horrible consequence of sin, which is eternal judgement and death.

His sacrifice is the supreme demonstration of His love for the lost and His desire that all be saved.

CHRIST'S REDEMPTION LEADS TO LIFE

John 10:10
Romans 5:21
1 John 5:12

Psalm 51:12–13
Jeremiah 30:17
Hosea 14:1–9
Micah 7:9

Romans 12:1–2

Hebrews 9:14
Hebrews 10:22

John 3:16

Romans 5:8

The redeeming work of Christ through giving His own life as a ransom not only delivers the captives from the curse, but also liberates them to a larger and fuller life under God.

The idea of redemption is to restore that which was lost back to its intended purpose. The aim of redemption is to lift men and women out of death toward life.

The darkened mind of men becomes enlightened by the Holy Spirit's revelation of the will of God for human life.

Our conscience is washed by Christ's sacrifice and re-enforced by the revelation of a Holy and Moral God who carries on all things in the interest of righteousness.

The human heart is stirred and won by the revelation of God's love which sent the only begotten Son of God to the cross for our redemption.

When we were helpless, lost under the curse of sin and awaiting impending judgement, Christ redeemed us and set us before God as righteous. Our lives were purchased and we were freed from the bondage of our own lusts to live according to God's plan for life and blessing. In the freedom of His love we are moved to share the Good News of His delivering power with those who are yet enslaved.

APPLICATION

What should we do in response to God's action on our behalf? What options do we have?

Being freed by Christ from sin and its curse, how are we to exercise the 'liberty' which has been purchased for us?

In view of the current focus on 'human rights', how should we define our 'rights' in the light of God's great salvation?

CONCLUSION

The Bible presents us with God's plan in creation and the vital role that men and women were to assume. The impact of sin and rebellion against God's laws resulted in devastating consequences to human life. Physical, mental, moral, and spiritual life suffered depravity and debasement. In this condition, mankind was lost and helpless to do anything to remedy the condition.

It is God's great love for us that he took the initiative to provide a way for us to be restored to His original purpose. The ultimate price for our rebellion – and the deliverance which we required – is demonstrated in the giving of His only begotten Son as a ransom for our sake. This 'payment' purchased us from slavery and restored us to His house and family.

LESSON 4 – THE CALL TO CHRIST'S MISSION

PURPOSE

Jesus Christ was sent into the world with a specific purpose and mission. This mission governed His entire life and led to His eventual death. His mission and purpose were confirmed by our Father in Heaven when, by great power and demonstration of the Holy Spirit, He raised Jesus from the dead.

This lesson will examine the mission of Jesus and His disciples to the world.

GLOSSARY

'Year of the Lord' – a period of time when God acts in a specific manner.

Mission – an assigned task; the act of sending.

CHRIST WAS SENT WITH A CLEAR MISSION

Matthew 5:18
John 3:16–17

Jesus came on earth to perfectly fulfill the requirements of the Law and the prophets in the Old Testament. He was sent as a result of the Father's great love for the world and His desire to save the lost.

Luke 4:43

Jesus came to proclaim the Sovereign Rule of God (the kingdom of God) in the earth.

Isaiah 61:1
Luke 19:10

Jesus came to proclaim to all who were lost that God had made a way for those who would turn from their own way and put their trust in Him.

John 10:10

Jesus came to bring spiritual and emotional healing to all who had suffered under the effects of sin and death. He came to bring abundant life.

Luke 4:18

He came to bring deliverance to all who were held in spiritual captivity to the works of Satan.

Luke 4:19

He came to proclaim the 'Year of the Lord', a time when God's great grace and mercy is extended in the earth.

John 12:48

He also came to proclaim a day of vengeance and judgement for all who refused the grace of God and continued in sin.

Isaiah 61:2–3

He came to bring comfort to those in mourning and to release praise and rejoicing in exchange for a heavy spirit.

CHRIST LIVED TO FULFILL HIS MISSION

John 4:34
John 17:4
Luke 4:43

Jesus was committed to fulfill the will of the Father who had sent Him. The guiding principle for His life was completing the purpose for which He had been commissioned.

John 9:4
John 5:30; John 14:10

Luke 4:1–15

Jesus' life on earth was governed by His desire to fulfill the mission given to Him by the Father.

Jesus had to overcome various temptations and distractions in the course of fulfilling the Father's purpose.

CHRIST FAITHFULLY ACCOMPLISHED HIS MISSION

John 17:1–4

John 19:33

Jesus completed the mission for which He had been sent upon the earth.

The sacrificing of His life on the cross as a ransom payment for our sake finished His earthly mission. It was finished.

Ephesians 1:17–23

His Resurrection from the dead by the power of God was the seal of God the Father upon Christ's mission.

WE ARE REDEEMED AND PURCHASED BY HIS MISSION

Romans 10:9

The fulfillment of His mission resulted in our salvation. His finished worked secures for us a place of acceptance with God and restoration to His family if we receive Him by faith.

Matthew 20:28

1 Timothy 2:6

His ransom for our sake purchased our lives from bondage at the great price of His own blood. As a consequence, we have been set free from the domination of Satan's rule and placed within the domain of Christ the King.

Galatians 5:1–13

The freedom and liberty secured for us through Christ's mission is not for independence but rather for the privilege of performing God's will and following Christ's example of commitment to God's purpose for us in His Kingdom. We are free to do His will, whereas before we were bound by our own weakness and Satan's control.

WE ARE REDEEMED FOR HIS MISSION

Philippians 2:9
Ephesians 1:20–21
Philippians 2:9–11

Acts 2:33

Ephesians 1:22–23
Romans 12:5
1 Corinthians 12:27
Ephesians 4:12

Colossians 1:24–29

Matthew 16:24

Philippians 3:10–17

Matthew 28:19–20

Acts 1:8

When Jesus Christ fulfilled His mission, God the Father raised Him to the place of supreme rulership.

From His position at the right hand of the Father, Jesus poured forth the Holy Spirit to establish His Body, the Church, on earth.

With Christ as Lord and Head of the Church, His will and purpose in the earth are given to and carried out by those who submit to His Lordship and seek to do His will.

We have been called to follow Christ and live by the example He has given us in His own life and ministry.

Following Christ involves the denying of ourselves and those things which are contrary to the will of God, even as Jesus did.

Knowing Christ and conforming to His image is the standard by which we are to live out our earthly responsibilities.

We are joined to Christ's mission of declaring the kingdom of God on earth by the Holy Spirit. The purpose for which Christ was sent is extended through us as we receive His great salvation and submit to His government. As citizens of His Kingdom and members of His Body, His mission becomes our mission and His will the guiding principle of our lives.

Our mission is not to proselytize – aggressive 'witnessing' with selfish motives. We are to be 'friends of sinners' – even as Jesus is – moved by the power of *agape* love to conduct ourselves in such a way that we offer 'living proof' of the truth of the Gospel.

APPLICATION

According to Galatians 4:1, Jesus has acquired for us 'liberty'. How do you apply that to your personal life and what privileges do you see that providing for you?

How would you describe the mission of Jesus recorded in Isaiah 61 as having practical application to your own life?

In what practical ways can you see your life as an extension of the mission of Jesus in the earth?

CONCLUSION

Mankind had been separated by sin and rebellion from a Holy and Just God. The vast chasm between God and man could only be bridged by satisfying God's requirement of condemnation and judgement upon sin. The only One capable of coming to earth and representing the Father was the pure and blameless Son of God, Jesus Christ. The only One who could become an adequate sacrifice in the place of those who were guilty under sin was the spotless Lamb of God.

Prepared with this purpose and mission, Jesus came to earth, lived a sinless life, and gave Himself as a ransom payment for our sake. In so doing, He completely fulfilled His mission and obtained for us salvation. Those who repent of their sin and acknowledge that Jesus Christ has been raised from the dead receive His Great Salvation and become citizens of God's household. They also become members of His Body and the extension of His mission to declare the 'Good News' in the earth.

LESSON 5 – CHRIST'S MISSION TO THE WORLD

PURPOSE

God the Father sent His only begotten Son into the world to redeem mankind from the devastating effects of sin and rebellion. The great liberating work of Jesus Christ opened the way for people from every tribe and nation to receive deliverance from spiritual bondage and a new life built upon God's laws.

This lesson will consider the 'world' as the object of God's love and His plan for reconstructing life on earth according to His divine pattern.

GLOSSARY

Bondage – slavery; subjection to compulsion (*Webster*).

Deliverance – to be liberated or rescued.

Depravity – a state of corrupt acts or practices, the conditions of fallen mankind.

'World' – the earthly state of human existence.

CHRIST'S MISSION IS TO THE WORLD

Genesis 1:28
Psalm 8:6

Hebrews 2:8

Romans 3:3–23
Ephesians 4:17–22

Genesis 3:1–24
Genesis 6:5–8, 12
Psalm 14:1–3
Matthew 5:19
Romans 8:5–8
1 John 5:19; 1 John 2:16
Isaiah 53:4–6
Romans 3:9–23

Genesis 6:5
Romans 5:8

John 3:16–17
Isaiah 61:1–3
Luke 4:18–19
Luke 4:43; Luke 4:14

Romans 5:6–11
2 Corinthians 5:18–19

In the very beginning, God made known His sovereign right to govern life on earth. Divine order was to be extended in all the earth through those whom He created to be His representatives in creation.

Rebellion against God's order resulted in tragic consequences for mankind and the earth in general. There was a loss of the vast privilege in stewarding creation as co-laborers with God. Expansive intellectual capabilities were exchanged for darkened minds and ignorance. The effects of sin and rebellion against God's will are marked by mental, moral, and physical depravity . . . and violence.

The 'Fall' of mankind produced an utterly helpless and hopeless condition. Apart from God's initiative to deliver and liberate, mankind was forever lost and bound to the impending judgement of a Holy God.

God's love for the 'World' is demonstrated through sending His only begotten Son into the world to proclaim liberty to the captive and a time of favor with God. Jesus proclaimed the kingdom of God and demonstrated by His own life how the Kingdom operated in the Holy Spirit . . . and how we should live. Jesus concluded His earthly mission by offering Himself as a sacrifice for the sins of the world in order that all could be reconciled to God.

CHRIST'S MISSION IS LIGHT INTO DARKNESS

Colossians 1:13
Isaiah 9:2
John 1:4–9; John 8:12
2 Corinthians 4:6

Isaiah 60:3
Isaiah 62:1

Matthew 5:14

Acts 13:47

Ephesians 5:8
Philippians 2:15

1 Thessalonians 5:5

Jesus came into the world as a light shining in darkness. The entrance of Jesus Christ brought light to those stumbling in darkness and revealed the way leading to eternal life.

The prophet Isaiah spoke hundreds of years before the coming of Christ that His followers would also be as a light to the nations.

Jesus told His disciples that they would be a light to the world to be observed by the nations.

Early Church leaders understood that they were set forth as light for the nations of the earth, showing the way of salvation. The call upon the followers of Christ is to recognize that once they were in darkness but are now called to walk as 'children of the light'.

CHRIST'S COMMISSION IS TO EVERY NATION

Matthew 28:19–20
Mark 16:15
Luke 24:47
Revelation 14:6

Ephesians 1:20–23
Mark 16:19
Luke 22:69
Philippians 2:9
Revelation 5:12
Matthew 28:18

Matthew 10:7
Mark 16:15

Jesus Christ joined His followers to His own mission to reach all the nations of the earth. Those who follow Christ are 'co-missioned' in fulfilling His ministry in the earth.

Following the Resurrection of Jesus from the dead by the power of God, all power was given to Him, both in heaven and on earth. Jesus exercised this authority and power to send forth His disciples to the 'nations' of the earth. Then He was seated in the place of supreme authority at the right hand of God the Father. Proclaiming God's redeeming love which leads to faith and repentance is central to the Christian's mission in Christ. Baptizing those who place their faith in Christ is His command. Training the 'nations' of the earth to observe Christ's commands is necessary to fulfilling this 'Great Commission'.

CHRIST'S COMMISSION IS TO TRAIN IN CHRIST'S WAYS

Acts17:26–28
John 14:6; John 1:12
1 Corinthians 2:14–16
Ephesians 2:9–10

Leviticus 20:10
Ephesians 5:22–24
Ephesians 6:1–3
Deuteronomy 6:6–7
1 Corinthians 11:1–15
Colossians 3:20

1 Corinthians 6:2–3
Ephesians 4:1–32
Ephesians 3:10–11

1 Timothy 2:1–2
Proverbs 8:15; Daniel 2:21
Proverbs 14:34

The salvation work of God begins with the individuals that make up families and the larger tribes – 'people groups' or nations. The redeeming work of Christ liberates the individual to discover and realize government under God.

God is the Author of the family units which comprise the fabric of a nation. God desires to reveal His divine plan for family government under God. Training the nations involves teaching families how to live in the light of Christ's Kingdom.

The commission of Christ involves teaching the nations of the earth concerning the role of the Church in the earth as the body of Christ.

Christ's Kingdom also provides the principles upon which sound civil government is established as well the principles essential for economic order.

Our motive for reaching out, training, and discipling others is not to dominate or 'lord over'. No, our motive for sharing this Good News is the same as Christ's – *agape* love.

APPLICATION

What role do you believe the Church should fulfill in society? Examine the Christian's responsibility to influence matters which may be categorized as 'public affairs.'

Do you make a distinction between that which is 'spiritual' and that which is 'secular'? Why?

CONCLUSION

Christ was sent into the world to redeem mankind from the bondage of sin and death. This great salvation, secured by the price of His own life, reaches to every race and nation in the earth. Every aspect of life requires God's redeeming love and the revelation of His will. Those who have been called by Him must go for Him to instruct nations in repentance from dead works and obedience to Christ's ways.

LESSON 6 – CHRIST'S AMBASSADORS TO THE WORLD

PURPOSE

The followers of Jesus Christ are commanded to extend His mission and ministry in the earth. Christ has equipped those He sends by giving them the authority of His name and the power of the Holy Spirit.

This lesson will examine what it means to be an ambassador for Jesus Christ and the responsibility that remains with those that follow Him.

GLOSSARY

Ambassador – an authorized representative or messenger (*Webster*).

Authority – power to command the thought; opinion or behavior of another.

Philosophy – a system of belief concerning life and reality.

THOSE CALLED BY HIM MUST GO FOR HIM

Matthew 28:19

The motivation to represent Christ to the nations is not primarily based upon the needs and conditions of people. Neither is it rooted in the blessings of the Gospel which would be of great benefit to all who share in it. These are powerful motives, but the basic reason for being His ambassador springs from it being the direct command of Christ, which springs out of His great love for people.

Mark 16:14–20
Acts 5:20
2 Timothy 4:2

The object of Christ's command is to 'go'. It involves an active and aggressive effort in carrying the Good News of the Gospel to all who have not received it.

Luke 24:45–48
Acts 2:22–32
Acts 4:1–2; Acts 4:33
Acts 3:14–15
Acts 10:39–41
Acts 17:2–3
Romans 1:4

The fundamental purpose for Christ's representatives in the earth is to bear witness to Jesus as the Son of God, crucified for the sins of the world and resurrected by the power of God. From His throne at the right hand of God the Father, He rules and reigns, establishing His Kingdom. His return to the earth will be the crowning act of His Kingdom on earth.

Matthew 24:14
Mark 10:13
Revelation 14:6

While waiting for His return, Christ's disciples are called to extend His Kingdom, proclaiming the 'Good News' of the Gospel, and disciple the nations in Christ's ways.

THOSE SENT ARE TO REPRESENT HIS INTEREST

Matthew 28:19–20

Christ's commission defines the message of His followers. Those things which He taught His disciples were to be the basis for discipling nations.

Matthew 16:19
Colossians 2:6–8
Hebrews 13:8–9
Acts 1:1–8
Acts 19:8

With the many philosophies that confront mankind into today's world, it is essential that Christ's followers be clearly committed to the

Kingdom message which Jesus taught during His earthly ministry. We must also be moved by the same love that moved Him. (See Lesson 16 of Section 3 in this book.)

1 Corinthians 2:16
Philippians 2:5

1 Peter 4:1

Matthew 16:23
Colossians 3:1–2
Mark 8:27–33

There is a vast difference between the thoughts of man concerning life versus the teachings of Jesus. It is having the 'mind of Christ' that enables Christians to live productively on earth.

Being mindful of the will of God as revealed in Christ is essential for fulfilling the 'Great Commission'. Peter received a supernatural revelation of Jesus as Christ, the Son of God ... but then immediately afterward responded to Jesus on the basis of 'man's thoughts.' Jesus rebuked Peter and called him up to embrace God's thoughts as the basis for fulfilling God's purposes.

THOSE SENT RECEIVE AUTHORITY AND POWER

Matthew 28:18–20
Luke 22:69
Ephesians 1:18–23
Philippians 2:9
Revelation 5:12

Luke 24:47
John 14:13
John 20:31
Acts 3:6,16
Acts 16:18

Luke 24:49
Acts 1:8
Acts 2:34

Acts 2:1
Acts 4:13–31
Acts 9:28
Acts 14:3
Acts 19:8

When Christ was raised from the dead, He was given a name above all others and all authority was handed to Him. This investment of authority by God the Father is the grounds upon which Jesus commissioned His disciples.

Jesus gives His name and authority to those whom He sends. Those who 'go' on behalf of Christ are not proceeding in their own capacity, but as men and woman who have been bestowed with the very authority of Christ's name. They are ambassadors.

In addition to authorizing His disciples, He empowered them to fulfill the task they were being assigned. Their mission was beyond the scope of human ability. They required supernatural authority, and power to accomplish their task.

The outpouring of the Holy Spirit on the Day of Pentecost filled the early disciples with great power, authority, and boldness to venture forth, proclaiming the Good News of Christ's Kingdom and God's power to deliver.

THOSE SENT ARE TO BEAR WITNESS

Acts 2:4
Acts 1:22
Hebrews 2:4

1 Corinthians 2:1–4
2 Timothy 2:2

Acts 10:39–43

Matthew 10:18–23

1 Corinthians 4:10–13
2 Corinthians 4:11
Acts 4:3; Acts 5:40

Following the outpouring of the Holy Spirit, the early Christians bore witness to the Resurrection of Christ with great power. Signs and wonders accompanied their message, attesting to the authority given them by Christ.

Witnessing for Christ is not restricted to the first apostles, but is the universal obligation of all Christians. All of those who were filled with the Holy Spirit became active in testifying about the saving power of Jesus.

Their testimony centered on the facts, the meaning of the earthly ministry of Jesus, and His power to save. This power was confirmed by His Resurrection.

The disciples were to be faithful in their witness without regard to their personal safety or welfare. Many in the Early Church were willing to endure much suffering and even death in the interest of being faithful in their witness for Christ.

Matthew 18:20
Matthew 28:20
John 10:11–15
Romans 8:38–39

Isaiah 9:7; Isaiah 54:3
Isaiah 55:5; Mark 4:30–32

Luke 10:19
Romans 8:35–37
1 John 5:4
Revelation 2:17–26
Revelation 3:5–21
Revelation 21:7

THOSE SENT ARE ASSURED OF FRUITFUL LABOR

Jesus promised to be with His disciples, even to the end of the world. He assured them that His presence would accompany them as they went forward in His name.

The promise of God is that the kingdom of Christ would never cease to increase in the earth. Even when appearances would indicate to the contrary, Christ's government is being extended.

Those who follow Christ and overcome the world are assured of ultimate victory. They are given power to be victorious in the present life and the promise of eternal victory at the end of this age.

APPLICATION

Describe your personal sense of responsibility to represent the claims of Christ to those around you.

Do you believe that you have received the power that Jesus promised to those for being His witness? Describe your personal encounter with the power of the Holy Spirit.

Identify several ways in which you believe that you could be a more effective witness for Jesus Christ.

Is God's love and mercy working in and through you towards those around you?

CONCLUSION

The command of Christ to disciple the nations extends to all who receive Him as their Lord and Savior. Jesus promised to send the Holy Spirit to empower His followers to be effective witnesses throughout the world. Until Christ returns to consummate this age, the call to be His ambassadors to the nations of the earth is the prevailing purpose of the Church.

LESSON 7 – DEMONSTRATING AUTHENTIC FAITH

PURPOSE

Jesus told His disciples they were 'salt' and 'light' in this world. The presence of sincere Christian faith, therefore, should be evident and visible to the nations of the world.

This lesson will examine different aspects of being an effective witness for Christ in the midst of a pluralistic society.

GLOSSARY

Philosophy – the beliefs, attitudes, and concepts of an individual or group.

Pluralism – the notion that there are more than one or several kinds of reality that deserve equal treatment.

Worldly – temporal, pertaining to this life in contrast to life associated with eternity.

LIVING FOR CHRIST IN A PLURALISTIC SOCIETY

Colossians 2:8

Many different philosophies and value systems exist within the nations of the earth. The Bible regards non-Christian philosophies as darkness. The salvation work of Christ delivers those who trust Him from the works of darkness and the foolish speculations founded in the traditions of men and not God.

Isaiah 29:14
Romans 1:22
1 Corinthians 1:19
1 Corinthians 2:6
1 Corinthians 3:19
Romans 12:2
Colossians 3:10
Titus 3:5

The wisdom of God is being revealed as Christ's Kingdom is extended in the earth. The plan of God is to allow worldly wisdom to perish as He does His marvelous work in the earth.

Followers of Christ are called to separate themselves from worldly patterns. It is in avoiding conformity to the world's pattern – and renewing the mind through Christ's instruction – that God's will and work is revealed in the earth.

EVIDENCING CHRIST'S CHARACTER

Ephesians 1:22
Ephesians 4:15
Colossians 1:18

Those who follow Christ are also members of His Body, the Church. Jesus Christ, as the Head of His Body, completes His purpose in the earth through those who are its members.

Galatians 5:22–25
Ephesians 4:20–24
James 3:17

The character of Christ is revealed through the lives and testimony of those who live for Him. The 'fruit' of the Spirit manifested in the lives of Christ's disciples is a reflection of Christ's own character.

John 15:1–7
Matthew 13:23
Romans 6:21–22

Through an abiding relationship with Jesus, those who are sent by Him are able to bear fruit which glorifies God and testifies to the presence and nature of Jesus.

John 14:12–14

Luke 24:49
Acts 1:8
Acts 4:13
Acts 9:28
Acts 14:3
Acts 19:8

Acts 2:43
Acts 4:30
Acts 5:12
Acts 8:13
Acts 14:3

Luke 4:33–39
Luke 4:40–44
Luke 5:17–26
Luke 8:22–25
Luke 8:49–56
Luke 9:14–17

Ephesians 4:1–13

1 Corinthians 12:1–11

DEMONSTRATING CHRIST'S POWER

Jesus taught His disciples that they would do the works of power that He had done during His ministry on earth. He promised that they would do even greater works because of His Ascension to the Father.

Jesus told the disciples to wait until they had been endued with power from on high ... then they would receive power to be His witnesses. It was the outpouring of Holy Spirit power that propelled the early Christians forth into the world.

Signs and wonders accompanied the ministry of the Early Church as it proclaimed Christ as the risen Lord. The anointing or ordination that had rested upon Jesus during His earthly ministry came upon the Church, demonstrating the very power of Christ.

FULFILLING CHRIST'S MINISTRY

During His life on earth, the ministry of Christ was characterized by diverse operations of the Holy Spirit. He moved in dimensions of knowledge and understanding that were supernatural. He performed acts that superseded natural laws and demonstrated authority over spiritual forces of wickedness.

When the disciples were baptized in the Holy Spirit, the gifts of the Spirit were set forth in the Church as it pleased Christ, the Baptizer.

The gifts of the Holy Spirit, as taught in the Scriptures, characterize the earthly ministry of Jesus and the Church. Supernatural revelation, wisdom, and knowledge is to be evident in the Church even as it was in Christ. Supernatural acts of power, healing, and prophecy are now to be revealed in the Church even as it was in the earthly ministry of Jesus.

APPLICATION

Define the ministry of the Holy Spirit in the life of today's Church.

Describe ways that you can see the person, character, and ministry of Jesus Christ being revealed in the Church.

How do you understand your place within God's work in the earth? What gifts of the Holy Spirit do you believe should be operating in your life?

CONCLUSION

The current ministry of the Holy Spirit is to reveal Jesus Christ in the earth. Through working in the lives of those that follow Christ, the fruit of the Spirit is cultivated and the gifts of the Spirit are manifested.

This is the extension of the very character and ministry of Jesus the King. The demonstration of authentic Christian faith in today's world is a proclamation of Christ supported by the evidence of His presence, character, power, and ministry at work in His followers.

LESSON 8 – THE PROBLEM OF MORTALITY

PURPOSE

Genesis 2:7
Genesis 3:19
Isaiah 40:6–8

Our perspective on the world begins with our perspective on ourselves. The purpose of this lesson is to help us to have a biblical perspective on our physical self – the body. Only as we see the nature of our physical being can we understand where our hope is and where it is not. Our hope is not in our physical bodies or our ability to fully demonstrate Christ's Kingdom in this life.

Mankind was formed from dust. And because of the disobedience of Adam, God has promised that unless we are alive at the appearing of Christ, our bodies will also return to dust.

The problem of mortality must not drive us to despair, but rather to faith in Christ. For He has not only taught us how to live in this life, but He has conquered death. Realizing our mortality moves our hope to higher ground: Jesus Christ.

GLOSSARY

Mortality – lifelessness, or being subject to death.

Sin – breaking the law, coming short, or missing the mark.

Flesh – our physical being.

Soul – our personality, consciousness, will, intelligence, and emotion.

Spirit – breath, dynamic, life.

Discern – to distinguish between.

THE LEGACY

1 Corinthians 15:22
1 Corinthians 15:48–50

Genesis 3:3–19

The problem of death is not an individual problem; it is a problem of all humanity and goes back to the first man, Adam. 'In Adam all men die.'

The Scriptures tell us that Adam willfully disobeyed the Lord and ate fruit from the Tree of Knowledge of Good and Evil.

With disobedience came death. While we do not fully understand all of the reasons, we do know that disobedience brought separation from God, and separation brought death. Death was like a disease that entered into Adam's body and soul until he in fact died. His days became numbered.

Disobedience brought death to Adam and Eve. But it did more; it affected their seed, or offspring. All of their offspring also lived with the disease of death and eventually died. Death was passed on to us; we are born with it in our genes.

Romans 5:12

The apostle Paul tells us that 'in Adam, all die.' He also tells us that sin entered the entire world through Adam, and spread to all men. Sin is a genetic problem. Man is born terminally ill and is limited by time.

Romans 7

Philippians 3:3

Romans 3:23

We are also born with another limitation; we are born morally imperfect or flawed. We have a tendency to disobey as Adam did. We are in fact incapable of moral perfection. We cannot keep all of the Law all of the time. This problem of sin is described in Scripture as being under a curse, sold under sin, subject to physical desire, and being unredeemed. To the apostle Paul and other biblical teachers, it adds up to a vote of no confidence for the flesh. We cannot place our trust in ourselves.

One might question the verdict of the apostle Paul if only one person, race, or nation had the problem. But Paul states the obvious – it is a universal problem.

There are many ideas, systems, and philosophies that men have believed which were supposed to save mankind from its problems. Many nations and generations have held out hope for a political, psychological, theological, or economic salvation. There have been many who promised a utopia. History confirms that the underlying flaw in every false hope is humanity – it is sinful; no system can save us from ourselves. Marxism is a most recent example of an idea that failed to consider man's mortality and sinful nature ... this failure was the undoing of Marxism.

THE LIFE

Matthew 16:13
Matthew 16:15–16
John 3:16
Luke 1:26–38
Hebrews 4:15

John 2:25
John 3:17
Isaiah 11:1–5
Luke 3:21–22
Luke 4:1–21
John 8:28–29
Acts 10:38–42

Isaiah 53

John 1:29–30

John 3:3–6
John 3:16
Acts 16:31
Romans 10:8–17

Romans 7:24–8:11

Jesus was and is unique among mankind. He is not only the 'Son of Man' ... He is the Son of God. While He was born of woman and conceived by the Holy Spirit, He did not share our genetic flaw – sinful nature. He lived in a physical body free of sin. Where Adam had disobeyed, Jesus obeyed.

Jesus was free from our problem of sin, yet He understood our problem. He knew what was in us and came to deliver us from it. Jesus resisted the Tempter and followed the Holy Spirit, living a sinless life. His entire life was given over to pleasing the Father and setting people free from their own sin by the power of the Holy Spirit.

But Jesus was more than an example of sinlessness ... He finally died in our place for our sin. He was the sacrificial Lamb of God who paid the price of our sin. So, He not only helps with our problem; He paid the price of our sin – our debt against righteousness.

The Scriptures plainly teach that life is not in us – in fact, death is in us. Life is in Christ! The Bible offers us this promise: If we believe in Him within our hearts and confess Him with our mouths, we will be delivered from ourselves and have eternal life.

When we are born of the Spirit, we are given the ability to see and enter into God's government in Christ. He becomes our Lord and guides us by the Holy Spirit into a life of obedience. The life is in the Holy Spirit. The apostle Paul warns us not to focus on ourselves, but rather to focus on and follow the Holy Spirit.

THE LINE BETWEEN

Malachi 3:13–18

Hebrews 4:10–13

It is essential for us to discern between self and Spirit; between our physical weakness and His eternal strength. Respect and awe for Him, and no confidence in our own ability, causes us to trust in Him. A lack of discernment will result in disappointment and disillusionment. The Word of God is alive and divides between our soul and God's Spirit. It enables us to be spiritually alive and spiritually sensitive to God.

John 2:23–25
Isaiah 11:1–5

The 'Adamic nature' is earthly, selfish, contrary, temporary, and oriented toward consumption and gratification. Christ's nature is heavenly, unselfish, cooperative, eternal, and oriented toward giving.

Jesus knew the line between; He discerned man's problem without judging or rejecting. He came to save us from ourselves. While He could 'see through us,' He nevertheless came to 'see us through.'

LIVING WITH THE FLESH

Galatians 2:20

We must not live for the flesh or in the flesh, but we do have to live with the flesh until we die. How can we live with the reality that our physical being is flawed and sinful?

Hebrews 12:2

(1) Most of all, keep Christ central to your life and thinking.

Colossians 3:3–10

(2) Reckon yourself dead; be crucified to self.

1 Corinthians 9:25–27

(3) Realize that even though you 'count it dead,' the flesh still lives and must be disciplined.

Romans 8:5–6

(4) Submit yourself to the Holy Spirit; put your mind upon Him and His will, not yourself.

Hebrews 13:7–13
Hebrews 10:23–25

(5) Be part of the redeemed community. Fellowship with other believers daily.

1 Corinthians 6:19–20

(6) Take good care of your physical body; it is the house in which your soul and spirit live . . . and is the 'temple of the Holy Spirit.'

2 Corinthians 4:7–5:9
Hebrews 12:1–29

(7) Spend regular time in worship and praise to Jesus Christ . . . 'fix your eyes upon Him.'

APPLICATION

Does sin exist in us before we commit it? Can a believer sin? Why do you answer that way? Do we have a choice? What will help us in our choices? What can you do about past sins?

CONCLUSION

Colossians 3:4

Romans 8:37–39

The physical body presents us with serious problems: sin, death, temptation, sickness, and other limitations. We must not, however, dwell on our failure. Personal failure and the failure of others should only drive us to faith in Jesus Christ. Christ is our life. We must put our sin behind us under His blood sacrifice, and look to Jesus, the Author and Finisher of our faith. In Christ, we are more than conquerors!

LESSON 9 – THE ETERNAL KINGDOM

PURPOSE

Matthew 6:33
Exodus 19:6
Daniel 7:27

The central theme of the Bible is God's Kingdom. It was promised to the patriarchs, taught in Israel, prophesied by the prophets, demonstrated in Christ, and proclaimed by the apostles. The final verses of the New Testament describe its fully revealed character in the heavenly city.

Matthew 4:23
Mark 4:11
Matthew 25
1 Corinthians 2:6–16
Romans 14:17

Matthew 8:12
Matthew 13:38
Matthew 25:34
Luke 12:32
Luke 19:14–15
Colossians 1:13
Hebrews 12:28

While we are told much about God's Kingdom, it remains a mystery. Repeatedly Jesus described it to His disciples as a mystery that is incomprehensible to the natural mind. The kingdom of God is revealed by the Spirit and lived out in our lives by the power of the Holy Spirit. It is spiritual in origin and nature, and can only be fully revealed in us after the Resurrection, as we will then be transformed and glorified.

The kingdom of God has been given to us who believe that Christ is King, and it works among us who submit to Christ's government. Nevertheless, in this life and on this earth there is still rebellion against His rule. Our own flesh is among the rebels, as stated in the previous lesson. In addition to our physical condition, the earth itself is in need of redemption and renewal.

Romans 12:2
1 Corinthians 15:58

The new birth in Christ has regenerated our spirits to obey Him. Our minds are being transformed and renewed daily in His Word. And our bodies will one day be transformed and renewed in resurrection; then and only then will the Kingdom be fully revealed in the earth. This lesson is devoted to describing God's Kingdom in Christ; how it works and differs from other kingdoms, and how it will be revealed in the future.

GLOSSARY

Kingdom – a realm of government.

Eternal – timeless, outside the realm of time; the spiritual realm.

Revelation – an insight inspired by the Holy Spirit.

Dominion – a sphere of reign.

Pharisee – a strict interpreter of Jewish Law.

ANOTHER KINGDOM

John 12:25
John 18:37
John 19:11–14
Acts 17:7

John 18:36
John 17:14–16

Kings are rulers over a realm or dominion. Jesus is a King and has a dominion which supersedes or transcends all other dominions. He is the promised Messiah and Deliverer of mankind. This is the claim of the New Testament and of our Lord Himself. It is also the reason that He was crucified.

Jesus' Kingdom however, is not of this world, even as He was not from this world. His Kingdom is 'other than' – it is different in nature

John 4:24
Romans 1:20

Genesis 1:26–28

Hebrews 1:1–12
2 Corinthians 5:2–3
Job 10:11
Psalm 104:1
1 Corinthians 15:35–58

Daniel 2
Daniel 7
Daniel 4:34–37

Colossians 1:13
Ezekiel 28:11–19

1 Timothy 1:18

James 4:1–2
1 Peter 2:11
Revelation 11:7
Revelation 12:7–17
Revelation 13:4–8

Ephesians 6:10–18
2 Corinthians 10:3–6
1 Corinthians 12
1 Peter 1:13–25
1 Peter 2:3–11

Matthew 16:18

Matthew 5:14, 16

John 1:4–9

Philippians 3:20

and operation from any other government. It is rooted in the Eternal God and operated by the Eternal Spirit. The kingdom of God, therefore, proceeds from the throne of God into the world through Jesus Christ and the Holy Spirit. Ultimate authority and reality are in the spiritual realm. Kingdoms come and go, but God's throne and God's government will not pass away.

The **invisible** God has made Himself known to mankind in **visible** ways. Creation itself reveals God and His nature. In addition, mankind is created in the image of God, distorted as it has become. And most especially, God has revealed Himself through the Incarnation, the birth of Jesus Christ.

The natural realm (the universe, physical things, and our flesh) are but 'clothes' that are worn by spiritual reality. Our clothes are temporary, but spiritual reality is eternal. One day, our physical clothing will be put away; we shall be clothed with a glorious body like our Lord's resurrected body. The next lesson will discuss that great truth.

The kingdom of God in Christ is not just another Kingdom; it is above all kingdoms. It proceeds from the throne of God and the spiritual realm into the natural realm with all of its political systems.

A CONTROVERSIAL KINGDOM

Jesus came to bring salvation; to deliver people out of the dominion of Satan into the kingdom of God. Satan, who resisted God before the creation of earth, continues to resist in the earth. Satan's main objection is to God's will and His dominion. Unredeemed mankind becomes Satan's pawns in Satan's battle against God.

In order to win man's affections, Satan promises fulfillment to our fleshly desires. In so doing, he buys our support to resist the Holy Spirit. By appealing to our pride, ambition, and lusts, he uses us to war against God's government. When we see our sin, repent, and submit to the Holy Spirit, Satan then wars against us because we represent the kingdom of God that he hates.

We are not without weapons in this war with Satan and his evil forces. The apostle Paul describes our armor and weaponry. John the apostle tells us that the enemy is overcome by the Word of our testimony, the blood of the Lamb, and a willingness to lay down our lives unto death.

The battle rages between God and Satan, light and darkness, and good and evil. It is a clash of kingdoms and soldiers for mastery of the human heart. The Church is the Body of Christ which is God's primary agent on earth to do battle with evil and reveal righteousness. It is the 'light of the world,' an extension of the 'Light of Christ.' We have confidence that the kingdom of darkness cannot extinguish the Light.

A BRIGHTER KINGDOM

Jesus is the 'Light of the World.' His Kingdom is enlightened by His own nature. His citizens have a better citizenship – an eternal citizenship.

Acts 9

The apostle Paul was a Pharisee prior to his conversion. He saw Christians as a threat and violently persecuted them. However, while on his way to Damascus to imprison Christians, he was struck by a light 'brighter than the noonday sun.' It was then that he fell to the ground and received Christ as Lord.

Isaiah 55:6–13

From Paul's conversion, he was 'enlightened' about Who Christ was – the Messiah – and what Christ's life was about – true righteousness. 'He saw the Light!' God's ways are higher than our ways. Paul's message was about Christ's Kingdom and Christ's ways as opposed to the ways of unregenerated mankind.

Matthew 5–7

In Jesus' Sermon on the Mount, He set forth the character of Kingdom people – humble, merciful, meek, hungry for righteousness, pure in heart, peacemakers, and a willingness to be persecuted, if necessary, for His cause. Such people would be the 'salt of the earth' and the 'light of the world.'

Matthew 25

In His parables, Jesus contrasted good seed and bad seed ... productive seed versus non-productive seed. He contrasted good stewardship and bad stewardship, and He contrasted mercy and callousness.

Romans 14:17

The effects of the Holy Spirit's leadership in our lives are incalculable. He not only gives us life, but the kind of life that serves, produces, cares, and endures. He produces righteousness, peace, and joy in our lives. He not only reveals a brighter Kingdom, but also a brighter eternity.

APPLICATION

What is a kingdom? How does God's Kingdom affect you? How does God's government affect family life? Business? How does natural and political government benefit from God's government in the lives of its citizens?

CONCLUSION

God is not only the Creator; He has revealed Himself in Christ as the rightful Ruler of all dominions. Christians are those who have repented of self-rule and submitted to Christ as Lord. His government and Holy Spirit leadership delivers us from the darkness of evil forces and fleshly weakness into His marvelous light and true spiritual righteousness. Our government is not mere rules, but a living relationship with the Ruler – Jesus Christ.

LESSON 10 – THE BLESSED HOPE

PURPOSE

Acts 23:6

1 Corinthians 15:12–23

In previous lessons we have discussed the problem of our mortality and the spiritual nature of the kingdom of God. Later, we will also review various theories of how this age will end. Our mortality is a fact observed daily – and Holy Scripture testifies to the spiritual kingdom of God. Whatever views one may hold about the end of the age, Scriptures give us the 'blessed hope' of resurrection from the dead. This is a hope in which all Christians can rejoice.

Acts 24:15
Acts 26:6–8
1 Corinthians 15:19
2 Corinthians 3:12

Galatians 5:5
Ephesians 1:15–20
Colossians 1:5
Colossians 1:22–23
Titus 2:13
1 Thessalonians 2:19
1 Thessalonians 4:13

The phrase 'blessed hope' appears many times in the King James Version of the Bible and refers to our resurrection. It is this hope that affected the lives of early Christians and enabled them to triumph in trials and persecution . . . even unto death.

The purpose of this lesson is to remind us that our hope is higher than the limits of mortal life; therefore, we should live for eternal purposes in this life. To properly understand our faith and its goals, we need to daily remind ourselves that Christ's call and promises extend beyond our fading flesh.

GLOSSARY

Mortality – the inevitability of death, unless the Lord appears first.

Gospel – Good News.

Resurrection – the raising up of our bodies in a changed state after death.

Hope – eager anticipation.

THE GOSPEL

John 14:6
John 3:16

Romans 8:11

Jesus Christ came to earth with Good News: there is salvation for mankind from the destruction caused by sin and from inevitable death. His salvation is to be received through believing in Him – His life, His death, and His Resurrection from the dead. Those who believe are forgiven of their sins and receive His life within them by the power of the Holy Spirit. They will be raised from the dead.

1 Corinthians 15:1–8
Luke 22:44–53

1 Corinthians 15:3–8

The Gospel is the story of Jesus and His power to save and establish His Kingdom in our lives. This Gospel was declared by Jesus Himself and the apostles who took up His ministry after His Ascension into heaven. The apostle Paul gives us a clear statement of the Gospel in 1 Corinthians 15: Jesus died for our sins; He was buried; He was raised; He appeared to His disciples; and He was seen by over 500 people at one time.

1 Corinthians 15:12–19
1 Corinthians 15:20

Paul declares that the Gospel hinges on Christ's Resurrection. Without the Resurrection, there is no forgiveness of sin, all perish, and there is no hope. Paul goes on to declare, however, that Christ has been raised and is the 'first fruits' of those who die and shall be raised.

THE FACTS

Matthew 26:31–32
John 11:23–25
Luke 3:21–22
Romans 6:1–14

Matthew 27:62–66
Matthew 28:1–9

Jesus predicted His own death and Resurrection. He not only predicted the events, but stated that He Himself is Resurrection and Life; resurrection power is in Him. He observed and commanded observance of baptism, itself a symbol of death, burial, and resurrection.

Jesus' death and burial isolated Him from His followers; they fled. Jesus' tomb was sealed and guarded. But He was raised by the power of the Holy Spirit and His Resurrection was a surprise to His followers, even though He had foretold it. He was then seen by His disciples and many witnesses.

Acts 2

After His Ascension, the apostles declared His Resurrection to many thousands of Jews and their testimony was believed by 3,000 people at one time in the city of Jerusalem, where it all had happened!

The story of Jesus had such credibility that it was accepted by multitudes in other nations who believed, in spite of persecution and martyrdom. The Church was established and grew on the basis of His Resurrection and the promise of ours.

THE HOPE

1 Corinthians 15:22

2 Corinthians 5:5
1 Peter 1:1–9
1 Peter 1:18–25

The apostle Paul declared that even as we die in our natural bodies, we will also be made alive in Christ. Peter declares that our spiritual birth generates hope in us as the Holy Spirit witnesses to our spirit, that as He raised up our Lord, He will also raise us up.

The blessed hope is tied to an event – the return of Christ. Our transformation awaits His return. Upon His return, Jesus will accomplish several things: He will defeat His remaining enemies and the chief enemy – death – and He will raise up all of those who have died in faith. Through resurrection, our corruptible bodies will be transformed to a body like His resurrected body.

The apostle Paul's account of events are as follows: The Lord returns to earth, He conquers death, He raises the dead and transforms their bodies, He judges His enemies, putting all things under subjection, and delivers up the government to the Father, who re-permeates all creation with His life and glory.

A REMINDER

The apostle Paul reminds us that we 'prophesy in part.' We see some things, but not all things. When Jesus' disciples asked Him about restoring the Kingdom to Israel, He said, 'It's not for you to know the times and seasons which the Father has fixed by His Own authority.' Neither Jesus nor the apostles tried to answer all of the questions.

We are not told when He will come; we are not told, nor do we fully understand all of the issues surrounding Israel, the Antichrist, the Millennium, and the various antagonists. We are told that righteousness and wickedness will both be present at the end. Whatever we believe about these issues, we must agree that our hope is not in a particular scenario – it is in the appearing of Christ.

APPLICATION

How does hope in resurrection affect us in this life? How could this hope affect nations? How does it affect us in the loss of loved ones? Do you believe that 'the blessed hope' should be emphasized more in our approach to life?

CONCLUSION

2 Corinthians 4:7–14

Romans 8:11

Christ's Kingdom is an eternal Kingdom. We enter through the new birth; a spiritual transformation of our lives. While our bodies grow old, our inner man is renewed day by day in the power of His Kingdom in our lives. Should the Lord's return be beyond our earthly years, we can rejoice in the blessed hope: the same Spirit that raised Christ from the dead dwells in us and will also raise up to be with Him.

LESSON 11 – GLORIFICATION

PURPOSE

1 Corinthians 15:50

1 Corinthians 15:52

The apostle Paul states: 'I declare to you, brothers, that flesh and blood cannot inherit the kingdom of God, nor does the perishable inherit the imperishable' (NIV). The last part explains the first. **The perishable does not inherit the imperishable**. We who are compromised by decay or corruption cannot possibly handle or contain the immortal and indestructible.

Romans 8:29–30

1 Corinthians 15:53

The Scripture shows us how Christ provides the answer, calling it **Glorification**. Paul explains that we believers – though predestined, called, and justified – cannot fully integrate the dimensions and holiness of God's reign in our daily lives, without this drastic restructuring called **Glorification**. It is like trying to inherit something that we are physically and spiritually unable to bear. Can a skyscraper fit into the local convenience store? Our bodies, our minds, our spirits, the very God-given faculties we daily use – these cannot fully cope with the immensity and intensity of God's personal rule in our lives. The fullness of God's Kingdom eludes us until such time as we shall be glorified – that is, clothed with immortality.

GLOSSARY

Corruption – the inexorable decay process that grips our physical bodies, due to Adam's sin of choosing his own way, instead of God's way.

Egocentricity – the natural and sinful state of mankind in which we see ourselves as the source, means, and goal of life on earth.

Flesh and Blood – a New Testament figure of speech representing our natural human body.

Glorification – the act of God's supreme power whereby, after death, we receive the same type of indestructible, perfected existence that Jesus enjoyed after His Resurrection.

Glory – reputation, radiance, power; at times used for God's Name.

DECAY IS BUILT INTO OUR MORTAL EXISTENCE

Genesis 2:7
Romans 8:20–21
Genesis 3:19
2 Corinthians 5:1–4

Flesh and blood refers to our mortal bodies, fatally infected with death and egocentricity, awaiting glorification by God's life-giving work. Though we are all designed in God's image, this physical life – animated by the natural forces of the soul – dies and remains buried, turning to dust by the natural processes of life. When God takes down this 'tent' of ours and replaces it with the glorified one, then we can fully express God's life and Kingdom.

ADAM AND SIN: THAT'S WHERE IT ALL STARTED

Romans 5:15

Romans 5:14
Romans 5:17–19

Paul explains that through Adam's sin, all people became infected with sin and so death spread to all. Death became the common experience of mankind, although we did not sin in the same way Adam did. Adam's sin also brought upon us the genetic inheritance that steers our lives into self-centeredness and rebellion against God's ways.

CHRIST'S RESURRECTION CHANGED US AND THE UNIVERSE

2 Corinthians 5:18–19
Romans 8:2

1 Corinthians 15:12–19
Romans 3:21–26

1 Corinthians 15:50–58

1 Corinthians 15:53–54

Although we all deserve the penalty of hell, Jesus' death on the cross brings us forgiveness and reconciliation with God. Christ's Resurrection sets us free to live by the Spirit of Life in Christ Jesus. His Resurrection from the dead forms the center point of our faith. The Father demonstrated His own righteousness and that of Jesus by raising Him from the dead. In the same way that He rose from the dead, we also shall rise from the dead. And in the same way that the Father gave Jesus a glorified body, so also the Father will give to each of Jesus's followers His own glorified body.

JESUS CHRIST'S RESURRECTED BODY SHOWS US THE WAY

John 20:26
Luke 24:42–43
John 21:1–14
Matthew 28:3
Luke 24:13
1 Corinthians 15:20

1 Corinthians 15:52

John 20:26

John 20:28
1 Corinthians 15:42–44

What do you do with a man who can pass through walls and then have a fish lunch with friends? The disciples on the Emmaus road fellowshipped with Christ's glorified body – without recognizing Him until He opened their eyes. At the moment of Resurrection, the Father transformed Jesus' earthly body into the glorified body. And that glorified body, amazing as it was to all who saw Him, shows us what we await.

Now as the Father transformed Jesus' earthly body into the heavenly one, so also He will change us. We, like His disciples, all stand in amazement at Jesus of Nazareth, empowered by the Holy Spirit. But imagine how His disciples felt that first time when Jesus came and stood in their midst, without using a door. Even Brother Thomas was impressed! Now just try and imagine yourself in your own glorified body; you were born into the world in a weak, perishable body, but then to be raised imperishable – glorious, powerful, and spiritual. Obviously, the physical sciences as we know them today have neither equipment nor world-view sufficient to account for the glorified body. For us, the fruit of the Resurrection is the glorified body – as for Jesus, so also for us.

JESUS CHRIST ENTERS HEAVEN IN HIS GLORIFIED BODY

Ephesians 1:20

Mark 16:19
Philippians 2:9–11

Hebrews 7:25

When the Father raised Jesus from the dead, He ascended to heaven and sat down at the right hand of His Father. At His inauguration in His glorified body, Jesus received all the rewards for His life of obedience. He reigns as Sovereign over all heaven and earth. He directs all activities of His Church, as well as all nations on earth. In that glorified

Acts 1:11

body, He intercedes for His Bride, the Church. And in that glorified body, He will descend to earth to be received by those who love His appearing.

THE GLORY OF CHRIST AS SEEN ON EARTH

1 John 1:1
John 1:14
Matthew 17:1–8
Revelation 1:14–17

John the Beloved saw clearly the glory that accompanied Jesus of Nazareth. It baffled him, as he heard, saw, and handled that glory. He speaks of a glory, 'as of the only begotten of the Father.' Jesus' face 'shone as the sun and His garments became white as light.' John saw the glory of the Living One: His clothing, head, hair, eyes, feet, and face. John fell 'as a dead man' before that glory.

John 17:5

John 17:22

Romans 8:17
John 18:6

John heard Jesus praying, asking His Father to re-introduce the glory He always had. And Jesus went on to ask His Father to give His own glory to His believers. Jesus' avowed purpose is to impart to us the very glory which He received from His Father and always enjoyed in His Father's presence. That glory shone, in part, through Jesus of Nazareth. The fullness of that glory is our inheritance in the glorified body. At the moment of His arrest, Jesus asserted that He is Jehovah, the living God of Exodus' burning bush. Such glory confronted His captors at that moment that 'they drew back and fell to the ground.' The fullness of that glory, unrestricted by our decaying bodies and old natures, transforms us into a glorified body.

INABILITY TO SIN

Romans 7:15–21

Galatians 2:20

1 John 3:2

God designed us, in the architecture of His eternal reign, for a lifestyle that excludes death, especially the law of sin. Innumerable Christian writers have displayed their inner struggle in devotional classics over the innate law of sin. What we desire to do, we don't do. And what we hate, we find ourselves doing. Life in the Spirit gradually teaches us how to put innate sin to the cross and live in the victory power of Jesus Christ. But in the glorified body, sin will not be an issue. The **inability to sin** becomes a reality. Our whole being becomes righteous: permanent, godly living, with no thought for sin.

NO WEAKNESS

Hebrews 5:2

1 Corinthians 15:42–44

The law, or power, of sin in our mortal bodies translates into a weakness that the High Priest carried. That weakness we also carry; we wear it like a mantle on our shoulders. The law of sin produces physical, emotional, and moral weakness that we all struggle to handle. But we never make peace with it.

Romans 7:17

Who of us learns and never forgets; works and never tires; eats and never gets hungry? When we sin, we disappoint ourselves, for it really was not our intention to disappoint our Lord. We feel intolerable isolation when we wound and offend our loved ones.

Romans 8:23
1 Corinthians 15:42–44
1 Corinthians 15:54–57
1 Corinthians 5:2

At funerals, we speak of the grave as the entrance into God's presence, but we groan within. Though we remain, we know very deeply that our beloved walks in a glorified lifestyle, one that is no longer natural, weak, or dishonored. And we look toward the day when, in God's timing, we will be clothed with immortality and sing the final victory song.

NO LIMITS

1 Corinthians 15:50

John 20:26
John 21:9
James 4:14

1 Corinthians 15:51

God destined our glorified body for His Kingdom: spiritual, not natural; powerful, not weak; glorious, not dishonored. For as awesome, complex, and marvelous this mortal mind may be, God's royal reign defies our full comprehension. Our bodies – unlike resurrected Jesus – do not travel instantly through space and yet eat regularly with friends. The starry heavens confront us with our insignificant, momentary and shadow-like life. All this changes in the twinkling of an eye, 'we shall be changed.'

APPLICATION

When was Jesus' body glorified? When will ours be? What purpose will glorification serve?

CONCLUSION

1 Corinthians 15:53

1 Corinthians 15:45
1 Corinthians 15:49

What beats within our restructured heart fits the architecture of a glorious, powerful and Spirit-imbued body. That new body – decay-proof, imperishable and immortal – we can only touch in part. But for those who are in Christ, the day will come when He shall take down our mortal 'tent' and clothe us with that God-made eternal dwelling.

LESSON 12 – CHRIST'S RETURN AND FINAL JUDGEMENT

PURPOSE

The return of Jesus Christ will fulfill the expectant longings of all who look for Him. It will also conclude a final and complete vindication of God's righteousness in the universe.

Christ's return as Judge will manifest the true character of all men and reward them, accordingly, to corresponding destinies. This lesson will consider the nature of the final judgement and how it applies to both the righteous and the wicked.

GLOSSARY

The Judgement – the final trial of the human race when God will decide the fate of every individual and award sentence according to justice.

The Righteous – individuals who have lived by faith in accordance with divine law, and in conformity with God's holy will.

The Wicked – individuals who have lived in transgression of divine law.

THE NATURE OF THE FINAL JUDGEMENT

Matthew 25:31–46

2 Corinthians 5:10

Acts 17:31

Romans 2:16

The final judgement of God in the earth executed through Jesus Christ will be an outward and visible event, occurring at a definite time in the future.

The justice of God, though partly revealed in history, requires a final judgement as its vindication.

God, as the omniscient Judge, already knows the moral condition of mankind. His final judgement in the last day will only be the revelation of His righteous, eternal judgement.

THE JUDGE IN THE FINAL JUDGEMENT

Matthew 25:31–32
Hebrews 12:23
John 5:22–27

Acts 17:31

Matthew 19:28
1 Corinthians 6:2–3
Revelation 3:21

God, in the person of Jesus Christ, is to be the Judge of all. This judicial activity has been given to Christ to be exercised in the last day as well as the present.

Christ's human experience enables Him to understand both the Law and the love of God. It is this union of perfect human nature and the divine nature which provides the grounds of true judgement.

Those who have been redeemed by Christ will also join with Him in executing judgement on earth.

THE SUBJECTS IN THE FINAL JUDGEMENT

All of mankind will be subject to Christ's judgement in the events of the last day. All who are living at that hour, those who were once dead but

1 Corinthians 15:1–51

1 Thessalonians 4:16–17

2 Peter 2:4
Matthew 13:41–42

Matthew 25:31

John 12:48

Romans 2:12

Revelation 20:12

now raised, and those who are alive, yet changed into His likeness will know the effects of judgement.

Angels, both good and evil, will be involved in, and subject to, the last judgement. Those angelic beings who have been steadfast in their devotion to God will serve as attendants to Christ as Judge.

There are two principle means which will serve as the grounds of this final judgement. The Law of God, as made known in the conscience and clearly set forth in the Scripture, will be the standard by which those who have refused God's grace will be judged. The grace of Christ will be at work in those whose names are found 'written in the Book of Life'. They will stand in God's approval simply because of their union with Christ and participation in His righteousness. Their works will be brought into judgement only as a testimony of Christ's blood and the measure of their reward.

THE FINAL STATE OF THE RIGHTEOUS

Matthew 25:46
2 Corinthians 4:17

Hebrews 4:9
1 Corinthians 13:8–10
Revelation 21:27
Revelation 22:3
Revelation 19:1
Hebrews 12:23
Luke 19:17–19
1 Corinthians 3:14–15
1 Corinthians 2:9
Revelation 3:12
Revelation 22:14
John 14:2–3

Hebrews 12:14

The consequence of final judgement will be the righteous entering into eternal life.

Eternal life, as described in Scripture, will involve glory, rest, knowledge, holiness, service, worship, fellowship, and perfect communion with God.

Although there will be degrees of blessings allotted according to the capacity and faithfulness of each person, all who share in eternal life receive as great a measure of reward as can be contained. Once eternal life has been entered, it will be unchanging and endless in duration.

Jesus promised to go and prepare a place for those who trust and follow Him. Though we are limited in our ability to comprehend 'heaven,' we are assured that it is the place where Christ manifests His glory through the glorified body which He has received. It is a place characterized by a perfect state of holy communion with God.

THE FINAL STATE OF THE WICKED

Matthew 8:12
Matthew 24:41–46
Romans 2:5
Revelation 14:10–11
2 Thessalonians 1:9
Matthew 25:41
Revelation 9:2, 11

Romans 2:5
Revelation 21:8
2 Thessalonians 1:9

Where the final condition of the righteous is understood in blessed terms, the final state of the wicked is described as eternal fire, outer darkness, torment, eternal judgement, wrath, and destruction.

Hell is understood in Scripture as a place and condition of utter abandonment from God's presence and hope. The consuming fires of hell and the torment associated with 'outer darkness' are as eternal in nature as heaven is to the redeemed.

In essence, hell is the loss of all good; an evil conscience banished from God. It is dwelling forever under God's curse in a place that serves as a penitentiary for the unrepentant. Whatever outward conditions may exist in hell only corresponds to the inward condition of the soul that has refused God's grace revealed in Christ.

APPLICATION

How do the thoughts of final judgement, eternal life, heaven, and hell influence your approach to daily living?

Why do you think that modern society is resistant to the idea of a God who could act with grave consequences at the end of this age? How do you respond to the question 'how could a loving God condemn someone to hell?'

In what ways do you think living life now in the light of eternity should be emphasized in the life of the Church?

CONCLUSION

People today live in cultures heavily influenced by humanistic thinking built around modern psychological models. This has projected man to the center of the universe with his concerns and welfare as the priority issues of life. The proclamation of the Gospel spells 'Good News' to all who recognize self-centered living as sin and rebellion against God. The grace of God revealed in Christ reconciles those who turn to Him. The Gospel also conveys the harsh realities of refusing God's benevolence. There is an ultimate day of reckoning which will result in great blessings to those who have believed in Christ and great torment for those who have spurned His love.

LESSON 13 – THEORIES ABOUT THE RETURN OF JESUS

PURPOSE

Titus 2:13
2 Thessalonians 2:8
John 14:3
Matthew 24:30
1 Thessalonians 4:16

Since the earliest days of Apostolic Christianity, believers in Christ counted His coming as the joy and hope of their earthly life. They awaited the moment when their risen Lord would literally and physically arrive on earth as the undisputed Sovereign over all forces ... earthly and heavenly, physical and spiritual.

GLOSSARY

1 Thessalonians 4:16

The Second Coming – the return; the physical, literal arrival of Jesus Christ on earth.

1 Thessalonians 4:17

The Rapture – a secret 'return' of Jesus Christ to remove His believers physically from earth, lest they experience the Great Tribulation.

Matthew 24:21

The Tribulation (Persecution) – a time of extra-ordinary upheaval, war, and suffering on earth.

Revelation 20:2–6

The Millennium – a thousand-year interlude in earthly history when Jesus Christ shall literally reign on earth. Satanic influence is removed and believers resurrected. This reign is separate from Christ's eternal Kingdom at the end of earthly history.

Matthew 16:27

The Judgement – the terminal point of earthly life when Jesus Christ evaluates all humans from all ages as to their faith, works, and obedience.

THREE PERSPECTIVES ON THE RETURN OF JESUS CHRIST

Titus 2:13

The fact of Jesus' return forms part of basic Christianity since the establishment of the Church. And believers since the Early Church have set down their opinions concerning just how the Lord Jesus would return to earth. The 'blessed hope' is the 'appearing of the glory of our great God and Savior, Christ Jesus.' In this brief survey, we present three general views of Jesus' return that revolve around the Millennium itself. May the Lord Himself encourage your heart as you look at amillennialism, postmillennialism, and premillennialism (historic and dispensational).

AMILLENNIALISM: WHAT DOES IT SAY?

Ephesians 1:20
1 Corinthians 15:20–28
Matthew 24:36
Revelation 20:11–15

These believers emphasize **that Christ's decisive victory over sin, death, and Satan brought God's Kingdom to earth in the Church.** 'We are in the last days now. We are in the Millennium now.' They see Christ's victory and inauguration as the greatest day in history – not

Revelation 20:2–6

John 15:19
Matthew 10:22

His Second Coming. His return consummates what has already been won at the cross. When the Father sends His Son, then Jesus raises the dead. He executes final judgement on all creation and sets in motion His eternal Kingdom. Therefore, the Millennium is not a literal 1,000 year reign on earth, but a figurative description of believers ruling with Christ during this present age. Believers now learn to rest in Christ's victory in the midst of the evil and alien world system. For the Amillennialist, the present Church Age is the Millennium.

Chronology

Church Age – Second Coming – Judgement – Eternal Kingdom

The Church in its favored political position in the Roman Empire helped believers see themselves as living in a full expression of all that Christ won for them. In 420 AD, St. Augustine formalized the amillennial view in the Western Church for the next 1,100 years. The major Protestant traditions of the Sixteenth Century Reformers (Lutheran, Calvinist, Anglican) all held an amillennial view of Christ's return.

Pitfalls

This view defines the Millennium as being the same as the Church Age; it makes no distinction between the Millennium and life in the Spirit as we now experience it. The amillennial view would require us to interpret Revelation 20 in a way that is totally symbolic.

POSTMILLENNIALISM

Isaiah 65:17–25
Isaiah 60:1–22

Luke 19
John 1:5

These believers emphasize **the Church's work of producing the conditions** which usher in the Millennium on earth. Christians themselves will bring into existence the Millennium by their diligent obedience to the Word and the power of God's Spirit. Violence, poverty, sickness, and ignorance fade before the overwhelming light of Christ's Word, Church, and believers.

Chronology

Church Age – Millennium – Second Coming – Judgement – Eternal Kingdom

Isaiah 2:1–4

Isaiah 61:1–11

Isaiah 62:1–12

In the postmillennialist's view, the Church enables governments to resolve the issues that divide and disintegrate nations. Christ's Kingdom on earth becomes a ruling factor among nations, without necessarily destroying all evil. As the Roman Empire received Christianity in 300 AD, so also the nations of the earth will, for the most part, yield to the rule of Jesus Christ and His Word. In the Nineteenth Century, North American preachers hoped to produce the kingdom of God on earth. The famous New England revivalist Jonathan Edwards emphasized the place of the North American Church in establishing millennial conditions on earth. He, among many, expected to bring in the Millennium on earth through technology and democracy. This civil millennialism seemingly thought of the United States and the kingdom of God as one and the same.

Pitfalls

Postmillennialism would require us to expect the Church on earth to bring about God's Kingdom apart from Christ's Second Coming. This view counts on our ability to redeem society.

PREMILLENNIALISM

1 Thessalonians 4:13–18

2 Thessalonians 2:12

Matthew 24:36

2 Peter 3:10
Matthew 24:5–14

2 Thessalonians 2:3

Matthew 24:14

2 Thessalonians 2:8

In contrast to the 'amills' and 'postmills', those who espouse **Premillennialism** emphasize **the return of Jesus Christ before the Millennium in a sudden and devastating way.** Their theory says that Jesus Christ Himself comes to earth and starts the Millennium. **Sudden,** because Christ will come unexpectedly, 'like a thief in the night.' **Devastating,** because He returns with angelic armies to eliminate all opposition to His Father's reign. He returns upon His Father's command, without regard to either Satan or an earthly kingdom.

Catastrophic happenings on earth precede Christ's return, such as earthquakes, wars, and famines. Radical persecution overtakes the Church; the antichrist emerges to lead opposition to Jesus Christ. The worldwide proclamation of Christ and His Kingdom takes place, as well as a radical apostasy from the faith. This viewpoint emphasizes **the sudden, supernatural establishment** of Christ's Millennium. Not the gradual conversion rate that ushers in Christ's Kingdom; rather a blunt invasion that terminates history as we have known it.

Chronology

Church Age – Tribulation – Second Coming – Millennium – Judgement – Eternal Kingdom

Revelation 20:6
2 Timothy 2:12

Revelation 20:7–10

Revelation 20:11–15

Revelation 21:10–27

According to the premillennial point of view, during this Millennium God will remove the curse from nature so that the 'desert will bloom like the rose.' Believers actively reign with Christ among nations. Yet toward the end of Christ's reign, God permits Satan and his followers to rebel once again. This final exposure of evil draws the cataclysmic demolishing of Satan's kingdom. Then all the dead are raised to face final judgement. God supervises the final disposition of all peoples: separation from His presence in hell, or eternity with God in heaven.

Pitfalls

Some believers emphasize the imminent and sudden return of Jesus by proclaiming this part of the Gospel as though it were the entire Gospel. They ignore their God-given responsibilities to serve Him in the midst of businesses, schools, and professions. A short-term view makes no preparation for God's mercy delaying Christ's return.

HISTORIC PREMILLENNIALISM

This most ancient view in Church history is called **historic** premillennialism. After the Reformation season, except for the Nineteenth Century, this view of the Second Coming largely prevailed in British and American Churches until the new teaching on 'dispensational premillennialism.'

Chronology

Same as premillennialism above

DISPENSATIONAL PREMILLENNIALISM

Matthew 13
Matthew 24
Matthew 25
Daniel 7

1 Thessalonians 4:17

American Evangelicalism held, through C.I. Scofield's notes in study Bibles, a dispensational view of Christ's return to earth. That is, God worked differently in seven dispensations, or ages, in providing salvation history. Further, God worked with Israel in ways distinctive from the Church. These adherents closely relate Daniel's prophecies with those in Revelation. Also, they emphasize the secret 'rapture' or catching away of the Church before the Tribulation as their entrance into a temporary state in heaven. After the Tribulation, they expect to return to earth with Christ and rule with Him. Most Evangelicals in the United States from 1880–1950 considered this view to be basic Christianity. Some of these teachings rely on doctrinal innovations from Nineteenth Century England.

Chronology

Church Age – Rapture – Tribulation – Second Coming – Millennium – Judgement – Eternal State

Guidelines to Avoid Pitfalls

1 Thessalonians 4:18
John 14:26

(1) **Comfort, do not harass** one another by these words.

(2) Seek the Spirit as Teacher of the Word.

(3) Insist that different interpretations of Christ's return not divide believers and establish new denominations.

(4) Beware of re-interpreting Christ's return to earth based on obscure or occasional verses.

(5) Reject personal claims of 'revelation' that define Christ's coming in ways not found in the history of the Church.

APPLICATION

What view do you hold? Do you see room for tolerating other views? Is it possible that the event will supersede all views?

CONCLUSION

The Bible does not base our hope on having the proper view of His Return. Rather, it is based on our faith in Him. His return is not for those who **understand** it all, but for those who love His Appearing. May God help us to grow in our understanding and in our love for Him.

LESSON 14 – CHRIST'S IMMINENCE

PURPOSE

The first Christians lived in the light of Christ's presence and the anticipation of His visible return. He was present yet coming again. He was near, yet due to arrive.

In times of great revival throughout history, Christ's return has received renewed emphasis. His presence revived the Church and heightened the anticipation of His Second Coming. In the light of the nearness of His coming, it is essential that Christians have a productive relationship with this present age as they anticipate the future to be revealed at His appearing.

This lesson will consider the broad issues concerning the imminence of Christ and the importance of a balanced view of biblical truth.

GLOSSARY

Acts 1:11

Ascension – the act of rising; here in reference to Christ visibly leaving the earth to be with the Father after the Resurrection.

Escapist – one preoccupied with being delivered out of circumstances accompanied by an absence of purpose or redemptive relationship to those circumstances.

Legalistic – in Scripture, having to do with a reliance upon works as a means of salvation or acquiring approval from God.

Subjective – having to do with feeling, perception, sense, interpretation, or intuition about something in contrast to an external and objective standard.

Proprietorial – a quality or attitude of exclusive title accompanied by a strong sense of ownership in determining outcome or disposition.

JESUS PROCLAIMED THE KINGDOM OF GOD

Matthew 4:17
Matthew 5:3
Luke 9:62; John 3:3
Acts 1:1–8

Acts 8:12; Acts 20:25
Acts 28:23–31
1 Corinthians 4:20

Throughout the earthly ministry of Jesus, the message of the kingdom of God was central to His teaching.

In the days following His Resurrection from the dead, Jesus instructed His disciples on the kingdom of God. The message of Christ's Kingdom became the central theme of the Church after Christ's Ascension.

JESUS PROCLAIMED THE NEED OF HOLY SPIRIT POWER

Luke 11:13; Luke 24:49
John 7:39; John 14:16–17

Acts 1:8; Acts 10:44
Acts 13:2–44; Acts 19:1–8
1 Corinthians 2:4–5
Hebrews 2:4

Jesus clearly taught that the promise of the Holy Spirit would come upon those who were His disciples.

He emphasized the necessity of the Holy Spirit's power to accomplish the mission He was giving them. The activity of the early Church was accompanied by the power and demonstration of the Holy Spirit.

JESUS PROCLAIMED THAT HE WOULD RETURN AGAIN

Matthew 26:64
Luke 21:27

Acts 1:11

1 Corinthians 1:7
1 Corinthians 4:5
1 Thessalonians 5:23
Titus 2:13

Christ taught that He would come again in power after His death and Resurrection.

The angelic messengers attending Christ at His Ascension proclaimed that He would come again in the same manner that they had seen Him depart.

The Early Church lived in the light of His presence and in expectation of His visible return to the earth.

A BALANCED EMPHASIS IS NEEDED IN THE CHURCH

Acts 1:1–11

The kingdom of God, the power of the Holy Spirit, and the visible return of Christ are each a vital part of the total message of Christ. Any one or two, accented to the neglect of the other, results in error by emphasis as seen in the following:

Mark 2:24–28
Luke 6:2, 9–11
John 5:10; Acts 15:5
Romans 10:2–5

Colossians 2:18–19
1 Corinthians 8:1

2 Thessalonians 3:1–18

- **Legalism** – Emphasis on the principles of the Kingdom apart from the presence and power of the Holy Spirit to effect those principles may result in a legalistic and lifeless application of divine Truth.

- **Subjectivism** – Emphasis on the presence and power of the Holy Spirit apart from the objective revelation of God's Word and Kingdom principle may result in a highly subjective lifestyle lacking order and discipline.

- **Escapism** – Emphasis on the visible return of Christ, apart from a proper understanding of the Christian's mission to extend His Kingdom on earth in the power of the Holy Spirit, may result in a desire to escape present duties as Christ's ambassadors.

- **Proprietorialism** – Emphasis upon extending the kingdom of God by the Spirit's power, without recognizing the essential role of Christ's return as the consummating event, may lead to an erroneous assumption that our own accomplishments will usher in the next age. It may lead to the assumption that 'it's our kingdom.'

A balanced emphasis of the Kingdom message, the power of the Holy Spirit in this present life, and the role of Christ's return in the future is necessary for a redemptive relationship to this present age, and a sense of accountability.

APPLICATION

Describe how you believe an emphasis on the imminent return of Christ could affect your local church.

All church congregations tend to be built upon a particular area of truth deemed important to its members. Define areas where you think you need a balance of emphasis.

Review what has been described as 'error by emphasis' in this lesson. If any area applies to you, what do you see as a course of action to achieve a more balanced perspective?

CONCLUSION

The coming of Christ to the earth, the coming of Christ in the Church, and the coming of Christ again for the Church are three related aspects of His imminent presence. By nature, we are prone to gather around one aspect of biblical Truth. The call to demonstrate authentic faith requires that we search out the Scriptures in the interest of stewarding, not just 'our corner' of truth, but the whole counsel of God.

LESSON 15 – THE HOPE THAT PURIFIES

PURPOSE

2 Peter 3:11

The apostle Peter raises the issue of how we should live in the light of the end of the age ... or the 'Day of the Lord.' In this lesson, we will look at that question and how the Bible answers it.

Hebrews 12:22–29

This entire series of lessons has focused upon God and His work in creation. The Lord God establishes His work by His Word, whether it is creating or sustaining what He has already created. God sustains creation by His covenant Word and His faithfulness to creation. God also reigns over what He has made. Hence, it is His covenant and His Kingdom that are established and shall never be shaken.

Isaiah 28:16
1 Peter 2:6

God's covenants and God's Kingdom affect us. If we accept His Word and His government in Christ, we are established and unshakeable in a changing and volatile world.

1 Corinthians 6:1–3

God's covenant Word and government are given to us in Christ Jesus. But as the Holy Spirit works in us, these qualities are also produced in us; that is, our word becomes a covenant word – faithful and true. And, as the Holy Spirit works in us, we learn to rule and reign in the matters of life. God's covenant and God's Kingdom come into us. Seeing that we have received an eternal Kingdom in a world that will pass away, how should we live in the midst of it? Let us examine that vital question.

GLOSSARY

Isaiah 2:12; Isaiah 13:6

'Day of the Lord' – day of reckoning, accountability and judgement.

Isaiah 46:10

Last Days – times of the apostles and thereafter.

1 Corinthians 5:5

Imminent – ready to take place.

THE PROMISE OF HIS COMING

Revelation 1:8
Acts 1:11

As the Lord began all things, He will also conclude all things. He is 'the First and Last.' We are promised by many biblical references that the Lord will return to bring destruction upon the wicked and salvation to the righteous.

2 Peter 3:7–13

1 Corinthians 15:23
1 Thessalonians 4:16

We are told that at that time, even the earth will be renewed by fire. This event is often referred to by Old Testament and New Testament prophets as the 'Day of the Lord.' Whether this is a 'season of events' that brings the final end of the age, or whether it all happens at once, scholars disagree. But the issue here is not sequence of events, but that He will appear and call creation to account.

THE PROBLEM OF DELAY

2 Timothy 4:8

2 Corinthians 4:7–5:11

The return of Christ was a firmly held teaching among early Christians. The dynamic of the Holy Spirit produced a love for His appearing, and the persecutions they endured reminded them that this present world was not their final home.

It is clear that early Christians saw the coming of the Lord as imminent, or at hand. They saw the return of Christ not only as a reunion with Christ, but a day of reckoning, accountability, and judgement.

Matthew 25:1–46

1 Thessalonians 5:23

Matthew 24:48

This view is put forth in the Parables. Therefore, Early Christians lived as though the coming of the Lord was at hand. The nearness of the Lord's coming had a profound effect. It caused them to live prepared to see Him as a Bride is prepared for the Bridegroom. Likewise, the sense of delay also had a profound effect upon many believers; it caused them to become bold in their devotion and behavior.

2 Peter 1:12

2 Peter 3:1–4

Peter is writing to the Church about this condition in his second epistle. In the last days of the apostles, some Christians arose to question the return of Christ or its imminence. The result was more emphasis on this earthly life, our bodies and desires, and the love of Christians for eternal things grew cold. 'The Lord delays His Coming' was an attitude that led to careless behavior and sudden judgement.

One of the issues that perplexes young Christians is the return of Christ. They have heard many messages and read much Scripture about His imminent return, yet He has not returned. Why did early believers and many Christians since that time believe that He was coming soon? What is the essence of the doctrine of Christ's imminent return?

Revelation 1:10–20

2 Peter 3:8
2 Peter 3:10–12

This question is best understood as we see the spiritual nature of the kingdom of God. When the Holy Spirit moves upon us, spiritual things become more real ... the spiritual world is 'at hand.' Many people, just prior to death, become very aware of the eternal world and find an amazing peace. When one sees 'in the Spirit' or is given a revelation of Christ, it is a window into eternal things. Things that are far off in a time-space world are near in the Holy Spirit.

Peter makes much of this truth in the third chapter of his second epistle. In the Lord, a thousand years is like a day. He warns Christians not to mistake the Lord's timing to mean He is not at hand. He affirms that the 'Day of the Lord' will come.

THE PURITY OF BELIEVING

2 Peter 3:11–14
2 Peter 3:14

2 Peter 3:15–18
2 Timothy 2:14–3:5

1 John 3:3

Peter asks a question that requires an answer: 'Since all of this is going to happen, what kind of people should we be?' This answer is, 'peaceful, pure, and blameless.' Peter also refers to the apostle Paul's teaching that the imminence of Christ's return should make us diligent and not prone to error.

The apostle John draws the same conclusion: 'Every one who has his hope fixed on Him purifies himself, just as He is pure.' The issue is clear in all apostolic teaching – a real faith in the return of Christ produces a godly life in us.

The issue in discussing the return of Christ is not what scenario do you believe, or when it will happen. The issue is, what effect does it have upon you?

Purity of life and good works makes us a light in the world. We are an extension of Christ's Kingdom in the earth. We are an expression of covenant faithfulness in our word, and Kingdom excellence in our work. Our lives – and the Christian community – should draw people to want to know Christ . . . to come out of the dominion of darkness into the kingdom of Christ. The Light of Purity in us is a powerful light to the world.

Matthew 6:10

Our Lord taught us to pray 'Thy Kingdom Come.' It was prophesied by the prophets; it was preached and revealed in Christ the Covenant King; it was proclaimed by the apostles and demonstrated in the Church. But the return of the King promises to fully and finally reveal God's Kingdom on earth. His will shall be done in earth as in heaven. Anticipation of this consummate event will cause us, with God's help, to purify ourselves in anticipation of the age to come.

APPLICATION

In what way does the kingdom of God exist now? Is it still correct to pray 'Thy Kingdom Come?' What are the effects of looking for His appearing?

CONCLUSION

2 Peter 1:3
Philippians 4:19
Romans 8:31–32
Ephesians 1:11–22

2 Peter 1:4
Romans 8:19–25
1 Corinthians 1:7
Philippians 3:20

God has given us His Word, His Son, and all things that we need. We have literally thousands of promises. The God of Creation and History has provided us with salvation and hope. He has joined us together with the Community of Christ which is to reveal His glory in this age, and will be glorified at His appearing. These promises are not only for our knowledge, but are resources for our living. Our prayer is that these truths will have made you a more equipped minister of Christ, living in greater anticipation of His Coming.

Recommended Resources

Aldrich, Joseph C., *Gentle Persuasion*. Multnomah Press, 1988

Allen, Roland, *The Spontaneous Expansion of the Church*. Grand Rapids: Eerdmans, 1962

Andelin, Dr Aubrey P., *Man of Steel and Velvet*. New York, New York, NY: Whitaker House, 1982

Augsburger, Myron S., *Practicing the Presence of the Spirit*. 1982

Barclay, William, *The Letter to the Hebrews*: A volume of The Daily Study Bible Series. Philadelphia: The Westminster Press, 1975

Barclay, William, *The Mind of St. Paul*. New York: Harper & Row, 1975

Basham, Don, *Handbook on Holy Spirit Baptism*. Springdale, PA: Whitaker House, 1969

Baylis, Albert H., *On the Way to Jesus – A Journey through the Bible*. Multnomah Press, 1986

Baxter, Ern., *God's World Purpose*. Mobile, AL: New Wine Tape of the Month

Beasley-Murray, George R., *Jesus and the Kingdom*. Grand Rapids: Eerdmans, 1986

Bennet, William J., *The De-Valuing of America*. Focus on the Family, 1992, 1994

Berkhof, Louis, *Summary of Christian Doctrine*. Wm B. Eerdmans Pub. Co., 1983

Billheimer, Paul, E., *Destined for the Throne*. Fort Washington, PA: Christian Literature Crusade, 1975

Blackwood, Andrew W., *The Prophets – Elijah to Christ*. New York: Fleming H. Revell Company, 1917

Blitchington, W. Peter, PhD, *Sex Roles and the Christian Family*. Wheaton, IL: Tyndale House Publishers, Inc., 1981

Bloesch, Donald G., *The Battle for the Trinity*. Servant Publications, 1985

Bloesch, D.G., *'Sin', Evangelical Dictionary of Theology*. Grand Rapids: Baker Book House, 1984

Boa, Kenneth, *God, I Don't Understand*. Wheaton: Victor Books, 1975

Boice, James Montgomery, *Foundations of the Christian Faith*. Downers Grove: InterVarsity Press, 1986

Bonhoeffer, Dietrich, *The Cost of Discipleship*. New York: The Macmillan Company, 1961

Boone, Pat, *Twixt Twelve and Twenty*. Old Tappan, NJ: Spire Books, 1973

Boyce, J.P., *Abstract of Systematic Theology*. Philadelphia: American Baptist Publication Society, 1887

Bridge, Donald, *The Water That Divides: The Baptism Debate*. Downers Grove: InterVarsity, 1977

Bright, John, *The Kingdom of God: The Biblical Concept and Its Meaning for the Church*. Nashville: Abingdon, 1953

Brown, Colin (ed.), *Dictionary of New Testament Theology*, Vol. 1, pp. 353–62. Grand Rapids, Michigan: Zondervan, 1976

Bruce, A.B., *The Training of the Twelve*. Grand Rapids, Michigan: Kregel Publications, 1971

Bruce, F.F., *Commentary on the Epistle to the Hebrews*: A volume of The New International Commentary on the New Testament (edited by F.F. Bruce), 18 vols. Grand Rapids: Wm B. Eerdmans Publishing Co., 1964

Brunner, Emil, *The Christian Doctrine of the Church, Faith and the Consummation*. Philadelphia: Westminster Press, 1978

Brunner, Emil, *The Misunderstanding of the Church*. Philadelphia: Westminster, 1953

Chilton, Bruce (ed.), *The Kingdom of God in the Teaching of Jesus*. Philadelphia: Fortress Press, 1984

Chilton, David, *Paradise Restored*. Reconstruction Press, 1985

Chironna, Mark J., *The Inner Dimension*. Destiny Images Pub., 1987

Christensen, Larry, *The Christian Family*. Minneapolis, MN: 1970

Christensen, Larry and Nordis, *The Christian Couple*. Minneapolis, MN: Bethany Fellowship, Inc., 1977

Ciervo, Ray, *The Local Church*. Destiny Image Publishers, 1992

Clark, Stephen B., *Man and Woman in Christ*. Ann Arbor, MI: Servant Books, 1980

Cole, Edward Louis, *Maximized Manhood*. Springdale, PA: Whitaker House, 1984

Cole, Edward Louis, *The Potential Principle*. Springdale, PA: Whitaker House, 1984

Coleman, Robert E., *Written in Blood*. Fleming H. Revell Co., 1972

Colson, Charles, *The Body*. Word Publishing, 1992

Colson, Charles W. and Jack Eckerd, *Why America Doesn't Work*. Word Publishing, 1991

Cullman, Oscar, *Immortality of the Soul or Resurrection of the Body?* New York: MacMillan, 1958

Cullman, Oscar, *Baptism in the New Testament*. Chicago: Regnery, 1950

Cullman, Oscar, *Essays on the Lord's Supper*. Richmond: John Knox Press, 1958

Cumming, James E., *A Handbook on the Holy Spirit*. Bethany Books, 1977

Dayton, Donald W., *Theological Roots of Pentecostalism*. Grand Rapids: Zondervan, 1987

Dawson, David M., *More Power in Prayer*. Grand Rapids: Zondervan, 1962

DeGraff, S.G., *Promise and Deliverance*, Vol. I, Vol. III, *Christ's Ministry and Death*. Paideia Press, 1979

Dobson, James C., *Hide and Seek*. Old Tappan, NJ: Fleming H. Revell Co., 1979

Dobson, James C., *Love Must Be Tough*. Waco, TX: Word Books, 1987

Dobson, James C., *Parenting Isn't For Cowards*. Waco, TX: Word Books, 1987

Dobson, James C., *Preparing for Adolescence*. Ventura, CA: Regal Books, 1978

Dulles, Avery, *Models of the Church*. Garden City: Doubleday, 1974

Edge, Findley, *A Quest for Vitality in Religion*. Nashville: Broadman Press, 1963

Engel, James F. and Norton, H. Wilbert, *What's Gone Wrong With the Harvest?* Grand Rapids: Zondervan, 1975

Ervin, Howard M., *These Are Not Drunken, As Ye Suppose*. Plainfield, New Jersey: Logos International, 1968

Foster, Richard J., *Celebration of Discipline*. San Francisco: Harper and Rowe Publishers, 1978

Gee, Donald, *Concerning Spiritual Gifts*. Springfield, MO: Gospel, 1972

Geisler, Norman L., *False Gods of Our Time*. Harvest House, 1985

Getz, Gene A., *Encouraging One Another*. Victor Books, 1981

Gray, Ronald, *Enter to Worship, Exit to Serve*. Revival Press, 1988

Green, Michael, *Evangelism in the Early Church*. Grand Rapids: Eerdmans, 1970

Gruenler, Royce G., *The Trinity in the Gospel of John*. Baker Book House, 1986

Hamon, Bill, *The Eternal Church*. Phoenix: Christian International Publishers, 1981

Hamon, Bill, *Prophets and Personal Prophecy*. Shippensburg, PA: Destiny Image, 1987

Hardenbrook, Weldon M. *Missing from Action: Vanishing Manhood in America*. Nashville, TN: Thomas Nelson Publishers, 1987

Harrison, Everett, *The Apostolic Church*. Grand Rapids: Eerdmans, 1985

Hayford, Jack, *Worship His Majesty*. Word Books, 1987

Huegel, F.J., *Bone of His Son*. Grand Rapids: Zondervan House

Hunter, Charles and Frances, *To Heal the Sick*. Kingwood, Texas: Hunter Books, 1983

Institute in Basic Youth Conflicts, *How to Understand Humanism*. Institute in Basic Youth Conflicts, 1983

Interpreter's Dictionary of the Bible, Vol. 4, 'Tithe'. New York: Abington Press, 1962

Iverson, Dick, *Team Ministry*. Portland: Bible Temple Publications, 1984

James, William, *The Varieties of Religious Experience*. New York: The New American Library, 1958

Jones, E. Stanley, *The Unshakable Kingdom and the Unchanging Person*. Abington Press

Jordan, James B., *Rebellion, Tyranny, and Dominion in the Book of Genesis*, Christianity and Civilization No. 3, (edited by Gary North). Geneva Divinity School Press, 1983

Jordan, James B., *The Law of the Covenant: An Exposition of Exodus 21–23*. Institute for Christian Economics, 1984

Jordan, James B., *Judges: God's War Against Humanism*. Geneva Ministries, 1985

Kesler, Jay and Ronald A. Beers (eds), *Parents and Teenagers*. Wheaton, IL: Victor Books, 1985

Kinghorn, Kenneth C., *Gifts of the Spirit*. Nashville: Abington, 1976

Kline, Meredith G., *Kingdom Prologue: Vol. One*. Meredith Kline, 1986

Kline, Meredith G., *By Oath Consigned*. Eerdmans, 1968

Kline, Meredith G., *The Structure of Biblical Authority*. Eerdmans, [1972], 1978

Kline, Meredith G., *The Treaty of the Great King*. Eerdmans, 1963

Kung, Hans, *Structures for the Church*. London: Burns and Oates, 1964

Ladd, George E., *The Presence of the Future*. Eerdmans Pub. Co., 1973

Ladd, George E., *The Last Things. Jesus and the Kingdom*. New York: Harper & Row, Publishers, 1964

Ladd, George E., *Crucial Questions Concerning the Kingdom of God*. Grand Rapids: Eerdmans, 1952

Ladd, George, *The Gospel of the Kingdom*. Grand Rapids: Eerdmans, 1987

LaHaye, Tim and Beverly, *The Act of Marriage*. Grand Rapids, MI: Zondervan, 1976

Lea, Larry, *Could You Not Tarry One Hour?* Rockwall, Texas: Church on the Rock, 1985

Lockyer, Herbert, *All the Doctrines of the Bible*. Grand Rapids

Marshall, I. Howard, *Kept by the Power of God*. Minneapolis: Bethany Fellowship, Inc., 1969

Marshall, I. Howard, *Last Supper and Lord's Supper*. Grand Rapids: Eerdmans, 1981

Martin, Ralph, *Husbands, Wives, Parents, Children*. Ann Arbor, MI: Servant Books, 1978

Martin, Ralph P., *The Spirit and the Congregation*. Grand Rapids: Eerdmans, 1984

McDowell, Josh, *Evidence that Demands a Verdict*. Here's Life Publishers, 1972

McMillen, S.I., *None of These Diseases*. Westwood, New Jersey: Fleming Revell Company, 1963

Meyer, F.B., *The Christ-Life for the Self-Life*. Chicago: Moody Press

Miller, Donald G., *The Nature and Mission of the Church*. Richmond: John Knox Press, 1957

Milton, Elizabeth, *Sarah: A Friend for the Journey*. Corner Pillar Publishing, 1991

Moltmann, Jurgen, *The Church in the Power of the Spirit*. New York: Harper & Row, 1977

Moody, Dale, *The Hope of Glory*. Grand Rapids: William B. Eerdmans Publishing Company, 1964

Moody, Dale, *Spirit of the Living God*. Philadelphia: Westminster Press, 1968

Morgan, G. Campbell, *The Teachings of Christ*. Old Tappan: Revell, 1913

Morris, Leon, *The Lord from Heaven*. Grand Rapids, Michigan: Eerdman's Publishing Co., 1958

Mumford, Bob, *The Purpose of Temptation*. Fleming H. Revell Co., 1973

Mumford, Bob, *The Ten Commandments in the Life of the Believer* (audio tape). Life-Changers

Mumford, Bob, *The King and You*. Life-Changers

Mumford, Bob, *The Purpose of Temptation*. Life-Changers

Mumford, Bob, *Christ in Session*. Fort Lauderdale, FL: Bob Mumford, 1973

Mumford, Bob, *Baptism*. Fort Lauderdale, FL: Christian Growth Ministries, 1973

Mumford, Bob, *15 Steps Out*. Plainfield, New Jersey: Logos International, 1969

Murray, Andrew, *How to Raise Your Children for Christ*. Minneapolis, MN: Bethany Fellowship, Inc., 1975

Murray, John, *The Atonement*. Philadelphia: Presbyterian and Reformed Publishing Co., 1962

Nee, Watchman, *Changed into His Likeness*. Christian Literature Crusade, 1967

Nee, Watchman, *The Glorious Church*. Los Angeles: The Stream Publishers, 1974

Newbigin, Leslie, *The Holy Spirit and The Church*. Christian Literature Society, 1972

Newbigin, Leslie, *The Household of God: Lectures on the Nature of the Church*. New York: Friendship Press, 1954

North, Gary, *Inherit the Earth*. Ft Worth, Texas: Dominion Press, 1987

O'Connor, Elizabeth, *Call to Commitment*. New York: Harper & Row Publishers, 1963

Packer, J.I., *Knowing God*. InterVarsity Press, 1973

Palmer, Edwin H., *The Five Points of Calvinism*. Grand Rapids: Baker Book House, 1972

Paterson, Ross and Elizabeth Farrell, *China: The Hidden Miracle*. Sovereign World Ltd, 1993

Paul, Robert S., *'The Atonement: Sacrifice and Penalty', Readings in Calvin's Theology* (Donald K. McKim, editor). Grand Rapids: Baker Book House, 1984

Payne, David F., *Kingdoms of the Lord*. Grand Rapids: William B. Eerdmans Publishing Company, 1981

Peretti, Frank E., *This Present Darkness*. Westchester, Illinois: Crossway Books, 1986

Peters, George W., *A Theology of Church Growth*. Grand Rapids: Zondervan, 1981

Peterson, Eugene H., *The Message*. Navpress, 1993

Pink, Arthur W., *The Attributes of God*. Baker Book House, 1985

Pratt, Richard L., *Every Thought Captive*. Presbyterian and Reformed, 1979

Pride, Mary, *The Way Home: Beyond Feminism, Back to Reality*. Westchester, IL: Crossway Books, 1985

Prince, Derek, *Faith to Live By*. Ann Arbor: Servant Books, 1977

Prince, Derek, *Foundation Series*. Fort Lauderdale, FL: Derek Prince Ministries, 1986

Prince, Derek, *The Marriage Covenant*. Fort Lauderdale, FL: Derek Prince Ministries, 1978

Ramm, Bernard L., *An Evangelical Christogogy*. Nashville: Thomas Nelson Publishers, 1985

Rainey, Dennis and Barbara, *Building Your Mate's Self Esteem*. San Bernardino, CA: Here's Life Publishers, 1986

Ridderbos, Herman, *Paul: An Outline of His Theology*. Grand Rapids: Eerdmans, 1975

Robertson, O. Palmer, *The Christ of the Covenants*. Presbyterian and Reformed Publishing Co., 1980

Rushdoony, R.J., *The Institute of Biblical Law*. Nutley, New Jersey: The Craig Press, 1973

Rushdoony, Rousas J., *The One and the Many*. Thoburn Press, 1978

Savelle, Jerry, *Sharing Jesus Effectively*. Tulsa: Harrison House, 1982

Schaffer, Francis A., *A Christian Manifesto*. Crossway Books, 1981

Schaffer, Francis A., *Baptism*. Wilmington: Cross Publishing Co., 1973

Schaffer, Francis A., *The Church at the End of the 20th Century*. Downers Grove: InterVarsity Press, 1971

Schaffer, Francis A., *The Church Before the Watching World*. Downers Grove: InterVarsity Press, 1971

Schmemann, Alexander, *For the Life of the World*. St. Vladimir's Seminary Press, 1973

Shedd, Charlie, *Letters to Phillip*. Old Tappan, NJ: Fleming H. Revell Co., 1968

Shedd, Charlie, *Letters to Karen*. Abington, 1965

Simpson, Charles, *Integrity from the Inside Out or Internal Integrity and External Integration* (audio tape). Mobile, AL: CSM, PO Box Z, Mobile, AL 36616

Simpson, Charles, *The Holy Nation* (audio tape). Mobile, AL: CSM, PO Box Z, Mobile, AL 36616

Simpson, Charles, *The Priceless Woman* (audio tape). Mobile, AL: CSM, PO Box Z, Mobile, AL 36616

Simpson, Charles, *Turning the Hearts of the Fathers* (audio tape). Mobile, AL: CSM, PO Box Z, Mobile, AL 36616

Simpson, Charles, *Your Home or His?* (audio tape). Mobile, AL: CSM, PO Box Z, Mobile, AL 36616

Simpson, Charles, *Christ the Entrepreneur* (audio tape). Mobile, AL: CSM, PO Box Z, Mobile, AL 36616

Simpson, Charles, *The Cost of Pentecost: Covenant, Conflict, and Unity* (3 audio tapes). Mobile, AL: CSM, PO Box Z, Mobile, AL 36616

Simpson, Charles, *Family: The Most Vital Issue in America* (3 audio tapes). Mobile, AL: CSM, PO Box Z, Mobile, AL 36616

Simpson, Charles, *The Home – A Cornerstone* (4 audio tapes). Mobile, AL: CSM, PO Box Z, Mobile, AL 36616

Simpson, Charles, *Lessons from the Life of Our Lord* (4 audio tapes). Mobile, AL: CSM, PO Box Z, Mobile, AL 36616

Simpson, Charles, *The Joy of Productivity* (4 audio tapes). Mobile, AL: CSM, PO Box Z, Mobile, AL 36616

Simpson, Charles, *Abraham: Eternal Values in Changing Times* (8 audio tapes). Mobile, AL: CSM, PO Box Z, Mobile, AL 36616

Simpson, Charles, *Christian Life Seminar*. Mobile, AL: CSM, PO Box Z, Mobile, AL 36616

Simpson, Charles; Foster, Carter; Strauss, Richard; Leggatt, Dick and Basham, Don, *Family*. Mobile, AL: CSM, PO Box Z, Mobile, AL 36616

Simpson, Charles, *The Challenge to Care*. Ann Arbor: Servant Books, 1986

Simpson, Charles, *Courageous Living*. Ann Arbor: Servant Books, 1987

Snyder, Howard, *The Community of the King*. Downers Grove, IL: InterVarsity Press, 1977

Snyder, Howard, *The Problem of Wine Skins*. Downers Grove, IL: InterVarsity Press, 1975

Solomon, Charles R., *Handbook to Happiness*. Wheaton: Living Studies Tyndale House Publishers, Inc., 1986

Sparks, T. Austin, *What is Man?*. Cloverdale, IN: Ministry of Life, Inc.

Sproul, R.C., *One Holy Passion*. Thomas Nelson, 1987

Sproul, R.C., *The Holiness of God*. Wheaton, Illinois: Tyndale House Publishers, 1985

Stedman, Ray C., *Body Life*. Glendale: Regal, 1970

Stott, John R.W., *The Cross of Christ*. Downers Grove, Illinois: InterVarsity Press, 1986

Sutton, Ray, *Who Won the Family?*, Biblical Blueprint Series. Ft Worth, TX: Dominion Press, 1986

Swindoll, Charles R., *Dropping Your Guard*. Waco, Texas: Word Books, 1960

Swindoll, Charles R., *Growing Wise in Family Life*. Portland, OR: Multnomah Press, 1988

Swindoll, Charles R., *You and Your Child*. New York, NY: Bantom Books, 1980

Tenney, Merrill C., (ed.), *Zondervan Pictorial Encyclopedia of the Bible*, Vol. 2. Grand Rapids, MI: Zondervan, 1975

Theissen, Henry Clarence, *Lectures in Systematic Theology*, Revised edition. Grand Rapids: William B. Eerdmans Publishing Co., 1979

Tomczak, Larry, *Straightforward: Why Wait Till Marriage?* Plainfield, NJ

Tomczak, Larry, *God, the Rod and Your Child's Bod*. Old Tappan, NJ: Fleming H. Revell, 1982

Torrance, T.F., *Calvin's Doctrine of Man*. Wm. B. Eerdman's Pub. Co., 1957

Truscott, Graham, *The Power of His Presence*. Burbank, California: World Map Press, 1969

Unger, Ken, *True Sexuality*. Wheaton, IL: Tyndale House Publishers, Inc., 1987

Vine, W.E., *Expository Dictionary of New Testament Words*, (re. 'love'). Old Tappan, New Jersey: Fleming H. Revell Company, 1940

Warfield, B.B., *The Person and Work of Christ*. Presbyterian and Reformed, 1950

Warfield, Benjamin B., *The Plan of Salvation*. Grand Rapids: Wm. B. Eerdmans Publishing Co., 1970

Weakley, Clare, *John Wesley: The Holy Spirit and Power*. Plainfield, NJ: Logos International, 1977

Webber, George W., *The Congregation in Mission*. New York: Abington Press, 1964

Wilderson, Rich., *Teenagers: Parental Guidance Suggested*. Eugene, OR: Harvest House Publishers, 1983

Williams, Rodman, *The Era of the Spirit*. Plainfield: Logos, 1971

Williams, Rodman, *The Gift of the Holy Spirit*. Plainfield: Logos, 1980

Wilson, Ken, *The Obedient Child*. Ann Arbor, MI: Servant Books, 1988

Wimber, John, *Power Evangelism*. San Francisco: Harper & Row, 1986

Wuest, Kenneth S., *Word Studies in the Greek New Testament*. Grand Rapids: Wm. B. Eerdmans Publishing Company, 1973